Confessions of a
Barbarian

Confessions of a Barbarian: These melancholy memoirs,
this crooked chronicle of my days.

— from the journals of Edward Abbey

Confessions of a Barbarian

Selections from the Journals of
Edward Abbey
1951–1989

Original Drawings by Edward Abbey
Edited and with an Introduction by David Petersen

LITTLE, BROWN AND COMPANY

BOSTON   NEW YORK   TORONTO   LONDON

First Paperback Edition

Library of Congress Cataloging-in-Publication Data

Abbey, Edward.
    Confessions of a barbarian : selections from the journals of Edward
Abbey, 1951–1989 / Edward Abbey ; original drawings by Edward
Abbey ; edited and with an introduction by David Petersen. — 1st ed.
        p.   cm.
    ISBN 0-316-00415-4 (hc)   0-316-00416-2 (pb)
    1. Abbey, Edward — Diaries.   2. Authors, American — 20th
century — Diaries.   3. Park rangers — United States — Diaries.
4. Naturalists — United States — Diaries. 5. Nature. I. Petersen,
David. II. Title.
PS3551.B2Z462   1994
818'.5403 — dc20
[B]   94-7042

10   9   8   7   6   5   4   3   2   1

HAD

*Published simultaneously in Canada
by Little, Brown & Company (Canada) Limited*

Printed in the United States of America

Contents

∞

EL MANO NEGRO ®

TRADE MARK

REG. U.S. CAT. OFF.

Introduction

∞

$\mathcal{E}$DWARD PAUL ABBEY began keeping a personal journal in 1946, viewing it as an important resource in his hoped-for career as "a writer of creative fictions." He was nineteen at the time, serving as an army motorcycle cop in postwar Italy. Abbey continued the practice of writing to himself until just days before his death on March 14, 1989. The product of those four-plus decades of "scribbling" (his term) was twenty cursive volumes kept in eight-by-ten and five-by-seven notebooks.

Would have been twenty volumes, that is, had not the three earliest journals, documenting the years 1946 through most of 1951, been destroyed by flooding while in storage in the basement of the Abbey family home in rural Pennsylvania. That leaves us with seventeen chronological volumes, numbered IV through XX, covering the thirty-eight years 1951 to 1989.

Additionally, four peripheral notebooks survive, one devoted to the specific topic of anarchy and the others to details of particular experiences (the daily routine of a fire lookout, a long solo walk in the Sonoran Desert, and a cross-country research road trip for *The Fool's Progress*), bringing the total up to the twenty-one volumes Abbey mentions in the introduction to his collection of aphorisms, *A Voice Crying in the Wilderness: Notes from a Secret Journal*.

Today, the original notebooks stand as the backbone of the Abbey Papers at the University of Arizona's Special Collections Library — a hefty assemblage comprising, to quote the official inventory, "12.1 feet, 30 manuscript boxes."

Retired University Librarian W. David Laird, together with Lawrence Clark Powell, a prominent southwestern literary figure and friend of Ed's, conspired as early as the spring of 1973 to acquire the Abbey papers as a premier collection for the school's new Special Collections Library. They were motivated in this, Laird says, by the shared conviction that *Desert Solitaire* was "a work that would last," and that owning the Abbey materials would attract other notable donors.

Powell phoned Abbey and arranged a meeting at the Big A, a popular Tucson lunch stop near campus. There, over burgers and beer, Laird put forth his proposition.

Abbey's initial reaction, Laird recalls, was on the order of "Surely, you joke." Ed couldn't believe posterity would have any use for "all those old papers." But Laird and Powell were persistent and persuasive, and by lunch's end, Abbey had tentatively agreed.

Yet even after he'd begun handing over material to the university, Abbey's uncertainty concerning the "external" value of his papers lingered. These doubts surfaced dramatically one day when Ed walked into the library and told Laird he'd like to see the journals. Laird rolled out the collection on a wheeled bookshelf, the notebooks standing in a row between bookends. Abbey picked up a couple of the oldest, most ragged volumes, briefly paged through them, then — grumbling that "nobody wants these" — tossed them into the nearest trash can.

After rescuing the discarded notebooks, Laird returned them to the cart with the others and hurried the whole lot back to the storage room and out of further harm's way.

After that, Ed visited the collection occasionally, lining out entries or writing in second-thought notes here and there. But he never again attempted to destroy the "worthless" journals. And thank the gods for that, for they not only contain some of the finest writing the prolific author ever put to paper but also compose an intimate record of this important and controversial figure's innermost thoughts and feelings.

For various good reasons, public access to the Abbey Papers — in addition to the journals, the collection includes article and book manuscripts, speech notes, correspondence, poetry, photographs, audio and video tapes, and various etceteras — is tightly restricted. Given the phenomenal interest in Edward Abbey, this restriction creates something of an information bind — a bind the volume you now hold in your hands will substantially relieve. For fans, these *Confessions* will provide some insight into the most often asked question about Edward Abbey: "What was he *really* like?" And for scholars, these journal pages will provide a whole new universe of primary resource material.

As editor of my old friend's journals — of his memory, as it were — my primary task has been to select approximately 130,000 words — a hefty bookful, as you can see and feel for yourself, yet no more than a quarter of the total — that best portray the flavor of the voluminous whole. I began by restricting the scope to the seventeen primary journals plus the two little pocket notebooks containing Abbey's scribbled account of his 1981 "Walk in the Desert Hills." From there, I selected those entries that seem most fairly and accurately to reveal the "real" Edward Abbey — right and wrong, joyful and morose, eloquent and crude, sensitive and coarse. With a single exception: The desert walk is presented here in its entirety.

In making the editorial choices necessitated by this nearly four-fold compression of the journals, I have taken great care not to "sanitize" Abbey by eschewing an inordinate proportion of material that may strike some as offensive. To cater to "correctness" would be to betray both Ed and his dedication to candidness. It would also be cheating readers both now and in the future, since a "correct" Edward Abbey would be — well, no Edward Abbey at all.

In order to keep the flavor of these *Confessions* pure Abbey, I've kept my editor's blue pencil leashed tight to restraint and respect, as have the editors at Little, Brown. Ed's artfully "anarchic" use of the language, particularly in the early journals, is an integral part of his voice; to force that unique style through the homogenizing sieve of *The Chicago Manual* would be literary travesty.

In the same vein, other than brackets [like so], which I've reserved exclusively to cage my editorial comments, all punctuation is Abbey's own . . . including ellipses.

With a few exceptions, the line drawings were reproduced directly from the journal notebooks; the exceptions are outtakes from a series of illustrations Abbey drew for *Down the River* and which, in common with the journal drawings, have never been published. Even the volume's title, *Confessions of a Barbarian*, was suggested by Abbey himself, in these journal pages and elsewhere.

Finally, I have tried to include entries from each date recorded in the notebooks; the occasional long temporal jumps between journal entry dates reflect the author's lapses in journal-keeping or date notation, not the editor's exclusions.

Throughout, I've endeavored to minimize my editorial intrusions, so that Abbey's *Confessions* remain, as purely as possible, *Abbey's* confessions. Nonetheless, temporal leaps, together with the fact that the journals are far more internal than external — that is, they deal more often with what Ed is thinking and feeling than with what he's doing — necessitate brief "road maps" at the opening of each journal, in addition to the occasional bracketed explanations within the text.

One considerable problem has been the difficulty of identifying all the many names Ed mentions as he goes along. Most are merely last names, even nicknames, mentioned once or twice in passing, and can be identified only in context — for example, "college friends." We do, however, primarily through Abbey's own descriptions, come to know all the major players.

Pulitzer poet Gary Snyder, an enthusiastic philosophical sparring mate of Abbey's, has said that Ed "was so smart that even when he was wrong, he was damned near right." My greatest hope is that my editorial carpentry, albeit minimal, hasn't made "Cactus Ed" appear less in these pages than the great soulful intellect he in fact was.

In preparing these *Confessions* for publication, I have been generously aided by and am deeply grateful to many friends old and new (you know who you are). Specifically, I wish to thank Clarke Cartwright Abbey; Jack Loeffler; Roger Myers, Peter Steere, and their wholly professional staff at the University of Arizona Special Collections Library; and, as always, Caroline.

DAVID PETERSEN

Confessions of a Barbarian

Road map: *After graduating from high school at Indiana, Pennsylvania, in 1944, and facing induction into the wartime military on his eighteenth birthday some eight months hence, "Ned" (as the Abbey clan knew him) embarked on a solo tour of the American Southwest, traveling by foot, bus, thumb, and "hopped" freight train. For the details of this adventure, see Abbey's own account, "Hallelujah on the Bum," in* The Journey Home.

Shortly after returning home — to Home, Pennsylvania — Ed was drafted into the army. He spent the next two years as a reluctant military cop, serving a year in occupied Italy.

After being honorably discharged (sans good conduct medal), Abbey returned to the Southwest, where he took advantage of the G.I. Bill to study literature and philosophy at the University of New Mexico, Albuquerque. After five years of off-and-on academics, adventures, and misadventures there, Ed graduated with a degree in philosophy and academic honors. That was in 1951.

In August of 1950, during his senior year at UNM, Ed had married his girlfriend, Jean Schmechal, who accompanied him in 1951 to Scotland, where he'd won a Fulbright fellowship to study at the University of Edinburgh. Ed's marriage to Jean was tumultuous from the beginning, and after a short time in Edinburgh she returned to America and filed for divorce. No children were born of their brief union, and their parting was amicable. The journals fail to make clear whether or not Jean knew of Ed's overlapping romantic involvement with another former UNM coed, Rita Deanin.

Journal IV, the earliest of the journals to survive, opens immediately following Jean's departure. Though a sometimes melancholy interlude for Abbey, it was a time nonetheless rich in exploratory thought and literary experimentation. This "first" journal reveals a formative Edward Abbey who is analytic, philosophic, and painfully romantic. Perhaps more than in any of the later journal volumes or his sizable body of published work, Journal IV details the coalescence of the Abbey weltanschauung. *Here too, more than elsewhere, Abbey experiments — plays — with the language.*

JOURNAL IV

November 1951 to April 1952

∞

November 10, 1951 – Edinburgh, Scotland

Oh! for love, for the painfully nourished, tenderly cherished, sweet frenzied illusion, the known-illusion within the globule of sentimental cynicism. For romantic love, then, I sacrifice honor, decency, human kindness, charity, honesty, friendship and the future — all (ah!) for love! Let this simple valediction be my benediction, and this nonsense my good sense in this, the latest and God help me the last, of my sordid adventures in humanity . . .

The grim grimy grisly details can be of little interest; look them up in my official biography. What matters is the heart of the affair, the whistling spirit behind the facade of surface data; guilt, the sense of guilt, and who am I to sacrifice not only my own but perhaps another's happiness upon the bloody stinking alter of romantic love?

Yes indeed, but here we go despite all. All for love? Again, yes again! Yes.

∞

The harlot's cry from street to street
Shall weave old England's winding sheet.

Edinburgh. A soft gray loveliness, fog-shrouded, gray-green, gray-blue, gray-gray, mauve, melting, misting over, grave. And old, with the stench of ages old, built up on packed and repacked mounds of human charnel: excrement, dead bones, blood-woven earth soaked in saltwater urine and piled over high the heaped-up bodies of the dead and dying.

Medieval, yes; dark-aged, grim ecclesiastical spire-populated, spire-pointed, steeple-spired, gothic-inspired, a clawing toothy saber-toothy jag-ragged sky-scratching skyline, spear-clutching sky-bound city; soul fleeing earth. The slimy streets, the smeary streets, the slime-smear-shining streets: dung, piss, spit, snot and ever-present wetness, water, fish blood, foggy sky, smoky, pressed down by its own weight upon the city's streets.

Dark.

Grave.

A dusky graveyard of the lithe lissome spirit, possibly — I'll make no verdicts there. Smoke-fog everywhere, a heavy foggy smoggy sky pushed damply down upon the city under its own foul-filthy fatness, dump-lidded bosom-sky.

Scruff from an itching scalp.

A shod horse on a cobbled street is a whistling echo from the dimmest past, a fifty-years = fifty-thousand light-years ago past. Lost voices windborne from the ghostly past. The ghostly ghastly past, aghast against the past.

*Prometheus Bounded Up and Down
From a Crag in the Caucasus*

NO MORE OF THIS NONSENSE, ABBEY!

∞

Three Tramps: A novel vindicating the philosophy of adventure & disorder, soaked in the democratic popular culture of contemporary U.S.A. (A modern *Huckleberry Finn?*) Three grown men, one a Negro, wander from California to Texas and Louisiana and back (maybe), singing, guitar-playing, whoring, stealing, talking, a paean to irresponsibility. The climax might be an attempted lynching in the South.

Philosophical Correlative = the values of the earthbound sensuous life (value in adventure, too) against a background of cosmic melancholia: freight trains, used cars, bad jobs, blues and hillbillies, out on the desert, mountain cabin, ghost town. Mexico, New Orleans, fine drunks (*Tortilla Flat* stuff?); rain on the tin roof, fire in the stove, venison hanging from the rafters, a case of beer on the floor; Pure Sentimentality, emphasizing equality, liberty, good living, brotherhood; change and adventure and uncertainty made both real and ideal.

Everything. I'll throw everything in. Whole hog. Hog wild. A great big fat beautiful obscene book, the most hilarious, tear-jerking, side-splitting, throat-choking, belly-busting, heart-breaking book ever written. Don't forget the book *in* the book. (The proper place for parody.)

Throw everything in? Maybe you'd better throw in the towel.

∞

[Manuel] de Falla's Harpsichord Concerto; *Greensleeves* — another of the farawaymysticalstrangelyhauntinghearttroubling melodies.

Imagine the thrill of the composer, hearing a smudgefaced child in the street singing a tune of his; hearing, by the sea — the great curve of sand,

5

leaning trees, clouds, gulls, crags, the wind-whistle, the waves larrup, the screebirds' cry, the vaulting distance echo — a personal music.

There is a music in me, too, not much yet but growing. I'll have to soon put in a stretch at some conservatory, getting the means to release this musical pressure. Nothing in the literary or ideational can fully express it. Two or three symphonies, a handful of songs, things for flutes, piano, guitar, timpani, harp, Indian drums, Indian themes, the Indian desert world.

∞

The Walking Wonder, the PENTARACHNID, the rolling pictographic crypto-man, all legs, arms, backwardlooking head, all feet and hands, quintesticled. [Abbey's sketches of this five-limbed anthropomorphic tumbleweed figure appear scores of times throughout the early journals.]

∞

Everything in the universe converges upon me.

I radiate light upon everything in the universe.

I am an egocentric predicament (and love it!).

I find arrows shooting, rockets streaming spaceward, most fascinating — no doubt because I am a sex-maniac.

∞

Needed: "A General Theory of Anarchism" outlining aims, methods, metaphysical justification and teleological value (Principle of Evolutionary Differentiation). Try H. Read, Bakunin, Geronimo, Proudhon, Kropotkin, Tolstoy.

∞

Society and Solitude — another significant polarity. What influence does or can a certain landscape have over a person? Should the great desert (for example) provoke moods, feelings and finally permanent traits of expansive openness, broadness, universality, oneness with the natural world, a cosmic (subspecies *eternitatis*) outlook? Or would it result in an analogous aridity, sterility, death-dealing and stalking? The mountain . . . the great space . . . what happens there to the human spirit?

The human world of artifice and imagination can never equal the richness and variety and wonder of the real natural nonhuman world. But man belongs to the world; he is no more enemy or alien than the saguaro, the jaguar or the spinning spider.

Science can tell us *what* is happening, and *how*, but surely not *why*. And even then, scientific explanations are always hypothetical, of limited certitude and subject to change without notice.

In other words, there is no good reason to assume that the world was constructed, or constructs itself, to fit an *a priori* mathematical scheme. Rather, we construct mathematical schemes to fit the world. (This looks like an unabashed nominalism.) An important question following this, then, is: What limitations does this place upon science and upon our knowledge in general?

If the world is irrational, we can never know it (either it or its irrationality)?

∞

The magnificence, the HEROIC quality of Beethoven's music, the glorious humanism of it, its HELLENIC shape & indeed . . . the great Humanist of music.

∞

The Abbey Curse: In my opinion all Abbeys suffer from a family blood curse, invoked somewhere in the dim past by unknown Enemies and as malignant and powerful in its operations today as ever it might have been in the past. Its prevailing effects are (1) miserable loneliness (2) constant disunity and friction, disintegration (3) heartbreaking aspirations (4) social failure and trouble.

∞

Not baby-killers, these latter-day Papists, but mother-killers. (What a monstrous "morality" it is that would let good mothers die for the sake of one more digit in the number of souls in Heaven! "Let the known and loved personality die; we *must* baptize that embryo!") The spiritual life.

∞

About time my friend about time to think about the book, the first spasmodic effort of the reluctant soul harrowing itself for something to say; do I have something to say? Your goddamned ass I have something to say!

What?

You call me, sir, a rank materialist — sir, I accept the appellation and I accept with pride, sir, and glory. Never shall this flower of the spirit reject the good earth from which it grows — never shall I live in an alabaster spirit-city, separated from my mother by concrete or gold, by white robes, ineffables, or multi-colored sewage and communication systems, not this nigger, no sir!

I celebrate the Earth, my home, my mother, my grave, and as long as men are Man they must, if they would preserve the integrated being, do the same — [and preserve] with it the body — this rank casual hungry smelly sweaty lusting transitory body, my oozy pulpy liquid-bag-swollen body, bones, blood, hair, glands, my bejeweled sex; I love and celebrate it all. Never to let men forget that they are animals as much as gods — that is one thing I shall say.

From the above, certain theorems naturally derive: If the earth and the animal are valuable, then every earthborn man and woman, every animal, has an inherent right to a portion of this earth, to its produce, to its free air, its seas, sands, mountains, deserts and sunrises — this means some kind of socialism, social justice, economic democracy, decentralized, voluntary, cooperative; and a spacious commonwealth, with lots of room for all (birth control) in the Green Utopia. Here is something to fight for that will never desert me in my lifetime.

The free man I sing, the anti-authoritarian, the libertine; material for several volumes in this theme.

The common man, too, the everyday ordinary hardworking family man — someone someday must write a book about him. Mine, perhaps, the small southwestern rancher with his starved cows, pickup, kids, windmill.

PASSION: passion-light must be brought back into Literature. If no one else can or will do it, I must.

∞

For the travel book on Europe (*Rolled Over on Europe?*):

France. France is that country which must be traversed by any traveler going from Britain to Germany, Switzerland, Italy or Spain, or by any traveler going from one of those countries to Britain. (If you can afford it, take an airplane.)

Paris. Paris is the capital of France.

England. After a few months in England, one finds that one likes the Scotch very much.

∞

I've decided to be a regional writer. My region will be the U.S.A., Mexico, Guatemala, Easter Island, Spain, Isle of Skye, Persia, Kenya, South Africa, Australia, New Zealand and Tasmania. Area posted. Squatters are warned. Prosecution. Fine.

Art of the Novel: Maximizing order in maximum chaos — complex symmetry as opposed to simple symmetry — simultaneity — counterpoint and contrary motion — the novel should appeal primarily to the intellect; for the emotions there is music, for the senses, color and form.

∞

Sibelius, the First [symphony] — the lean prelude and then the lightning's flash, the thunder's roll, the strike and strike again! Then later, quiet interludes, tho always present the sense of tension, of something coming, something straining to be free, to . . . how the distant music plays upon, pulls at, turns over and echoes thru the listening heart — the incredible wistful dim dreaming distant impossible promise — how sure and certain that here, for once, the music speaks of something more than itself, of something beyond itself, not a place, not an idea, not a story, but something, some kind of deep aesthetic intuition — a memory? An anticipation? A vision? A symbol of emotion?

But what kind of sentimental gush is all this? Am I taking a cue from the music and drifting down into pretty fantasy? Possibly — oh, but why should I not? There is too much simple loveliness here to be scorned, too much meaning and truth to be ignored. I'll not be the one to try to back down the old man — let him stand. Love him. And listen. Listen. Awake, sleepers, dogmatic slumberers . . . listen here to the voice of innocence, the song. . . .

December 10, 1951 – Edinburgh
TIPS FOR ANARCHISTS:

Law derives whatever moral authority it may have, not from its origin, but from its end and substance. Likewise, government derives its moral authority from those whose ends it serves. My moral allegiance to a given State (and the State is the body of men and law and power which composes & comprises the government) is directly proportional in degree to the extent to which the State senses my needs, and inversely proportional to the extent to which the State violates or disregards my ends, needs, principles.

God help me, I will never sacrifice a friend to an ideal. I will never betray a friend for the sake of any cause. I will never reject a friend in order to stand by an institution. Great nations may fall in dusty ruin before I will sell a friend to save them. I pray to the God within me to give me the power to live by this design.

∞

The poets are like sheep; they scamper around in flocks. In the '20s, [they were] all experimental aesthetes; in the '30s, all social revolutionaries; in the '40s, all Anglicans. The philosophers are considerably more reliable and independent-minded, I'll say that for them.

∞

The paradox of life and death: Not only is death essential to life, and the converse, and not only is reproduction charged with the death "force," but for the sake of more abundant life the reproductive drive itself must be chained, restricted, channeled by sterility.

The world needs a good sugar-coated Sterility Pill.

The Man in the Mackintosh must be captured and controlled, the rubber sheath unsheathed, shriven by life and for.

∞

My favorite melodramatic theme: the harried anarchist, a wounded wolf, struggling toward the green hills, or the black-white alpine mountains, or the purple-golden desert range and liberty. Will he make it? Or will the FBI shoot him down on the very threshold of wilderness and freedom?

∞

A web of spiders in her hair
And spasm in her eyes.

∞

"When I see a mountain like that, I know there *must* be a God."

When *I* see a mountain like that, I know we don't *need* a God.

∞

Philosophy — a witch's puddling brew, a big black battered cauldron full of a heterogeneous stew, odd bits and scrapments tossed in by various philosophical cooks, all heated from below by the fire of controversy. From the purling bubbling mess ascends a steam, a heavy vaporous cloud, obscuring somewhat the bearded cooks squatting around the huge pot. Every now and then some old man throws another chunk of fatty meat into the mixture, and though occasionally some indomitable dogmatist jumps up, tries to kick the fire apart, declaring the stew finished, the truth is that the stew is *far* from finished and probably never will be.

∞

The poets are like lawyers — they lie too much. (Excepting a noble handful of each.)

There's only one thing as good as society — solitude. (And conversely.)

What was the virgin Mary's escape velocity when she made her physical Assumption into outer space?

10

December 15, 1951 – Edinburgh

At the concert last night, listening to the orchestra open the affair with the British anthem ("God Save the Bloody Fucking King") but wordless see, no singing, and the simple tune also, that of my country, *My country, 'tis of thee I sing*, I was amazed and a little embarrassed as a strange emotion welled up from the heart, obstructing the larynx and troubling my eyes . . . a wave of homesickness and loneliness, yet more than that — an immense and inordinate and tearful tragic pride in my land, my country, America, *sweet land of liberty;* immense and inordinate with a profound and swelling love of the physical land, of the towns and farms, of the many folks I know — tragic with a sense of America as a promise yet far from complete, far from realization, and as a dream menaced by ugliness and by mean little enemies masquerading as defenders of that dream and armed now with the most awful POWER the world has ever known.

Conscious in heart and mind of all this, and of far more that only music can symbolically express and words cannot, I nearly cried, I nearly wept under that great burden of loneliness and alienation from my home, and with it the pride and joy and anger and sorrow which, combined, prove me to be a patriot of a most earnest kind and, I hope, a patriot of a most dangerous kind. Me, a patriot! It's true, my soul, it's true.

∞

Jeanie is gone. Jeanie is gone. I'll never see Jeanie again.
O, o, o, what have I done?
What have I done?
What have I?
Have I?
I?
Aye.
I have.
I have done.
What I have done.
O, o, o, what I have done.
O Jeanie; O Jeanie; Jeanie O; O; O; O Jeanie O; Jeanie.

∞

So, you're a Mozart man? Well, you take your thin little slice of cold ham over in the corner and nibble away; I'll have a sirloin of Bach, well-aged, thick & rare; or a Beethoven porterhouse, big, warm, bloody; or a *filet de* Bartók, spicy, juicy and chewy as an old horse.

Alban Berg — now there's a musician for you — maybe he's better than Bartók, maybe as good as Schoenberg — maybe — anyway, he has made some marvelous music — *Wozzeck* I've got drunk on before, and for a second time just last week, and tonight — piling it on — I heard his little six-note "Lyric Suite." Well of course there's doubtless much more there than can soak into the amateur ear at first listening, but even so I lapped up enuf to get a good glow on — better than Bovril for that — there's music for you, man, if you can take it! Sensuous as purple grapes, sensual as reproduction, palpable and mute, a thing you could eat, maybe, if it were as tangible as cloudstuff.

∞

HOW TO DIE — but first, how not to:

Not in a smelly old bloody-gutted bed in a rest-home room drowning in the damp wash from related souls groping around you in an ocean heavy with morbid fascination with agony, sin and guilt expiated, with clinical faces and automatic tear glands functioning perfunctorily and a fat priest kneeling on the naked heart.

Not in snowy whiteness under arc lights and klieg lights and direct television hookup. No never under clinical smells and sterilized medical eyes cool with detail calculated needle-prolonged agonizing, stiff and starchy in the white monastic cell, no.

Not in the muddymire of battleblood commingled with charnelflesh and others' blood, guts, bones, mud and exrement in the damp smell of blasted and wrung-out air; *nor* in the masspacked weight of the cities atomized while masonry topples and chandeliers crash clashing buried with a million others, no.

Not the legal murder either — too grim and ugly such a martyrdom — down long aisles with chattering Christers chins on shoulders under bright lights again a spectacle an entertainment grim stickyquiet officialdom and heavy-booted policemen guiding the turning of a pubic hair gently grinding in a knucklebone an arm hard and obscene fatassed policemen everywhere under the judicial — not to be murdered so, no never.

But how *to:*

Alone, elegantly, a wolf on a rock, old pale and dry, dry bones rattling in the leather bag, eyes alight, high, dry, cool, far off, dim distance alone, free as a dying wolf on a pale dry rock gurgling quietly alone between the agony-spasms of beauty and delight; when the first flash of hatred comes to crawl, ease off casually forward into space the old useless body, falling, turning, glimpsing for one more time the blue evening sky and the far distant lonesome rocks below — before the crash, before. . . .

With none to say no, none.

Way off yonder in the evening blue, in the gloaming.

[At this point, Abbey took a monthlong European vacation. Therefore, Journal V — the "Spanish Journal," which covers mid-December 1951 to mid-January 1952 — chronologically precedes the remainder of Journal IV.]

January 29, 1952 – Edinburgh

Today, old man, you are twenty-five years old. A quarter of a century. One-third dead. Judgment Day approaches. What, it might not be inappropriate to ask, though indiscreet, have you accomplished, precisely, in your allotment, your rare precious slender portion of years? What, if much of anything? Come, let's have a thorough *Inventory of the Self.*

A: LOVE. I have, deservedly or not, loved and/or been loved by a handful of people whose lives I value almost as much as my own — my mother, Milly, that wise small fragile lovely loving selfless and angelic woman, mother of four sons, a daughter, innumerable school-brats, and a husband; my father, Paul, a man with a heart too big for this world, and anger, too, and a quiet tragedy; a small troupe of girlfriends — Priscilla, Ione, Brunetta, Betsy, Joyce (the most beautiful girl I, or any man, has ever loved), Helen, Carolee, Liz, Elaine and Charlotte; finally, and too important, almost, too near, for words, I have known (perhaps still know) the love of, and do myself love, two women whose goodness, magic, nobility, beauty of soul and heart have quite conquered my finest sensibilities — I refer to Jean (a man's woman, a fair creature of many talents) and to Rita, my devil, my demon, wicked and lovely beyond all bounds of common decency, a mad girl with a touch of hell in her.

Sex. Not much — a mistress in Italy, a wife in America, a sweetheart in the desert, a few semi-whores here and there.

Tastes: Orthodox, but with poetry.

B: ART. *The Picture.* My training and background [here are] meager, despite the historical fact that I started as an "artist" myself, doing doodles, watercolors, ink drawings, cartoons, comic strips, charcoal and crayon before I was ten years old and still doing it as late as secondary school. But it died, and with good reason — no talent. I never was, probably never will be, in spite of old stirrings, more than an amateur cartoonist.

Tastes: I like Marin, Orozco, Tschelitchev, Braque, Rattner, Diebenkorn and Norman Rockwell among contemporaries; the troglodytae, della

13

Francesca, Mike Angelo, El Greco and Van Gogh among the old-timers.

Sculpture. I once did an imitation of the Sphinx in clay for a bookend. Good likeness. My favorite sculptors are Rita Deanin and the fellow who made those Negro gods in Africa. Not to mention Mount Rushmore.

Stage. Another world little known to me, tho I once played in *A Christmas Carol* to a packed house. Packed in. I was Ebenezer Scrooge and loved the part. Favorite playwrights: Euripides, Kit Marlowe, Shaw.

Movies. A more familiar world, from an extremely limited point of view. [I harbor a] great ambition to write a few scenarios and direct a few pictures, [though I've] done nothing but look at movies so far. Haven't seen much so far, either.

Music. I play the harmonica, in an elementary manner the flute, in a crude improvising way the piano. Have composed about thirty tunes of various types and shapes. Outlined a symphony. Have participated, as a member of chorus, in some magnificent musical experiences — *Messiah, St. Matthew's Passion, Mass in B Minor,* Mozart's *Requiem.* Once had a chat with Ernst Krenek; admirable fellow.

Preferences: Among the regulars, Bach and Beethoven. I have a weakness for modern Romantics like Vaughn Williams, Sibelius, Shostakovich. But the best composers of our time are undoubtedly the new men — Schoenberg, Berg, Stravinsky, Bartók; possibly Harris, Sessions, Ives in U.S.A. are best. I'm full of musical ambition. Intend to master the flute, get acquainted with the timpani, cello, harp; master theory at the University of Mexico and compose four symphonies.

Architecture. I will someday build a desert hideout (Baboquivari) in the most naturalistic indigenous functional and fortified manner possible; also, a mountain home in Montana or Alaska; also, a seaside villa in Baja California or Sonora. I'm a great admirer of Frank Lloyd Wright. I consider most of the world's great cathedrals and public buildings to be in need of atomic bombing.

Ballet. I once knew how to square-dance. Can still do the two-step fox-trot and the Supai Shuffle. Ballet and modern dance frighten me, but I'm going back for a second look.

Literature: Poetry. I've written seventy-five to a hundred poems, most of them terrible. I intend to write a lot more, including a few good ones. Intend to write a version of *The Philosophy of Romance* in verse, as well as a verse drama about Giordano Bruno. Have read about five-thousand to 7,500 poems; admire most those by Anacreon, Lucretius, Will Shakespeare, Andrew Marvell, Billy Blake, Shelley, Robbie Burns, Heine, Walt

Whitman, Jeffers, Frost, and Dylan Thomas. I despise T. S. Eliot, the biggest fraud who ever lived.

Literature: The Novel. Have written one-fourth of a magnificent novel, will have it finished by October; afterwards, about eight more even greater. My favorite predecessors: Mann, Dostoyevski, Mark Twain and, above all, JOYCE.

Aesthetics. I have stolen, borrowed, dreamed up innumerable ideas and theories about Art with a capital A. Novelty, Form & Mystery; that's my only contribution in systematic form to date, however. Something should be done about the lamentable state of aesthetics; my opinion.

C: ADVENTURE. Ah, so little, so little. Fell out of a tree one time and got all scratched up. Slipped while fence-walking once and badly bruised my testicles. Hitch-hiked around the U.S., got robbed, was put in jail for vagrancy, rode a freight train from Needles [California] to Gallup [New Mexico]. With the infantry in Italy I shot rats, bullied terrified chickens, ordered people around. Almost fell into Vesuvius. Got drunk in the Toledo area of Naples and made a big row. Went AWOL once, for two days, in Milan. Stole a .45 from the army. Rode a motorcycle. Once arrested a colonel.

Had my tonsils out when I was ten or so. Got into a fight with Buddy Woolweaver, was badly beaten. Burned down a shithouse one time. Trapped skunks, shot squirrels at dawn. Went bear hunting once.

Have climbed a few hills — Shasta, Wheeler, Ben Nevis, Craig Mayor in Majorca. Had a few close calls on rocks. Once got nearly trapped in a cul-de-sac in Havasu Canyon [Grand Canyon]. Swam in the Gulf of California. Got arrested in Pittsburgh campaigning for Henry Wallace. Went down South lookin' for trouble, didn't find any. Have painted live high-tension towers, worked as a roughneck on oil rigs, helped fight a forest fire, helped Bud Adams [a college friend] break and train a mean horse. Have never got lost in the woods, on mountains, in canyons or even in cities. Boy Scout, second class.

Have traversed about forty of the forty-eight states; have been in or touched upon sixteen countries: U.S.A., Canada, Mexico, Italy, Yugoslavia, Austria, Switzerland, England, Wales, Scotland, Ireland, France, Belgium, Germany, Sweden, Spain (anticipating by just a month).

[During] two years in the Army of the United States, I rose from the rank of private to private first class; was not given a Good Conduct medal. Wounded once in a fencing duel with T/5 Turner; no medals. Have defied my selective service (conscription) board and so far got away with it.

[Abbey was concerned about being re-drafted to serve in the Korean conflict.] Love is adventure. Art is adventure. I've explored some interesting places: Grand Canyon, Majorca, under ladies' skirts, central New Mexico, the heart.

Numerous plans for the future — want to see the South Pacific, Australia, New Zealand, Easter Island, Baja California, more of Sonora, Alaska, Guatemala, Kenya, Sinkiang & Nepal, Russia, Persia, Timbuktu, India, Antarctica, the moon, Mars, Venus. I want to drive a jeep from Nome to Tierra del Fuego. Climb McKinley, Cabezon Peak, Las Truchas, a few active volcanoes. Want to see an earthquake or tidal wave, or at least a volcanic eruption. Want to live in wilderness awhile. Want to spend a few weeks in a prison. Want to own a good horse. And have a good woman . . . someday. Want to blow up St. Peter's. Want to edit another magazine. [Abbey was fired as editor of UNM's literary magazine, *The Thunderbird*, after printing the Voltaire quote "Man will never be free until the last king is strangled with the entrails of the last priest" on the cover, and attributing it to Louisa May Alcott.]

D: ACADEMY. An unreliable scholar. Mediocre schoolboy — failed [high school] journalism twice, almost failed geometry. In college I failed Spanish and Handicraft. Graduated, however, with a flourish, with honors, Fulbright scholarship and so forth. [My] field is supposed to be English literature and philosophy.

I wrote a few brilliant but superficial essays in college. Edited a literary magazine. My academic ambition is to get a Ph.D. in philosophy and never use it; that is, never teach, only write semi-popular books in the manner of Bertie Russell.

My gallery of great philosophers — Pathegoras, Plotinus, Anselm, Bruno, Spinoza, Schopenhauer, Bergson, Bertie Russell.

My gallery of great literary scholars — L. V. Wicker, Ben Duncan, Coleridge.

My favorite schools — Yale, Edinburgh, Wittenburgh, Mexico City, Moscow Institute for Advanced Study in Revolutionary Technique and Guerrilla Warfare, Wimpleton State Teacher's College in Wimpleton, West Virginia.

Would like to organize, someday, an informal little study group in literature, art and philosophy, say a meeting in the sunlit plaza of some Mexican village. Sandals and wine.

E: CATCH-ALL. I have made a few good friends in my first twenty-five years . . . but it's all kind of vague. I haven't really ever had much to do with any of them. Except for my women, I have been alone for most of my life so far. And sometimes it seems strange to me that this should be so, for I have felt for quite some time, for years, that I am ready to love my fellow-man — a few of them, I mean. Why must my love be restricted to women? I have enough love in me, not only for two women at once, but also for others, other women or men. By love, in this context, I mean simply a powerful and intimate friendship, a joining of minds and spirits in affection and comradeship. I imagine myself ready — but it doesn't happen.

Why not? One obvious reason — I make no move myself. Because I generally feel indifferent to other people — interested in them as phenomena of great philosophical interest but little more. My behavior is consistently neutralistic. I make no effort to make friends, none whatsoever; I wait for the other man. And of course he often doesn't show up. In fact, he hasn't showed up yet. And he probably never will if my life continues in its present haphazard fashion, which I seem to like. But there are better things than this and don't think I don't know it, pardner. I'm sleepy as hell. . . .

F: SUMMATION. Looking back over the first twenty-five, seems to me I've had a pretty damn good time. Oh, I've been unhappy — God but I've been so unhappy, and I've been and am lonely — oh Mary but I've been so terribly lonely. But even so, I *enjoy* being unhappy and lonely, and I've enjoyed it just about all — the trouble, misery, tears, dust, boredom, frustration, anger, fear, shame, horror, pain and failure — it's all been rather interesting.

In everything that has happened to me I've found something worth chewing over, speculating about, though always, always, I mean always, there has been, over everything, the great starry universe included, the hint of tragedy in the human role and tragedy in life itself. The spiritual aim becomes the transcendence of this imminent tragedy — a flight beyond tragedy, beyond joy, to . . . what?

O come sweet death, soothing undulating death, the ideal serenity of nothingness?

Against this dark background, like diamonds on purple velvet, have been my moments of glory — alone on a hill at night, on snow like frozen moonlight, on cold snow glittering with frosty jewels under a shower of moonlight from a full moon, alone on top of the hill, skis on my feet, and I just standing there, looking down the hill at the small dim light of home below, standing there, waiting, waiting for the miracle, my mind and heart still with enchantment, waiting there, under the moon, alone and beauty-filled.

That April in 1945 when I first fell blindly, hopelessly, completely as I never have since or can again, in love with a girl, that thick dream-syrupy golden month when time suspended itself and I walked every night through twilight and darkness for miles and miles and miles, just to see and touch a girl.

The time I pitched against Marion Center for the Home Hellions and struck out fifteen batters.

Night-skating on Crooked Creek.

A flight through the green woods of summer, the body-shock and sensation of cool moss and the depths of leafy green.

That day when, like stout Cortez, I stood on Red Cloud Peak in the Bighorn Mountains and, looking westward, saw for the first time the great range of the Rockies blue with distance and dappled with perpetual snow.

The first time I heard a great symphony and thought the world must end, my tears of unutterable sorrow and joy, and I a mere boy.

Awakening in and looking out of a boxcar, seeing for the first time the red and yellow world of Arizona baking under a sun I had never seen before.

Bathing, swimming, alone and naked, in a huge blue secret pool under a hundred-foot waterfall in a red canyon where only Indians live.

The day I trapped myself in a trick canyon in the middle of nowhere and thought I was going to slowly die; my escape.

Going to jail for Henry Wallace and Peace, Prosperity and Progress.

That April in 1951 when I fell in love for the last time, those warm dark delirious nights, the complex troubled time of love and early sorrow, love against time and love against love, and music.

Returning home, climbing the green hill through fields and over wild places of grass and briars and down the hill through the heavy green woods and across the little stream of water from the pasture and under the great maple tree and through the kitchen's open doors to the final triumph and tragedy that has never failed me and will never fail me — returning home.

Twenty-five highly entertaining years, the best by far that I've ever had. On the planet Earth, too . . . where is it likely to be any better? Earth is the place for love. Twenty-five years I wouldn't trade for anything — except the next twenty-five.

February 1952 – Edinburgh

I've been reading Delacroix's *Journal*. Considerably different from mine. Much more orderly, straightforward, restrained, limited and, I would say, much less interesting. However, the lad did have a gay time, it seems, in his early days, going to bed continually with house-maids and models. "Helene arriving today . . . I made a series of studies for the picture, 'The Massacre at Scio.' Unfortunately, she carried away with her a part of the energy I needed for my day's work."

And though he resolves an honesty at the beginning, writing, he says, only for himself, still, I think his honesty a cowardly and unsatisfactory kind. No doubt he writes the truth; but how much of the truth he has surely omitted! Except for the quote above, there is little indication of humor (in the first twenty pages), and a rather priggish prim air of self-admonishment. "I will write nothing that would make my dear Mother blush." "Control yourself; don't judge by first impressions." Parts are good, tho, even interesting, and it should get better as he moves forward in time, becoming more a man and artist, less a self-conscious petty philanderer.

And look at your own journal, Abbey; what about those first two or three parts [accidentally destroyed in storage] devoted almost wholly to highly emotional and maudlin reminiscences of one girl-passion after another.

ശ

Girls. Since returning from Spain, about two weeks ago, I've kept myself fairly busy — writing, fluting, going to classes and the theatre, worrying about my novel — and consequently have not been subjected to the attacks of sickly melancholy which fastened upon me so frequently in Spain, where I had nothing to do but eat, sleep and gaze at lovely landscapes and buildings. I was genuinely lonely there; I missed Jean, honestly and painfully missed her, even though I had just completed a year or more of married life with her, during most of which time I could barely endure her presence at all, and made the affair so unpleasant for her that she finally gave up and went home to get a divorce.

But, as I have said, no sooner was she gone than I wanted her back; such is the adolescent perversity of my nature. She had become a habit, I suppose, a dependable fixture, ever a staff and base of my daily life; thinking I did not want her I had actually become quite dependent upon her, unconsciously, of course, and was made painfully aware of her value and importance to me only when she had gone for good. Ah, then did I moon and moan, and weep wet and dry, wax cold and hot, speared by loneliness, as is plainly and mawkishly apparent in my "Spanish" journal. But time dries up the wound; already Jean is on her way to immortality as a memory, a memory and nothing more.

Absinthe makes the heart grow fonder — not absence. On her way; she's not yet actually there; she's not yet been sacked and sunk and buried as novel-material in a writer's sketch-book (which is what this thing actually is — a sketch-book rather than a journal).

No, for even now, almost two months after her departure, I can still experience, when properly stimulated by some appropriately associative sensation — a song, a walk under the trees, a certain obscure fragrance, like fermented rose-juice — the need for Jean. I remember her suddenly, deeply, poignantly, and long for a look at her (tho I can hardly remember her face) and for the feel of her warm heavy solid body in my arms, pressed against me, and the smell and tickling caress of her hair against my face.

My wife — my dear sweet loyal wife, how fine you are, how good, and how foolish and stupid I was . . . and am. For I am not yet convinced that marriage to you was, or could be, a good thing for either of us. No, as the days shuttle by like fence posts, faster than birds, and leisure and irresponsibility become a new pattern of habit, I learn to enjoy my new liberty, my new freedom, so different from what I had known before marriage, when I was a vibrating bundle of lusts and longings incapable of sober thought. (What foolishness I'm writing!)

I'm in love, that's the only relevant truth. A new love; that alone, were it not for my novel [*Jonathan Troy*] and my big dreams, is all that sustains and enhances my life at this time: Another love, the devil-girl, Rita, the little-known mad girl.

February 10, 1952 – Edinburgh

I heard and saw the proclamation of a new queen the other day at Mercat Cross. Lots of scarlet and gold, gray wigs, soldiers, swords, bayonets, cannons booming with gay puffs of smoke, flags flying, trumpeters blaring royally.

"And other gentlemen of quality . . . given this day . . . Eliza the Second . . . high and mighty princess Elizabeth Alexandra Mary, one thousand nine hundred and fifty-two . . . God save the queen! Hip! Hip!"

The streets were jammed with middle-aged women and schoolchildren. The British monarchy, I would say, is an institution like Sunday School in the U.S.A. — supported mainly by middle-class housewives and middle-class schoolchildren. As indeed it should be; for what is the Royal Family but bourgeois domesticity enshrined, a waxen group of animated dummies under glass, carefully dusted and tenderly handled every morning including Sundays.

Yet royalty has another aspect in this country which must not be overlooked — glamour. In this way it is analogous to the part Hollywood plays in the lives of millions of adolescent females in America. They, the common girls of the nation, lead drab and dreary lives — dull, wearisome and ugly. But here, up above and not so very far away, is Heaven, where men with fantastically handsome faces and women with angelic faces ("everyone remarked on how serene and radiant the Princess looked") lie about in lives of leisure and luxury, where the women will take a wardrobe of three hundred outfits on a flying trip to Kenya, where nobody ever works, ever gets sick, ever goes hungry, ever goes without love and adoration.

So the working girl shambles on, living only in a dream in the illustrated magazines the life that should be hers by natural right; living her life through others — in the case of the monarchy, through a small group of persons who have no more business living the foolish, unproductive, artificial, hot-house existences they do than a group of monkeys have monkeying with a cyclotron. Yet some nations, and most people, will probably never grow up.

Britain has never had a thorough-going revolution. And that is undoubtedly what is wrong with Britain.

Has my Anglophobia lessened since coming to Britain? Yes, of course. For one thing, the power of Socialism here puts me in an awkward position; I cannot be satisfyingly Anglophobic without to some extent undermining my support of Labor. Besides, I like the people too much. The Scotch, I mean.

∞

Resolved: On my next tour to the Continent I will submit to every available temptation. What I need to purge my brain and soul is an orgy of flesh and drunkenness.

The novel creeps along from day to day, a petty pace, lighting the way. Oh, it's such a huge undertaking; sometimes I get discouraged, my heart sinks at the appalling prospect of so much labor (that it might be effort in vain is a thought which I firmly suppress — most of the time). So much hard labor, so much planning and arranging, so damned many parts and elements to worry about and try to harmonize into a cumulative whole with a powerful effect.

I am disheartened by the psychic difficulty of getting outside my book, of looking at it with a critical stranger's eyes, watching it grow from a distance. I am sadly aware of confusion in my aims, of perhaps too much ambiguity and too many inconsistencies, of doubtful characterizations and dubious motives. I am always in danger of internal sabotage by the most sly and insidious of enemies, the one who says:

"Don't despair if this time you don't get it just right; don't waste time and sleep in a struggle for perfection; you're young, my lad, and this is, after all, only your first attempt; you'll have many more opportunities to write better novels. Take it easy; your faults are those of immaturity; you'll do better next time; eventually, in the dim distant future, you'll create your masterpiece. Be patient; relax." The voice of the tempter whispering in my ear, slick and sleek and sinister.

So very slowly goes and grows the novel; even the little creative ecstasies that I used to know, in composing a wad of verse or rattling off a short story, are here mostly denied to me. The thing is so big, so many-dimensional, so complex and unruly and restless — I have to look in a dozen directions at once, I need compound and independent eyes, I need several brains — that there is seldom a chance for me to feel the whole story, to know it overall, and thus experience the big thrill that comes with creation and contemplation.

Maybe later — near, with or immediately after the ultimate climax — I'll get the inward charge, know the lightning's hour, the inward pride, the certainty of power, come running with the old aesthetic orgasm. But tempt me no more with idle promises. Get thee hence, dear Lucifer.

The lazy and reluctant mind sometimes tries other tricks on me: I may find myself gaping vacantly out the window at the sky and thinking about the novel finished, and fame and honor and wealth and power already mine. Fame-honor-wealth-power; is that what I'm writing for? Be honest now, be frank, old chap. Well, the answer is, yes — but not for those ends alone. I have other things in mind: the achievement of beauty, the satisfaction of a deep and mighty desire, understanding.

VERSE PROVOKED BY A RECENT VISIT TO THE STACKS

All the forlorn futile faces
Drifting, ghostly, thru the iron and book-filled cages
In a sunken filtered light remote from day —
How often in these melancholy places
(so like old dungeons in the Middle, Dark or Christian Ages)
Am I impelled by fearful piety to pray:
O Lord, preserve me from the fate of these poor hacks
Who waste their lives within library stacks.

February 12, 1952 – Edinburgh

What can I say about love? For I am in love, and if I am ever to understand it I'd better make the effort now — this kind of love may never come again to me. And while I'm not sure that it can be explored and analyzed from within with much success, I am *certain* that little will ever be discovered in analytic approaches from the outside. (Love, where is thy sting? And *what* is it?)

The obvious physiological symptoms of love I think I have described before: an acceleration of the pulse rate, a flush of blood to the face (in my case, at least), a certain amount of sweating in the palms and armpits, a slight loosening of the bowels, other unspecifiable churnings and glandular gurglings throughout the body. All of this is in addition to the customary signs of sexual excitement, which are not always present anyway, up to a certain point of intimacy. Fear and trembling, stagefright, intense longing, intense joy and pleasure, a sense of power and triumph — these are emotional concomitants of love related in some subtle way to the purely physical disturbances mentioned above.

Ah, but what's the use? The more I think about it, the more I doubt that I can say anything which hasn't been said much better a thousand times before. I don't suppose love has changed much in the last four or five hundred years; the essentials remain the same.

Fundamental, of course, is sex. Though I have now fallen in love some fourteen or fifteen times, I have never loved a girl who was not physically attractive, by modern Western standards; every one of them, as Schopenhauer could easily have predicted, were full female specimens, well-equipped for copulation and designed for eventual maternity, without exception. No question about it, the flight of the arrow is bent on one target.

Yet there's so much more; obviously, there's more, for though every good-looking girl instantly appeals to my reproductive instinct, I do not go thru the emotional traumas of romantic love with every good-looking girl I see.

Reflect, however: Is it not possible that, with just a little favorable push, the right circumstances, you *would* "fall in love" with every pretty girl you meet? But if true, love is reduced to nothing but the sex drive. Nothing but. And if that is so, then love is either a complete illusion, or else it is something quite different from what I have been fooling with for nearly ten years now. (Saw a young waitress today with fine firm breasts, long legs, a pretty face — almost at once I felt a tender regard for her.)

Why sir, just why *have* you been in love so often? After all, fifteen affairs in ten — no, actually just seven — years, seems to indicate that love comes easily; indeed, it seems to answer the question. For if you will examine your memories closely, I think you will discover, possibly to your chagrin and astonishment, that every time, *every single time*, that you met, prolonged an acquaintance with, really talked with, played with, got to know a little some pretty wench, no matter how dissimilar she might have been intellectually, socially or culturally, that every time you *met* a pretty girl you *did* begin to admire, to long for and, in the usual way, to love her. Without exception.

Well, that might be true; it looks likely, but I'll not take the trouble just now to give my memory the thorough ransacking that would be necessary. Anyway, I'm not doubting the purely animal-life-repeating basis and origin of love; what I would like to investigate is the lovely and stirring aura, atmosphere, poetry, feeling and emotion, built upon and around sex by Western Man in modern times.

What is that? Be it simply association, a connection of a series of extensions of the beloved's dark and mysterious sex organ? Why does the glimpse of an envelope addressed to me, containing a letter from, say, Rita, send such a thrill of magic thru me, tingling my hair, charging the heart, clouding the mind with dim visions of scarcely imaginable delight? Why? Simply because that envelope contains a letter, and that letter displays the actual handwriting of the girl I love, her physical imprint upon paper, and because that letter contains a message from her mind, from her emotions, and because I know that her mind is in her head, and her emotions there too, and because I instantly associate her head with her body and her body with the small aperture that is the whole point and purpose of all my sweating scrambling yearnings, of all my dreams, bold gestures, fantastic rhetoric, need for service and loyalty and a display of each myself, of all my big plans, sunny honeymoons, music, bawlings, songs, shivers and shakes?

IS THAT ALL IT IS?

Impossible! Monstrous! And yet . . . what is the goal of it all, what is it that I really want, more than anything else, with the girl I love? What is primary and central, to which all of my other aspirations and desires, no matter how fine and noble, are but secondary added-on effects? The answer is bald and obvious — all dreams end in bed. Love ends in marriage and the death-by-smothering of love. Life ends in death. Everything, probably, ends in stasis — in still perfection — Heaven or Hell — or the same thing, the all-inclusive final peace of Death.

I haven't begun to answer my original question — I've let myself be shunted off on a tangent by unignorable elementals. Happens every time.

∝

Journey to the Moon: Ten miles of flaming billboards lighting up the night; bandits in a jeep. [An embryonic reference to a philoso-fantasy that will eventually mature into Abbey's 1975 novel of comedic eco-sabotage, *The Monkey Wrench Gang.*]

February 13, 1952 – Edinburgh

I really should stop wasting time, ink and paper by writing so much flabby drivel. This Journal might actually be of some interest and value to me later if I would devote more space to describing the events and scenes of my daily life. That is what, fifty years from now, I will be most keenly interested in.

Received today a letter from Jeanie — a letter and official documents officially decreeing us officially divorced. Fantastic. Incredible. Actually, I took it quite calmly — not a ripple of emotion, only a slight ease of relief. This has taken so much time I was afraid something might have gone wrong; that Fred Black [a mutual college friend, with whom Ed had recently had a falling out] had got hold of her and talked her out of it — something ridiculous like that. But no — there it is. Complete. No more matrimony for me for a good long time.

Received also a letter from Stockholm in reply to my blind advance: a girl named Ami wants me to come and live with her (and, also, with her family) for a few weeks. The letter is written in most exuberant English. She promises me a "fine time," significantly (?) underlined. The goatish devil of lust, smelling sex and seduction, immediately dominates the situation. With sly craft I send her a gibbering foolish letter, striving already for intimate relations — I include a photograph of myself on the chance that she will reciprocate, providing me with the means to look her over (at least her face) and to see what I may be getting into, figuratively speaking.

∝

The wanderlust, tho it's only early February, is seeping up from the ground into the soles of my feet, thence rising by capillary action up toward the heart. First, there's the Austrian ski trip in March — I'm excited enuf over that; then, there's the Stockholm invitation, sex and socialism, for April; then, capping it off, setting the head a-twirl, the idea of a trip to Australia, passage free, courtesy of the Australian government — I would masquerade as a would-be settler (maybe genuine?), necessarily, but that's nothing — and maybe a job on a cattle ranch deep in the wilderness interior of the continent.

Three million square miles and only eight million people! Marvelous. (Maybe Australia *will* be my home.) And almost all of the eight million concentrated in a dozen cities on the east, south and southwestern coastal areas. Superb. A land fit for a free man to breathe in.

I must see Australia sooner or later; why not take off this spring? How pleasant it would be, all my family and friends expecting me back in the U.S. in June, to jolt them a little with a cheerful letter from Singapore, or Milbourne, or Alice Springs.

Ah, but. But the novel. I must finish the novel. Would I do it in Australia? Could I? Not likely. And Rita — my passion-fireflower: I can't run off from her like that; we need an idyll of some sort next summer. A few weeks on the beach somewhere.

After completing my novel, and after making a big stake on it, or in Alaska or the oil fields, and after settling, if possible, my destiny with Rita — I don't see how we'll get together much in the next few years; she seems determined to study in, and not get far from, New York. And besides, I'm not sure that I want to drag her around with me from Alaska to Australia to Kenya to South Africa to Brazil (I'm working out my itinerary already) to Mexico and "home." What I'm planning is a little rough for a girl: deck passages, cattle stations, travel inland by motorcycle, merchant marine, the tropics, etc.

My God, I've got so damned much to do in the next few years. I want to do my traveling while I'm young and tough, yet I don't want to give up the novel or music study or Rita. Of course, if war comes, my problems will be greatly simplified — then I will have to choose between the mountains or prison. Simple. And I should be making preparations for war and hiding in the hills — caching supplies, training myself more intensely for outdoor living and, more important, for outdoor subsistence. And some research in guerrilla warfare.

My God, sometimes I delude myself into thinking a bandit life would be extremely romantic and adventurous (maybe it would), and as I foolishly let it grow more attractive (no responsibility) one wicked devil in me begins to anticipate with something like pleasure the coming of war. Childish, criminal stupidity.

∽

Tragedy: Surely an essential element in tragedy is the sense, the presence of, the dark and omnipotent background of *doom;* the foreknowledge of death and defeat enhances and glorifies the struggle.

For there must be struggle, youth, or beauty or nobility of some kind opposing, defying and opposed by great and malignant power, the issue of the contest foreknown, the contestants unequal but the struggle nonetheless glorious.

There must be greatness and nobility *and strength* present in the hero. The foredoomed battle of the little man, or foolish man, or evil man, is not tragic but pathetic. Pathos is of course an element of tragedy but not in itself a sufficient condition of tragedy.

What about Socrates? Is his death, as described by Plato, a tragic one? No, I think not; the element of struggle is absent, the serenity and the acceptance of fate too easily arrived at, the hero too smugly confident of some kind of pleasant second life in another world. The wishful dream of personal immortality makes true tragedy impossible; death must be death, complete and final, without illusions.

Which brings up an incidental point: Tragedy is impossible in a Christian framework. As Dante realized, in the Pauline-Augustine-Thomist world only comedy is possible, though comedy of two varieties — on the one hand, Heaven, perpetual and perfect and static and perfectly inane bliss; on the other hand, Hell, the apotheosis of the hideous and ugly and grotesque, eternally prolonged horror without relief, without grace, without humanity.

Tragedy: The foredoomed struggle of the good, or young, or beautiful, noble, against an overwhelming and malignant POWER, with defeat and final death for the hero as the physical end; with poetry, serenity and solemnity the aesthetic end; with grandeur the final end.

A genuine tragic hero: Giordano Bruno. Another: Bartolomeo Vanzetti.

Is *Hamlet* a tragedy? Or a muddled farce? A little of both, I would say, though a little more the latter. First thing, of course, the Christian metaphysic underlying the play has to be ignored; for how can death be taken seriously if it is merely the gateway to Hollywood? (I need not specify an alternative; Heaven and Hell are fundamentally identical, and Hollywood easily embraces both.) And death, real and honest death, is essential in tragedy. Since Shakespeare himself thought of *Hamlet* as a tragedy, and since most Englishmen have followed his suggestion, it seems obvious that, at least while watching or reading the play, most Englishmen have suspended their Christianity and taken death, not the doctrine of immortality, as something real and important.

Good. With Christianity on the shelf, we can look at things clearly. It soon becomes apparent that the essential conflict in *Hamlet* is that between order and disorder, with good, personified by Hamlet, identified with the former. The theme is the necessity for the restoration of order, the duty falling upon Hamlet. Unfortunately, both theme and conflict depend to a critical extent upon the Christian or medieval concept of the world, which had to be rejected previously in order to make *Hamlet* eligible for consideration as a tragedy.

An immediate and fatal inner contradiction is now revealed: In the Christian frame of reference *Hamlet* cannot be regarded as a tragedy, yet without it *Hamlet* falls apart as a meaningful dramatic structure, crumbling and disintegrating into nothing more than a complicated adventure story of court intrigue with lots of swordplay, sex and a sad ending.

The foolish flurry of carnage in the final scene cruelly exposes the play's crucial weaknesses, revealing it as both a literal and dramatic shambles. Observe, among the numerous and aptly described "casual slaughters" at the end, the careless, pointless and almost incidental death of Hamlet himself; if he had survived to reign alive it would make no substantial difference so far as the play's point and purpose are concerned. Lives are too cheap, political stability too dear — *Hamlet* cannot be considered a tragedy, either with or without its Christian substructure.

Furthermore, whether taken with or without its Christian background, *Hamlet* cannot honestly be considered a very good play, as a play. Of course, this fellow Shakespeare had a genuine talent for the fine phrase and the memorable speech; there is more than enough poetry in *Hamlet* to keep it in the repertoire of the legitimate theatre for many years to come.

Not that Shakespeare was unable to write tragedy; *King Lear* is a tragedy, and a good one. Well . . . pretty good.

February 14, 1952 – Edinburgh

Went to the U.S. consulate today to see about visas for Austria and Germany. Looks like I'm gonna hafta write to London — damned nuisance. Also tried to get information on entering the Soviet Union — the consulate had none whatever. Not very encouraging, eh? Maybe I can make a quick surprise-dash from Stockholm to Leningrad. I must have at least a glimpse of the Workers' Paradise before I go back, reluctantly, to old Commercia, to the land of the chrome-plated dollar grin.

∞

At the Golf Tavern today for lunch: I went primarily to stare at one of the waitresses, but ordered lunch and ale out of common courtesy. What an appealing creature she is. Her name is Elsie. She's blue-eyed and fair-haired, speaks a thick Scotch, has fine ankles and calves, solid-looking hips and a splendid pair of breasts — big, full, fore-thrust; they jiggle most delightfully as she jogs about on her high heels.

Shall I take her out? Or is a point of loyalty involved? Rita is the girl who dominates my mind, and heart, *and* sex; she is the only girl I know, at the moment, for whom I would swim the Bosphorus, or climb Ben Nevis or compose a sonnet. But yet, I keep thinking about that waitress — what she must look like undressed — she must have a fine body. How I wish I were a painter. There are so damned few good-looking girls here in Edinburgh; it's disgraceful. Seems, in a way, a shame, perhaps a kind of sin, to neglect a potential source of pleasure and quiet companionship like Elsie.

February 15, 1952 – Edinburgh

Today, with much fuss and flowering, we buried old King George. I don't know — the spectacle disunites me. On the one hand, the pomp and pageantry has an immediate aesthetic appeal to which I respond with pleasure; on the other hand, my democratic and republican instincts are deeply repelled by so much fuss over one man. He was, after all, a very ordinary man: He loved his wife and kids, he went to church on Sundays, he did his strange and rather ridiculous job to the best of his ability, he suffered quite a bit from bad health and as far as we know he never complained about it.

A very common man — there, perhaps, is the key to the business. The symbol — everybody's symbol: To the middle-class housewives who support the monarchy he was domesticity enshrined; to the politicians and brass hats, he was Britain . . . old, lordly and triumphant. To all the others who were, in some way, moved by his death, he was the solemn symbol of death, of the common man's common lot.

I listened to part of the funeral service over the radio. The comment and commentators were sickening, but the other sounds — feet tramping, crowds whispering, horses clattering, slow muffled drum beats. And seemingly from far away — wild, green, over a mourning drone — the wailing then keening of the Scottish bagpiper in old dim lament — oh sad, sad — were intensely real, vivid, human and sad, oh so sad. Oh weep for man, oh weep!

∽

I am filled with admiration upon recalling my last semester at New Mexico University, when, in addition to being alive, I was carrying on the following activities simultaneously: (1) taking six full-time academic courses, working hard enough to get A's in everything but French (that ugly language!), completing a double major in Philosophy and English and graduating "with Honors" (two projects in independent research); (2) writing the first hundred pages of my novel; (3) editing, contributing to, getting in trouble with and getting fired from the student literary magazine; (4) working part-time in Riddle's tile factory; (5) separating from and trying to divorce my wife; (6) falling in love and carrying on an intense affair with a crazy girl sculptor and painter; (7) spending the last six weeks of the semester without a roof over my head, living in a sleeping bag on top of a small hill in Tijeras Canyon.

February 25, 1952 – Edinburgh

It's ten minutes 'til midnight in old Edinburgh. The night is dark as primeval night; what can I see through the cold glass of my window? Blackness and blackness only — except for one window, high up, an attic window higher than mine, across the inner courtyard, illumined dimly by a light within, the orange translucent blinds drawn down; one other soul, at least, is awake and ... perhaps, thinking, or even writing as I am. A small wind is blowing over the roofs, disturbing the air currents in the chimneys; every now and then a puff of dirty coal smoke comes out of my miniature open fireplace — even tho there's not much of a fire in it, mostly just red glowing coals — and floats up past the mantle, adding there to an old film of dust, up, over the mirror above the mantle, up to the ceiling, there to flatten and diffuse and apparently to disappear. Just smoke.

It is midnight in Edinburgh and I am haunted by a dim sorrow, a sweet sad gentle little anguish as soft and lovely and impossible to touch as the glowing coals in my fireplace. I am tenderly haunted by a mourning ghost, by the most elusive and ineffable of melancholy spirits ... and by a girl's face, by a girl's face under a flowing veil of music, radiant and transfigured, mysterious with love.

∞

Dear God, dear Mother, dear Earth, dear Sweetheart — madly we rush, headlong with breakneck speed, furiously we hurl ourselves and are flung forward over shining and always narrowing tracks out of night through morning, noon and twilight, under whirling cloudy, clear or starred skies forward into darkness, into an eternal darkness, out of the night and into the night.

It's a troubling thought, the fantastic dash of time, the bitter-cruel brevity of our mixed-up, lonely, unhappy lives; so little time, so very much to do, so wide the world. I can almost, at certain times, feel a surge of panic when the knowledge oversweeps me: You, Edward Abbey, Paul Abbey, whatever you call yourself, you are going to die, and the day of your dying is not so very far away. You are going to die, and all the world's loveliness — the love of young girls and old friends, the taste of cold water on a hot afternoon, the smell of green willow leaves, the molecular dance of fireflies over the swamp in Bennett's pasture, the feel of warm rain in April, rain falling across the sun like a kilt of gauze, like a maiden's hair, like a film of smoke, like a morning dream, like transparent silk, the sound of the river and the sea, the flow of poetry, the touch of old black leather, of fair fresh hands, of moving air — all the world's loveliness, the heartbreaking beauty, is going to die with you and for you and in you and forever. Forever, forever, forever (what a gracious tri-syllabic wave of tone and meaning in that forever over-woven ever-wanted and unwavering word).

Oh night, weave riddles in my head, fill my heart with restless ghosts, but do not, I beg you, do not, please, penetrate the weary world halfway between the mind and the emotions' well with old, sick and dying spells and thralls and creeping enchantments from the black forest of ancestral memory — there is something in that too faint, too overgrown with rusty briars and seedy weeds, with tangled scrub-thorn and crab apple and hawthorn and wild vines, all snarled and jungled together, and crawling over my dreams smothering all hope, and from the other room the whining snore, the sad wind-whistle, the night's evocation of empty black haunted old farmhouses falling and drifting through space in wild yards among dark pines along old pointless rutty roads.

O, there are no words for what I mean. I am lonely. I am unhappy. I cannot say what it is that I am feeling. There is no music for it, there is no art . . . I cannot tell you what I mean. I know that I am alone, that I am lonely, that I am haunted by a vague cloud of sorrow and by a fading floating image of a breathless loveliness which sings not hope to me, not warmth or happiness, nor meaning or end, but only is, only is, and never will be more. I am heavy-tongued, slow-worded, thick and halting and nearly dumb. I cannot say it. I am unhappy. I am lonely. Give me your hand, whoever you are.

February 27, 1952 – Edinburgh

It seems rather a shame not to commit suicide, not to cap with tragedy (brilliant youth struck down by sorrow) the lovely and pathetic sentiments on the preceding page; how fine they would look as "his last words." But here I am, two days later, still alive, with my dandruff as bad as ever, my head aching with a good solid blocked-up cold, and me needing a bath badly — I haven't bathed or showered for a week.

Foggy as a whore's history outside: bluish-gray, smoky yellow, dirty, pale, filthy, hovering air of Edinburgh, the Athens of the North. Cold, too, clammy-damp cold that soaks through walls, through wool and through flesh and lodges in the marrow of the bone.

Well . . . not actually for me, but it probably feels like that to the old and dying. Anyway, I've got two fires going and I'm sitting between them — in front of me, on the floor at my feet, a small electric heater with resistance coils hot and glowing, warming my bony shanks; behind me, the little coal fire, yellow flames streaming endlessly up out of soft-looking, intensely softly radiant, golden-orange coals and hard black coals yet untouched by the fire.

So I should be warm enough, and I am. My lips are stiff and chapped, with a small crack in the upper lip, a reliable source of a kind of interesting, tiny, dry pain which I take continual delight in experiencing.

∞

The novel, my terrible novel, will drive me to ruin. It's almost five-hundred manuscript pages long now, well over 100,000 words, I imagine, and yet not more than a third complete. A frightful labor!

And the worth of it, the quality — the problem worries me night and day. At times I'm afraid to read what I've written, almost superstitiously afraid — and then at other times I do work up enough courage to hastily read snatches chosen at random. The effects are mixed — parts of the book seem to me hilariously funny, beautifully written, packed and quivering with life. And then I'll read the same passage again, or another, and it will seem dead as junkyard iron, pretentious and false, weak, thin, spineless, empty and hideous.

Who is right? The critic or the author? I swing constantly, if erratically, between power and confidence, and antipodal despair; between surges of triumph when I look at myself grinning at me in the mirror and can say, "Abbey, oh Abbey, you monstrously clever fellow," and dank glooms of dark defeat, convinced of failure, crushed by doubt, with nothing to do but wonder how I'll ever make a living, if I can possibly tolerate a suburban life with wife and family and a dreary job, or if I should march off at once into the wilderness, like Troy himself, and fling myself picturesquely from some high and lonesome cliff. It's a problem all right.

The very fact that I am subjected to fits and attacks of doubt is in itself enough to harass my will to go forward. I ask myself: If the thing were truly good and worthwhile would not my confidence be sure and untroubled, my creative drive strong and unflagging and steady, my will to work irresistible? I ask myself, and worry and wonder, not sure, not knowing.

At times I try the heroic approach; I go walking at noon, or at night, under the Georgian lamp posts, and mutter and mumble sternly to myself: "I will not. I will never surrender. I will fight through to the finish, whatever the outcome. I will not quit, I will not betray and desert the best thing in my life. No, no, I will not surrender."

And another part of the mind, looking on, grins and jeers: "Thataboy, Abbey, make it dramatic, make it melodramatic. Make yourself some kind of a hero. If it's not really important, persuade yourself it is. Talk to yourself; convince your lazy soul that it holds a power for which all humanity is tensely and hopefully waiting. That's the way. Keep talking."

It's enough to drive a good man to drink. But not me; I'm not a good man. Nor am I, much as I would like to be, an evil and wicked man. Damn it, no; I belong to the great mass of the in-betweens, hapless and impotent, slow and dull and awkward, sentimental, easily moved to tears, full of big hopes, bigger doubts, gigantic fantasies. What's going to become of me? I have no idea. Who cares? I don't know. Does it matter a good goddamn? Probably not.

No wonder the first novel is so often a writer's best — the poor bastard pours the first twenty or thirty years of his life into it. What subsequent work can ever be a condensation and distillation in so compact a space of so much material?

/March 1, 1952 – Edinburgh

Sunshine — real live sunshine — is pouring through my window. And beyond the glass I can see a sea-blue sky and clouds in a hurry. Is spring possible? I can't believe it — it's been years, I would say, since we last had a spring in our faces, the blood steaming and curling with the old swampy fluty desires, the indefinable longings. Just the mere sight of sunshine, so many are the vague associations, cooks up a broth of nostalgia and idiot happiness in my soul.

Love and sex spring first to mind, of course, but immediately after comes the incredible heaven of boyhood remembered, when every hill was a big rock-candy mountain of delight and mystery, every woods full of trees, a forest of the ancestral history, conquest and sweet terror, hide-and-seek, battle, ambush, secrecy. And running downhill upwind. And rolling on warm damp grass and weeds — the smell of oiled leather and the smack of the baseball in the palm, the solid smash of a good hit, the long loping runs in the outfield hauling down a high fly ball — the smell and texture of spring air, spring air in motion, breezing through the stickly little leaves, winding among the hills like an irresponsible ghost, blowing mouths open and eyes shut and hair apart.

Spring is a dangerous topic; almost impossible to write about it without lapsing into literary conventions and girlish gush and false, absolutely false statements. I prove it myself. Yet. . . .

Yet the power and compulsion of spring is true, true as ever, and cannot be ignored. Perhaps . . . rather than strive too hard for originality, if I could just observe accurately myself and spring, and remember truly my boyhood and spring, and then report simply and straightforwardly what I have discovered, I might do quite well.

Unless spring is something which cannot be handled so easily. "Straightforward reporting" suggests simple factual prose — is that enough? Surely poetry is necessary — for what can be more straightforward, direct, immediate, inescapable than *good* poetry? Descriptive reporting is insufficient — only the vivid crashing impact of imagery hammered out under stress and packed with fire and emotion, rough, harsh, jagged-edged — Hart Crane! — only that can tell the truth, or enough of the truth to demand attention. What shall I do then? Attempt both simple reporting and sensuous picture-painting? Combine the two somehow? Give up? "I will never surrender." Then I must choose and act; I think I'll try the combination method. (Not here and now — sit still.)

∞

The novel has languished in stasis for three days. I've been busy with love. The fact of Rita. The dawning of a miracle — I think she really loves me. The thought is enough to make a man yodel in church, cry in his beer, step over trees and look down chimneys. *Jesus Christ!* And I thought I was getting too old for such spasms of blind foolish blurry whirring joy. *Mon Dieu!*

But even here I'm itched by creeping doubts: Does she really love me, or just the shade of me? Is it love for me, of me, or love of love in love with her and love? I mean — does she love me steadily and honestly, or does she love me only for the comfort I administer to her soul? Does she reach out for me only when I seem to fade a shade, to turn away, to withdraw a few steps? Is it possessiveness rather than love that inspires her effulgences of breathless emotion? Surely not, I don't for a moment think so, never — but the little brown doubts, safe in their particular cells, cannot be exorcised by the confidence that fills the rest of my mind.

There is this certain pull and tension in love at a certain stage, when one lover, in order to draw out the other more fully, threatens with a feigned wandering of the attention, mutters vague doubts, suggests hazy and possibly insufferable difficulties, pretends to be losing interest.

Then the other lover, all too easily deceived, nearly overwhelmed by the heart-crushing soul-smashing bleak black blank prospect conjured up by the scheming one, comes rushing desperately forward, crying out with anguish, pleading for solace and reassurance, pledging a sweeping love, demanding concrete promises and alabaster lies.

To this the first lover, unless so base and mean as to be unable to resist the temptation to play out the line with further agonizing doubts and withdrawals, responds magnanimously, perhaps joyously, certainly with an inward happiness that washes away all sins. And the two live happily ever after — unless there are a few more bouts of tugging and pulling destined to precede the longed-for consummation, with the role of initiating the goad alternating regularly between the love-ensnared couple.

I mention this not because I think it funny, but because I think it childish, and perhaps wicked, and because I wonder if I have not been guilty of the very thing I've described. If done deliberately, with knowledge, it's an act of cruelty — plain cheap cruelty.

If I were to charge myself with that, I would plead not guilty, but I am aware that I may, semi-consciously, caught in a flush of general excitement and independence, have said or written things which could affect the one I love and who loves me just as painfully as if it had been an act of calculated malice. Of such sinful recklessness I may well be guilty, and the possibility troubles me greatly. To play with, to twist and stretch and rack, the grave emotions of another human being — that is an awful thing. And I'm not so sure as I was a paragraph ago that love, even great and joyous love, can wash away such a sin.

In fact, I don't believe sins can be washed away by anything, not by the Blood of the Lamb, not by Christ on or off the Cross, not by love of God or God's love, not by a billion Hail Marys or a Milky Way of candles or a thousand ages of penance or a million miles of contrition on broken glass and burning coals and leprous bodies.

In fact, I indignantly reject, with horror and with loathing, the dark, ancient, vile and filthy lie that another man or God-Man can redeem us of our sins by his own suffering, or that we can purify ourselves and start over again by compounding our sins with more suffering, more ugliness, more filth and gibbering faith.

What an utterly horrible doctrine! What a contemptible and nightmarish horror-story to preach to grave, thoughtful children. It's time we stood up like men and faced our responsibilities, admitted and lived with our past sins, and cleared our hearts, in so far as we can, not by atonement or by condemning someone else to die for us, but by refusing to cooperate with evil and insisting upon doing good.

I think I'll go outside and walk through some of that sunlight. I feel like I've been rummaging through old dark closets and cubby-holes and damp cellars. Breathe some of that honest air. Taste the wind. Have a closer look at that cloud over by Arthur's Seat [a huge basaltic (volcanic) core and prominent Edinburgh-area landmark]; it might go away any minute. Try to forget that I'm suddenly angry and full of hate. What can I do in that condition? Might go see a movie later on. There's one at the Playhouse Theatre I ought to see: *Detective Story* with Kirk Douglas and William Bendix.

March 10, 1952 – Edinburgh

The Delights of Melancholy: O, I grow younger, more beautiful, every hour! What do I mean? Why is it that almost anything troubles my trembling heart to the very depths; where is the old steady eye and crafty cynic of the mind? I wobble all over the tracks, like a drunken bum, like young Shelley falling and fainting on the grass under his love's window. My eyes hang on the verge, continually, of tears.

Tears! There is too much beauty in the world! O, there is too much to love, too much to desire! The fantastic wordless longings go singing and screaming out, the mind reels drunkenly far behind and body crawls after mind. Too much — I can't take it any longer. Something's got to give, break, snap, burst.

My God, I go to the window for a breath of fresh air and what do I see? A great silver disc passing through shining clouds of sea-air, the other world, the moon, under the purple night-sky — Jesus Christ! It's too much! I glance at the fire: a cluster of fire-roses, luminescent, velvet-radiances of quivering semi-translucent melting liquid fire, yellow flames pouring upward and dying in gray smoke, transformed to invisible spirits! No!

I turn on the goddamned radio, hoping to hear something ugly and sobering — instead, I hear a consort of viols, a lute, an Elizabethan melody, sweet, serene and pure! I shut my eyes, turn off the radio, stop breathing, taste nothing — and at once, from nothing coming swiftly, appears to mind an image, a face, the eyes of love and the magic hair, a faraway mysterious smile!

Nothing can destroy these ghosts and spirits of the adolescent heart, the beautiful romantic heart, but writing — writing can do it, for a short while, at least. Yes, the effort to grasp, understand, capture and communicate in words — *that* frightens my haunts away! Unless I have, in some wondrous metaphysical way, succeeded in transferring them from my own emotional apparatus through pen and ink onto these pages here — which I can scarcely believe. How can anything so vague, fleeting, elusive as my twinges of melancholy, of love, of tearful awareness of beauty, be spread out in words like a specimen on a slide?

I don't know — I don't believe it — yet now they, the ghouls of romance, are all gone, or nearly all gone. I've nothing left to do now but go get a drink of water, urinate, blow my nose, stoke up the fire, take one more look at the moon . . . and get to work.

The Flute-Girl: A lovely, fantastic creature, tall and slim, with black hair surrounding her head and *brilliant* eyes; she wears a gown of black velvet and carries a silver flute. (One of the darkest and most obscure of my passions and one that will, I am afraid, haunt me with mingled wonder and regret all the days of my life.) Viewed and loved for long from afar. Met? Never known? The Ballad of the Flute-Girl.

Those love letters I write, dreadful things — I shudder as I lick them shut and drop them in the mailbox, like a man disposing of a dirty diaper. I don't know why I hate them so much — I get a big kick while actually engaged in the writing of them. Yes, I know; it's because I try to do so much and fail so dismally.

I love that girl, I truly and deeply love her. When I write a letter to her I try then to communicate the emotion, naturally. Prose will never do, nor the flat stale repetitious monotony of simply stating over and over again, like a silly gibbering unbrained parrot, "I love you i love you i love you." . . .

No — poetry is necessary. Only poetry can tell the truth. In this situation. So I try to write poetry — but in a rush. You can't write poetry in a rush. But I can't wait. So I write rhetoric, bombast, great empty booming shells of sound without content, fury without object.

It must be sickening stuff to read — how false and fraudulent she must think I am. How can she love such a windy furnace of noise as I? (But she does.) Verbal exuberance without control, without form, the spring unsprung and wobbling wildly, the breezy blowing in all directions at once. (If only she can understand my weakness and, understanding, forgive.)

I don't see how poetry can ever be easy — possibly a few fragile lyrics have been blown off like spray, but even then there were probably several years of unconscious preparation behind them. But real poetry, the thick dense intense complicated stuff that lives and endures, must require blood and sweat; blood and sweat are essential elements *in* poetry as well as behind it.

March 17, 1952 – Edinburgh

Tomorrow I'm off to Austria and the Tirolean Alps. Nothing to do but ski skate and eat for two weeks. What a wretched life I lead. What have I ever done to deserve this? A painful question. *If I am to have so much I must have more.*

April 15, 1952 – on the North Sea

Sicken and die, friend, sicken and die.

Lusterless the world, damp and gray . . . all that once seemed beautiful is dead, all is desolate. This is the worst time of all, when everything, everything lacks interest . . . art, love, adventure, justice, sex, beauty, tragedy; all has — for the moment — faded, Earth and all upon it seems dull and drab . . . I cannot even feel satisfactorily melancholy about it.

Now, I suppose, I am as close to suicide as I am ever likely to get; it will pass, I'm sure; I have a sore throat or something, something has upset the mechanism, turned the mind against itself — a bad time — two days now. The loveliness of April, and I am dead to it. From far away a beautiful girl calls to me, and I am deaf. The novel waits, incomplete, not growing, and I am dumb, fingers paralyzed.

I can't do anything; utterly listless, lethargic, disinterested, dying on my feet; an awful condition. Nothing compels, everything waits; I might as well be dead, I might as well be dead. God, I hope this sort of dun pall doesn't come upon me very often. Powerless, impotent, finally still.

What is more beautiful than red streaming
Banners on the wind
Screaming —
"Fire! Revenge! Death to Kings! Life
To the new world of the heart's
Dreaming!"?

END OF JOURNAL IV

OUR FRIEND

EL SALVADOR. DE ESPAÑA

Road map: *Journal V covers approximately one month, during which Abbey took a break from his Edinburgh studies, and from keeping Journal IV, to enjoy a Spanish vacation, via the Channel and France.*

JOURNAL V

The Spanish Journal December 1951 to January 1952

∞

December 21, 1951 – Paris

The night train to London: A dismal ride, a dreary old long dismal ride it was, with the mist and the fog flowing ghostly by beyond the glass panes and the engine squealing occasionally and the compartment too cold for a long time and me not able to sleep — not able to sleep for thinking about so many terrible deeds I have done, and loneliness too.

An old man on the train, smiling, grinning, going down to Edinburgh to have a new rubber throat installed. He couldn't eat — lived on beer and tea; funny — he laughed — just couldn't swallow real food — something wrong with his gullet — food got stuck down there. Without his new rubber throat, he would starve to death — funny — everybody laughed.

At Victoria, I saw an impressive number of pretty French girls, jolly pretty Frenchy girls so nice and fresh and flowery and sexy-looking compared to the ugly women of the British, the poor peaked homely English girls.

Met a Frenchman on the train who's going to be a Bendix engineer — loves automatic dishwashers.

Stepping through customs, on the docks and onto the mediocre little ship . . . the smooth and mediocre sea.

The poetic beauty of the gulls, seen by me in true understanding for the first time — the poetry of motion, gull-motion, a sea gull soaring, streaking down, flapping along behind our boat-tug-garbage scow with his perfectionist wings and his torpedo body and his invisible splendid arcs and curves still alive in the air behind him. "The storm dance of gulls." (Why am I suddenly so lonely?)

Dieppe was simple — the long surprisingly clean and comfortable train to Paris ... two dour Englishmen, myself and four homeward-bound Italian girls, piling the compartment to the corridor with too much shabby baggage, talking away like mad, eating candy, drinking tea, cackling and clawing at each other, and finally singing sad and sentimental Eye-tie songs, "Sorrento" etc. I nearly cried, and I nearly loved them all. It's a sad shape I'm in ... half-sick with fatigue and loneliness.

Then Paris, after plowing through, tunneling through more fog, more mist, so that I have no idea what France is like yet, except for glimpses of dull-green, small-hilly, Scot-like country.

Paris. More ugly business. Couldn't find a taxi, got hooked by a fake *porteur*, gypped out of half a pound for a miserable Metro ride and the privilege of watching the sly little weasel tote my miniature handbag. Ugly scene. The bastard wanted seven hundred francs for his half-hour's work — I wanted to give him a hundred — finally compromised on half a pound, about 450 francs. Never do that again. Always take the taxi.

Finally got rid of him, got a room, a rather dingy one though equipped with a basin and a tiny balcony, here at L'Hotel Cavour. Does Thomas Cook really bring his protégés here!?

December 30, 1951 - Barcelona

On the train from Paris to Irún ... an effort at conversation between me and a blind Lithuanian. Interesting fellow — blond, tall, slender, rough Slavic face, smoked incessantly, talked of the Russians (hated them, naturally), of his future schooling — going to be a cabinet maker. Had a hideous old middle-aged redheaded girlfriend of a woman — red hair, roguish rouge, *rojo, rioja*, ugly, hideous, oh Jesus ugly 'twas that hair, and the face under it just as bad. [The Lithuanian] talked in French, German, Russian, even a little English — the effort at communication was intense, genuine, if halting, crude and limited. The train rambled on through the night — the blind Lithuanian got off at Bayonne.

Irún — the strange thrill, unforgettable, of hearing *Español* blaring from the loudspeakers; so different, so incredibly different. (Did you think it would be the same, idiot?) So foreign yet familiar — so military yet agreeable — so Spanish, so suggestive of trouble.

The grim-looking otherworldly looking *soldados* — old antique uniforms, shiny boots on the officers, long coats flapping around the ankles. The private [enlisted] soldiers were miserable creatures — dirty, sloppy, beaten, doglike. But that voice at Irún blaring forth in genuine *Español* — Jesus how I thrill at the sound of it — so much better than English English, Scottish English, French French. (French — an ugly fucking bleeding goddamn language!)

At Irún I lingered only a few minutes. (I'm now on the boat for Palma, a mere table away from a lovely precious luscious lovable Wellesley-type blonde, with her doltish loutish American male, and another Wellesley girl, very burstful of Spanish but not very pretty.)

And then I was off to San Sebastian, accompanied by three Ceylonese I met at the Irún station — they *looked* a little helpless (I was to find out better later), speaking no Spanish at all, and I thought I could help; student naval officers for the Ceylonese Navy [which] consists of one destroyer.

(She's married, she's married, just found out, she's married. Goddamn.)

So we [Abbey and the Ceylonese] went to San Sebastian — a town, city, rather attractive. After some consultation of a list, we headed for the Correo Hotel, preceded by a *porteur* pushing a cart loaded with their, hardly my (so little) baggage.

San Sebastian: surprisingly clean, bright, white — I expected the worst in *España* — San Sebastian: every window, every room with its iron-grilled balcony. People all over the place, surprisingly healthy looking, well-dressed, though not particularly happy looking — very Puritanical in fact.

At the hotel, confusion: the Ceylonese went barging boldly into things; didn't wait for or expect any help from me; thus, confusion. They thought that by speaking English with a Spanish accent, by adding a vowel to every word, by dabbling in a little French, by mobile faces, by waving hands, they could communicate anything and everything. On the other hand, the old woman running the hotel tried to make herself understood by increased volume of voice, by a louder tone, by shouting, by getting irritable and excited and talking at an incredibly rapid jabbering rate, gibberish to our ears.

Nevertheless, plunging thickly in, while I stood by near-helpless with amusement, the three Ceylonese managed to get something like what we wanted.

How familiar those three were to become: Paul, just perceptibly the leader, light olive skin, black hair (of course), a pronounced British accent, a mad cocky swaggering manner — got drunk easily — highly curious, argumentative, especially with Spaniards who couldn't understand what he was saying. (Sometimes I wish I were back "home" in Scotland, warm and cozy in my little room with the fire going, music, a good book nearby, tea and biscuits.) Overflowing with mock British mannerisms: "I say, old chap," and "What a bloody mess," and "God save the bleeding fucking King." Why can't I capture the fellow; what's his essence?

January 4, 1952 – Palma de Majorca

Goddamnit, I'm still cold. I've got a cold. Hot sun here but it's amazing how the Christing clouds keep obscuring it — they go to all the trouble, in fact, of drifting in circles. Never saw the like. Joints, hotels. Food, ah food, what and in what excellent quantities am I eating. (My hands are cold; I can hardly write.) At least one steak every day; and fine smooth potent wines.

How do I feel? Not too bad. When engaged, involved, I'm mighty glad to be alive. Only when doing nothing, thinking nothing important, do I begin to mourn for my past sins, to whine for the future, to whine and whimper for my women, to be lonely rather than alone, to crawl through the tunnels of the heart begging forgiveness from unknown and known victims. (Ah, Jean, what have I done to you? And Rita, what shall I do to you? Forgive me if you can, for I know what I do, and if you can't I will know why. Light a candle for me. Hail a few Marys. I sure need it, and them.)

Hail a few Marys for me, *compadre*. Whistle one up.

We're all Brothers in the Bowels of Jesus Christ.

∞

A Proposed Improvement on the Wedding Rite:

The couple stand alone together on some great and beautiful escarpment facing the setting sun, attended only by the rocks and trees, by the sky, wind and sun. Before them, at their feet, burns a small fire of pinyon and juniper. As the sun, poised on the western horizon, is about to disappear, the to-be-wedded pair, standing clasped together, address the sun with the following oath of marriage:

> *"O, our beloved sun,*
> *Supreme source of light, of life, of love;*
> *Never rise again if we two,*
> *I, __ __, and I, __ __,*
> *Are not united in body and spirit this night*
> *And do not remain so united,*
> *With affection and comradeship,*
> *For as long as love shall endure."*

The sun sets, completing and sealing with twilight the elemental ritual.

January 5, 1952 – Soller, Majorca

What's this I'm in now, some little old mountain valley in Majorca? Rain, too. Late night now. Cold, wet, dark.

Where was I?

The other two Indios — Ceylonese — Mahsin: short, squat, very dark, a square serious face, excitable talker, squawker, irritating at times I must say, sad imitations of British college wit, also a neat dresser. Wanted to know if I took him for a Spaniard when I first saw him. Voluble, full of gestures, too, talked too fast for me, often unintelligible — heavy black brows, the promise of a lovely heavy black beard, a sort of gray-black skin, not Negro at all, rather . . . Drividian, I guess. Fond of singing various national anthems. Much more sober than the other two, I think. Frantic questions: "Shall we? Shall we?"

Reyo — an altogether different type: Smooth, slick, sharp, jazzy-like, a very American type, sharp dresser, cigarette holder, sang American pop songs, a crooner, mooner over love, like the American drugstore corner Negro maybe, but he looked the most *Indian* of the three — smooth brown skin, shiny black hair, big white eyes, rather handsome actually. Fond of women, phono-records, has some sort of vague interest in art and architecture, very likable and consequently not very interesting.

They became brothers as I got to know them — I never thought about their darker skins, their different voices, shorter stature, blueblack slickback hair, no, honest, I didn't. Still, a bizarre trio, with their queer combined British-American cultures and their Ceylonese bodies, eyes, voices, spirits. Very modern. All three were professed atheists or agnostics. Odd types, really. And their powerful driving genitals.

∞

In a Little Spanish Whorehouse:

Christmas Eve in San Sebastian. Full of steak, primed with *vino y cognac*, the boys were baying for a cunt-hunt. Lots of wine we spilled in that dingy little back-street bar-*restaurante*. The frightened little waitress. One apiece not enuf, we ordered and consumed a second round of beefsteaks and French fries. Okay. Hokay. Goot. Hungry boys, us.

Drunken by now, barging forth into the evening two went, while one and I lingered, fingering our penises in the *urinario*. Outward. Cool warm night. Off staggered us. Eventually came cascading on wheels Paul y Reyo in Taxi-Baby. Off.

Already, somehow, in their incredible jargon, the boys had made the frightened-looking driver understand what we wanted. On Christmas Eve.

Rushing off through the night in an unknown foreign city, destination SEX. With a capital X. Speeding. Turns. Suburbs. A continual babble bubbled, crowded us, cigarette lighters, matches, all flaming, jab-jabber jabber-rapid frantic talk, the Oriental coming to the fore as gonadal pressure rose — blind drunken anticipatory excitement.

On the outskirts of the city, hill-climbing sharp-turning, headlights coasting over white plaster, red tile roofs, blue-tiled walls, flowers, gardens, balconies, iron-grilled gates, the handsome villas of the middling European rich. Christmas Eve. (At home the stockings dangle before the ruddy blinking fire waiting glowing to singe the fat ass of Santa Claus.)

What was I doing? I had not the faintest desire to go a-whoring — I've seen too many of the mask-face bitches. But the carefree excitement carried me with it — no harm in just lookin'.

In front of a gracious-looking villa we stopped; the driver got out, rapped on the gate. After a few minutes a light went on and a middle-aged woman in a kimono came to the gate, frowning. The Madam, irritated. Christmas Eve. A hurried whispered gibbering conversation twixt Mad and cabby. The Madam disappeared, leaving the villa's garden gate locked behind her. Light went out. The boys were flabbergasted.

In we piled, off we went, through the dark vagina of the night. Another swanky-looking villa. Here no response at all, no lights, *nada*. Off again. Third joint. Same no-result. The boys were astounded, angry, incredulous.

The driver had no more ideas. Sadly, quietly, apparently accepting his ass-chewing as deserved, he drove us back to the center of town. Softened by his resignation, somebody offered the driver fifty pesetas. He took it, drove off, disappeared, doubtless headed home to a warm bed and a hot woman.

The boys, het up, changed, went looking for pimps. Every man on the street (there weren't many at this late hour, midnight) they took for a pimp. Lots of confused conversation, hopeless conversation in their fantastic mixture of Ceylonese, British, pidgin, American. Several contacts were apparently found, but all said the same thing — tonight no, tomorrow yes.

One sad-looking specimen was found, a sickening dog-like character who spoke a bit of American. Questioned, he promised *senoritas* at ten the next day, Christmas morning. The boys took up his offer. Back to bed.

Morning. Sightseeing. We had all forgotten about the promising pimp of the preceding night. Much to our surprise (not mine, really), the gray-haired soft-faced pimp showed up for the ceremony. Nobody was interested for a long while. Like a damned sheep dog, he followed the four of us on our walk around the beach. When I stopped to contemplate the surf licking over the sand, he did the same.

Eventually, the hotboys relented a little and let the old man guide us to a whore villa on the outskirts of town — one of the same ones we'd visited the night before in the taxi. Again, no business. Girls all sleeping, the Madam said. Come back in a few hours.

Off we went, the boys hopping hot and mad, the old man contrite, profusely apologetic. For a while we let him tag after, patient, expectant, talkative. Finally, to get rid of him we paid him a few pesetas and shooed him off.

Rain. Cognac in the *restaurante* bar. Another taxi. Mounting excitement with the mounting genitalian demand . . . twenty-four hours put off and delayed, the boys were hot for women. I must confess that I began to share their anticipatory fervor, though I didn't expect anything palatable to be found. This time the big iron gate was wide open — we streamed in.

The Madam greeted us, grinning, chuckling, making wisecracks, ushered us into the waiting room. Silence for several minutes. We glanced at each other, grinning. The room was heavily curtained with cheap frayed pink drapes, furnished with worn stuffed chairs, carpeted with a worn floral-figured rug. There was also a faded wallpaper in flowers or something pink and gray — peeling here and there. From the ceiling hung a chandelier fitted with a few low-watt bulbs and covered with a pink satin Victorian-fringed Victorian-looking skirt of some kind. The room looked old, heavy, too warm, dark. We waited.

I noticed *beaucoup* cigarette burns in the sad rug. The boys smoked nervously, grinning, talking rapidly to each other. Still, I had the impression, later backed by their own testimony, that this sort of thing was old stuff for them.

In came, finally, the girls, the young *señoritas* we had been promised, four of them. Well, they had undoubtedly been young at one time, but now — ! What a sleazy crew.

There was a Cuban with a short muscular-looking body, big breasts and ass, brown skin and black eyes and hair. She wore a black skirt, a white blouse and a hastily made-up face that failed to disguise the original underneath — hard, tough, professional — whom I judged to be about thirty-five years old.

There was an artificial blonde with a bony face, hollow dark-ringed eyes, flat skinny bony body.

There was a big fat mama type with a round friendly face and big blubbery billowing breasts.

There was a sad slut of a blonde, also artificial, with curlers in her hair and a nightgown on. A pale flat face, dead eyes, white skin and bad teeth.

The "girls." No doubt about it.

Instantly, of course, the boys registered disgust and demanded to see *mas otras* [literally, "more others"]. Argument and confusion as usual. The Madam gibbered and waved her arms. The girls looked thotful, a little hurt, and played with the boys a bit, teasing them some.

As soon as it appeared that no more *señoritas* were coming, Mahsin and Reyo gave in with perceptible embarrassment to the wigglings of two of the wenches, the Cuban and the skinny blonde. But Paul held out for something better, and I — I thought the whole situation too funny for further words or debate.

I tried to talk with the fat one but she wasn't interested in conversation; she gave me quite a shock by seizing me suddenly in her arms and lifting me about three feet above the floor. First such experience, that. She finally gave up, went away.

Paul's patience was, in a fashion, rewarded. Another sleepy-eyed wench was finally ushered in, looking slightly better than the others but not much; Paul went upstairs with her after only a moment's hesitation.

I was left alone for about thirty minutes in the heavy-aired darkish room, bothered by no one any longer, free to think, if I chose (and I did — I had and have plenty to think about) and listen to the distant muted jangle of upstairs beds.

Thirty minutes — it seemed to me an unconscionably long time, but later it turned out that each of the three Ceylonese had banged his respective selection twice, pausing for about ten minutes of recharging between attacks. Determined, all of them, to get their money's worth, which was 110 pesetas apiece. (The management must have had English currency strongly fixed in mind, for at the time the pound sterling was worth exactly 110 pesetas.)

In parting, the whores buttonholed the boys with gardenias. I was spurned, however; no gardenia for me. A taxi was called, and after a round of incoherent farewells, we were off. Back at the hotel, they rushed off to the *baños* to clean themselves, although Paul told me that in his opinion the best VD preventive was a good healthy piss immediately after indulging. That had always been his practice, he said, and he had yet to get anything worse from all of his adventures than a moderate collection of crabs one time.

Followed a wild drunken night on the train from San Sebastian to Madrid. With a bottle of potent *vino* apiece, we worked ourselves into hilarious condition and spent half the night singing. All sorts of songs — everything from national anthems to cowboy songs. For part of the fiesta we were joined by three Spanish boys — hopped-up fellows they were. They sang Spanish cabaret songs and taught the boys all the bad words in Spanish. Great fun. Everyone laughed, roared, drank, shouted.

The only awkward moment came when politics appeared and I made vigorous anti-Franco remarks and gestures. That jarred them into awful silence, then whispers, then signs and signals of taboo to me, eyes (theirs) wide-open, white.

Madrid — rather striking at first. Quite different from the sometimes charming but always dingy drabness of London, the smoky pall of lovely old Edinburgh, the green springtime gaiety (so I'm told) of Paris. Quite different, Madrid. Raw, red, white concrete everywhere, new-looking. Semi-skyscrapers going up within sight of empty plains. Big winged creatures with riders poised on building-tops. Lots of hack-modern architecture, the whole thing vaguely suggestive of Houston, Texas, or Mexico City, two cities I've never seen.

On strolls thru the more ragged parts of the city I was struck by the old familiar Latin note of poverty and sloth and careless ugliness and reckless song. Sign on a wall — *Es Prohibido Se Hace Agua Aqui* [No Urinating Here]. It's a tough world for most people.

The old familiar smells: fish, rotten fruit, sewage, urine, fresh fruit, perfumed girls, sausage frying, *pan* [bread], something burnt, the fragrance of a pastry shop (unpassable).

The little old women, hideously ugly wrinkled shriveled hairy bony starving miserable life-clutching faces, dressed, shawled, stockinged, shod completely in dirty dusty faded worn and rag-patch-fringed BLACK, the obvious color of Death, of suffering, of the Church — The Black Pestilence that feeds on Spain and Italy vampirelike and will not be shaken off.

The gray and greasy faces of the poor. The occasional soft, flowery, deep-eyed face of a young girl. Little ratlike boys. Little girls with hair all over the place, dirty fat faces, drooping drawers. Innumerable fat old women operating chair and table shops on the sidewalk, selling cigarettes by the cigarette, or raw oysters, or roasting chestnuts. Trim young priests striding importantly by with stern pale faces painstakingly shaved, wearing the long black cassock and the wide-brimmed furry hat — the fashion here. Fat old rather dirty priests shambling by, looking over-fed, under-educated and ill-tempered. A sight that never fails to appall and sicken me — a full-grown man bending from the waist and kissing the ring on a clerical hand. Can't quite stomach it.

Onward.

Pressing crowds in narrow twisting streets. Smells and vapors mount, the senses tingle, tangle, jangle and then, over-battered and bombarded by it all, subside numbly into lethargy. Only the eyes remain open, and they begin to fail to see. Back to the hotel for a decent meal, a warm bath, a good stiff drink. To bed then, for a long night's sleep.

January 8, 1952 – Soller

Saw some rather striking scenery between Madrid and Barcelona — still in Castille: big, brown and yellow hills, grottoes, canyons; a long flowing brown desert with a great horizontally striped mesa in the north; bare spectral pueblos rising out of the rock on distant hills, looking lonely, uninhabited, dry and cold as old death in the evening sun. Raw, red, rocky land under a gloom-gray sky. Cold winds sailing by. Old ruined towers and castles here and there. A man on a horse moving slowly, almost not moving at all it appeared, along a narrow rutted road a great distance away. Where was he going in that empty land, in that red winter's light?

(Goddamned pictures of Franco — fat, balding, mustached, with a noble distant haughty stare in his eyes, "*El Salvador de Espano*," everywhere.)

January 9, 1952 – Soller

Had my hair cut and my beard trimmed today, by a barber allergic to hair. At least he seemed to be allergic to mine; he kept suppressing sneezes. Two *paisanos* [peasants] sat by watching the delicate operation, apparently fascinated. Beards are quite a novelty in 1952 Spain — I'm stared at everywhere, by young and old alike. Girls stare with peculiar interest, as if wondering what it would be like to be nuzzled by that hairy face.

Palma, an antique city, sunny-colored, orange, yellow, amber, golden. Narrow cobble-slimy streets; thousands of little booth-shops; fruit and nut vendors everywhere. A rather mediocre cathedral, lots of soldiers and police as usual in *España*. A miniature trolley car on a narrow-gauge railway groaning slowly up and braking squealing down incredible curves, tunnels, hills. Lots of movie theaters with all the actors speaking Spanish — imagine Gary Cooper speaking Spanish in a buckskin shirt (dislocated phrase there). A long pebbly seaweed-littered beach; all of the old traditional Mediterranean charm. After a few days I'd had enuf of it; took to bicycle tours through the surrounding countryside and up and down the coast.

Short of the northern mountains, the country displays an appalling picture of humanization. Not anywhere is there visible, except on mountain tops and along the edge of the coast, free land, virgin terrain, land not mutilated, not defaced, not tortured into domesticity by the ingenuity and patient labor of generations of hungry men and women. An awful devastation, and horrible though it is to remember, most of Europe and half of Asia is in the same condition. Someday the Americas, too, I fear; my only consolation is that I will probably not live long enough to see it happen there. I fervently hope not.

∞

One thing I must, shall and will do in the immediate future is go to the head for a hearty good piss. (And here I go. . . .)

Gawd, I wish they'd leave the windows of that WC open — it's a fucking foul stink of a stench-hole. I noticed also that the bowl is clogged up again — somebody using *Life* magazine for toilet paper (poetically apropos but too practically slick and heavy) — well, that should teach the management to keep toilet paper on hand. Call the plumber, Pablo. If any there are in this land. Ah, my friends, it's quite true about European plumbing. Life must be hell for chambermaids.

And how I miss, how I long for — as dearly desperately as for home, mother, love, friends — Music, real music. I hum, whistle, sing endlessly to myself. I can enjoy, mildly, for a while, the exotic Oriental and extremely limited singing of the local yokels. But oh Comrade Jesus what I would give for the song of a noble singer from the North, for MUSIC true.

Why, I don't know, but it seems to be the Northern Barbarians — the Slavs and Teutons — who discovered, developed and perfected MUSIC, and who keep it alive, growing and beautiful, to this very day. Why I don't know — the Dark Forests? The Caucasian Steppes? Wild movement, horses and battle, loneliness and fear, triumph and exultation in wilderness glens? I don't know. (Curious, isn't it?)

I could fill pages and pages with this rambling pointless drivel. Shall I? This is supposed to be a Spanish journal; that is, presumably, an account of my travels and discoveries in Spain, not of my loose-lippy wobbling heartrind rendings. But you know me — always waggling on. Sickening.

January 12, 1952 - Valencia

What a dirty dusty city. And windy as hell, blowing all the dust into your eyes. A big ragged rugged sprawling city, crawling with people, lots of churches, indescribable, baroque nineteenth-century architecture. The two old gates, tower fortresses, are mildly impressive. Most eye-appealing are the old bridges across the desultory, muddy, half-dry *Río Turia,* and the fruit stands.

Immense numbers of blind and crippled lottery-ticket vendors (what a cruel business, *el lottería* — feeding on, bloodsucking on the starved helpless souls of the mediocre poor with its opiate miracle promise and its god-knows area of profit and graft for the warlords who run this country), as usual, beggars and shoe-shine boys; pimps, tarts and thieves; old women selling cigarettes.

Half the population of *España* wear black bands of mourning on their sleeves — why are they so numerous? High mortality, big families, long mourning periods? A minor civil war of sloganeering appears on the many bare plaster walls of the city — *"Viva Franco"* versus *"Viva la Republica"* — the former having much the greater mass. Why? Is Republicanism truly dead in Spain — shot or exiled? Or is it merely dormant, buried but alive, awaiting the opportune moment to reappear? Or are the people just sick of war and trouble, worn down to passivity by poverty? That the mass of the people in this country are too poor to make life worth living I cannot any longer doubt — the evidence is blatant, flagrant, omnipresent, impressive.

Tomorrow we see a bullfight. It's long from the season — this is a special one for the benefit of the American Sixth Fleet, which is visiting six or seven Spanish ports this week. Sailors are all over the place — looking big, tough, healthy and casually amused by what they see. A big friendship drive is on, *un gran armistad.* The American warlords seem determined to make us love Franco. What can be done about it? Should anything be done? *Quien sabe* [who knows]? That's the Spanish attitude — might as well adopt it for a while myself.

January 13, 1952 - Valencia

At the bullfights:

The great circus, the drama of life and courage against Death and Fear, the tormenting and slow butchering of a big, beautifully angry black bull — six of them, that is.

High on the *Sol* side I sat — quite clever of me; I sat in such a location that I was one of the last to be plunged into chill shade. Warm and sunny. First thing I missed was "The Virgin of (whatever it is)," the *toreros'* theme song in Mexico. Instead, I heard "Anchors Aweigh, My Boys" played by a small American naval band, followed soon by a Navy helicopter that circled the plaza a few times, much to the delight of the spectators.

About half an hour later, the fun began: Two old men on white horses cantered in, saluted the judges and the guests of honor (Navy officers). The doors of the Death Chamber were opened — a long pause — then out comes a snorting and quivering glossy black bull with the ranch colors pinned to his hide. Lots of sloppy passes by the *picadores* [mounted bull-fighters armed with goads rather than swords], the long and arduous killing. None of the three matadors was much good at swordplay. (My God, if they can't learn to use their swords they should be given guns. GUNS.)

Not one of the bulls was killed on the first try. Two were killed with two or three stabs each, the other four required at least half a dozen apiece. One bull, even then, with the sword sunk in him to the hilt, still refused to die. The matador kicked the sand in disgust, while his aides whirled the blood-frothy bull, the roaring bellowing bull, round and round, trying to make it tire and bleed itself to death. Finally, the brave bull folded and sank to his knees. But his head remained up; he stared at the ring of gaudy tormentors around him. With a different kind of sword, the matador jabbed the bull three times in the back of the neck, trying to find the vital nerve. He failed; the bull remained stolidly, stubbornly half-alive.

The flunky with the knife was then called in, the man supposed to convince the bull that he is dead. He stabbed the bull once in the nape of the neck, viciously and efficiently, and the bull finally died. Three flashy horses dragged him, amid a sea of cheers from the delighted audience, out of the arena.

One *picadore* was hurt, how badly I don't know, when the bull pushed his horse over on top of him. How the crowd howled with joy when the bull went after the horse!

The best part of the whole show was impromptu — some white-shirted kid ran into the arena with a red cloth and took the bull on for a pass before one of the second-string matadors grabbed him by the shoulder and shoved him toward the gate. Just before he went, however, the kid did a salute to the admiral in the box and knelt to salute the ladies. He was enthusiastically cheered.

One matador, the one with the indestructible bull, had a tough time all afternoon: Once he slipped and fell in front of the bull — I thought sure he was done for, but no — he lay still, prone, and the bull couldn't seem to get his horns into him and after a few moments lost interest as the other matadors rushed up flourishing capes. Another time this same fellow tripped on his own cape and fell on his face in the sand. Whistles and jeers for him.

Only one of the three matadors put on a good show. Clearing the ring so that he and the bull were alone, at one side far from the bull, he would begin a slow mincing prancing teasing almost feminine dance obliquely toward the bull; challenging the bull, daring him, inviting him. The act always impressed the bull as well as the mob; he'd begin to bellow, paw the sand, snort and shake his head menacingly, then charge. The matador then broke into a run, toward but not directly toward the bull. As he passed the charging bull, he leaned in over the horns and drove home the pretty darts that always infuriated the bull and thrilled the crowd, including me. It always looked good, dramatic, beautiful.

This same fellow got a rousing show of approval when he killed his second and final bull on the second sword thrust. He got the ear, he got bouquets of flowers, a lady's shoe, a sailor's hat, somebody's overcoat, innumerable packs of cigarettes from the sailors, all this thrown into the ring as he walked around it holding up one hand in triumph, followed by his personal retinue of aides, *picadores*, managers, waterboys. He passed the old hat to the admiral too, getting it back full of — money, no doubt. Anything else? Much wenching, later, I lust-trust.

The second matador, though he generally was pretty poor, pulled off one hair-lifting stunt: He waited on his knees directly in front of the Death-cunt, waiting for the bull to emerge in thunder, and when it did, he took its charge with his cape, moving not a muscle so far as I could tell. Hair-lifting. Otherwise, mediocre.

The whole show was mediocre. No flashy smooth Veronicas like I saw in Juarez, no passes of punishment *galante*, no kneeling back-facing the bull, very little *ole* material. The crowd felt as I did . . . it was a mediocre fight, on the whole. Six bloody bleeding bulls for the butcher, six. And those fat mean ugly foul-cigar-smoking mediocre commercial men who sat around me — how I detested the oily faced swine. The damned cigar smoke. And me with dysentery.

Yes, I had it, dysentery in Valencia — must get us a good St. Christopher's medal for our future travels, keep the bacilli away.

The wench with the butter-colored hair screamed with delight as the spermy sea swirled around and between her thighs — which reminded me of that time in Venice-on-the-Gulf when . . .

∞

END OF JOURNAL V

Road map: *Abbey has completed his studies at Edinburgh, and is embarked on an extended Scandinavian vacation before returning to America, via England.*

JOURNAL VI

April to June 1952

∞

April 23, 1952 – on the North Sea

The old ocean is as cold and gray-looking as ever today, gray gravy-bilge, effervescent sewage, salt-foamy dishwater. Iron-slate-blue gray, hard-looking, sprinkled lightly with whitecaps.

The water is tiring — why can't I learn to love the sea as other poets do? I do love the sea gulls, and the seashore — surf, sand and long horizon — and ships, the gracious and lovely ships and the rusty old tubs — and the clouds above the sea, and the sea-air, and sea-music, and the sea's depth — its old mystery, dark crawly inhabitants, metaphysic's spiritual significance, romantic history, its womb-source-ballad power and wonder as the Mother of All. And I love the sea breaking around and over the ship's prow, and the sea-change, and the sea as the waterway to romance and adventure, and the sea at night, and the sea at sundown with its glittering track of fire leading to the west, and I love sea-poetry and sea-stories, and I love the sea's storms and fury and the sea's mobile peace.

But the goddamned ocean leaves me cold, unmoved, or else makes me sick. The great heaving expanse of wavy water leaves me uninspired. What I love is not the ocean itself, but all the things and events and magic associated with it.

The ship throbs on, the *Astrea*, steaming steadily over the gray North Sea, Bergen-bound under a solid mass of gray-blue stormy clouds. Vibration; everything vibrates with the pumping effort of the great marine engines, the laboring diesels. Slight pitch, little roll — the sea is steady as a duck pond so far.

I'm traveling second class for a change — wallowing in luxury. (There weren't any third-class berths available.) A fine big meal we had: Norse soup, thick and dark, full of spices and pieces of boiled egg and mysteries — delicious; then thick slabs of roast beef with potatoes and gravy and cabbage and carrots; then a big fat obscene yellow pudding with some kind of berry-laden sauce; finally, moving to the salon, we had Norwegian coffee, strong enough to satisfy a horse. A simple meal, big and simple, the kind that lucky workingmen or merchant seamen eat.

April 24, 1952 – on the Nord-See

A few sea gulls winging about in our wake, eyes peeled for garbage. We must be getting near the coast; good thing too — the damned boiling ocean is beginning to turn my stomach. I guess I'll never be a sailor; have to stick to mountains and prairies, canyons and forests. Too bad, perhaps, though I'm really no more susceptible to motion-sickness than the average ship's passenger. Hell, I never get a chance to get my sea-legs. Just when I'm getting immunized to sea-motion I'm cast ashore for a few months and lose all that I've learned.

I still want to circumnavigate the world someday, with Volpe and Kieffer [college friends from UNM], in a little sloop or schooner. *Old dream* . . . with a motorcycle or two, or a jeep on board for inland exploration. I'm not interested in rounding the Earth just for the sake of seeing a lot of identical mucky scummy salt-water seaports. Hell no. I want a lot more than that. Jungle and desert, mountain and steppes I want to see, and queer funny people with rings in their noses and innocence in their eyes. If any such remain anywhere on earth; I doubt it. Palm trees will do, and a few Azbak hogans in deep Turkestan or on the Great Kaloo. Karoo.

Memories of Austria:

I'm still dazzled by that rare experience, those magic few days on the snowfields near the sun among the stunning peaks of the Tirol. The unforgettable heights, the vivid air, the fanatic sun, the brilliant virgin snow and me swooping down to the valley among the pines, following old leathery Rudolf, our instructor. Fantastic. Burned deep, seared and branded on the memory those glittering hours of simple pure adventure. Better than sex, higher than music, as good as good poetry.

Better than sex? As might be expected, I fell in "love" for a few days. I met a girl from South Africa named Penelope. Ostracized by the English in our tour party, I found her most delightful and refreshing company. Someone to talk to. She turned out to be very much like me; though a couple years younger, on an intellectual par with me. Interested in everything, all facets of human experience, she was not always interesting herself. Mildly talented in a variety of ways but with no genuine ability in any one field, she was, like me, the perennial hapless self-amused dilettante, half-worried by the slippage of time but determined to enjoy failure anyway.

"A non-Stalinist Communist" she called herself; under cross-examination her Communism turned out to be nothing but a vague Utopian liberalism. Not without integrity. Her ethical system, boiled down, was "be kind." A modest proposal. But understand: she was well aware of the insipid quality of her Categorical Imperative, of its apparent childlike simplicity, its distressing lack of passion, glamour, fire.

And yet . . . like Forster, the quintessence of liberalism. To be more extreme means conflict. Life is dangerous, dogmatic, sure to make trouble. Not so easy is "Love thine enemy . . . love thy neighbor as thyself . . . do unto others . . ." the Christian ethic, going too far, demanding too much, accomplishes too little. No tyranny of hatred has ever been as complete and systematic as that presented on the stage of human history by Jesus and his imitators.

"Be kind" is perhaps actually more difficult than "Love everybody." Love is treacherous, really easy, and the lover a tyrant. I would rather be tolerated than loved — wouldn't I? — as I prefer to tolerate rather than love. I'm another tepid liberal myself, despite extremist inclinations and fanatic aspirations. Liberalism and rationalism *seem* too simple, easy, soft, comfortable. But what is so rare? Anywhere? Anytime?

Besides, like Penny, I want nothing to do with God the Benevolent Father. Like her, I prefer comradeship to brotherhood. I'm a Communist myself, a signal honor of which I am pleasantly conscious. Man of the future. Insofar as Communism does not conflict with my more basic Jeffersonian Anarchism, I mean. Not much, though this confusion of labels makes it all seem ridiculous. Communism means, to most people today, Stalinist totalitarianism, the police state, philosophic materialism, unscrupulous and ruthless opportunism. Is that what it is, if that is what everyone means by it? The democratic semantic?

Well, it doesn't mean that to Asiatics, or Africans or about twenty million Europeans. So perhaps Communism still means what it should mean anyway. *Quien sabe?* The lazy thinker; always content to let problems dissolve into a universal euphoria of doubt. Sheer sloth.

Penny talked a lot about South Africa, and I plied and supplied her with plenty of questions. Naturally, she was a violent racist — hated the white race. Altho, as she admitted, on the finally darkling plain, if it ever came to outright war, she thought she might be overwhelmed by old blood loyalty and finish standing by and dying with her "own" people, the superior Europeans.

I argued with her on this point — what are our "own" people? To what group, if any, do we owe our loyalty? And she agreed with me, but felt, nevertheless, that she would fight with the whites, shoot down the advancing browns and blacks. (What about the beige race of the future? She concurred, but still. . . .)

Well? What would I do?

There's a core of violence in me that might, I feel, take an intense pleasure in looking at Malan [Daniel François, South African prime minister, 1948–54] and other Afrikaners over gun-sights. But could I pull the trigger? In cold blood? I don't know. In a hurry, in the rush and confusion of battle, I'm certain I could maim and murder my fellow men about as easily as anyone else can, and it does seem to be easy. But I don't think I want a job on any firing squad. No, I certainly don't.

Where were we? I've shifted the subject. Would I stand by the white race, as Penny was honest enough to admit that she would? I don't know. I think I'd rather not participate in an inter-racial war at all, unless it's a nice bloody revolution, such as is needed in most parts of Africa at present; in that case I would join with the blacks against their white oppressors. (I'm in favor of settling the African problem by violent revolution, if at all possible; and by peaceful negotiation if all other means fail.)

The only trouble is, as Penny herself suggested, I would probably be murdered myself by my black comrades — in their flush of enthusiasm and fervor in shooting at white faces, they would probably have neither the time nor the desire to discriminate between enemy whites and ally whites. Who could blame them? I'd feel the same way myself. Might as well shoot all whites in Afrika, friend and foe alike — make a good clean job of it. That's the way they would — or perhaps will — reason about the problem, insofar as they reason about it at all. God knows there will be little room for reason, as the blind fools in Afrika, the ruling Europeans, have little use for reason now. They'll continue to kick the dumb Negroes around until they wake up some nice morning with their necks slashed open from ear to ear — grinning in blood from ear to ear.

We talked about Art too, of course, and Love, and the Tragedy of Life, as we sat there in the Arlberg Bar or the Hotel Tirol Club Bar night after night, drinking Rhine wine and Rotwein and nameless aperitifs, occasionally getting up to dance — well, Penny would dance nearly every dance, if not with me then with one of the numerous young men always breathing down her neck.

A very attractive girl, Penelope; wherever she went she was surrounded by lust-eyed men (including myself), like a fisherman surrounded by a swarm of mosquitoes. But I monopolized her time shamelessly. Though she spoke French fairly well, and some Deutsch, I was her only English-speaking friend in Saint Anton. I was the only man with whom she could converse on topics more complex and profound than skiing, the weather, surface politics, sex and home life. So that, eventually, when she surrendered to the vital force and the adventure of being away from home and far from Mother, it was with me that she went to bed.

April 25, 1952 – on the train from Bergen to Oslo

The train seems to be full of Norwegians — a handsome and healthy-looking people: tall, fair-haired, steady-eyed, quiet and calm, fine-featured Viking faces. The Nordic human is a good one. But any better than the Bantu, or the Neapolitan or the Mexican? A problem; we get into all kinds of anthropological, axiological and il-logical difficulties the moment we begin thinking of human beings not as unique personalities, but as types, breeds and races, as though men were manufactured like automobiles, coming out in different but standardized brands, as though we could compare one nationality with another and discuss their relative merits in the same manner as we compare Fords with Buicks, Chevrolets with Dodges and so forth. Foolishness.

And yet, as a devout environmentalist, I cannot ignore the existential reality of such things as national traits, characteristics, etc. Cultures certainly differ, and to the extent that men are determined by their culture, which in most cases is to a pretty great extent, we can reasonably expect the members of one culture to differ considerably from the members of another culture. But that may not justify comparative evaluations.

Norway looks very woody; lots of trees and almost all the buildings are made of wood. Typical hill-country architecture, whether Swiss, Bavarian, Tirolean or West Virginian. Fancy scroll-work and filigreed trim on porches and window frames, eaves and ventilators of barns. Green grass, black cows, board fences, big shiny milk cans by the road in front of every farmhouse, just like rural Pennsylvania. In fact, from what I've seen so far, Norway looks amazingly like parts of Pennsylvania, West Virginia, New England — now that we've left the fiords and the black cliffs behind.

Quantities of raw new timber and lumber are stacked along the railway; piles of manure in the fields, a few farmers out dragging and harrowing plowed fields. When the train stops you can smell the manure — strong powerful stuff — makes me nostalgic. Must be planting time in Pennsylvania now. The folks there must be busy, perhaps hopeful, emerging from dreary winter.

Springtime: In the Rockies the snow is still piled high — not much activity there; in the New Mexican desert spring must be in full glory now, the cactus blooming like crazy and the sycamores and cottonwoods coming out, budding green. Or spring may even be on the wane in the desert; certainly it is in Sonora and lower Arizona; already the specter of desert summer must be edging toward Yuma and Sonoita and High Lonesome Wells and Nogales and Quitobaquito and Baboquivari. Something to think about, old desert rat, *compañero*. . . .

∞

Radio Moscow: Speaking of propaganda, this is just about the most naive, incompetent and boring I have ever heard. Surely the Voice of America is not as childish as this. God, I hope not. National pride. Truth crushed to earth on both sides — will it ever rise again?

April 26, 1952 - Stockholm

"The city without tragedy." Perhaps . . . I doubt it. When the weary horror and monotony of poverty are forgotten, the human spirit faces new and greater problems — the problems of the soul and human destiny, which are the greatest of all. That's why it so irritates me that we, the majority of the human race, should waste so much time with mere housekeeping, which is, after all, what economic misery finally comes down to — a problem of efficient housekeeping.

Now the Swedes are obviously good housekeepers. Everyone looks healthy enough, well-fed — much better than Britain, somewhat better than the U.S.A. in this respect — most of them are well-dressed, nobody in rags, nobody peddling cigarettes on the street; automatic machine-type vendors everywhere, a good sign of economic well-being. No, the Swedes have other problems, more interesting.

A few tables away from me sits a squirmy middle-aged mother and what appears to be her fidgeting exasperated twenty-five-year-old son. She is counting her money over and over again, moving her lips, while he watches her, obviously furious, glaring, muttering, growling at her. He kicks at her under the table. She gets up, scampers sullenly away, comes back in a few minutes and resumes counting her money. Previous scene repeated. Finally, clutching his beer, the son stares moodily and sullenly away, beyond anger now, and Mother turns her pocketbook inside-out and upside-down in an effort to find some missing money. Well can I understand his stubborn fury, his hopeless futile bottomless rage.

Here I sit in the station buffet, waiting for Ami [the Stockholm girl who, as recounted in Journal IV, invited Abbey to spend some time with her] to come and get me. A teasing game — what will she look like, what will she *be* like? I have never been in a situation quite like this before: interesting. Naturally, I hope she is beautiful and charming.

Well, if she's beautiful she *will* be charming. If she's beautiful she doesn't have to be charming. If she's beautiful I will be charmed whether she is charming or not.

I've seen some lovely girls in Stockholm already — the Nordic blondes, tall and muscular, clean tan faces, honey-and-brown hair, clear keen eyes, dark eyebrows. A splendid type of human, as I said before, and I meant it and I still mean it. Just a matter of taste, perhaps, but there it is, and no less important to me for all of that.

SKOAL! *Alla vaca flickor* — to the girls of Skandia, the world's most beautiful, most generous and hospitable, most memorable. (At least from the point of view of a young, handsome and charming *Amerikansk* like myself.)

Where was I? Yes, the efficient nearly self-sufficient Swedes. Ah, it's much too soon for any judgments. Wait 'til you've been here an honest country week, at least.

Do the *Swedes* worry about the state of their souls? Then why the hell should you?

April 27, 1952 – Stockholm

The Steenhafs — Ami, Mama and Papa. Ami is a girl, certainly a pretty girl, perhaps a beautiful girl. Conviction hesitates. She is blue-eyed, fair-skinned, with dark brown hair, black eyebrows, long black lashes, making her look almost French rather than Swedish. She is a small girl, too — short and very light. A fine figure, well-proportioned, but quite small all over. A little girl, though she's twenty-one. She speaks English with a strong American accent — the result, I suppose, of her three-month stay in America.

Alas, I don't see much of her: she has a Big Examination coming up in about three weeks, the culmination of a two-year course, and her whole academic career hinges upon the result, so that she spends all day and all evening curled around a book.

Besides that, she's in love with the Bishop of Stockholm — I mean the Bishop's son — and is barely interested in other men. I'm beginning to wonder why she invited me here, conscious of a slight disappointment. You thought — yes, you *thought,* you lecherous scoundrel. Apparently . . . a simple uncomplicated act of kindness, generosity, hospitality; considering the other circumstances, it was an exceedingly kind, generous and hospitable thing to do — inviting a complete stranger, simply on the strength of his being a young American student, to come and live in your house, share your bread for two or three weeks. And she busy preparing for an examination, besides.

Well, this makes it easier for me to be faithful to my moon-mad demongirl way out there in the desert. But Ami has not ignored me; already she has taken me to a movie (with her mother); she has introduced me to a gentle little girl named Yorval, and to her [Ami's] boyfriend Erland; and the three of them, last night, took me on a tour of the city in Ami's automobile.

Come Wednesday, the four of us are going up to Uppsala to participate in the annual University Spring Drinking Festival — how's that for International Living? A three-day orgy of drinking, dancing and singing — and love-making too, I suppose.

So what are you complaining about? Do you want the little girl to wipe your nose for you? Display some initiative — get up and get out and forage for yourself — go find Olvig. Olvig . . . oh my god, what a funny little adventure that was.

On the train from Bergen to Oslo, I met Olvig. She got on at Voss and sat down facing me. A pretty girl, though rather large in the hips. For miles we said nothing to each other — tried to avoid each other's curious glances — the omnipresent shadow of sex. But eventually one of us said something to the other — it was me — I offered her an *Amerikansk* cigarette and she accepted. We started a conversation — of sorts.

It immediately was apparent that she spoke no English — hardly a word — and no *Français, Deutsch* or *Español*. I tried her on all of them. And of course I speak no *Norsk*. But nevertheless, we managed to communicate a lot to each other, somehow, some way. I learned her name, her occupation, nursing student; her age, twenty-five; her destination, Stockholm; her Norwegian address, her Stockholm telephone number and her ambition in life — to be a nurse.

By the time we reached Oslo, though we had been unable to exchange more information than what I have listed, we were good friends. We talked a lot to each other in totally incomprehensible terms. I played my harmonica for her and quoted all that I could remember from Hamlet and Macbeth, with appropriate gestures. In Oslo we had a four-hour wait.

In the station lobby, after checking my suitcase, I hesitated, uncertain. I wanted to ask the girl to join me for *kaffe* somewhere, and for a stroll about the city, but I wasn't sure whether I should or not . . . and besides, she was busy jabbering with some Viking who might have been her uncle or something.

So I started to leave the station alone — and up she came running, Olvig, and grabbed my arm, laughing and talking excitedly, unaccompanied, and hauled me off to a restaurant and bought me a dinner and insisted on paying for it, and then we went sightseeing around Oslo — I haven't the faintest idea of what it looked like — and then we had to catch the Stockholm train and by midnight the train was half-empty and we had a compartment to ourselves.

By that time she was ready for kisses, as was I. We spent most of the rest of the night in each other's arms.

Coming into Stockholm next morning — daylight, green trees — I awoke to see Olvig combing her hair with my comb. I experienced, suddenly and vividly, the old sensation of domesticity, of matrimony. When she saw that I was awake, she gave me a tender little wifely kiss to reinforce the illusion. In the chilly gray light of morning, with her lipstick all kissed away, her hair a mess, her eyes dim and her eyelids fat with sleepiness and fatigue, she no longer looked so pretty. Friendly and gay and intimate she was, but no longer so bright and new and pretty. The old familiar tragedy.

At the station we parted — friends took her away — and I guess I was a little relieved to be through with her. And I haven't seen her since. Too many other things to think about.

But I shall not forget you, Olvig. We are good friends forever. Forever. The spontaneous and native love, the simple animal love of animal human-beings — us — and natural friendliness, open and unselfish, I cannot forget. And you are that — and Norway — Northgirl, you.

/May 6, 1952 - Stockholm

> *Ja, ja, we Wikings fierce will rise again*
> *To torment Bretagne's coastal plain.*
> *Let it never more be said*
> *The spirit of the North is dead.*
> *Wikings once were worse than wolves,*
> *Worse than wolves again we'll be,*
> *And rape, ransack and ravish Europe*
> *From Calais to Napoli!*

(A little occasional composition, the occasion being a party to celebrate my departure from Stockholm; this anthem sung to the tune of the *Uppsala Studentena* drinking song. My Wiking friends liked it and sang it with totally unexpected enthusiasm. Imperial Sweden.)

/May 11, 1952 - Arjang, Sweden

How in the hell did I get here? Way off in the tail end of nowhere, somewhere in the piny hills near the Swedish-Norwegian border. A quiet little town now, on Sunday morning — dead quiet. All the local boys got drunk last night — I didn't for a change — and now everyone is hard at work sleeping it off.

I'm hungry for breakfast but almost nothing is open and I can't get anything. I'm hungry and irritable. I hear a cuckoo off in the woods somewhere — damned silly bird. There's some other bird with a thrilling cry — I'm not sure what it is — perhaps a curlew.

This little town at the intersection is so much like about a million American small towns that it's disgusting. Two run-down little hotels — I must have been in the worst one last night — something much like an American drugstore without the drugs, a small movie house showing *Winchester 73* starring Mr. James Stewart of Indiana (Pennsylvania), a bus station without buses most of the time, a train station without trains going anyplace.

The most striking resemblance, however, was Saturday night, last night, with the young men in town all dressed up and driving around, two to a car, in their old shined-up junked-up ornamented smoke-throwing oil-burning second-hand American cars. Old Nashes and Mercurys and Terraplanes, mostly about fifteen years old, painted new with tire flaps and long radio aerials and chrome-plated gas-tank caps. Haunting.

Doing the same, too: Driving slowly around town, or just parking with the radio going, they would stare at and comment on the girls who walked around in pairs or groups of four or five, staring at and talking about the boys. Only occasionally would there be a joining of the sexes.

Also present were a multitude of middle- and old-aged men of the sulky-racing fraternity, all uniformly drunk, wandering in loose ellipses and getting lost.

Most of the girls are genuinely pretty; the boys and men are not — they have crude red faces with little blue eyes, albino eyebrows and hair, short bodies, big mouths and ears, murderous-looking hands. But very friendly. Everyone, or almost, is extremely friendly in this cheerful and friendly, dark and piney and lovely country. (The first phrase refers to the towns and cities, the second to the vast tracts of lake and forest with which Sweden is blessed abundantly.)

But how did I get here?

I thought I was hitch-hiking to Oslo. The signs said so, the map said so. But the traffic said no. I'm on the right road, all right, but there's practically no traffic on it. Nothing but local farmers going about three or four kilometers into the country. So I guess I'll have to take a bus if I really want to get to Oslo. And I'd been doing damn well, too; I hitch-hiked from Stockholm to Karlstad Friday, and in about eleven hours. Yesterday I came from

Karlstad to here; not very far. But I didn't leave Karlstad until four in the afternoon, for reasons which I may or may not divulge to the silences of my journal. An interesting and shameful story, anyway. Eh, Lila?

Same day - Oslo

I made it. The bold break I had been expecting. Just when Arjang was at its dullest and deadest, along came a paunchy businessman in a two-door. He stopped and I got in and now, about six hours later, I'm in Oslo.

Oslo's a striking town. Straight lines and bold effects. Signs of design, an architectonic mind at work. Oslo is small and bravely beautiful, the impressive harbor-side area well laid-out. I've always maintained that nothing is more contributory to urban beauty than form, design, shape — in a word, planning.

Just when I'm beginning to like Oslo so much, I see something both depressing and infuriating: toy soldiers in front of the king's castle stepping back and forth like machine parts working. Only they're not toy soldiers — inside the gaudy black and green livery are live thinking human beings. What a horrible way to misuse and abuse the services of a loyal citizenry — making some of them behave like tin monsters.

It's just for show, I know that. If the king must be guarded (though why supposedly grown-up men and women should tolerate even a make-believe king like Haakon is beyond me), the job could best be done by a couple of experienced G-Men sitting at strategic points of defense, each man with a tommy-gun in one hand and a comic book in the other.

Look at the poor devils: jaws strapped up in leather, long bayoneted rifle, white gloves, plume falling into the eye, they pace smartly back and forth on a concrete runway and in line with each other — when one reaches the end of the concrete they do simultaneously a sharp about-face and step off until the other comes to his end and so on and so on. Surely no human being, let alone some kingly parasite, is worth all this trouble, but on they go; no doubt they've been told that what they're doing is a Great Honor for the poor boobs who make up the King's Army. Perhaps they even believe it themselves. Though they look faintly restless around the ears.

∞

Incidental intelligence: These Nordic women, no matter how golden their hair, blue their eyes, white their skin, do not have blonde pubic hair. At least not in the cases which I personally have investigated; theirs is a light brown, curly and crinkly like anyone else's. I'd wondered about this for some time.

May 12, 1952 – Finse

Now I've done it. On the way to Bergen, Skottland bound, I saw all this snow still here, skis sticking up in it, and acting on a fanatic impulse I grabbed my coat and suitcase and jumped off the train. At 4:30 in the morning, in the long gray sub-arctic summer dawn.

To the south stands the white dome of the Hardanzer, two-thousand meters high. I'm looking at it now — the sky is cloudy, almost solidly clouded, but through a hole a slow-moving pool of golden summer-warm light is spangling the frozen snow. It's lovely, and miles away.

I sit here in the lobby of Finse's only hotel, warm enough but terribly sleepy. Awfully sleepy; it's a great effort to write these obscure words; my eyes are heavy as pinballs. It's about 8:00 *klocken* now; once again I'm waiting for breakfast. After that I hope to hit one of those ski trails and slide up and down a few mountains. If I can get boots. Stupid of me, but I didn't bring any.

Seems cold, though there's almost no wind — about five degrees centigrade's worth of temperature — so it should be quite warm when and if the sunshine comes through that cottony layer of clouds; a typically European sky.

I had a violent shock last night. Went to a restaurant, found the menu totally incomprehensible; I ordered the most expensive item on it: *Smorgasbord och Hummer*, feeling certain that. . . . But *mein Gott!* — *Hummer* turned out to be a boiled lobster. There he was on a big silver platter before me, stashed up on his tail, claws extended, mandibles open, antennae aloft, stiff and red and boiled, presumably dead, though his little black seedy eyes watched me intently. All in one piece! What a monster.

I could not look at it — the very sight of it turned my stomach — people *eat* complicated hairy brittle segmented things like that? I don't believe it. I summoned the surprised and startled waitress; waved it away. She didn't believe me at first. Of course, her feelings were hurt. Too bad; I couldn't stand having that lobster at the same table with me — one of us would have to leave. She finally took it away, The Thing, after I ordered something simple and cheap and stodgily conservative: *smorgasbord och weinerschnitzelkammer*.

No doubt I should be heartily ashamed of myself, being frightened — terrified — revolted, by one old boiled lobster. I understand that many people not only can tolerate the crustacean's appearance but can also crack him apart and eat him, guts and all. Well . . . the Congolese love

68

fried caterpillars, the Digger Indians whole roast rat. All sorts of tastes. I beg to be excluded.

Ah, the sky is opening; more of that celestial dusty atmosphere, the blue primeval with which our rare planet is graced, is now appearing, as the clouds drift, part, thaw, melt, resolve, *adieu.* Acres and acres of snow, black cliffs, cloud and sky; and somewhere beyond it all, God — the sun. The cool loveliness of morning.

I'm in danger of becoming some sort of shabby Don Juan; not in the number of my sex-love affairs, God knows they're not numerous, but in my reaction to them. Gradually, I find myself getting more satisfaction from the mere possession, the "conquest" (though the word, in connection with my adventures, is simply fantastic — I never conquered a girl in my life; they conquer me — I submit, or at most, merely encourage their voluntary cooperation and the innate pride of every pretty girl in her own body and its appropriate use), from the successful pursuit than from the sex-act itself. The psychic becomes more important than the physical; not that the latter is becoming for me any less pleasurable, not at all, on the contrary . . . but the other drive, the spiritual, is becoming, or may become, primary.

Which I want to avoid, squash, submerge — honest sex is a wholesome and harmless diversion, but the mania for counting the women, collecting trophies, cutting notches — that's bad, that's a disease. From which preserve me, Mary.

My last day of skiing in Europe. I'm glad I stopped here at Finse for a final fling. It's a splendid day, bright and warm, and the snow, not so good as it could be, is good enough for the merry month of May. The snow is, in fact, rather treacherous: alternatively fast and slow, icy and wet.

I went to the top of the Hardanzer this morning and enjoyed the climb almost as much as the descent. The sun was so warm that I took my shirt off and climbed the mountain — on skis — stripped to the waist, absorbing solar energy. I needed it. On top though, it was windy, quite windy — I had to put my shirt back on and a sweater to boot. Cold too; my hands and nose nearly froze. But in about five minutes I was halfway down, into the warmth again.

A swift descent, marred by one unnecessary fall — instead of staying on the trail I wandered a little and hit some blue ice. Nothing hurt but my pride and dignity. The rest of the flight down was a lark, a breeze, a swoop. I sang "Careless Love" the whole way down — once. That's all the time it took; about two hours going up, ten minutes coming down. A fantastic game. Foolish? Not to me. Let the uninitiated think so if they wish — no worry to me — to us. The fanatics.

Getting cloudy now, and cold. I'll have to leave this balcony and get inside where it's warm. Or better yet, go up the mountain for one more run. That's it. One more time.

May 13, 1952 – Bergen

Going up the Hardanzer for the second and last time yesterday afternoon, I overtook a woman — a handsome, distinguished-looking lady of about fifty years. All alone for miles around, we naturally fell into conversation.

A Norwegian, she spoke excellent English. When she asked me where I was from I told her what is at worst a half-truth: "New Mexico," I said. She was pleased to hear it; her husband and she had been in New Mexico only a year before; she had, she said, been charmed by Santa Fe and impressed by the New Mexican landscape.

I said some nice things about *Norge*. The talk got around to American politics — I said there was only one man I knew of fit to be president, and that was Justice William O. Douglas. That delighted her; she also was a Bill Douglas admirer — what's more, she was a personal acquaintance of his!

It turned out that her husband, Ferdinand Schjelderup, was a member of the Norwegian Supreme Court, also an admirer of Douglas, a long-time student of American law and quite an outstanding figure in his own right. (She didn't tell me that last item — I learned it myself later when I met the justice.)

Anyway, the Schjelderups had gone to America, had been invited to meet the members of the American Supreme Court, and had finally been invited by Bill Douglas to meet his family, to stay with him for a while in a place of his in the Cascades, and to meet the little band of eccentric and thoroughly admirable individuals who figure in Douglas's book, *Of Men and Mountains*. Douglas had also planned a tour of America for them, emphasizing the mountain and desert country of the West, which they had followed and highly enjoyed.

In return, the Schjelderups had invited Douglas to visit them in Norway, and he accepted — he's coming this summer.

Mrs. Schjelderup and I, as we herringboned slowly up the snowy slope, discussed the important question of how best to entertain the justice. We agreed that it would not be difficult, not in Norway — just give him a rucksack and turn him loose in the great forests and mountains which make up most of *Norge*. The Schjelderups are also mountain climbers and wilderness cultists — like myself and Douglas and Ralph Newcomb and Everett Reuss [Southwestern desert explorer and writer] — so they would be able to show him a pretty good time.

About then, halfway up the mountain, Mrs. Schjelderup had to turn back toward Finse — she had to get ready for dinner at the hotel.

Since I had nothing to do but catch a train an hour or two from then, I went on up alone, hoping to get to the top before the sun went down or a storm came up. The sky looked fierce and beautiful, swirling with dark purple clouds, and the violet-blue and amber light of the sun. The snow was half-frozen, dazzling, glittering with reflected fire. Across the valley I could see another range of mountains — white snow, black rock — with huge cloud shadows moving over them, shadows of the most fair fragile pastel blue I have ever seen. A strange color, somewhere between blue and purple, really, and light, a tint, a shadow of color, a hint of tone. Impossible to forget, difficult to recall in words.

I never made it to the top; within a half-kilometer or so of the summit the clouds came down and I was in a blizzard. I simply reversed my tracks and skied down out of it, at about thirty miles an hour I would guess. Anyway, I reached the bottom in six minutes, a faster trip by far than the previous one. But this was by a different route — I went straight down, straight as a geometric line, and I had no falls. Breathless, breathtaking — the wind felt like it was tearing my hair out, whistling through my ribs, burning my face. At the bottom I hit a rotten patch and lurched to a stop.

Except for that ungraceful finish, a minor matter, it had been a splendid ride. I wish I were going up again today.

⤬

Delia is her name; for chrissake. Delia Rhum.

SKOAL! to Thomas Mann, who puts the cause of humanity before the cause of God.

I've found a use for my necktie: I can dust my typewriter with it. Even when I'm wearing it.

Same day – on the boat

When I returned from my evening ski run, working up a lather trying to get back in time to catch my train (at Finse you have to ski over a frozen lake about half a mile wide between the village and the foot of the mountain), I found the Schjelderups waiting for me outside the hotel. (The village of Finse consists of a railway station, this big first-class resort hotel, snow sheds and about three houses — everything painted a brilliant Dutch-barn red.) They invited me to miss the train, have dinner and drink and discussion with them, and go to Bergen the next morning on another train. I accepted at once.

No, I didn't — I was momentarily confused, thinking about seventeen other matters simultaneously. But I accepted.

The justice muttered a few words to the hotel manager and I was instantly transformed from a common vagrant into a guest of honor. Though the hotel was supposed to be full, a room with bath was found for me at once, I was surrounded by excited chambermaids; somebody carried my suitcase, which had been setting all day long in a dark corner of the lobby, up to my room; somebody filled the tub with warm water; somebody handed me a towel about as big as a parlor rug and just as thick, and soap — and there I was, still sweating from my hard-pressed dash across the lake. There I was, alone again.

I bathed in my leisurely navel-contemplating way, changed into other dirty socks, put on another dirty shirt and went down to the dining room, where I found the Schjelderups patiently waiting for me just outside.

We went in, escorted by a convoy of waiters, and had a pretty decent meal — some clever varieties of smorgasbord to begin with, and the rest in the same style, together with a fragrant and penetrating red wine. From then until midnight we never stopped talking — about a covey of fascinating topics.

After coffee and an hour or so of talk about American politics and Norwegian scenery, we went up to the Schjelderups' room for a few stiff slugs of upper-class cognac and more talk.

Something that Mrs. S. let slip gave me a hint of the stature of the man I was talking with. I began to question the justice about the Norwegian resistance movement during the Nazi occupation, and gradually, though I had to pry at him some at first to overcome his modest reticence, a good sound adventure story came out.

He and most of the others on Norway's supreme court had resisted Quisling and the Nazis from the beginning; within a year Schjelderup had got himself into so much trouble with the puppet government and with the Gestapo that he was forced by the intensity of the hunt for him to flee to Sweden, together with his family, which included a one-year-old child.

As they were rowing across a lake to Sweden, at night, not far from a German camp, the baby began to squall. They silenced him by sticking his face underwater — for just a few seconds, of course. The justice seemed amused by the memory, but it must not have been very funny at the time.

He and his wife and child came through the occupation physically undamaged, but he had a brother who was not so lucky: the Gestapo agents beat him so badly that, though still living, he is a helpless cripple, the nerves of his neck and back irreparably and permanently injured. And Mrs. S. — I mean the second or present Mrs. S. — had two sons who had been kept in concentration camps for a combined total of six years.

We finished the evening by talking some more about Douglas. We all agreed that he was a good man, possibly a great man, the one outstanding successor to Justice Holmes and the man who should be, though he won't be, the next President of the United States of America.

The Schjelderups, with much delight, told me about a Washington diplomatic party that Douglas had nearly disrupted. It was a formal affair at the Indian Embassy, with everyone dressed in the most severe of evening dress and seating arrangements handled according to the strictest traditional demands of protocol.

Douglas arrived late, straight from his office, wearing an old western slouch hat and a dirty raincoat, both of which he forgot to take off. He ignored the place reserved for him among the ambassadors and insisted on sitting with a friend of his, a minor congressman from Washington state, back in the back rows.

Mrs. [Vijayalakshmi] Pandit was having a private Washington premiere of the film *The River*. After the movie, instead of circulating among the ambassadors as apparently he was supposed to do, and still wearing his hat and raincoat, Douglas spent the rest of the evening with the Schjelderups and his friend from Washington state, talking about mountain climbing and horses.

Mrs. Pandit, said Justice S., was not at all disturbed — she apparently knows Douglas well and loves him as his other friends do. But some of the important people present — senators, ambassadors, socialites — were not at all pleased, even though it was behavior characteristic of Douglas.

I'm not sure what this homey little story proves; I guess it depends mostly on the nature of William Douglas. If his eccentricities are affectations, done deliberately for the mere sake of shocking, and to build up his reputation as a folksy character, then the story is not a likable one.

But if, as the Schjelderups by their manner of telling about the incident proved they believe (they gave no sign of the doubt which I have suggested), and as I myself really believe, if Douglas is the sort of honest, simple and in a way simple-minded man, absent-minded, who acts the way he acts sincerely, because it seems to him the friendly and obvious thing to do, then the story is further proof of the man's democratic character.

(That is one of the worst sentences I have ever written. I should start all over again — it reads like a speech by Governor Olaf Olafsen of Minnesota.)

We skoaled Douglas with cognac and went to bed. Four hours later, at about four this morning, I was awakened to get the Bergen train. What a sensation; I haven't had a full night's sleep for nearly a week, it seems. Oh well, here's to Douglas, man's best friend; to the friendly and courageous Schjelderups; to *Skandia*.

Again. We are now backing and sculling, like a furtive crab, out of the Stavanger harbor. With the Salvation Army as a stateroom companion.

Yes, again I got a fat old man as a cabin-mate. This one is a Lieutenant-Colonel or something in the Salvation Army. Very friendly and quiet. A Norskmann, too. A Wiking of the Lord.

Sail on, sail on, sail on and on, O Edward Abbey — on. The heaving bloody ocean never changes — eternal. Eternally be-damned, for all I care. The surface of the sea is all we see; what I want most to see (next to land) is the sea beneath the surface. Where ragged claws scuttle . . . where the hooded polyp dwells . . . and where the seamaids linger, like a dream in slow motion, over sunken ships half-buried in the sea-floor's sand.

∞

The Art of the Novel: If I could write the damned thing in notebooks — like this — my powers of mobility would be nearly squared. The typewriter hangs from my neck like an anchor — I have to carry it with me everywhere I go and when I want to write on it I require a roof and walls, a chair and table, paper, carbon, ribbon. A bloody nuisance. In good weather I must always make the unhappy choice between staying in to write the book or going out to breathe the green air and kiss the gilded sun.

Of course, I can always go out in the backyard with my machine — if a backyard is available — but it's a lot of trouble and by the time I'm settled and ready to write, the rain comes, or a wind or something.

A notebook and a pen are nothing — I can carry them with me anywhere I go. Now if I could only write my novel like I'm writing this. Why can't I? Because the typewriter inspires me as nothing else but money can, or love. I write more carefully on the machine, and think and feel harder — the typed words have such an impressive appearance of authority and finality — I *have* to try harder. When I write with a pen, any old junk is liable to come out. Just look!

∞

Remember Vienna? When Penelope and I . . . but we had to get there first. And we went separately; Penny, being a South African, was not allowed to go to Vienna via Lenz through the American Zone. I, being

American, was not allowed to go through the British Zone. (I'm getting confused — both routes to Wein go through the Soviet Zone — the trouble was this: one route was reserved for Americans, one for British. Yes, that's it.)

So we said good-by at Salzburg, took different trains and met again in Vienna, about ten hours later. But getting there was interesting; it was my first opportunity to see real live Russians — with boots and Tommy-guns, I mean. I was not disappointed.

There was a small detachment of them at Lenz, on the border between the American and Soviet Zones. I saw four; the rest were in a little green barracks, sleeping, I suppose. The train stopped and the Russians came aboard to check passports and permits. They looked surprisingly alike — short and stocky, blond, healthy and well-fed, round outdoor faces, blue eyes, slightly bored expressions. All were very young, surely not over twenty, any of them. They wore heavy woolen uniforms, leather boots and Tommy-guns, just as advertised. It was a hot day and they were all sweating some, obviously uncomfortable.

But they behaved like good Communist gentlemen, treating the passengers with scrupulous courtesy. No; I mean they were painstaking about not being discourteous. As far as I could see, they never said a word to anybody. They moved through the hot crowded coaches like young bulls bent on disproving a proverb would move through a crockery shop. Saying not a word — gently, very gently touching passengers' elbows to get by them in the jammed train corridors — patiently and expressionlessly and sweatingly waiting while passengers fumbled nervously for passports — occasionally re-adjusting the positions of the Tommy-guns slung across their backs so that no one would be inadvertently poked in the eye by a muzzle or nudged in the ribs by a buttstock.

Almost, but not quite comic, these Russians. They looked too tough and competent to be comic, but not cruel and arrogant in the manner of American MPs. Their Tommy-guns, Russian-made, looked efficient, simple and well-cared for. I examined them with considerable interest, being very fond of such weapons myself.

Though rifles are really much more fun, much more interesting. To use, I mean. Operating a sub-machine gun, if I remember correctly, is much like having an orgasm — sensually thrilling, pleasure quick and concentrated, but almost devoid of intellectual interest. Rifle shooting requires thought, patience, much calculation and skill, and involves more precise, detailed and mathematical results and operations. Sex and logic; fire and ice; the water pistol and the .22.

Where was I?

It took the Russians an hour to go through the train. Then they got off, we went on, and I didn't see any more of them until we got into Vienna.

The country we went through getting there was not particularly interesting — at least I don't remember anything particularly interesting. Just low rolling hills, neat little villages, neat little farms, neat little people. Nobody looked like they were suffering under the Russian occupation. But of course police states do not set up concentration camps where they can be casually inspected by passing tourists. Russia remains a mystery. Under a blanket of Siberian snow. "The depth of it is unknown," says Santayana, "but the silence is impressive."

I suppose so. I still sometimes fondly hope . . . wishfully imagine that . . . wistfully suggest — but what's the use?

We'll see yet, old comrade. We'll see.

Vienna was a big disappointment. I'd been expecting a city something like Paris. Instead I saw old bombed ruins, dead empty unlit wide dusty dirty streets, grim shell-pocked walls and dreary buildings, unhappy and hunted and haunted and hungry people, too many Cadillacs and not enough Fords, too much neon and not enough grass, too many nightclubs and not enough trees — too many surefire signs of injustice, economic and social.

I thought of Madrid and Rome and New York. But those three cities have beauty, much great beauty, which partially obscures, though it does not justify, the human misery upon which it is based.

Vienna lacks any such balance; the contrast is raw and ugly, the faces of the overworked and underfed too numerous, too prominent. Beggars and shoe-shine boys, and old women peddling cigarettes — things you would never see in *Skandia*, for example, or Switzerland, or even in Britain. The old old story. How tiring it becomes. How much longer? What has happened? How, why, have we been betrayed? Man is born free and everywhere he is in chains. Arise, ye prisoners of starvation. Why not?

A couple of hours later - North Sea

I've been playing old frayed tunes on my harmonica and am immersed and half-drowned in a heavy sea of nostalgia, washed over by remembrances, rolling heavily and pitching badly in a syrupy ocean of sentiment. I kid myself, but it's too true to be false. I play those simple but delightful little melodies of Ralph [Newcomb]'s and think of cool nights by a hot fire drinking hot black coffee under the stars among the junipers out in Tijeras Canyon, and Ralph playing and singing in his thin, wan but intimate and appealing and unforgettable way — playing his old guitar and singing his homely little sad little beautiful little songs. His own personal music, better than the whole jukebox repertoire of all time combined.

Ralph Newcomb — a genuine full-blooded human being, and consequently somewhat of an anachronism in modern commercial-atomic America. A kind of misfit, like I hope I am. A queer guy who rolls his own cigarettes, and shaves when he feels like it, which isn't very often, and shoots and cooks his own meat, and sleeps on the ground and likes it, and paints pictures in his own way, and writes his own songs because he doesn't like the ones he hears on the radio, which machine he never listens to, and has a wife and two kids just as friendly and independent as he is, and makes his own bows and arrows, and likes Indians better than people, and knows more about horses than horses know about themselves, and doesn't own a wristwatch or alarm clock or much of anything else, and goes where he likes when he likes and is all in all a full-fledged practicing Philosophical Anarchist.

Huckleberry Finn Newcomb. One of the half-dozen people I really know and really like.

Which reminds me of other people, other [UNM] friends — Bud Adams and Alan [Odendahl] and Dick Volpe and Riddle and Shook.

And places — Tijeras, Cabezon, Red River, the San Juan River, the Sandias.

And adventures — riding and racing through the Canyon, exploring in the White Mountains, Taos, roughnecking in the oil fields in the San Juan Basin, climbing the tower in the Sandias.

My God, the near-past hangs over me like a golden haze, dusty with glory and trouble. Complex and bulging with problems, unexplored significances, crucial and secret-laden experiences.

Oh Lord! And Jean, poor Jean, that sad and sorryfull affair, which reminds me of what a selfish, careless, irresponsible sonofabitch I am. And Rita — the spring magic of love, the essence of happiness and ecstasy, of heartbreak and sorrow — an unresolved and swirling cloud of mystery and promise.

I dare not think of it anymore, or as anymore, not yet, not yet. Forget it, friend; begin anew.

All of that is the desert world, the land of purple mountains and sun-transfigured life. There is another, the primal one, the source, where the earth is dark and fruitful, and the hills green, and where love began and must always return. Not where I now belong, but where I am always welcomed, no matter how evil I become; not where I choose to live, but where I must continually return, if I am anything at all. Far from there, long away, I easily remember my home. Yes, yes, I think of home, I think of Home. [The foregoing foreshadows, by nearly four decades, the central premise of Abbey's "fat masterpiece," *The Fool's Progress*.]

Same day, same fucking place (North Sea), several hours later

What else did [Penny and I] see in Vienna? The filthy Danube; the dank dreary dull Vienna Woods; some ugly old churches.

And we heard and saw a Communist mass-meeting at the huge Red Army Memorial in the Stalinplatz. Searchlights, flags, speeches, band music, singing, thousands of people — also a stirring performance, if largely incomprehensible to us. Lots of Red soldiers lounging around in small groups, paying not the slightest attention to the speeches, and looking bored or homesick or joking among themselves, like young draftees in any army anywhere in the world.

The Russian officers looked decidedly different — they were older, of course, and often fat and thick-necked and red-faced and mean-looking, and they were stiffly attentive while the speeches rasped and crackled and roared through the P.A. system — they looked like officers in any army anywhere in the world. No question about it, all things considered, the Russians constitute the number one tourist attraction in Vienna.

The same thing is true of Berlin; even the travel agencies and airlines have been bright enough to catch on. I have seen little leaflets, inviting tourists to Berlin, which lay stress on the adventure of a tour through the Russian Zone of the city. Come and stare at the wild barbarians from Asia! See genuine full-blooded Russian Reds with Tommy-guns and Cossack boots!

I understand the emotion — part of my eagerness to go to Vienna was based on the same crass and childish curiosity. I wanted to see the polar bears in the zoo, too. If the Russians themselves are aware of this attitude, they show no sign of it. The ones I saw seemed utterly indifferent to the people and activity around them. As I said, not cruel or arrogant (not even the officers, exactly), but tough and competent, bored or homesick, or concerned with their own affairs and nothing else. And not stolid; among themselves they talked and laughed pretty much like human beings, and they sang even more.

Most of them, I imagine, are sealed off from the Viennese, and from other non-Russians, by the wall of language. Nobody speaks Russian but Russians, and most of the Russians speak nothing but Russian. I tried to talk to some of the soldiers in English and got nothing in return but sullen stares, or amused shrugs, or dull grins. I tried out my Russian on some of them — my Russian consists of about six words or phrases — and got pleased smiles, which rapidly faded when my vocabulary was exhausted and the soldiers realized that I had nothing more to say. Conversations limited to "Hello" and "How are you, comrade?" and "Good-by" are not particularly interesting to anybody.

The Russian officers, some of whom probably know a little English, I didn't bother with; they looked too unfriendly. So that was that; the Russian mystery remains a mystery — I got no further than Napoleon or Hitler — nowhere worth getting to. And there is no country in the world which I would rather explore than the Soviet Union, and no people I would rather live with for a while than the people of Russia.

It's a tragic situation; the Iron Curtain seems impenetrable. And it's a two-way curtain. Not only will the Russians not grant me a visa (I've tried three times: in London, Vienna and Stockholm), but now those swine in Washington — who have already smudged my passport with restrictions making Czechoslovakia, Hungary and Bulgaria "off limits" (the phrase is quite appropriate for personnel of the new U.S.A., the garrison state) — are planning to make the whole Soviet empire a forbidden territory, including China. That's too damn much! I strenuously object! Acheson, you dirty dog, I object! You hear me?

I heard the Russians sing. Walking at night alone through the dim and lonely streets of Vienna — where are all the people? — I heard, seemingly from a great distance, a spasmodic wild vulpine howling, a chorus of drunken Cossacks, wild and strange, barbaric and complex, subtly beautiful. It *was* coming from a great distance; I had to walk about ten blocks before I came within sight of a Red Army barracks, a huge old palace or something with sagging walls and shell-holes and blinded windows.

But there was light beyond the blinds, and much noise, and every few minutes one of these short choral bursts of sound, of musical howling — there must have been a hundred men or more, but the harmony, highly chromatic and subtle, sounded as true and far more thrilling than any professional chorus.

Outside — listening in. How I longed to join them, those barbarians, and share their songs and vodka, and share with them the heart's yearning for home, for the open steppes and plains, for the great skies and distant mountains of Russia — or western America. Does it matter where? Of course that's what the strange songs were about — home and wind and vast space and wilderness and mystery — there could be no doubt about that.

For an hour or more I stood outside listening, and never in all of Europe, at any time, have I felt more deeply the trouble and longing of exile, and never have I felt, on this horrible old continent, such comradeship with other men as with these, my fellow non-Europeans. And never, finally, was I more aware of what a tragedy a war between Russia and America would be — of what our two nations could share, could do together, far more than Europe ever could.

Emotion quite overwhelmed the intellect; for an hour the heart ruled the soul. And then the singing stopped and the lights, one by one, went out, and the old silence and the customary darkness came rolling back.

May 15, 1952 – New Castle, England

I stumbled on deck this morning for a charge of that fresh English air. First thing I got was a cinder in the eye. Sun shining gamely through the smoke and fog. A lot of happy Englishmen running around making joyful sounds. One of life's many curiosities — the genuine happiness with which Englishmen respond to a return to their native land, poor smoky benighted ugly little England. Poor little England . . . world's worst food, world's homeliest women. No question about either proposition — both readily verifiable, and already verified.

No wonder the men of Britain have been so brave and restless, so far-wandering, so resourceful and energetic in commerce, war and empire. They have literally been driven away from home, forcibly expelled by the horror of British cooking, by the dreary faces and bony bodies of the British females.

Poor little England. I must be understanding, kind, compassionate — there is much that is good here, much that is fine and new and courageous — but so heavily presses down the dead weight of the centuries, of the dark medieval past, that the good and new must half-exhaust themselves in mere survival.

Oh to be a poet now that spring is here!

Oh to be in April now that spring is there!

May 24, 1952 – Edinburgh

Anguish. Not a deep or great anguish, not an important or lasting anguish, not, perhaps, a real anguish. Rather, something soft and gentle and caressing, a light, melancholy, passing and wholly transient anguish — the most painful of anguishes. Well — what's the cause of all this maudlin moaning? The usual thing — a girl.

A girl?

A woman, then. For nine months I have been in love with the second flutist of the Scottish National Orchestra, a tall slim woman with magic fingers and dark-brown piled-up hair and soft shadowed brilliant eyes and a silver flute and a black velvet gown. Every Friday night (except when I was away from Edinburgh) for nine months I have been in love with this dark mysterious woman. But a silent secret love it has been — she doesn't know I exist. Nine months should be sufficient time for the most timid of lovers to speak to the woman he loves — but it has not been long enough for me. I had resolved to speak to her tonight — I came within three feet of her — and my heart and nerves failed me. I could not speak.

In a few days I leave Edinburgh for good — while she, at this moment, is on the train to Glasgow, headquarters of the orchestra, home of the players. It is quite certain that I shall never see her again. Tonight was my final opportunity to attempt to contact directly this tall and lovely woman who has haunted my Friday nights for nearly a year; my last chance and I failed to respond. Failed myself. Failed love and the romantic heart. Thus, my anguish comes.

At least I came close to her tonight, looked hungrily at her face and hands and hair — saw, for a moment, her eyes meet mine, our souls interlock — then break, and I moved on while she stood there smiling gently in a circle of talking and laughing friends, listening to them perhaps but waiting — waiting for me? Did she see me, then? Does she know me, think of me? Dear world, I will never know. Oh the intolerable lostness of it, the anguish.

Now she flies through the night, westward. What is she doing now? . . . Thinking? . . . Feeling?

GLUTTONY — that's my vice and my curse. I want too much of everything.

Women — every time I pass a pretty girl on the street my heart gives a lurch of regret — regret that I *passed* her.

Books — there are not enough great novels, great philosophic treatises, great poems, to more than dampen the bottoms of the cisterns of my lust; I must write my own.

Music — I cannot hear enough, I cannot understand enough of what I do hear, I cannot over-exploit my own musical resources, there are few instruments I am not eager to master, no songs I will not sing.

Color and Form — I must draw, too, and paint, and here I have so much to learn, so much. The world's great paintings puzzle me, disquiet me, rob me of comfort. Jungles of mystery I have not begun to explore, yet whose secret heart I must find.

Philosophy — the world of ideas is my particular province, yet here I am as hungrily ignorant as everywhere else.

Travel and Adventure — the oldest and principal dream, as far away as ever. The more cities I see and mountains I climb, the more I want, and trouble and danger tempt and torment me.

The result of this bestial lust is an indiscriminate and promiscuous splaying of my energies — wanting all, I accomplish nothing; desiring everything, I satisfy nothing and am satisfied by nothing. Balloons, celestial telescopes, saddle horses, lunar exploration, sex in the afternoon on the desert's seashore, the feel of a book, the power of a name, the concatenation of spells of imagery in a poem, the comradeship of brave men, the love of noble women, the founding of a dynasty — too much for a nation of aspirants to glory. Too much for a nation — not for me.

God, to be able to do one thing, and do it well. To be familiar with freshwater fish — to know how to make a good bow — to be able to scale a rotten-rock cliff — almost anything. I look back at the pathetic devastation of my twenty-five years — and am nearly sickened. A third of my life gone up in smoke, nothing to show, and I haven't started yet. Oh, these are black ugly thoughts — and not wholly true — but they verge on panic; if I don't master myself soon, there'll be nothing left to master.

And I must do something about this inflationary rhetoric of mine — I seem incapable of writing a paragraph of sturdy, straightforward, honest prose. There's far too much reliance on bulging generalizations and vague romantic-heart words. And a monotonous and ostentatious sentence rhythm — the cursed iamb! All the old sins of sophomoric writing are mine, still mine, dearly preserved. Writing from the ink-bottle rather than the head — gushing over feeling rather than tabulating and ordering sensory data.

Try using your eyes on the world, blind man; they're quick enough to spot a wench's wiggling rump, to consider and evaluate the curvature and substance of nodding breasts and springy thighs — why in heaven's name can't you be as crafty and diligent in the observation of old faces, the attitude of trees, the texture of grass and soil, the new light on old walls, the color of water? And your hands and their ten fingers — put them to work. In unaccustomed places, I mean.

May 29, 1952 – Edinburgh

Farewell to old Edinburgh. Such a beautiful day, with a deep-blue dramatic sky, and cumulus clouds scudding along before a fast cold sea-wind, and the sun burning like brass, and the green of the trees and grass like the heart and essence of all that green should be — simple, vivid, fresh, juicy, vital — and the blue-and-white flags of Scotland flying from high poles all along Princes Street, and the great castle standing out bold and gray and romantic on its cliff-sided hill, and the flowers blooming in Princes Street Gardens, and a band playing in the park, and a million people on parade — a glorious city! Athens of the North! So beautiful, it nearly breaks this poor heart to be a-leavin' ye.

Aye, but I must be movin' on, me fair bonny city. Good-by good-by good-by, sweet city, my Old World Home, good-by.

June 3, 1952 – Cornwall

The way these short-skirted English women display their knobby knees and hairy shanks, you would think they thought they had something to show. You would think they thought. How'd I happen to notice? Well . . . just habit.

Where am I? I'm on the north Cornish coast by the seashore near a little town called Bude, looking west, at the moment, toward America — the Promised Land.

The sea is beautiful. It's a revelation: I'd almost forgotten how powerful and mysterious and beautiful the shore, the beach, the sun, sea and charging surf can be. Genuine surf here — big breakers three feet high, and a sandy beach walled in by gray-green cliffs. Gulls and crows. Dark brown kelp sprawled wet and limp on the rocks, algae the color of pea-soup, pale blue English sky, mild English sun, wistful little English clouds floating around listlessly on the horizon. A pleasant charming setting, England at its best.

I'm all alone on the beach now. The English have all trotted off for three o'clock tea. An amazing people. If I didn't admire them so much I could despise them far more satisfactorily.

June 5, 1952 – Bude

The next time she looks up at me that way, I think I'm going to kiss her.

She looks up at me that way and I kiss her — a long lingering and exploring kiss. I had expected at least a token show of resistance but there is none. We break for breath and she smiles at me, her big eyes wide open.

Oh dear, she says, oh dear. That raspberry flavor, I am thinking, where did I meet that before? Oh dear, she says again, laughing a little.

What's so funny?

Why, I was just thinking — we've only just met about an hour ago and here . . . we are.

The most natural, inevitable and beautiful thing in the world, I say. And you kiss quite charmingly.

You taste as sweet, I say, as you look.

Oh dear, she says, what a shameless flatterer you are!

We can hear the old ocean beating on the rocks below us. A slice of blue moon is floating among the purple clouds. Up north, toward Clovelly, the anti-aircraft boys are practicing. Shooting at sea gulls, maybe. The heavies; they flash like bursts of lightning in the clouds far out to sea. A minute later you hear the burst, the rumble like thunder. East of us the lights of Bude shine like Christmas. Whitsun holiday — they've strung colored lights along the canal.

Ten o'clock in the evening, the air is warm and full of moths, the sun is down but twilight hovers over the beach. I look at it, thinking of the warm sand, and at the foaming surf sweeping in, wave after wave.

Let's go for a swim, I say.

Now? she says.

Yes, why not?

But I haven't got my bathing costume.

Doesn't matter; it's dark now; nobody out here but us.

Oh dear, she says, I don't know. . . .

Don't you like to swim at night? I say, thinking of the warm sand.

Oh yes, she says, I love it.

Well, let's go.

It's not dark enough yet.

Oh? When will it be dark enough?

In about half an hour. . . .

June 7, 1952 – Bude

The novel is shambling along — I'm in a big scene now, the murder of Jonathan's father, but there are so many distractions and interruptions here that I can't really get rolling — every time I think it's about to rain, the sun comes out instead and I surrender to the overwhelming compulsion to go swimming in the surf — then when I get in at night I'm too tired to write. Damn thing is 625 pages long now and I'm not halfway finished. What a monstrous heap of rubbish! — or genius and artistry! — or both.

About three more days and I'll be leaving Cornwall, and Britain and Europe. Will I ever come back? Who knows. I want to, of course — yet not as much as I want to explore Asia, and Australia and the Americas. But I'll probably be back — not alone, I half-hope.

Thinking of girls, and sex and these brief parting little flying affairs of mine — I suddenly realize that I am tired and sick of simple animal love. I begin to long for something better, and more complicated, and more enduring. Every other thought or so — half-dream, vague emotion — is of her, the girl I love, the demon-possessed Jew-girl back there in the Promised Land, waiting for me.

Yet with the longing for the comradeship of a real live heart-and-brain-

84

shared love comes the old feeling of restriction, constriction, a dragging weight. I still wonder if I am man enough for love, good enough for marriage, worthy of her. When I wonder I doubt, and doubt makes wonder. I'm still filled and bulging with adolescent urges and lurches, afraid of responsibility, afraid of hard work. But what *would* it be like — with her? Not this pedestrian and mediocre association, surely, but rather something grand and growing, full of beauty and creating for both of us not less but ever more freedom. Surely . . .

June 8, 1952 – Bude

Do I occasionally long for death? Not very deeply — I'm much too interested in the investigation of the human situation, in trying to discover the root-cause of my own and others' misery. After all, I'll die anyway, probably — no need for impatience. The final gift of life, at least, never fails us.

Again I am grateful that I have abandoned — no, it would be more accurate to say "never acquired" — Christianity, with its appalling and horrible promise of immortality which makes Heaven and Hell indistinguishable, and life a vale of dread. It's not immortality I crave, no, never — what I want is understanding. Gladly, joyfully would I sacrifice all eternity for one bright flash of terrible and godly omniscience.

This traditional Western bawling after immortality — what is the meaning of it? Why the insane desire to perpetuate through and beyond all time the identity of the person and the personal consciousness? The Orientals know better — they have the spirit *merge with* the world, not buzz over it forever like a bored and boring fly.

I can hear the sea: the roaring surf, the waves, the wind.

I haven't seen a newspaper, read a magazine or heard a radio broadcast for nearly two weeks: I haven't the mistiest notion of how the Russian situation is coming along, or whether Eisenhower is beating Taft or how many atom bombs were last dropped on poor old Nevada. I don't know, and for the time being anyway don't give a good goddamn — all such matters, when compared to my own thoughts or to the curl of a sea wave or to the memory of a girl's touch, seem ridiculously unimportant, pathetic and foolish, pointless.

∞

Eleven o'clock at night, and all but my own lamp is dark, dark, dark.

I should resume work on the book, get poor old man Troy killed off — he's longing to die — it would be an act of mercy. Tonight? Ah, it's too sad a night for violence and death. Tomorrow? When? Ever? Never? Soon, quite soon, I swear.

I think of my own mother, my father, almost as real to me as the characters in my novel. How will they receive me when I return? Bearing no gifts — without a wife? Will they — do they — despise me? Pity me? Still love me? A cheap whoring drinking shiftless would-be playboy like me? (Ah Abbey, you dramatize yourself again — break that filthy habit. Take more cold showers.)

June 9, 1952 – Dorchester

What is it about Europe — thinking of Europe now, the whole continent — what is it here that oppresses the heart, that sickens and turns the stomach of the soul? *It is the stench of the Past, dead but not yet buried.*

So many, for so long, have suffered so much — jammed together here on this narrow hook of land like maggots on a carcass, without room to breathe or stand upright, proliferating on their own filth and excrement, crowded and shoved by sulfurous ghosts and trembling bones, trapped under a low sky filthy with human smoke and human breath and human misery and fear, swept by periodic plagues of war and madness, corroded by hatred and distrust and poverty, only half-awakened from the long nightmare of a thousand years and more of a life-denying faith, half-smothered under the heavy pall of history, cut off from the green Earth-mother by the spreading blight of concrete and steel and poisonous sewage.

No wonder the European is a short slink-eyed hard-mouthed gray-skinned man with a brain like a rat in a cage.

The European atmosphere of ugliness and hatred is all-pervasive, seeping into everything. I see that it has even gotten into my ink. Seldom have I blurted out such a huge and perilous generalization as that in the preceding paragraphs. My God! the problems raised by it, the implications, the suspicions generated about the health of my own mind, are so many and so complex that the task of working them out in thought and words staggers me, makes me want to drop the whole thing like a live centipede.

Significant biases: When I think about it, it seems to me that the peoples or places or cultures of the Old World which I find most appealing or admirable are those on the *fringe* of European civilization — the Scandinavians, more American than European; the Spanish, more African than European; the Russians, more Asiatic than European.

The heart of Europe, and indeed the heart of Western Civilization — Italy, France, England, Germany — *that* is what strikes me as being rotten and evil and ugly to the very guts, beyond hope, not worth saving, stinking to the skies. Nothing but a flood of fire can make Europe clean.

Sometimes I frighten myself, the way I slip so easily into irrational anger, blind misanthropy, provincial prejudice. Sometimes I sound like a Nazi or a Jesuit, or a Communist (standard brand), or a Republican congressman from Indiana. It's so pleasant, though, to satisfy the lyric and romantic impulsion to make wild and savage and extreme accusations — so much easier than the other course, the only one I respect and trust.

I mean the cool rational liberal approach — the balancing of argument and fact, the reasoned and qualified and documented statement, the honest suspension of judgment in case of insufficient, contrary, contradictory or doubtful evidence; the empirical investigation guided by strategic hypothesis and theory. And above all, by that which is supposed to be the essence of the philosophic temperament (why, I don't know; the history of philosophy illuminates the conspicuous absence of the "philosophical attitude" in professional philosophers) — detachment, disinterest and serenity — wisdom seasoned with humor and irony.

A sweet reasonableness. One touch of it and anyone would realize that an immature manure-slinger like myself, fresh from the farm, with the smell of cow-dung still under his fingernails and buckwheat in his trouser-cuffs, is hardly qualified, on the basis of a mere two years in Europe (counting the army hitch), to indict a whole continent and to condemn its inhabitants to Hell for the sake of sanitation.

But to dispose of me so easily would be to underestimate my garrulity — I'm not through talking. That Europe is vile and corrupt is an opinion based on my firmest intuitions — I will not retreat or modify one syllable of it.

But I am not so innocent as to suppose that Europe is unique in this regard — I have heard of a land called Asia, where a human life is as valuable as that of a swatted fly; I am aware of Africa, where a dying king would take with him to his grave a thousand wives and slaves; I am a citizen of America, the last great nation in the world to abolish human slavery (a partial abolition, of course).

No, I do not for a moment mean to suggest that Europe stands alone in the field of evil — wherever man is, there is evil. What makes Europe remarkable is the combination of neglected opportunities of breathtaking dimensions with the world's most pretentious aspirations and declarations and proclamations and inspirations (second only to the U.S.A.), and the unyielding suction with which this lurid double-beast is attached to a deep solid base of misery, injustice, murder, torture, hunger, insult, humiliation, filth, superstition, hatred and insanity.

The truth is, I am fascinated by Europe, in love with its rich dark complexity and foul wickedness, infatuated with its depravity, enamored by its putrid sophistication and cognac-breath and over-ripe corpus and treacherous eyes and dirty ears and syphilitic vagina and greasy lips and oily stinking hair and sweating armpits — a diseased old rum-drum of a whore is Europa, and I hate and loathe and love her.

But for the love of Christ, don't let her get into bed with America — debased though we are by our own slimy lust and sly sneaking sniggering immorality, we are still a young country, still half-open and big, with room to breathe and a gigantic sky, still wild and lonely in patches, still new and daring and unique, still a Land of Promise; even though the rats and vermin are having a field-day at the moment — don't let them make that Big Promise fade, and don't let that stinking old whore Europa get her grimy claws into your pockets and her lousy hair into your eyes.

The old bitch is beautiful, boys; in her rotten-ripe way she still has her points. Come on over and take a good look, but keep your hands in your pockets and go home before you pass out.

Yes, I admire Europe very much and I am honestly, sincerely, genuinely reluctant to return home, to Old Commercia, so soon. I would like to spend at least five, perhaps ten consecutive contemplative and observing years on this glittering continent. But I would no more live my whole life in Europe than in Alcatraz or Sing Sing. Nor in America. Or Russia. Or any other one place.

Fond of America, proud of her, curious and hopeful about her future, I nevertheless renounce America. My loyalties will not be bound by national borders, or confined in time by one nation's history, or limited in the spiritual dimension by one language and culture. I pledge my allegiance to the damned human race, and my everlasting love to the green hills of Earth, and my intimations of glory to the singing stars, to the very end of space and time.

June 10, 1952 – Dorchester

Cranes and herons are more beautiful than swans. I saw several of each this afternoon — England flutters with birds and wildfowl — and came to that conclusion without hesitation. Seeing a swan waddling around on dry land, I suddenly realized that the celebrated bird is nothing but a big fat duck with a tube neck and a conceited temper. Who ever saw a swan fly? As likely an event as an Allegheny pig-iron barge taking off for a spin over the Triangle around three o'clock in the afternoon on Mother's Day.

Of course, even though they have no business at it, swans *will* fly — but what an effort! Anyway it's esthetics, not aerodynamics, that I'm talking about. Not that the two may not be inseparable. Down with swans! I wouldn't wipe my nose with a swan. But a crane! Or a heron! Or a flamingo! Or a Great Speckled Bird! Now there's a creation worthy of dawn-hour adoration.

Quite late in the afternoon, along toward sundown, I saw it — the blue heron. Wading in the dark slow water on its surrealistic legs, stabbing at a fish with its rapier-beak, craning and twisting its knob of a head and skinny neck, shaking its blue feathers and blue tail, occasionally taking a one-eyed look at me to see what I was up to — looking at me first with one eye and then with the other, as though each eye observed life in its own perspective.

The fragile and fantastic bird, like something dreamed up by Paul Klee or Rita Deanin or . . . it stepped delicately through the shallow stream over reeds and cress, moved through the thick English light on yellow stilts, a feathered marionette, nothing but sticks of bone and tatters of blue feather, nothing but hunger — clean craw hunger, and clean splintered shakes of grace and zealot-eyes, nothing but life cut slim and light and precious — more valuable than the tears of Mary, the blood of Christ, the love of God.

About then the creature left the water and flapped slowly into the air, floated away like a fading dream.

What a bigot I'm becoming; I can't even report on a bird-watching expedition without giving the poor old doddering Christian religion a sneaky jab in the groin. The conscientious way I go about it must breed a gloating suspicion in some crinkled minds. "He's almost ready for us," they're thinking, "he's fighting off Heaven's bloodhounds now — the harder he kicks, the sooner he'll tire and collapse."

I can see them watching me as I write these lines: They're hunched in a row on the cemetery wall watching me, huddled in their ragged black wings, claws exposed, red sore eyes gleaming, around their scrawny necks the clerical ruff that hides the ugly separation of head and body, and inside their bald skulls, locked like a corpse in a coffin, the scheming little brain. Eaters of carrion, parasites on death, idolaters of fear and decay — the vultures.

"He's coming," they're thinking, "look at him sweat. Soon now, the supreme unction, the oil on the eyelid, our beaks picking out those rebellious eyes."

But oh my lean and hungry cousins you are wrong — dead . . . wrong.

∞

END OF JOURNAL VI

Literary Cricket

Road map: *Journal VII documents the opening of an unsettled period in Abbey's life. From England, he crossed the Channel to France, where he boarded the* Queen Elizabeth, *bound for America. Arrived, he visited his parents in Pennsylvania and Rita in New Jersey, then settled temporarily in Washington, D.C., having grudgingly accepted an office job arranged by his old college friend Alan Odendahl. As Journal VII closes, Ed and Rita, recently married, have returned to New Mexico.*

JOURNAL VII

June 1952 to August 1953

∞

June 11, 1952 - Dorchester Station, England

The birdshit on the cover [of this journal notebook] was not meant to serve as a rubric for the contents. Just a parting token of appreciation from Little Old England, delivered personally by a common bluetit.

A few more hours and I must crawl despondently aboard the *Queen Elizabeth.* Being hustled back to Old Commercia. I'm feeling bitter (now that it's too late to do anything about it). Snatched away from Europe after a measly nine months! It's like an aborted seduction — I've got the girl all spread out on Grandfather's bed, she's naked as a plucked peacock, her eyes are foaming with love and I am just slipping out of my jockstrap, inhaling deeply, when there comes this knock like thunder on the door: *HEY YOU!*

June 11, 1952 - Cherbourg, France

The sun is low over Cherbourg now; we're at the big pier gathering in a flock of expatriates, patriots, artists and Frenchmen. Beyond the city, the dirty-green Gallic countryside — between here and there the smoky little city. A mediocre light, the tone and substance of cheap beer. Frenchmen lean out of windows, shirt-sleeves and cigarettes, idly curious.

The clouds are like fish scales now, fine and silvery, blue and gray and beery from the sun. Idle [cargo] cranes turning black against the western light, complex machines pointing like skeletal fingers at the sky.

June 12, 1952 – on the North Atlantic

A letter from Odendahl was waiting for me on the *Queenie*. The kid seems to be having a pleasant time not bothering to be a brilliant scholar. He's like me — brilliant but fundamentally lazy — slothful geniuses. He still hangs around in Washington; he's in severe danger of becoming a minor bureaucrat. And he has the audacity to invite me to come to Washington and do the same! For $3,400 a year! I'd rather be a roughneck in the oil fields any day. Or a sheepherder in Australia.

I like Odendahl; there's something about that Viking I particularly like. What? I mean there is something unique, particular, peculiar about him. What is it? There are other obvious reasons for our casual but genuine friendship — a common respect for liberal and rational thinking (thinking is not necessarily, merely by definition, rational — certainly not liberal), a shared appreciation for the unusual beauty of the desert and a sense each of us must have of a complementary quality in the other; we fill, to an extent, vacancies in each other.

Alan has a keener quicker mind than I, and a healthy passion for precision and logic and detail; I have a better ear for music, for the sensuous and aesthetic. Insofar as we can share what we have, we enrich ourselves.

But none of this answers the original query — there's something more significant behind my affection for my friend. I think it is this: In Alan is the character of innocence and the direct and unflinching honesty born of this innocence. (He might be surprised to read this, perhaps not feel flattered despite his oft-professed disdain for what he means by "sophisticated.") But I think I've come close to what I was looking for — guilt-laden myself, I am conscious of his integrity.

Our friends the Browns [this could be a reference to either Malcolm or Tom Brown] and Boves and Bakers [all of the old New Mexico crowd] sink deeper daily in the mire of domesticity. Thank God I'm not married anymore. How truly satisfying it is to be responsible only for myself, to be alone and solitary again, to have the whole world as my private park. Society is good — in the clash and mesh of heated minds is born philosophy and art and human glory — but there is one thing sweeter, purer, deeper, higher, lovelier — and that is solitude. Bookless wordless solitude.

June 13, 1952 – Atlantic Ocean

Reasons I don't like white:

White is the color of sterile paper, of hospital interiors, of fungus, of toilet paper, of winding sheets, of T. S. Eliot, of cadavers, of Roman collars, of God, of chastity, of tombstones, of lilies, of pus, of government documents, of albinos, of skeletons, of salt mines, of The Cross, of fish eggs, of surrender, of morgues, of civic monuments, of glazed eyeballs, of stuffed shirts, of soft soap, of His Holiness, of false teeth, of trusses, of plaster casts, of abdominal supporters, of bone ash, of swans, of Englishmen, of quick-lime, of sleeping pills, of pisspots, of maggots, of termites, of the Ku Klux Klan, of poison gas, of false fronts, of John Foster Dulles, of birdshit, of kitchenettes, of gymnasiums, of military cemeteries, of leprosy, of the creeping scrofula, of theology students, of classicism, of metaphysical idealism, of small lies, of big lies — white is the color of the Absolute. The absolute Absolute.

June 14, 1952 – North Atlantic

Science has made the world a sweeter cleaner fresher place in which to live. I mean physics, not chemistry, and the world, not the Earth. The old gods have been swept like so many mildewed spiders out of the skies, out of space. And the frontiers have been pushed way back; the stars, stripped of adolescent fantasy, are brighter and bigger and a thousand times more beautiful. And the universe is big and open now, with ample room for adventure and mystery, novelty and breathing and speculation.

The moral: The human imagination, when it feeds only upon itself, as in the Dark Ages, does not liberate — it confines and poisons the imprisoned spirit. (It was against this disease that [Giordano] Bruno [16th-century Italian philosopher and martyr] revolted.) But when the imagination can break through the wall of its own desires and fears, and can embrace the naked beauty of the real world, then we have discovered Paradise. Natural happiness.

A girl's foot: In my roosterlike obsession with that luxurious portion of a woman's body that happens to be the focal point and functionally primary centripetice [sic] of sex, I have tended to overlook or at best to give only passing consideration to the extreme or incidental members which adorn a good woman. (Good, I mean, from the point of view of art.)

Such as the foot. I've long been dimly conscious of the charm and attraction of a healthy and shapely foot, not when abstracted in any but a mental way of course, but as a necessary appendage to any terrestrial automotive organism, with its aesthetic goodness as much a product of its connections and teleology as of its intrinsic substance and form. Not necessarily small, nor falsely arched, nor extended in the gesture of ballet, but straight out, at a slightly obtuse angle to the ankle; not necessarily clean, definitely not painted on the nails, but naked and firm-fleshed and young, the foot of a girl becomes extremely interesting, and not merely because it suggests the calves and thighs leading to better things.

I am contemplating such a foot at the moment. This very moment.

The naked foot has a quality of impish carnality, of devilish innocence and sweetness, of tender lascivity and child-like sensuality and utterly unselfconscious seductiveness which I find prettily amusing, cajoling like a golden child to the affinitive sentiments of gonad, heart and brain. Why have I deprived myself of so much for so long in my unseemly haste to get to the point?

But caution, ungulated-one, soothe thy wounded pride lest it lead thee into the veriest stews and pots of the sinful flesh — would thou become a sybarite, indolent on oily luxury, a sly voluptuary unfit for anything as clean as granite or pine or airy mountain . . . ever again? Sweat, crawl, pant, grunt like a mired pig — it'll do thee no good then for thou shalt be trapped, stuck like a worm in decadence and Hell's mud. Keep free, lad, stand back; it's not worth it!

June 15, 1952 – mid-Atlantic

Things I have seen, which I now can see no more:

The harbor of Valencia at dawn — iron ships, fishing boats, beggars' skiffs — under, or rather well within the horizontal Mediterranean light, the pale-gold winey light. Ancient, classic, Byzantine, familiar with towers and turrets and tall masts, blue hair and black eyes, all the glory, grandeur and ugly horror of several thousand human years — Valencia — old as misery and looking it, giving off the hard desolate light of Spain. The intense terrific cruelty and loneliness of Spain sticks in the mind, and the desert beauty, and the haunted unhappy people, and the stale fragrance of the tomb.

The Parnassus in Paris. Picturesque as a Technicolor movie set — the narrow winding uncertain cobbled streets, the leaning-walled overhanging pastel-tinted little buildings all with grilled iron and green shutters and yellow-red doors, the tiny cafes swollen with song and business and students — all kinds of students, including numerous Existentialists with thin jawline beards and haunted eyes, and temporary wistful expatriates from Des Moines and Boston and Albuquerque, and girl art students from places even more improbable.

A wind blowing and a dark night — from a point on the hill we could see all of Paris spread out below us, glittering softly, undulations of light and color coming and going, glowing and burning under that heavy old

European sky — the great million-faceted jewel of Paris, whirling through time, through space, waiting for the final possible impossible triumph.

Such meaningless thoughts strayed through my head as I looked down on the fabled city, everything universalizing rapidly, individual character melting quickly and easily, and I saw Paris as not Paris but as symbol, or rather, as more than Paris, more than symbol, for here the symbol is not only symbolic but also a concrete objectification of that which it symbolizes — human civilization lit up like a reflection of the stars, burning hopefully, or perhaps desperately, all night long.

Paris — the city of light and light-hearted laughter, of gay champagne and perennial spring and blossoming girls, of all that is brightest and most lyrical in men. Exactly. That's why it's so tragic. The sweeter, the more poignant; the more beautiful, the more pathetic. There is more tragedy in the kiss of young lovers than in all the murders of all the royal clowns who ever lived.

Nothing tags after happiness more closely than sorrow. The full heart bursts most easily. And so on and so on. Then what do you advise, grim weeper? Caution? Shall we retract, contract, shrivel and wither interiorly the exposed sensibilities? Play it safe? Oh go to hell — you get on my nerves. Go soak your head in a bucket of cyanide.

July 26, 1952 - Washington, D.C.

This life of mine, I don't know, the dreary vagueness of it — the imprecision. It's enough to drive a man to his own death; if I ever lose my taste for humor, the thing may happen to me. I can't stand too much of it.

This is another of my bad periods, when prospects are bleak in every direction. For one thing, I'm homesick, desperately homesick — for the wild free skies and spaces of the great Southwest.

I suppose it's immature, adolescent, this infatuation with a certain landscape, air, color. I suppose it is, but it is real for me. There's nothing I can do about it; even though I find beauty everywhere — even in darkest Washington — I don't find it everywhere in the same value or intensity. The variations, in fact, are extreme — great enough to make my heart burn with desire for the deserts and mountains of the land I love.

It's heartbreaking, this sick yearning, and the pictures with it, the old remembrances: riding through Tijeras Canyon [on the edge of Albuquerque] in the late afternoon sun, watching the shadow of my horse and me flowing over the golden dust and stone . . . alone on Wheeler Peak, far from man and near to my God . . . the ravishing loveliness of the white waterfalls and blue water and red walls of Havasu Canyon . . . wandering in the terrible desert along the Sonoran border . . . the great emptiness of Big Bend . . . the memories!

Then there's the girl again, adding to my troubles. I spent a week with her in Provincetown and the love that had weakened somewhat in Europe flagged and fluttered there, was set on fire once more with the ardor of madness and passion — not merely resumed, taken up, but enhanced, magnified, glorified. So that when I left her and came here, I suffered horribly from loneliness and the hungry cry of unsatisfied love. As if that alone were not enough, she chose that moment to reveal — in her first letter to me — a new plague of doubts and conflicts to which she was subject.

For days I wandered in a near-delirium of loss and anger and hope-lessness, convinced that everything was conspiring against me. Now that is slowly passing — I know better now; besides, she's coming back — but it leaves a cloud on my soul. My hollow battered soul. Wrung-out, smoked, un-nerved.

My claustrophobia, the sense of live-smothering, live burial, here in this festering city. As if I could barely breathe. Closed in, oppressed, weighed heavily upon. Allied, of course, with my desire for the West — its com-plement.

Heavy heat, and masses of bodies, and thick air and dull brown light, and smoke and smells and bone-jarring noise. Terrible. No wonder I'm sick. Disgusted. Tired. (Although the old therapy of writing is beginning to take its usual effect, transferring my feeble miseries from my stomach to this notebook. Most of them — not all.) Like an underground or shut-in life. Be like the eagle, or the mole? I can't take it — the latter's way of life.

4:30 p.m., Tuesday, July 29, 1952 – D.C.

I am so sick and tired of the "preparatory" life; that is, enduring present tedium or misery for the sake of something hoped to be better in the future, on which the eye of the mind and the inner eye of the heart are constantly fixed. I want to learn to live in the present, in the living present. Not like a simple animal, with *nothing but* the moving present occupying the attention, but like a true human, combining the animal and the spirit in a fused delight in both the present and the future.

Today I rejected an offer of a better job. Acceptance would have re-quired, on my part, a promise of staying in Washington for at least a year, something I cannot possibly do. I hate this hot smothering eastern city. You know what I need and want, O friend — well, you already know.

∞

For lunch today: apple pie ———— .15
glass of milk ———— .10
Total ———— .25
(Nearly broke again, but not yet starving.)

July 30, 1952 – D.C.

My adolescent and shaking soul: I seem never to be firm in decision. Whatever I do, I regret doing, wish that I had chosen a possible alternative. Now a part of me is sorry that I did not accept the job, the "good" job that was offered me, and the security with it and the novelty of being in a supervisory position, bossing other people around and — and of course, a living burial in Washington for a year.

But that's it, of course. I will not smother myself in the present for the sake of a possible future good. In a year I will be a year older and a year nearer death. Topics for reflection. But still, there's this cowardly or sensible element in my mind that continually reminds me of what a crazy and irresponsible fool I am, which dreads the uncertainty of the future. It's a weak part, thank God; I got the best of it yesterday when I obeyed my impulses and instincts rather than my common sense, when I did what I wanted to do instead of what I "should" do (e.g., declined the "good" job offer).

After all, I remind myself, the life of adventure is the only life that makes sense. Adventure interpreted broadly, of course — to include not only physical action, exploration, but also human love, ideas and ideals, the arts, and the common and daily motion and conflict and trouble of everyday people doing the world's hard work, making everything else possible.

Interpreted broadly, but not so broadly as to exclude the physical and the bodily active — true to my own romantic naturalism, I insist upon the essential value and uniqueness and beauty of the body and of sensuous activity and of the real manifestations of the slow-evolving earth. The man climbing the mountain, in other words.

August 2, 1952 – D.C.

Is music my own worst enemy? I'm almost forced to think so at times. Nothing urges me to destruction with a fraction of the enchantment outspun by music — except desert mountains.

This sick romanticism . . . I am afraid that I may never outgrow it — I might not live that long. Or I am afraid that I *will* live through and beyond it? It's a soul-curse I am deeply reluctant — would be — to surrender, even though the torment is exhausting, possibly fruitless and perhaps wearying to my friends and enemies.

Without this electric charge in the spirit, the world would not be the arena of infinite possibility and adventure it seems to me to be. But with the joy in that, comes the murky miasma of sadness, melancholy. Two aspects, insunderable, of the same image. And music animates and shines upon the form, the ever-changing but omnipresent symbol of this attitude.

Music is the moving and living ghost — no less real for being ghostly — of this turn of the mind and heart. Music makes my misery . . . makes it endless and promising and disturbing. "Urges to waterfalls," she [Rita] said. Urges to waterfalls. My Gawd, that's close. The old immolation impulse. She, too?

I want to do something good and intelligent. Something saintly. Something true. To whom shall I do it? In what manner? With a minimum of violence? Or no? I wish strongly to give point and purpose to my wistful bridge of days on Earth, to make them in some way memorable and valuable, at least in the opinions of my friends and enemies.

August 3, 1952 – Washington

Today Alan and I went for a walk to Rock Creek Park and back. We discussed: techniques in courtship — forms of courtesy, pursuit, capture and departure; relative merits of bachelorhood and "husbandry"; names, if any, of America's most beautiful cities; the worth of a certain motion picture; reactions, neural and motor, to traffic signals; Alan's phobia of high places; the resemblance of Washington apartment buildings to an ant civilization; the possibility of telepathy; the nature of flying saucers; my strong and his growing distaste for the oppressive mass-crowding of Washington; ideal home-sites in the Southwest; modes of transcontinental transportation; my marriage and divorce; power lawnmowers; civic beauty; the number of different places in which I lived while in Albuquerque — twenty in thirty-one months; poison ivy — its prevalence and effects; cars fording a stream; Washington's vague resemblance to *Roma*; the superfluity of magazines and consequent timber depletion; my desire for universal experience; the horror of quiet suburban life in Washington; islands of beauty in the U.S. East; specialization vs. dilettantism; stealing cars; mechanical difficulties in sexual congress; architecture — home-building, materials, costs and design; my tendency to slovenliness in personal appearance; the possible debilitation of Alan's mind; biology vs. mathematics as proper complements to the study of philosophy; how to make a living in the Southwest; beauty in machines — jet planes vs. Greyhound buses; persons — Ben Duncan, Tom Brown, Diana (Alan's girlfriend), a few others [all old friends from New Mexico]; the church as offering marital possibilities; my apparent claustrophobia; varieties of loneliness; the dreariness of boarding-houses; the evolution in Joyce's writing from *Dubliners* to *Ulysses*; air-conditioning in drugstores; semi-obesity in young women; European universities; the beauty of Sweden's women; the 1952 Olympics; Alan's need for physical exercise; the value of muscle in sexual attraction; the displacement of science by sex in Alan's mind; the grim future for me if I should renounce marriage; where to go to eat dinner.

August 9, 1952 - Washington

Had a letter from Jean the other day, informing me that my little red box of books is still in storage in Albuquerque. That's about all. Oh yes, she wishes me luck in whatever I'm doing, inquired about my recent travels, hopes I'm happy and well.

She (Jean) has almost disappeared from my world. I remember her occasionally, but with no little disbelief. To think that we were once actually married is to think too much. (I still haven't recorded that story.) That I once imagined myself in love with her now seems improbable, unreal. (The dull heart of the animal.) That we were central in each other's lives for almost two years seems incredible. (Swiftly, swiftly flying. . . .)

Yet I still remember her, I cannot forget her, for I owe her so much — for she is truly an admirable girl — for I was a villain. (Make it dramatic. Make it mellow-dramatic.)

∞

Another tale of tortured love, betrayal, etc. — I steal Alan's girl, then drop her, having never really wanted her.

Imagine this fellow — young but not very young, desperately in love with a shy winsome wench who also loves him, strangely enough, since he is homely, awkward, a bit grotesque, backward with women and incompetent, pessimistic in this area with good reason; all said, rather pathetic.

Then along comes this handsome dashing fellow, supposedly a friend, who unleashes his overpowering charm on the girl and breaks up the affair out of sheer meanness. (This story must be old as God. The sultry tango, heavy with sensuality, drooping with sin and desire, dark with a hint of sorrow.)

August 20, 1952 - D.C.

I've got a lump in my throat; maybe I've caught a cancer. Maybe I'm gonna die sooner than planned; where's my alpenstock?

My dear and good friend Little Robin Redbreast [an unidentifiable coworker, mentioned in the journals only this once, and only by this esoteric moniker], after seeing some hasty and facetious drawings of mine (nude men chasing nude women), suggested that I am in need of psychic therapy. (The little pig is a student of psyche-demonology.) I thanked him graciously for the compliment but openly confessed a suspicion that he was joshing me, to which apprehension he replied with assertive and apparently sincere negativeness, and in negation. He said — no.

Human Behavior: Men like to scratch their balls, adjust their penises, especially in public, watch women jiggle, bobbing mechanically, idiotically, without pleasure, when the jukebox music bleats and blares — rhythm without sense, purpose — blind and empty.

September 1952 – D.C.

Chilly days in September — the odor of corn husks, a taste of bitter winter in the air, immortal autumn, smoky, rich, bountiful.

I am enamored of the sound of crows — the far squawking, the flapping wings, the old dim southern husky rural dead-pine rail-fence sound of them. And of dead trees, the deader the better — big, silvery, hollow, old ghostly characters, crawling with ants, bees, locusts, vermin, parasitic life, saprophytic fungoid (old Gothic in a dead sycamore) and a multitude of sins in the form of cancerous burls, naked roots, desperate resigned limbs.

You read Spinoza for a long time before you get the feel of that admirable mind: patient, explaining the obvious yet difficult truth to the inert minds of his readers; thorough, repeating again and again the same argument in all possible syllogistic combinations and permutations; kind and gentle, appreciating, understanding and forgiving the lameness, the weakness of the poor minds trying to follow his; firm, too, dealing justly, courteously but mercilessly with his opponents and enemies in all fields, of all shades of learning, in all ways; blessed, aware of, full of love, an intellectual intoxication, a splendid generosity and charity and serenity; an ideal philosopher in almost every way one should be. Almost. (A good man.)

Rita was here last Saturday, looking a little sad and wistful, as she usually does. She loves me; she wants to be a mother, me the father. (Good Gawd! Am I ready? Am I worthy? Do I want to — yet?) But I do love her, the sweet small wild thing, I do love her. To the point of impotence, almost.

Too much fuss has been made about experience? How is that possible? What else is there to talk about?

The gods come and go; man remains.

∞

I've been enduring this monastic life for a long time now — nearly three months, and a month to go. I'm getting tired of it; I need a woman. I'm going to have to go out and get me a woman. Here I am, twenty-five years old, at the peak of my sexual powers — why should I condemn myself to temporary celibacy?

For honor? Loyalty? Something like that?

If I were really the villain I sometimes think I am, I would probably be a much happier human animal. Much happier. Probably.

October 4, 1952 – D.C.

The constant wailing of sirens — someone is dying, something is burning, all the time in this unfortunate city — is characteristic here, familiar, omnipresent: the moaning crying howling screaming sirens — the mere premonition of what is to come, the terror and the fantasy, when the bombs start falling and the flames rising.

Good Gawd, will I never be free of this tenacious noisome coiling city, this federal bog, this miasmic fen, this unraked muck-heap? Surely, by this long-over-drawn-out agony I've exasperated my hosts as well as myself.

Well, why don't you stop whining about it, get up and leave, as the Old Man would say? Well, I will. Just one more week after this one; by God that will be the last. I don't belong here; I don't fit at all.

∞

Dylan Thomas is the poet of this time, this frenetic lyric time, this spasm of nerve and instinct. No one comes nearly as close as Dylan Thomas, the baby-faced blue-eyed young dog of a Welshman. "Poetry is a statement made on the way to the grave."

Can I do in the novel what he does in verse? No, of course not — if I could, he'd be writing novels too. It's too intense, tight, green-earthed, tough-blooded, dense, compact for the novel. No, he knows what he's doing, and I won't fool or betray myself.

Perhaps the story should not grip, overpower, fixate the reader, but rather, induce in him a condition of purposeful reverie . . . and reverence. (Reverence for life.) A good story suggests much more than it tells, implies far more than it explies [sic], is surrounded by its own insinuations in infinite gradation like the expanding concentric waves on a sheer-smooth pool of water, or like the endless chain of overtones and undertones following the sounded tone, the fading but unlimited ring of connotation.

A story is as substantial and durable as a cloud, and is continuous with all life, as a cloud is with air and sea. A story moves but never arrives — strives for but never reaches completion — turns and turns and never stops. A story is as indefinable as the code in a girl's eyes. As hopeless.

∞

The Brave Cowboy (Don Quixote de Newcomb): The anachronism rides again, this time in the modern West. A young man, perhaps, who has read too many old books, seen too many movies; self-hallucinated, he rides the range alone (no Sancho) among the billboards, across the highways, under the telephone wires, seeking adventure, finding ridicule, indifference, a death without dignity. [This concept will become Abbey's second novel, *The Brave Cowboy*, published in 1956.]

October 1952 – At Home [Pennsylvania] on the farm again

Smoke hangs heavy over us; there's a big forest fire alive over near Ebensburg. And it's cold; it'll snow in hours. Now the proud immortal American autumn seems finished — the gold and death-fire of leaves is gone — all is black, drab lusterless brown, gray, under a bleak smoky sky. The leaves are down; the trees are black, wet, naked, cold. A somber hour, this late act in the change of seasons.

A huge yellow moon floats beyond the haze — silent, dull, impressive, greater now than the poor lost horizon-wandering disappearing sun. But even now a few cicada are left; you can hear them at twilight, few in number but still alive; their hopes are eggs. Last night we heard the wild geese. Over in the woods there's something else — something none of us has ever heard before. Nobody knows what it is.

October 30, 1952 – aboard "The Chief"

A stainless-steel luxury streamliner, half-empty, half-full (excepting me and a pair of pretty young ladies who may be movie stars or oilmen's mistresses) of rancid-faced ulcerous middle-aged unhappy-looking Republicans, male and . . . the other kind. (Sexless now, or rather, permanently never-sexed; laid, screwed, seeded perhaps, mothering perhaps, but essentially sexless. *Sans* — passion.) The wealthy are generally old — white-haired or bald, fat and morose. Too bad. A waste, it seems. How superior I feel — young, healthy, reasonably aware, poverty-stricken. The new plant.

Retrospection: My life in Washington was celibate, philosophically true and austere, right up until the last week. Then I went to Al's party and met this pretty little Italianate virgin named Paula. My life took on new purpose; deliberately, almost cold-bloodedly, I devoted myself to her seduction. She was intelligent enough to appreciate my purpose; we discussed it frankly and often. I talked of adventure, living a fantasy, daring (the same dreary old line). But true to my honor I made no promises, no vows, said nothing of (emotional) love. (I remembered, of course, old loyalties — obscurely troubled I was, but the animal need — or psychic need — was too great.)

She pleaded, begged for time; she was in spirit the very first evening, but her sense of propriety, her vaginal honor, required time. She would (she said), but she could not yield at once. (Though we had only a week and both knew it.)

She played Bach and Mozart on the phonograph and appealed for time. I was gracious, understanding; I allowed her five days.

I am going to Rita now. What does it mean? What do I really want? What does she? What is the meaning of us? I don't know; we're two blind creatures in the dark, each uncertain, a little cautious, worried. We each have our literary fictions to be true to — the legend-builders. We are reluctant to abandon our personal romances for a common romance. Yet I love her; I would love to sing for her, suffer for her, be heroic for her. Set me a task, my Jewish princess!

Looking at my terrible wedding picture (of Jean and me): what an indictment. How could any girl — or friend, anyone — see that cruelly revealing photograph and fail to hate the very lining of my guts? (Mustn't forget that sententious swine of a High Church Christing preacher who calmly, after the service, refused my champagne and accepted without offering any change in return my ten-dollar bill; $10 for a wedding! I had expected the dog to return $5, at least. No doubt he was getting even for the laugh. . . . A few evenings before, he had suggested that I teach Sunday school at his church and I, to my shame, replied with loud crass gross vulgar laughter.) Truly, I am indicted.

October 31, 1952 – aboard "The Chief"

Return: On the last day of October, 1952, I am returning to New Mexico.

First the sage. Before anything else, the blue or purple or silver of the scattered sagebrush. And of course a new clarity in the light, a purity of the air, so gradually subtly coming into being as you move west, you scarcely discern it at first, so that other things, more obvious and visible, strike the attention: the sage, then an occasional cottonwood — at this time of year a dull burning orange. And then, as you ascend the great plateau, the first of the cactus: cane or tree cactus, a few small yuccas, some prickly pear.

Higher up, pinons and junipers. And also now you see another sign: the dry wash — broad, shallow, sandy, dry or with a little trickle of water, diffusions of white alkali and sharp-cut vertical banks intricately fissured, sensitive to every rivulet, every stir of water.

And the barns change; spread out, flatten and, as range displaces farmland, disappear. Fences are fewer now; windmills more numerous: a windmill, a thicket of scrub oak, a cottonwood, a water tank — that's home to a beef cow.

The hills become queer: bare, rocky, rough-shapen, steep-sided, some of them flat-topped, others sharply peaked; their slopes may be studded with low-growing junipers, perhaps a few pinons. The light, the sun, becomes more obvious, the shadows blacker. Huge lava flows, now frozen: black rock, sharp edges, talus slopes of tumbled rock, disintegrated rock, weeds, cactus, junipers.

Houses are small and poor — little clusters of them make a city — Trinidad, Raton, Valmora. Along the track the Mexican workmen look up, grin at us as we go by, their faces as tough and dark and leathery as old jerky. Boys lounge around stations wearing tight jeans, high-heeled boots, tight shirts, big flat-crowned wide-brimmed side-flattened hats. They try hard to look unfriendly.

A hundred miles of rolling cattle-country lies beyond Raton: endless grasslands, dusty yellow, bare, empty, occasional cows. The plains are dotted, pebbled with black lava rocks — ten or twenty miles away you can see the dead volcano that brought them up (basalt?) and poured them out.

Overhead, above me and the others on this fast gleaming train, stretches the great western sky — pure blue, deep, a hundred-mile dome nearly cloudless. (The damned conductor just now chased me away from the vestibule between cars, where I had opened a window to stick my head out into the desert sun and "The Chief's" eighty-mph wind. "Very, very dangerous," he said, and told me about the bits of flying steel, ground from the wheels and rails, striking upward, hot, sharp and minute.)

November 20, 1952 – Albuquerque, New Mexico
Today I married Rita Deanin.

December 25, 1952 – Albuquerque
Mount Taylor looming over the western rim — like the greatest mountain in the world. And the *Ladrones* [Thieve Mountains] — not so grand, but vague, hazy, mysterious, lost in legend.

The soft undulating glitter of the city at night.

Vapor trails scored on the sky by Thunderjets. The jet fighter plane, wicked and vicious, is one of the most beautiful things made by man.

January 15, 1953 – Canyon de la Sol

The Pure River of the Water of Life . . . flowing clear as crystal from the great white throne of Gawd . . . truly a splendid revelation, though not as magnificent as that which mine own eyes reveal to me . . . when I open them . . . beholding the mountains of Arizona, the Colorado and, farther, the Sea of Cortez. . . .

January 29, 1953 – [?]

I'm as old as Keats now [twenty-six] and haven't even got consumption. On the other hand, I have yet to write a decent sonnet.

I am not Keatsian. (Though I've got my Fanny.)

Writing a novel is like the seduction of a woman: It begins with strategy, with a campaign, but soon — if the affair is genuine — all plans are lost in the rush of passion.

To the Mannerists — Racine, Austen, James Eliot, *et al*:

Character is determined by and values expressed through, not the *form* of behavior — "manners" — but by and through the pragmatic *substance* of behavior — its consequences, for good and bad, in the lives of the persons involved.

February 15, 1953, Friday – [?]

My mother on marriage: "Crises are easier to survive than the daily routine."

Malcolm [Brown, a New Mexico painter and close friend of the Abbeys] pointed out one day that married couples who fight continually may really need each other as desperately as those apparently desperately in love — the fighting fills an important vacuum in their otherwise empty vows. You get the idea.

June 1953 – Taos, New Mexico

Where are we now? Rita and I — adrift on a strange sea of uncertainty, disorder and trouble, mixed in purpose. Yet I love this wild queer little girl more than ever. What does it mean? What will happen to us?

It seems like the actualization of an ancient literary melodrama dream — in the grand hall, over the moors, along the cliff by the sea, among the tortured canyons and hills of the desert — a voice far distant crying my name, a space between us, the gulls shrieking, the echoes mocking and laughing, dying and floating and returning, the moon and the sun waiting above us, and all loneliness, all love, all terror and passion and lostness now electric in the air and blinding my eyes and expanding, exploding my heart until I die. Lost, running, calling out to me, the voice far away but pursuing, and death there watching us. An old dream. With a gray blue and austere music — six violoncellos. . . .

∞

I can say it now: Edward Abbey — Writer.

A few days ago came five hundred dollars from Dodd-Mead to make it legal, certificate. But my joy was quiet, or almost null; I knew a definite steady pleasure — steady for a day or two — but no exultation, no sense of triumph or liberation. Perhaps this hour was too long, too gradual in coming; perhaps too inevitable; perhaps not fully earned.

They'll release the book [*Jonathan Troy*] in about ten months; all I have to do is proofread and dedicate. (No trivial problem in this case!) But I find myself no happier, no more content, no more proud than before. A trifle more confident, considerably more determined to make a try at a great book. But no exultation, no triumph. I don't understand. For ten years I've dreamed of this victory. I don't know.

∞

Einstein, invoking the spirit of Gandhi, advises non-cooperation with the Investigators: When they ask you whether you are or ever have been, tell them the truth — "None of your goddamn business." I agree. I heartily agree. Don't cooperate with the bastards. [A reference to McCarthyism.]

This filthy country — I no longer feel any loyalty toward its institutions. I only wish I were free, had the power to live elsewhere. Hiroshima, Nagasaki — this — the moral power of this country is low, terribly low. Worse than in slavery days.

And law or not, no matter how legal, the murder of the Rosenbergs violates a higher law.

What loyalty I still have for "America" takes this form:

I love the land — its great rivers, plains, mountains and the ineffable desert; I love my friends, my kin, my unknown allies — I will stand by them to the end.

But for the cities, for our schools and churches and industries, for the government, for the meaningless documents embalmed of the past, for the mass of hucksters and enterprisers — no love. Fuck them. No loyalty. I will not defend them.

June 1953 - Taos

A vegetable. I do nothing, with so many things — admittedly trivial — to do: (1) Study French and German for [entrance exams for graduate study at] Yale. (2) Brush up on my logic and philosophical history. (3) Practice flute. (4) Swim, climb mountains, explore. (5) Make a little money. (6) And something important, possibly worthwhile: a second book — *The Brave Cowboy.* Or something. (7) The journals and notebooks. (8) [Compose] "Inventions & Speculations for Solo Flute."

None of this I do. Schedule: Perhaps I should construct a daily schedule of activities.

How to live. How to live a full, meaningful, joyous life. To be a saint, or an artist. Anything less is suicide in my case. And Rita's. The "reasonable" life; what is that? Fit to live? Contemplative, disinterested, philosophical.

July 14, 1953 - Taos

Bastille Day. As if the world cared. The meaning and hope of that sublime revolution have been lost, or buried, or distorted beyond recognition. Liberty, equality, fraternity have been ridiculed, scorned, nearly destroyed. The aesthetes and purists find it naive, amusing and inartistic. Our glorious leaders find it subversive. The mob of the people find it incomprehensible. The intellectuals find it impossible. I find it necessary.

Might as well go to bed.

Taos, on Divasdero, overlooking the Penitente village:

Great cumuli thunderheads above us. Us. Rita sits on a rock a few yards away, sketching. Chickens complaining from down below, at the San Geronimo. I can see for fifty miles or more into the "strange mystic unknown" Southwest. There's a mesa out there on the horizon, a beautiful high steep-sided flat-topped mesa. Blue, purple, dark, far-away, never-to-be-known-looking.

(Ah Gawd, I can't write, I can't think; the throng of impressions, remembrances, associations, aspirations, illusions, dreams, odors, visions, sounds, sensations, expectations, losses, disappointments, discoveries — multitudinous, too subtle and varied, too grand or too infinitesimal, too elusive, allusive, illusive and vague, indefinable and non-spatial, non-temporal, non-thinkable — impossible. I only know that something I expected, I have not found. Something never dreamed of, I *have* found, or it has found me.

The purpose of art: distillation, simplification, formalization, shaping of this huge chaotic ever-onrushing mass of experience; to make it meaningful, or understandable or at least beautiful to perceive. But if I am right, most art is wrong. Because. Because the greatest music, pictures, poems, are almost as mysterious and disturbing and perplexing as the rest of life, aliveness, experiencing. Art presents more questions than answers.

A terrible paradox of understanding — with every advance in knowledge, the unknown area, the perhaps-infinite sea of our ignorance, seems to grow. A truism, a cliché of thought: The more we know, the more we know we don't know. So that if wisdom, understanding, knowledge, is the ultimate end of men (if the three are the same), we seem to be self-defeated already, falling through space in acceleration.

Perhaps we should relax and enjoy what we now have.

But being human we won't, can't. Not while alive.

July 28, 1953 – Taos

Bud Adams tried to seduce my wife. I'll never speak to the bastard again.

I guess Malcolm Brown is the nearest thing to an all-around human I know. Though he's not without flaws: I don't like his mysticism; I don't like his puristic theory of painting; I don't like his intimacy with my wife — the devil's too good-looking. But still, he's a fine person, and compared to all others I know, he alone seems fully honorable, balanced, mature, good, sane, with a chance for a truly satisfying life.

And then again — his very equilibrium, his humorous and ironic intelligence, may be his major defects, and serious ones, perhaps: They may prevent him from becoming great; that is, a great painter, or thinker or actor of some kind in the human melodrama. He may end up as nothing but a good father to his children, a good friend to his friends, a good man in a small and inconspicuous way.

"Nothing but"?

Maybe that's quite enough. Assuming we have but one life, and that personal immortality is impossible and the immortality of fame a meaningless and tasteless joke, then one is surely justified in — leading a life of virtuous humble mediocrity?

The old question. And the only answer I can think of is the old answer: A man must be true to the best that is in him, and he must know what he is doing. In that way and in that way only can he act honestly, joyously and in liberty. Let Malcolm paint and raise chickens and father handsome sons — that's his vocation, perhaps; if it satisfies him, it certainly is, and the only guide is that he do it as well and as beautifully as he can.

Man turned inward, in love with himself, indifferent to the world around him, becomes pompous, grotesque, ugly; the same thing is true of art. The more it strives toward purity, the nearer it comes to failure and disaster. Art is not only a part of life; it is *about* life.

∞

The *scherzo* from Beethoven's F Major Quartet: What a clean clear fresh and celestial piece of music that is — completely inhuman; an ideal world of logic and number and crystalline radiance. Pure music and marvelous, and I seem to contradict or deny what I said before. But I can't admit being wrong; say rather that there is an art which escapes all categories, and that this is an example of it.

The ideal is most readily made the real in music, and then in painting, and then in literature. Musicians and painters are much freer than writers, those poor souls, who have to drag the whole weight of humanity with them wherever they go. *Have* to — can never escape it.

The past that can never be recovered, the future that never can be known, the elusive mystery of the quivering present — no wonder our existence is so fraught with poignancy, pathos, tragedy.

August 1, 1953 - Taos

Literary criticism — that dismal swamp where myth and metaphor angle for the darker truths. Modern criticism viewed charitably:

Contemporary literary critics have donned the vestments of high priests and presume to instruct the writer not only in literary method but in what he shall and shall not write about, and in what he shall think about what he writes and does not write. All [critics] assume that man is under the curse of some original or aboriginal sin, and that Evil stalks the world as an independent force comparable to lightning or the old Christian Devil.

The most shameful thing about the critics, and too many of the poets and novelists, is the way they huddle and graze in compact herds. Fashions in literature are often as arbitrary, whimsical and slavishly submitted to as fashions in women's clothes. The modern critic's nearest social equivalent is the local dressmaker and clothing shop proprietor. Both classes are parasitic and more or less pernicious.

∞

END OF JOURNAL VII

Be It Ever So Humble...

Road map: *During the seven-week silence between the closing of Journal VII and the opening of Journal VIII, Ed and Rita moved from New Mexico to New Jersey. There, she was happily reunited with her family, while he indulged an impulse to pursue graduate studies at an Ivy League university.*

But before the year was out, Ed's love for the Southwest and distaste for the urban East became overwhelming, and the Abbey family returned to New Mexico. There, Ed continued his graduate studies at UNM and Rita gave birth to their first son, Joshua. By journal's end, the Desert Solitaire *days had begun.*

JOURNAL VIII

September 1953 to July 1956

∞

September 20, 1953 – New Haven, Connecticut

Today, after two weeks of dilettante study, I withdrew from the graduate school of Yale University. My reasons are several: (1) Disenchantment — I had expected, somehow, so much more than is actually here, that the professors would be Platos, the students Aristotles. (2) Realization — I can no longer play at being an academic scholar; from here on, it would require intense and genuine effort, and after all, I want to be a writer, not an academician; I must choose and I have chosen. (3) Financial and temporal expediency — balancing a year at Yale against a year of writing, a year of travel in Europe, a year's delay in returning to the West, I'll give up Yale. (4) An Inner Voice — the sense that my calling and my study lie elsewhere, in the sweet air and under the open sky of the broad world, among my friends and folks, in space and movement and adventure. (*A posteriori* rhetoric, this last item; I felt a necessity to offset the anti-climax.)

Actually, in a sense, I don't know why I do anything. I can't introspect my own feelings accurately; or there are some things I *know* but cannot bear to admit even to myself. (That inner ticking of the soul — that divine inadequacy?)

I've *got* to live long, because I have so much to do, and am lazy and sentimental.

∞

The true genuine Western novel would be one in which the landscape, the climate, the peculiar physical environment of western America plays a crucial, essential, necessary part; a story that could not "have happened" anywhere else in the world. Can it have this characteristic and still be "universal" in the sense that is supposed to underlie artistic greatness?

October 10, 1953 - Rochelle Park, New Jersey

In the heart of the Great American Blight; about to go to work in a factory, a true prole. Regrets? Yes: loneliness and the vacuum await me — to live I must observe, record, try to understand.

For example — the subtle sense of inferiority the unskilled worker feels in the presence of the operators, the brains, the engineers, the men with clean sharp suits, white shirts with ties, unsoiled hands, stern mouths full of clean white teeth, briefcases, blueprints, slide rules, leather books full of logarithms; laughing talking lounging while WE work — THE FACTORY — Dumont Television.

The job itself, so far, has been ridiculously simple and easy: sitting at a bench winding fiberglass around transformer coils, laminating the cores, jig-boring modified specs, wedging one coil inside another, testing. The shop has the interesting, faintly exciting smell of steel and oil, an electrical hum and whine, soft fluorescent lights, hundreds and hundreds of television receivers stacked in the aisles.

The five others in the shop are what you'd expect: ignorant, foul-mouthed, pleasant, genial, dirty-nailed, unambitious, lazy, completely uninterested in their work, concerned mainly with home, family, sex, bowling, cars, payday.

Have I mentioned the music? Cheap pleasant meaningless music interlards the atmosphere at Dumont, stirring up production, soothing the nerves, making for contented workers. Then there was the woman who just loved to tape coils — wouldn't share the work with anyone; finally retired at age seventy-two. The greedy grubbing for overtime; working overtime in a TV factory so they can buy more television sets.

∞

Book: *Confessions — Confessions — Confessions! Confessions of —*
Confessions of a Tall Dog

Confessions of a (Middle-Aged) Barbarian (Young,
    Amorous, Melancholic, Insouciant, Aging, Inferior,
    Green, Blue, Red . . .)
Confessions of a Young Man with Three Red Eyes
Confessions of . . .

I repeat, I must tell what I think to be the truth in this Journal, no matter
what the cost. No matter whom it hurts or how much. For if I don't tell
the honest truth, this book will not be worth a damn to me in the future.

Why should the truth be painful? Because I lead a double life. Because
there is a part of me that wants to be good, to be kind and generous and
gentle with others, to be tolerant and forbearing, not to hurt, not to alarm.
Because there is that other part or faculty or demon, my cynic self sitting
on my left shoulder, seeing into myself and others, or merely observing
unpleasant externalities, and reporting harshly and directly what is under
observation.

Why cannot the two be combined? Insight and candor should not,
ultimately, be the enemies of love. Right. But the key word is "ultimately."
Time, depth, intensity. At some point in the heart of the object the two —
analysis and sympathy — converge and meet, fuse in understanding, which
we will *assume* is not complete without love.

But time is mixed up in this. And movement. So that few of the objects
under my inspection will receive all the study they may deserve. Consequently, the union of impression and love will not be made: The former
goes on, inevitably, involuntarily, while the latter hovers above and behind, an abstract ethical formula devoid of content and direction. Too
bad.

Is the Grand Canyon truly the "*locus Dei*"? Perhaps so. The gorge and the
God-term have much in common — both are vast, awesome, incomprehensible . . . and entirely devoid of content.

Can feelings be exchanged, shared, truly joined? I doubt it. They can be
communicated by an infinite variety of signs and symbols — words, tones,
tunes, color, form, bodily movement, facial twitches, manipulations of lip
and eyelid, touch, dead objects variously arranged, cries and outcries —
but there can be no genuine *communion* of feeling. How can there be?
What's the line, the link, the conduit of emotion between persons? I have
yet to hear of it. That's why two people are two people and not one people.
Arithmetical necessity.

November 1953 – New Joisey

The silent struggle. Temptation. The underground warfare. The skated-over tension. Me and Rita. Simply a matter of geography, really. She wants to go east, I want to go west. Simple. So we're stuck, a perilous equilibrium, here in this land of smog and bog, New Joisey, enduring what is (for me at least) a prolonged, dreary and meaningless bad dream. Not a nightmare, really, but just a bad dream. A dreaming hibernation. Injuring eternity.

It's mostly my own damn-fool fault, of course; if I hadn't got the half-hearted notion of going to Yale, we wouldn't be in this sick mess. Not exactly. But if we were still in New Mexico, my little Rita would be in a state of constant agitation, as she has admitted, longing for home, Hofmann [Rita's art teacher] and Europe. Little peace we'd have either way.

I feel like an alien in my own home. I don't belong. I'm an outsider. A barbarian! A fuckin' barb!

December 1953 – Rochelle Park, New Jersey

Rebellion. The furtive urge. How shall I, how can I say it? Without a little shame? (Required, you know. The rules.) Our first anniversary. One year married to Rabbit Rita Deanin. She seems to become more lovely, more womanly, more . . . with each passing week. In direct inverse ratio is the waning of my own primitive passion. The guilt of being a man!

∞

Confessions of a Barbarian:

Proofreading the galley prints of *Jonathan Troy* was a discouraging task. The book seems even worse than I had thought. Very juvenile, naive, clumsy, pretentious. I tried to do everything at once, and succeeded in almost nothing. Too much empty rhetoric, not enough meat and bone. Not convincing. All the obvious faults of the beginner.

I must be patient. Between the conception and the creation falls the shadow. Falls the shadow.

December 1953 – Rochelle Park

Last night I went to this Greenwich Village party and there was Norman Mailer, surrounded by a circle of listeners and interlocutors. I was too timid to butt in, though I wanted to very much. Fortunately, my pretty and resourceful Rita was there to help me out; she tapped the celebrated young man on the shoulder, calling out his name like a respectful acquaintance, and without wasting breath on apology or self-introduction informed him that there was someone here who wanted to meet him, then cheerfully introduced him to me and a couple of others.

A pleasant young man, Mailer. He shook hands firmly, grinned, looked at me for a moment with apparently friendly, interested eyes. (Not remarkable eyes, if I may contradict myself.) My nervousness vanished almost at once and in a moment we — three or four of us — were talking about books (his), Shakespeare, the theatre, the last war. He told us about some of his wartime experiences, how they were connected with his famous book [*The Naked and the Dead*].

I can't recall that he said anything particularly brilliant or memorable, perhaps because he did more listening than talking. I thought him unnecessarily patient, tolerant; he had to listen to some dreadful crap: A simple young man talking about *his* easy life in the army, how he couldn't understand how anyone could dislike it (he was drafted after the war was over); another guy, an insolent jerk, blowing smoke in [Mailer's] face, in his wine cup, describing in prolonged detail his experiences as a taxi driver (Mailer appeared to be sincerely interested). And so on.

Mailer has short curly sandy hair, a kind of pale fuzzy unhealthy-looking face, soft brown eyes, big flapping ears, round shoulders, small hands. He is not tall, stands always in a slumped position, head between hunched-up shoulders, hands in pockets, chin on chest, cigarette dangling, the attitude and posture of a listening, centripetal man. He wore a dark brown suit, not too clean, rumpled, a shirt not too clean, shoes as badly in need of a shine as my own.

[Mailer] had a very sexy black-haired sensualist hanging around him, a Tom Wolfean Jewess, warm, half-naked, luxurious. Protective.

I didn't really get to know him, to exchange much with him. I had a bad headache all evening; too many pretty girls around. Didn't want to impose.

What a consolation is death. I am not afraid, I believe, only I want it clean and alone and dramatic. And not premature, or if it must come early, to give me warning, that I may glean my teeming brain of the thoughts that oppress and delight me. In time, a pleasure is death, not the event actually but my present contemplation of it. Something to look forward to. The day of. A treasure of mine, and something that no one, *no one,* can take from me. The grand privilege of death. Mine, perhaps, when I want it, if I so choose. When everything else fails me, or I fail myself, I have always within my power the ultimate and inevitable resolution. Death, death, death, death.

The death you want, when you want it.

∞

The indifference of nature! Better yet, the hostility of it, the positive resistance! I like it that way. The enmity of the mountain. I like it tough.

∞

Is genius hereditary? Apparently not — where are Beethoven's heirs? But perhaps some families describe a cycle of growth, a development of power that culminates in a child of genius. A great build-up, then a relapse into customary mediocrity. I believe the Abbeys may be ascending toward such an end; not in me, I'm no genius, alas, nor am I, in important respects, as good a man as my father. But still, there's a discernible growth, a progress toward something powerful. Perhaps my son . . . or a grandson?

∞

Confessions of a Barbarian:

I'm so complicated a person I don't know *what* role to effect, and I'm not clever enough to pass myself off as what I truly am, a complicated person.

The Great Mathematician at Greenwich; my awe; I noticed he spent most of his time staring at my wife's breasts.

Art as a refuge, a retreat. Perhaps the best form of outlawry . . . next to mountain banditry.

The poor are materialistic. It takes money to be romantic.

Comes the revelation! Things will be different.

Is there a Gawd? Well, is there an Angry Unicorn on the Dark Side of the Moon?

Do you believe in ghosts? Those that haunt the human soul — yes.

Music clouds the mind but clarifies the heart.

My country, right or wrong? I'd rather be right than patriotic.

So much to do, so little time. The insurmountable disparity of the two. The gulf. Books to write, places to discover, truths to be learned or invented. Love to be learned or discovered.

January First, 1954 – Rochelle Park

Tradition? My father taught me something different — love of independence, justice, the future. Hatred of the past. The past, we thought, is pure evil.

Tradition! Let them have their cathedrals, coronation carriages, picturesque starving peasants. We've got our own sacred images — the iron stake, the secret press, the strangled bloodhound, the dusty wine bottle under candle, the cup of hemlock. They've got Authority but we've got

Disobedience; they have taste but we have fun; they have ritual, we have sex.

∞

Good writing is based solidly on knowledge. Sympathy, instinct, intuition, conscientious craftsmanship, ardor, dedication — all are very well, are well-nigh indispensable; but without knowledge, they are not enough and can lead to disastrous error. Take the case of Henry James.

Henry James — rebuked by Flaubert! I should have been there!

∞

Amazingly, I sometimes feel that the negative outweighs the positive, that I'm more concerned with what I have *not* done than with what I have done. Women, for example. I may be mistaken, but I sometimes feel that my displeasure and regret attendant upon the recollection of the girls I might have had but did not have, is stronger than the opposite linked to the contrary. Baffling and amazing. Is that another characteristic of the nature of a man? Or one peculiar to me, honest Abbey?

∞

Hearing a Brahms piano concerto, I don't know which one but a familiar one, brings an inevitable chain of associations, in this case the little community of South High in Albukerk [Albuquerque], where Volpe and I and Kieffer and Bove and Stevenson [college friends] once lived, dreamed, swore, fought, drank, suffered and rejoiced.

I can almost smell the smell of that small cramped dirty chaotic little wooden shoebox we lived in, can almost see purple-skinned Volpe on his upper bunk, dying horribly, and Kieffer storming and cursing over steak in the kitchen, and Stevenson pawing his girl in the dark miniature parlor in front and playing one stack of records after another on his machine. A shotgun blast in the night. Tequila in square bottles among the books. B. M. Adams swaggering in, staggering out, grinning laughing roaring fighting. Odendahl in an occasional diffident and tentative visit — nobody liked him but me.

The women, the music, the food. The old Ford sedan. The Mexican cemetery beyond the ash-heap, scarcely distinguishable from a garbage dump. Me sitting outside in the sun, burning and sweating, pounding away on my little Trent typewriter, page after page of fantasy and love and anger. Steve gets married and a small tragedy immediately after. I leave, go to Tijeras [Canyon], have a short career as a college playboy. Then back to the shack.

What all happened to me, anyway, in those college years? Can I ever forget? Is it worth remembering? (Blasphemous question.) Let's begin — but where shall we begin?

1941: Highschool — Indiana, Pennsylvania; four years of intellectual adventure and social misery. A hitch-hiking tour of the U.S.

1945: U.S. Army, Italy — two years of misery, frustration, exploration, growth, physical adventure.

1947: Home — a year of baseball, pallid love, ambitious writing, desultory study, painting high-tension towers, Phil Uhler, Stabley [childhood friends], knocked down by my genial brother Hoots [Howard] in a brief dispute over choice of radio program.

1948: New Mexico University — life begins at last. Life in the barracks at Kirtland Field. I meet Odendahl; the first delightful explorations of the Land of Enchantment in my old Chevvy [sic]: the Sandias, Bandelier, Chaco and Aztec, El Paso and Chihuahua, the White Mountains. Sex with Jo A. The Wallace agitation [Henry A., vice president under F.D.R., 1941–45, then replaced by Harry Truman, only to run for president in 1948 on the Progressive ticket]. Philosophy and anthropology. Poor old Elisa Ball Bull of Monck's Corners, South Carolina. Student politics. The great blizzard. I go to Taos, have a wonderful and beautiful summer, fall in love three times, learn to dance *La Raspa* ["The Scrape"], meet Volpe and Lash and Jacobs and Scobie and Charlotte, climb Mt. Wheeler (no visions), write lovely poetry, innumerable stories, make a resolve. Return to Pennsylvania, a sickening bus ride from Denver, campaign for Wallace, a week in sad and lovely Venice, Florida, then to GE at Erie and six pointless months of hell.

1949: Return to New Mexico — life resumed. Summer session [college], drive with Volpe, listen to Christopher Salmon in the mornings, swim in the afternoons, chase girls at night — Caroly, Liz. Practice flute, five strange haunting weeks alone in fantastic Havasu Canyon — flirtation with death; waterfalls and rattlesnakes. Back to school, the playboy days with Adams — charging into town every morning at seventy mph in a black Lincoln Continental. Horses, women, night rides. Adams gets married, I move in with Volpe & Company; life with Odendahl — we share a car. The long affair with Jean begins, deadly serious and trouble from the beginning; almost lose my "B" average.

1950: New Mexico University — the Jean affair continues. Phil Summers and his motorcycle, rock climbing in the Sandias, my first brush with logic, I fail to get an "A" to match Alan. Odendahl sells out to Jean and I'm in real trouble (talk of marriage begins).

I write poems for the *Thunderbird* [U.N.M. student literary magazine], brilliant papers on Shakespeare for [Professor] Simons, establish a kind of reputation. I move from one place to another, spend part of the summer in Scobie's fabulous hacienda in Carnuel. A terrific hot dusty summer in Albukerk. I take three deadly English courses. Marriage with Jean is scheduled — I am not altogether unhappy.

We visit Volpe-As-Hermit in his log cabin retreat high in Sangre de Cristo Mountains near Red River — a beautiful and unforgettable place, the retreat: he has a horse, pasture, barn, aspens and pines, a clear snow-fed brook in his backyard. Jean and I go beyond Bluff [Utah] to approach Monument Valley, low on water and gas, turn back without seeing it. We get married in August; champagne ceremony. Live in the mountains in Tijeras; fights begin almost at once.

1951: I edit the *Thunderbird,* meet Riddle, sing in a chorus, meet Rita Deanin — more trouble (I fall in love immediately, hopelessly, more desperately than ever before). Trouble with Popejoy and Smith [more college friends] while pursuing Rita, fighting off my wife, beginning a novel and living in a sleeping bag on top of a hill in Tijeras Canyon; separated from Jean. Have fun at school.

Rita and I have a preliminary semi-experimental and poetically lovely honeymoon going to Carlsbad [Caverns] and back (the forest fire, White Sands and the unreal mountains, the girl, the motels, the cavern, a sad and reluctant return to Albukerk). Rita goes East; I am stuck with wife.

Flight to oil fields, life as a roughneck. I go home, have a hopeless meeting with Rita. Jean and I go to Edinburgh; the delights of Scotland; Jean gives up, leaves me, divorces me, and I am free again at last. Free to love and wander.

∞

The Seven Joys of Poverty: (1) discomfort, (2) irritation, (3) hunger, (4) crime, (5) prison, (6) flight, (7) death.

∞

Not to avoid Death, but to put him in his proper place: at the end, not the beginning, of my life.

∞

Romanticism: the search for the intimate in the remote?

January 1954 – Rochelle Park

Out of work. Unemployed through no fault of my own, for once. A strange feeling, not too far from desperation and panic. Of course, I understand it's not important, only a temporary "readjustment" of the economy. Still, one wonders and fears. Suppose it were really impossible to get a job?

Suppose I had not only myself but several kids to feed and clothe and shelter? No easy task.

July 11, 1954 – Provincetown, Massachusetts

ON THE BEACH: These women with their narrow shoulders and huge bulky rumps — constructed like ants — the little round knobby head and tremendous powerful squat foundation of belly, hips, pelvis, ass. All those big saddles — like so many plow horses.

The fat hairy men with pink nipples.

But almost as bad as the slop-sow type women are these new monsters from Fifth Avenue: the terra-cotta dolls out of department store show windows — no meat — hipless, stomachless (how can they eat? they don't — they're not animals, they're toys) and flat-chested as ironing boards — inhuman brutes — with their tight dead brittle little painted faces — makes me shudder to see them: the machines! What's happening to the human race?

By the sea, sprawled on the shore under a moderate sun and a whiffle of breeze. You know, we're having our troubles with *The Brave Cowboy*. Primarily a matter of credibility. What the Brave Cowboy is up to hardly makes sense. How can he hope to persuade Bondi to give up his martyrdom in prison for the ridiculous life of the outlaw? Yet that is exactly what he proposes. And if he fails to convert Bondi, as he surely must, how are we to believe that the BC takes this business so seriously he'll come back to town and manage — somehow — to *kidnap* Bondi? Impossible. Not credible. Is there any compromise?

Confessions of a Barbarian:

Why does every American with any sensibility and wit despise Texas? Is it merely a joke, a national gag? Not at all — there are good and sufficient reasons for this serious and widespread attitude. Why pick on Texas? Because it typifies, concentrates and exaggerates most everything that is rotten in America: it's vulgar — not only cultureless but anti-cultural; it's rich in a brazen, vulgar, graceless way; it combines the bigotry and sheer animal ignorance of the Old South with the aggressive, ruthless, bustling, dollar-crazy brutality of the Yankee East and then attempts to hide this ugliness under a facade of mock-western play clothes stolen from a way of life that was crushed by Texanism over half a century ago. The trouble with Texas: it's ugly, noisy, mean-spirited, mediocre and false. (Confusion of quantity and quality.)

July 27, 1954 – Provincetown

Any connection between the novel and democracy? Why has literature been relatively successful in relatively democratic America, music and painting comparative failures? Almost everyone thinks he could write a novel if he really wanted to, and almost everyone is right. The other arts require far more time, training, materials — in other words, money. Anyone can buy a book; few can buy paintings, few can afford concert-going, etc. Any casual connection in these obvious correlations? No doubt the novel, child of the printing press, is the typical and essential art of democracy.

December 27, 1954 – Albuquerque

A Brief History of My Adventures Since Leaving New Jersey:

We came by way of the Big Smokys, New Orleans and Big Bend. Magical places, visions, sensations. Rediscovery of something thought forever lost. But a something unbelievable, inexpressible, of the nature of a Platonic reminiscence. Those wild lonely hills, smoky valleys, abandoned cabins of West Virginia, Kentucky, Tennessee. The swampy forests of Mississippi, Louisiana.

New Orleans — exciting, strange, esoteric, hot and windy and a glaring light, the smell of the sea and the heavy soul-troubling perfume of magnolia, lilac and unknown growths. A stirring, sense-quickening and in parts lovely city. Someday we'll return there, live in the Latin Quarter or on a houseboat on one of the muddy somnolent rivers in the bayous beyond. A winter in New Orleans.

After Louisiana, the vast dreary desolation of east and central Texas — then the magnificence, the terror, grandeur and deathlessness of Big Bend: there too I must live someday, for a winter, spring, fall. The summers must be incredible there, like or worse than Death Valley, the Sahara. The Badlands. Mountains like romantic dreams, canyons all yellow and red and gray and blue, utterly lifeless: poisonous alkali streams.

On arriving in New Mexico, our first act, practically, was to burn down a splendid old adobe mansion. As caretakers we lived there rent-free. The place belonged to an old lady named Minnebo or Menopause or something. We were there about two weeks when, one Sunday morning, I built a wood fire (scrub oak, yellow pine) in the livingroom stove. That evening the place was a heap of smoking ash. Alas! No one knows. A superb, an excellent conflagration, a blazing spectacle. Sightseers came from far and wide, and the press too.

We moved into Malcolm Brown's studio and life became more charming, cooperative, fundamental. For a goodly while we lived on pinto beans, home-baked bread, potatoes.

I went to jail for three days: reckless driving. A grim, tedious and illuminating experience. Judge Alexander Cheroot, that dapper dainty little man with the eyes and lips of an adder. A puff adder. Mean-spirited and not very bright. He put me there. Field research, I called it then.

Rita and I have periodic fights, then delicious emotional reconciliations, weeks of comparative peace, delight, happiness. Of course, melancholy is the prevailing mood, the mode of our acts and manners.

Jim Gilbert and Homer the hound and me — we hiked clear across the mesa one day from the edge of the city to the heart of the mountains. Four hours under a fiery sun. Trying to recapture my sense of distance, attain a physical, kinesthetic idea of the space separating me from the specter on the eastern horizon. About ten miles I guess, maybe twelve. An effort and imagination impossible to measure.

My book has been published, faintly reviewed, virtually ignored, generally unbought. Those who have read it maintain that they like it. Jacobs and Wicker and Stabley insist that it's a good book. But the press has ignored it — just two summary reviews so far as I know — disappointing, of course. How can I deny it? More or less expected but still disappointing. And we need some money.

Some progress on *The Brave Cowboy;* 125 pages written so far. Pretty good — tight taut compact stuff, I believe. But not so much fun in the writing of it as in *J. Troy.* Why not?

Personalities:

Malcolm Brown is my friend. I am proud to be his friend. I no longer regard him as a saint or minor god, however; he's human, like me, I've discovered, with several and considerable faults. But I love him the more for it. And I'd say that our mild experiment in cooperative living has been a mild success — we've helped and consoled each other very much. Especially successful considering the austere, irritating bout with poverty that both families had for a spell of five or six weeks back there. All four of us unemployed, without money. Not starving, of course, but doing a damn lot of worrying. The ugly rasping pressure of poverty. I can find no charm in it. Not in poverty coupled with fear, insecurity: and how to separate the two?

Ralph Newcomb seems more charming, delightful, interesting, complicated, deep and important than ever. A man of talent and parts, with an honest, engaging soul; rewarding. I haven't got near the bottom of him yet; I don't know how deep he is, but I know that he's deep. Profound? Riddle, like a grinning ghost, flits in and out of my ken. I still like him very much, though it's sometimes difficult to respect him. Some pathos in his life. And some raw comedy.

F. E. Black I have not seen for over a year. We do not seek each other out. He is my enemy. I am still faintly subject to the awful fascination of his eyes, grin, monologues. A brilliant talker; that's the best I'll say of him. A treacherous friend: that's the worst.

Wicker I love. A charming and gracious and generous old gentleman and scholar. He helped rescue me from the Duke City [Albuquerque] bastille. I'll never forget him. I owe him twenty-five dollars.

Bud Adams, that enigmatic sonofabitch. With him I have formally and solemnly pledged eternal comradeship. Steeped in alcohol, we have proclaimed our love. Yet I do not truly love him. I would do most anything for him, yet I do not truly love him. He needs me more than I need him; if I could help him I would.

Jim Gilbert I'm beginning to respect as well as like. I've always thought of him as a big, lumbering, likable kid. But he has been growing or I've been receding: I now see much in him worthy of attention and respect. A promising artist and man. (Curse the army!)

Confessions . . .

All these bonny wenches around here — the bleating voices, the twitching tails: makes me nervous, irritable, difficult.

Bird-watching: Birds can't count — if two men come, one goes away, birds assume no man to be present.

On Plato's *Republic* — The trouble with perfection: it leaves no room for improvement.

Beauty in death: A civilization, nearing its end, may burst into all the transient and melancholy glory of a cottonwood in autumn.

Roggoway [a college friend]: When the party gets dull, R. gets up, unbuttons his fly and lays his penis on the table. "Mine," he says, "all mine."

The soul that feeds on itself must die of starvation.

Yes, I believe in Total Immersion. I believe that all Baptists should be totally immersed. Or, as we say in Lubbock, the only good Baptist is a totally immersed Baptist.

FEUDALISM

The Duke & his family,
Proud ancestral name of a thousand years,
And all around the earth they owned,
Worked by the squat brown peasantry
Who sprang, spontaneously generated,
Without pasts, from the soil itself.

[This poem no doubt refers to the Duke of Alburquerque, Viceroy of New Spain, who in 1706 named the new pueblo after himself. The initial "r" was dropped from the spelling a century later.]

March 1, 1955 – Albuquerque

Back in graduate school, University of New Mexico, working — slaving — for an M.A. — *Masturbatius Artisticus* — and then on to other parts for a Ph.D. — *Philosophicus Diabolus;* shall call my thesis "An Inquiry Into the General Theory of Anarchism." Already approved by Bahm, Anton the Grik (one of those who came to this country to fry our hot dogs for us, and ended up steaming our brains), and somewhat grudgingly by Don Miguel Jorrin [professors at UNM and members of Abbey's master's thesis advisory committee].

(I'll never pass the French test. Gawddamnitt!)

Gawd but I hate school. Most of the time. Occasionally it's entertaining, even exciting. But mostly tedious and painful and full of gray smog and hateful to life. Surely life — a more abundant life — is possible! Must be. A life of violence and action and passion, sensation probed to its heights and depths, the soul stretched like violin strings over the arch of mountains and women and conflict! Of that, now, of that I dream. That is how genuine life appears, looking out wistfully through the bars of my cubicle window.

∞

Rita and Me: Two-and-a-half years of marriage. Incredible. I'm still in love with her, attached to her by invisible threads of sentiment impossible to break. I often become impatient, swear that I'll walk out and leave her, never come back, run away to liberty and masculine adventure! But I never do. Much as I sometimes want to, I cannot. I'm a slave of many things. Rita is the most powerful. It's a sweet and blessed slavery, though — I cannot bring myself to leave it.

Until recently, we were living in Malcolm's little mud studio. But now we're in town, enjoying the obvious yet involved advantages of gas heating and hot-and-cold running water and eleektrissitie and such. I despise myself for enjoying it and if *I* had to *work* for it (Rita does that), I would hate it. I still insist on plain living and high thinking. I enjoy chopping wood; I love wood fires; I don't mind carrying water; I find ecstasy in *building* a fire. Like Lawrence, I am taken by the primeval charm and fascination of the simple mysteries: fire, fucking, building in mud, rain, sunlight, the smell of greasewood and live oak after a cloudburst, the luxury of a sleeping hound. I require openness, space, economy, natural resistance, red meat, women, fire, water — the essentials of liberty.

A day like spring today. Nostalgia. Sun and violet sky, and a southern wind that whispers — "mountain, desert, yucca and lava rock, space, wildness, and the Gila monster, the vinegaroon, Big Bend and Mexico and freedom." O! brother, that southern wind!

The more I dim my eyes over print and frazzle my brain over abstract ideas, the more I want and appreciate the delight of being basically an animal wrapped in a sensitive skin: sex, the resistance of rock, the taste and touch of snow, the feel of the sun, good wine and rare beefsteak and the company of friends around a fire with guitar and lousy old cowboy songs. Despair: I'll never become a scholar, never be a decent good Christian. Just a hedonist, a pagan, a primitive romantic.

But what's an honest soul to do? I don't know. I can say this: Be loyal to what you love, be true to the earth, fight your enemies with passion and laughter.

Saturday morning, March 1955 - New Mexico

A yellow day, cold and bitter with sand-dust and wind. The dog is by the door, whining, whimpering, complaining. Wants in. The hell with him — let him freeze.

Rita is sending me to the laundry with two pillowcases full of filthy socks and underwear. Why this continual excrudescence of grease and grime from the human body? It's enough to make one a Platonist. Well — one sackful for one machine, another for another. Hot water with bleach. That's the ticket. Pick up laundered blouse. Send off my pink dress shirt. Right. Absolutely.

April 20, 1955 - Albuquerque

Sunrise! A canticle of blue and gold, a cantata of color and clean air and the cries of meadowlarks, mockingbirds, bobolinks, finches, blue jays. . . . Jesus but this can be a pretty world! Can be — could be.

Drugged. I'm drugged, sense and mind, by desert thoughts, canyon thoughts. I've been thinking of the Colorado Plateau, the country around the Green and Colorado and San Juan rivers. Planning a boat trip — from Shiprock to Mexican Hat, perhaps, or from Hite's Ferry to Rainbow Natural Bridge. (An expendable raft — that would be just the thing for a journey through Glen Canyon.) Thinking of those great canyons, and of the terrible and grand and unearthly wilderness of rock that surrounds them, my nerves and brain get taut and sharp and hot — Christ! I've got to go there, be there, live there: it's become an obsession with me, a passion! Those places, those names. . . .

∞

The literary crickets. Crackets. Clickets.

Bach on records: 33-1/3 revelations per minute.

Tolstoy's prophesy has been fulfilled: The advance of scientific technology has aided more the tyrant than the free man. Example: Every man can own and operate a rifle, but tanks and planes and atom bombs are and must be the property of the State.

∞

The baby: our little bungle from Heaven.

Babies . . . you can always eat them, can't you?

Seuder, the great philosopher: "False sophistication, fake sophistication. All you young ones have it. Don't you know [to Roberts, who had complained about his baby] that if you had the power of ten Shakespeares you could never produce such a work of art as a human child?"

Well . . . maybe the old man is right. Or is he merely being sentimental? Falsely simple? When 68,000 babies are born each and every day, what is left? See what I mean? Like in economics. Man in the mass tends to devalue himself. Men are too common. Life is sweeter when rarer. No?

Confessions . . .

What is the artist? He is a miracle worker: makes the blind to see, the insentient to feel, the dead to live.

"The Housewarming Party" — the story of our Peralta affair. [Peralta is the tiny Mexican village just south of Albuquerque, where the conflagration described under the December 27, 1954, entry took place. Abbey would eventually semi-fictionalize this story as one of the more torrid episodes in his 1988 novel, *The Fool's Progress*.]

Ideas, words, like a cloud of gnats befog the senses, smother the emotions. Ideas whining like mosquitoes around his brain.

Automatic Prayer Service: dial 7-1161 (recorded); next, Gawd in a vending machine, absolution for one thin dime.

One's sense of honor should be immediate, spontaneous — almost reflexive.

Poem, essay or story: "The Art of Dying."

What is Anarchism? Nothing as remote and melodramatic as most people imagine, thinking of Bakunin and the Russian nihilists; [rather, it] means simply the widest possible decentralization and dispersal of power, political and economic. Both, necessarily.

Surely the most ignoble of attitudes is that which sometimes makes us capable of suggesting to *others* that they sacrifice themselves — for *our* ideals.

Christmas in Hoboken: Piss on earth, God's swill to men!

Gawd: If He did exist, 'twould be necessary to circumvent Him.

Mystery, yes! But make it a tough mystery — the sea of space, the miracle of life — not some trivial man-concocted parlor-game like the Trinity or transubstantiation.

Sweet Jesus! Swap? Not one hour on this sweet Earth for an eternity in your stiff gilded Heaven.

Instead of polygamy, we have serial monogamy.

April 12, 1956 – Albuquerque

Today I became a father. Eight pounds twelve ounces and his name, it is called —

JOSHUA NATHANAEL ABBEY

May he be blessed by sky and earth, Heaven and Home; may he be brave and lucky and good.

May 11, 1956 – Arches National Monument, Utah

Desert Journal:

Wind blowing sand in my teeth, as usual. But the desert is very much alive — exultant, you might say. Great big yellow mule's ears blooming by the road; the cliffrose, gay and fragrant as a pretty girl, blossoming everywhere. Even the little hedgehog cactus has produced a flower, a fair and exquisite thing, lovelier than any orchid — purple petals, yellow stamen and pistil: herds of ants and fleas crawling through it, dusty with pollen; and the yucca too, small as it is, sends up a stalk heavy with big pendulous buds, big as plums, soon to open. That most miserable and scrubby of plants around here, the blackbush, even it is producing little yellow flowers. (Yellow seems to be the favorite color around here.)

What else?

First to appear, some three weeks ago, was a straggly weed with tiny pale blue or lavender flowers, four-petaled. Soon after that, the desert primrose — there's a pretty thing. Then, almost all at once, the yellow borage. Pepperweed [peppergrass] and desert buckwheat. A little later appeared the scarlet trumpet (or is that Indian paintbrush?), the rash of turquoise berries on *some* of the junipers (are there male and female junipers?), miniature yellow flowers on the green ephedra (Mormon tea), the strange pink-and-lavender blossoms of the tamarisk along the washes, some kind of purple lupine, and at least a dozen other little blossoming herbs I cannot identify.

Also attractive, though not yet in flower, are the single-leaf ash and sand sage. The former puts a dash of fresh green — a startling living green — in the desert drab; the latter, blue and silver, is as beautiful in its own way as the other. And of course, more traditional — the purple sage.

Any others? Well, the little sand verbena, the noxious snakeweed, some kind of desert daisy. And of course, my good old cottonwoods along the wash: more honest clean green in this hot land.

Birds? I'm not much of a bird-watcher: ravens, magpies, hawks, blue jays, sandpipers, Mexican finches, cliff swallows and the "bow-down" bird — sounds something like a whippoorwill — only it says "bow-down, bow-down," instead of "whip-poor-will, whip-poor-will." I've never seen it.

And lizards, black widows, doodlebugs, gnats, flies, scorpions and millipedes. And cottontails, jackrabbits, deer, with signs of bobcat. Christ, will I never see a living coyote? They've killed them off so heavy, what with cyanide guns, poison tallow balls, traps, shooting, etc. . . . it's a wonder there are any left atall. Are there?

And the wind, and the sand, and the rock: sandstone — Wingate, Entrada, Carmel, Navajo.

Moab: The big shiny uranium-reduction plant; hills of gray ore; fat asphalt paved roads; slick new motels, cafes, office buildings, gas stations. A woman shortage.

Saw an eight-point buck last evening, silhouetted against the western sky; I whistled at him and he stopped, waited for several long minutes searching out the sound, unable to see me. Some of his does, whom he had been herding along ahead of him, came back to see what was the matter. I whistled again: they stared about, could not see me; finally all trotted off over the brow of the hill, dropping in perfect silence into fields beyond my vision.

(To be God!)

Wednesday evening, May 16, 1956 – Arches

Christ, I'm lonely! At least at times I am; oh the long lonesome hours — dreaming of Rita, whom I love and who has gone away. Why?

Hoboken, New Jersey! She'd be closer on the moon.

Why has she gone away? Partly because of the baby — in order the better to care for him, close to doctors, hospitals, her mother. But mainly —

Got up at 4:30 this morning, if that means anything to you. Yes, I beat the sun, which, scheduled to appear around 4:50 — by my reckoning and the almanac — actually came to view almost ten minutes late. Dock him.

There's a point in rising early out here on the semi-desert: early morning is the coolest, sweetest time; even the gnats aren't biting. Gnats? Yes, we've got gnats here; since the country's so dry, they live on the blood of other animals, like me. Saw deer bounding away in my backyard when I went out to take my dawn piss. Had pancakes and bacon, pineapple juice and coffee for breakfast. I'm becoming an excellent cook, I believe. (Wan consolation for the deprivation of women!)

Women: there, I've mentioned that fatal subject again. Fatal? Annoying, then, or haunting, or itching. What can I do about it? Now? Nothing, I guess, except try to bury myself in work, forget them, the dear soft sweet gentle panting things.

The raven's wings paddling through the air — *huff, huff, huff, huff* — they sound. He haunts me, my raven — big, dirty, raucous, ugly . . . the raven, not me; living off my garbage, maybe waiting for me to die.

Saw a young rattlesnake yesterday, in my backyard; half-emerged from a slit under a rock, soaking up some sun. Eyes filmed over — he couldn't see me but his nervous sensitive tongue was out, licking at the air: perhaps he could taste my smell. When I approached him, he oozed back into his hole, like — like . . . similes fail me; nothing on earth can match the undulant slithering glide of a snake. I've gone back several times to visit him again, but he never appears. Has he left? Frightened away? Or in hiding? Ambush?

A big wind the other day broke off most of the budding yucca stalks: a minor desert tragedy.

∞

Style: Not for me the exaggerated tortured smoldering rhetoric of Faulkner, nor the spare artful diction of Hemingway, nor even the heavy blunderbound groping of Dreiser — though that has its own magnificence and poetry. (Dreiser is one of the great Americans; others: Melville, Mark

Twain, Jack London, maybe Faulkner. When I read Trilling on Dreiser I doubt, but when I read Dreiser on life in America I am convinced.)

What then? Precision, accuracy, a hard honesty — no bunk or hokum — an eye and ear for the ironic, a fidelity to common speech: let these be my guides and the truth will make its own poetry.

∞

Glen Canyon will soon be lost. The dam-building maniacs. The hogs and pigs win again. Glen Canyon, beautiful beyond any telling of it, to be drowned forever. O the filthy scheming greedy fanatical scum! *The Pigs.*

May 20, 1956 – Arches

This business with Rita: it's breaking me in two. Christ, I don't think I've ever suffered more than I suffer now. What does it profit a man — art? glory? adventure? — if he denies love, negates honor, mutilates his heart?

SUMMER LIGHTNING:

Lavender cumuli floating like armadas of men-o'-war over the arid canyons, bombarding them with lightning bolts; hisses and shouts of wind; the irritable whining of flies; clear open seas of blue and green to the west and north; the charged stillness, the heat, the sudden flurry of a whirlwind; the sand verbena and scarlet buglers nodding their brilliant heads; the flick of a tiger lizard over the baked unshadowed rock; the red Moenkopi sandstone that looks even hotter and redder than it feels; danger, pressure, tension, anticipation in the air. . . .

∞

Hell! Look at me, a young brown god, virile as a panther, lusty as a goat, bepricked like a veteran stud, and no women within twenty miles. What a shame, what a crying shame, what a parlous crying shame! (What a non-fukking shame, eh Tovarish?)

∞

Art? Don't talk to me of art! I don't give a shit for art! It's only monkey-business, and not the best kind at that. No, I don't give a hoot in hell for art! It's artists that matter. The people who sweat over the stuff. The poor crazy slobs who waste their lives away over an easel, a typewriter, a piano.

∞

Rhapsody on Farts: plaintive farts, resounding farts, explosive farts, reverberating farts, timid muffled farts, fluid farts, farts vigorous and robust, farts masculine, farts feminine, beastly farts, grim farts, lethal farts, poisonous farts, crushing farts, deadly farts, vicious and cruel farts.

There are the honest manly unabashed farts of plumbers and locomotive engineers, the candid farts of farmers, the masculine and solitary farts of cowboys and sheepherders and rangers, the bold united farts of factory workers. There are the talented aerobatic farts of schoolboys, the bemused abstracted farts of college students, the soft mellow farts of old professors of philosophy. There are the farts protracted and sullen of infantry soldiers, the farts peremptory of sergeants, *a la militaire* of captains, pompous and brassy of colonels; the stern, powerful and prolonged artillery of generals.

There are the plaintive wistful farts of clerks, the suffocated farts of secretaries and stenographers, the nervous farts of switchboard operators, the farts pallid and timid of office receptionists and airline hostesses. There are the casual, indifferent farts of ward bosses and precinct captains, the ingratiating well-meant farts of candidates, the loud cheerful farts of governors, the forensic and embattled farts of congressmen, the magnificent thundering farts of senators, the proud stately farts of ambassadors and cabinet officers, the grave and politic farts of presidents and prime ministers.

There is the deliberate insolent fart of the pimp, the bitter fart of the whore, the aggressive fart of the car dealer and realtor, the stealthy fart of the burglar and the smug, satisfied fart of the money-lender, the insidious fart of the pornographer, the cruel fart of the model, the vulgar and brazen fart of the huckster, the sly vile fart of the mortician and swindler, the startled fart of the pickpocket. There are the farts dull and sorrowful of policemen, harsh of desk sergeants and detectives, crude and brutal of screws, wary and apprehensive of police commissioners.

There is the diffident fart of the seminarian, the gritty fart of the Bible student, the fart loud and exhortatory of the fundamentalist preacher, the incriminating and revealing fart of the evangelist, the mellifluous fart of the TV theologian, the impromptu fart of the organist and the fart *sotto voce a la tempo* of the choirmaster. There is the discreet and sanctimonious fart of the priest, the consecrated fart of the nun, the inadvertent fart of the altar boy, the irritable fart of the bishop, the arch-fart of the archbishop, the painful and self-conscious fart of the cardinal, the solemn apostolic liturgical and infallible fart of the Pope himself. There will be finally the final divine omnipotent pretentious imperial fart of God. After that, nothing fartable will remain to be farted; for the mystery beyond God — the All-Source, the Brahman — does not fart.

June 15, 1956 – Arches

Old Rita's really puttin' the pressure on me these days, even has her head-shrinker writin' me letters: Promise, swear, to be a good dutiful obedient husband, or forever foreswear your wife — and son.

Here's the rub: Joshua, my son; my only son. What right have I? What right has anyone, to . . . ?

And then, anyway, with Rita too: I simply cannot make up my feeble mind. Do I want her or don't I? That solved, the rest would follow naturally.

God knows I'm lonesome here, I miss her — at times, at bad times — with an almost desperate pain, poignancy. And yet, there are other times — the good times? — when in action, in creation, in music and beer, I can rejoice in myself and my powers and my world and feel no need of Rita nor of any one particular woman. ("A man should stand alone." But should he? And can he?)

And then I remember our history and all the unhappiness I've caused her, and I begin to feel I owe her so much — that I must somehow do something to balance her grief and my guilt — with good. (But what? How?)

∞

On Gawd: This citified religion is no blame good; if they can't find him (Gawd) in the woods or swamps or mountains, or along the seashore or in the desert, they sure as hell won't find him in their stinking old theological libraries.

On wilderness preservation: *Don't* rely on the Park Service; all they can think of is more asphalt paving, more picnic tables, more garbage cans, more shithouses, more electric lights, more Kleenex dispensers. Those bastards are scared to death of congressmen, who in turn are representatives of and often identical with local chambers of commerce.

∞

[Sign at entrance to an imagined] Abbey's Ranch:

MEN ON FOOT OR HORSEBACK, WELCOME
MOTORISTS AND COMMON TOURISTS,
NOT WELCOME
FBI AGENTS, SHOT ON SIGHT
∞

I like to go swimmin
With bare-naked wimmin
And dive between their legs.

—Traditional

Tourists [thick as] flies on a dead hog.

"Thot you said it wouldn't rain," the tourist says to me. "Did I say that?" I answer. "Yes, you did," the tourist says. "Well doggone," I say — "that just goes to show, you can't trust the weather around here."

July 1956 – Arches

Me and the Tourists:

O, I'm a comedian. A tourist says to me, "That's a lousy road you got in here," and I say, "If I had my way, there wouldn't be any road atall in here," and they laugh and laugh. "You have TV here?" another tourist asks, and I say, "If I saw a TV set in here, I'd shoot it like I would a mad dog," and they laugh again. "Well," says a third, "what do you do for entertainment?" and I say, "I talk with the tourists," and they laugh and laugh and laugh.

There I am, deadly serious, and they stand there just a-laughing at me. "Don't you get lonesome out here?" says another tourist, and I say, "I like my own company, I get along with myself pretty good." And another tourist says, "You got an awful job," and I say, "I'd a lot rather be doing this than what you're doing," and they all start laughing again. Nobody takes me seriously.

Tourist says, "Does it ever rain out here?" and I say, "I don't know, I've only been here twenty-eight years." They go for that one, too. Laugh, Christ!

END OF JOURNAL VIII

Road map: *In a continuance of the frenetic road-tripping that had by now become an Abbey lifestyle, Journal IX documents the completion of Ed's first summer (1956) at Arches National Monument, near Moab, Utah, followed by his desperate flight east to reconcile with Rita and Josh. That accomplished, the Abbeys return to Utah for a second summer at Arches, at the close of which they move to coastal California, where Ed had won a Stegner fellowship in creative writing at Stanford University.*

JOURNAL IX

August 1956 to November 1957

∞

August 25, 1956 – Arches National Monument, Utah

News from nowhere. All these desert roads, laced with idiotic care and trouble over and around the red cruel deathly loveliness of the desert — to where? To nowhere. Down that nowhere road jeeps crawl, skittering puffballs of dust, dump trucks rumble in the van of moiling funnels of flying sand, tourists in fat gleaming automobiles creep along with absurd desperation.

Bound for what? A pocket of [uranium] ore in the gray Shinarump [sandstone], maybe, or the rumor of ore — or less, for a view, a picture, a transparency of the mute and timeless and implacable and sinister and incredible and heart-troubling mind-stunning canyons of the rich Colorado. Why? Jesus Christ, dad, do not ask why. . . . You're killing me; I bleed. Listen to that croaking black bird in the dead pinyon pine!

∞

Dreiser the Magnificent: Prose like a glacier of truth, massive, powerful and beautiful; shall not slide easily, oilily, oozily down the tender gullets of twiddling aesthetes, no; but rather, hammers on the door of the mind like Beethoven knocking, thunders, silences with glory, soaked in awe. Thus Theo Dreiser is America's third great novelist-poet: Melville, Mark Twain, Dreiser.

Faulkner now, almost all poetry and passion, had only a moderate regard for truth. That was his trouble.

All the clever little writers with the pretty names: Flannery, Robie, Carson, Truman, Tennessee, Twiddledee, Fiddletree, Picklebee . . . !

∝

Chesler Park in the Needles country [of Canyonlands National Park, Utah]: Green pastures without still waters; a dry Elysium; a Paradise for the bodiless, the invisible, for poetic spirits and romantic ghosts.

August 26, 1956 – Arches

A high excitement in the air and sky today: wind wind wind blowing all day long, no ceasing, no pausing, a continual singing whistling moaning wind. All day long, while the sun glares like — day's eye! fury incarcerated. Portentous wind, thrilling to blood and nerve and heart, portending . . . ? autumn? departure? victory? doom?

These magnificent oh splendid oh terrible oh charmingly futile summer storms of the desert!

Just a week ago, a rich thick glowing double-rainbow arching over the red-golden sunlit rocks of the Windows — one end in the canyon of the Colorado, the other ten miles north in Salt Valley; or was it Cache Valley? And then lightning jumping, dancing, glittering, sparkling be- hind — within! — the arc of the rainbow! Somewhere over Castle Valley and Fisher Towers. *Jesu Cristo!* While a mere dab of rain flickered at my face. . . . And west, searing the horizon, the sun going down in flame, dragging vast envelopes of gold-purple-blue-black-orange-gray-yellow cloudfire with it — immolation! — celestial suttee! And oh not a wretched common tourist, not a base villain of a shutterbug within miles of this grandiloquent display — all the craven varlets ran — run — for cover. . . .

This is the thing: The desert is a good place — clean, honest, danger- ous, uncluttered, strong, open, big, vibrant with legend.

It's the evenings that are kinda bad; mostly around supper time; I sit down to my steak and beans with only a can of beer for company. Ah then, then I miss her, miss my friends, miss all the crazy irresponsible delights of my old society. But most of all, then I miss her, the one true love-passion of my life on earth.

I mean — Rita.

∝

Two old men, sixty or worse: "Can't live forever, *compadre.* Down the nowhere road. End with a bang. I say, *cuate* ["pal"], let's head for the hills — go *bandido,* eh? Romantic and mad to the very end. Die in gunfire, eh?"

∞

Glen Canyon: latrines & register-books! O Christ! Born fifty years too late. But the most painful thought — even eight years ago I could have found the Colorado in its primitive state. In such a brief span of time has the virginal wilderness been insulted, despoiled and desecrated.

∞

On the Negro question: I don't like 'em. Don't like Negroes. As far as I can see, they're just as stupid & depraved as whites.

September 3, 1956 – Arches

Brave tourists go home. Oh brave and profligate tourists go home now. Go home now please. Thirty thousand tourists can't be stopped.

In the cabinet above my kitchen sink: gin, vodka, bourbon, scotch, rye.

I'm weary of grandeur. I long now for the grime, noise and confusion of the cities, for little touches of Nature — like a potted geranium on a windowsill, or a dead tumbleweed rattling over an asphalt parking lot. Such is the fickle whim of this human heart. Oh for the taste of hashbrown potatoes, oh for the smell of the men's room at Minsky's.

Sobering thought: Of all the world's two billion or more people, none would miss me very much if I were to die, except my parents and possibly Rita. No one else. Odd that I never thought of this before. But that's why a man — an ordinary man — needs a woman: only a woman is fool enough and great enough to love a man despite his obvious worthlessness.

To the question — AM I NECESSARY? — therefore, the answer is — NO.

Solitude is a great and difficult gift; loneliness is a sickness; and to be condemned to be alone is a terrible thing — madness follows.

∞

The tourists drift in and out of here like turds floating through a sewer. The simile could be extended easily, in several directions. And I? I am a watcher of turds.

Fragments of Kleenex flutter before the wind like an armada of butterflies.

A pretty girl from Oregon, alone in a new convertible, passing through — and I missed her. Christ! I'll be regretting this on my deathbed.

∞

For this world that we have made, none of us is bad enough. But for the world that made us, we are not good enough.

September 15, 1956 – Arches

[This entry opens with scattered quotes from a letter Ed has just received from Rita, saying, in effect, that their marriage is finished. In eloquent prose, Rita explains that she feels Ed is an unfit father, an untrustworthy husband, and frustrating to live with.]

Terrible words; they make living rather difficult. Therefore, I must go back to her at once, even though she writes that there is nothing for me to come home to except "a glimpse of what could have been." I must go back; three or four more days, then I leave this place. Probably forever. A lovely place, but tourists have come to depress me terribly. I can't bear to look a tourist in the face anymore.

December 6, 1956 – Hoboken

What am I doing here for gawdsake? An uncertain reconciliation with my family — Rita and Josh. A beautiful child; I love him now as I should have loved him from the beginning; a strong lively cheerful little boy — blue-eyed, fair-haired and well-shaped in every particular — all that a seven-month boy ideally should be.

And Rita I love now more than ever — not so much with the emotional desperation of a sick romantic isolation, as with a deep appreciation of her character, her essential beauty of mind and spirit as well as body, her courage and great strength.

Micaber. There's too much Micaber in me. I'm really a bum at heart — I'd be willing to spend my days in reverie and booze, floating along on a raft, eating catfish. Too much Huck Finn in me.

∞

The phantom world of TV; reality reduced to flickering shadows on an illuminated screen. Every home a platonic cave. Shackled by indolence, fatigue, habit, perhaps men work harder now than they ever did in the rural past — possibly die sooner, too. Undoubtedly, women have it easier, which is why their chief problem in life is how to keep from getting fat without doing something useful. The growth of the lottery, of pornography, of institutional authoritarianism — all the sure signs of another Roman decay. Our civilization has obviously entered its Tiberian phase — the barbarians mass in the East, merely waiting.

Lower Manhattan on a cold clear evening, approaching on a ferry: ten degrees above zero. Cold frozen tomblike grandeur: A fearsome and inhuman spectacle, more like Death Valley or Skull Canyon than any human habitation. Those powerful towering tombs crowded over dark and narrow and almost totally deserted streets — Wall St., etc. — a frozen nightmare. Sunset shining somberly on their windows — phosphorescent cadavers — horrible magnificent terrifying. And in that icy air and dread silence [Manhattan seems] more than ever like an island in Hell. Nowhere on earth has man created anything more ugly more terrible more useless and impotent — skyscrapers, impotent phalli, "granite cocks." Ten degrees above zero — almost sublime in its fearful inhumanness, almost beautiful?

The cold choppy waters of the Hudson, hard and scaly like lead frozen instantaneously from its molten state.

How can anyone *love* this absurd monstrosity? Even Hoboken is preferable. Even Newark. (My thoughts fly to the south — the Mediterranean lands: Sicily, Arizona, Greece, Libya, Baja California, New Mexico, southern Italy, Spain, Sonora, Crete — immortal Crete!)

Metropolitan dialect: "Sow, I *told* yuh. Gimme niyun apples please. Pawk da caw ovah deah. Not heeyah — ovah deah! Sow, I tole da fukkin cocksuckkah, I says look heeyah, yah dirty fukk! Yah cunt. Yah simple sonofabitch. Yah coksukkah. Yah schmuck klutz schlmiel. I *sore* it! Yeah, ah *sore* it myself!"

And oh the pure joy the bright beauty the holy clean hunger for life of our little boy Joshua — at nine months.

America's contribution to civilization? I mean, besides rubber gloves and atom bombs? Why, jazz of course — and jazz? By whom? Why, the Negroes, those people we've enslaved used abused tormented scorned humiliated and insulted. . . .

Love of Heaven slanders earth; be true to the earth.

No regard for the *quality* of life. No respect for the natural world. No love for other forms of life.

We in America are being systematically robbed. Robbed of the most elementary decencies of life — clean air, sunlight, pure unmedicated water, grass & woods to play in, silence solitude and space, even time, even death. Instead . . . ?

Insanity.

Tee Vee. Hi-Fi. Super-Duper.

Glittering shit. And, finally, morphine.

Not socialism, not capitalism is the enemy but — industry and technology carried to excess, to and beyond the point of madness. The monster is number — abstractification and quantity made gods, overwhelming bread and wine and life itself.

The delight, the satisfaction, the vital necessity of the primal mysteries: a wood fire, walking on leaves, rain in the desert. . . .

(Anarchism is a secret yearning toward brotherhood. Anarchism is the *demand* for community.)

Every man has two vocations: his own and philosophy.

With every pretty girl, a pang of anguish.

Confessions:

Perhaps the most horrible thing about the Nazis' massacre of Jews was the failure of the victims to resist. They too dishonored mankind.

My good friends (Bruno, Jesus, Shankara et al) of the Invisible Republic.

The greater our dreams . . . the more terrible our nightmares.

The MAD SCIENTIST — once a baroque villain, now a dominant, honored and commonplace figure in modern life.

SLOTH: one of the seven Deadly Sins; my deadliest.

April 8, 1957 – Arches, Utah

Back in Abbey's country again. I walk in beauty. I go in beauty [phrases from a Navajo holy song]. Once again. And this time my wife and my son shall share it with me.

Red naked rock again, the enormous and dazzling sky, the mountains east west north south blazing with snow; magnificence everywhere I look.

And the miniature beauties of the cliffrose yucca primrose and sage about to explode into life and color and mystery: sex and death and life, the dance of Shiva all over again.

Sweet sweet wilderness! Soon ah too soon to vanish under noise dirt and confusion — one incredible crime after another: attack murder dishonor and befoulment follow greed, overwhelm this wild innocent and defenseless beauty. . . .

∞

Guaranteed best-seller: *The Jesus H. Christ Story*, by Fulton Sheen, Jr., with introduction by J. Edgar Hoover and illustrations by Walt Disney.

O Christ of revolution and of poetry! Revolt? Of course! For what? For anything — for the sake of revolt!

Conceal thy rage, *cuate* — hide it under a casual contempt, a generous scorn.

The rule of LAW means the rule of Lawyers. That's all.

∞

My first girlfriend — Sarah Jane Dieffendeffer.

Ike — a tepid vapid insipid old man.

WHITE CANYON, UTAH:

A harsh cruel land; stark, naked beauty; terrible and deathly, untamed and untamable, lovelier than any song; a man's country.

White Canyon: population seven. One store post-office beer-joint gas-station garage home community-center combined. Joe the Bum, *descamisado* [ragged fellow], sitting on an empty crate, beer can in one hand, fly-swatter in the other. "Whaddayuh do?" I foolishly ask him. He stares at the floor for a while, considering the question. Swats a few flies. Then, "Nuthin," he says, looking up at me. Lives on bass, catfish and mud salmon [carp].

"Not enough money to get out," the others say when asked why they live in White Canyon. Old derelict village on the river bank, *abandido*. Store owner chaining his church-key to the counter — too many have been stolen. Birdlike old ladies debating what kind of pickup so-and-so had back in 1953. Silence; water trickling across the narrow dusty road.

The [Colorado] river — Chaffin's ferry, slung on cables, powered by an old Model A Ford. The gong signal; $5 fare.

North Wash: wild winding desolate fantastic labyrinthine, the green cottonwoods, cool water, the sheer golden overhanging cliffs.

The Henry Mountains: remote mysterious inaccessible.

White Canyon: a harsh cruel land — stark naked beauty; terrible and deathly, untamed and untamable, lovelier than any song; cruel; a man's country.

The land belongs to them that love it (and will fight for it?).

DICTUM: NO AUTOMOBILES IN NATIONAL PARKS.

Let's make them parks and not parking lots.

FOR HUMAN BEINGS ONLY.

God Bless America. Let's Save Some of It!

DENUNCIATION (inspired by [my] presence at a party in Berkeley, California, October 12, 1957):

"I say, oh you young fuddie-duddies, you young fogies, you prematurely middle-aged! Where are the gray flannel suits to go with your gray flannel mouths? You crumb-eaters! You knuckle-gnawers! You cappuccino drinkers! What right have YOU to be so wise, so dull, so blase and jaded, so conservative, so timid, so morose and defensive? at your age! So bored with protest, so disdainful of revolt, so tired tired tired of the straight and angry statement! What have you done to EARN your indifference?

"*I* say, hurrah for Ginsberg, hurrah for Rexroth, hurrah for Kerouac, hurrah for Miller and Jeffers and Mailer and Abbey and Williams and Dean Moriarty!"

October 1957 – Half Moon Bay, California

On the shore of the ultimate.

On the shore of the ultimate sea.

Here the bulging Pacific glitters and sparkles, surges and roars, crashing on the sand, green waves translucent with sunlight, creamy foam, salt to the taste, the seminal smell of the sea, pregnant as ever, powerful with its sound of eternity, its smell of birth and death, its tireless cycles, its calamitous sense of doom.

Under the bank just beyond reach of the tide we see the litter of the multitudes, the newspapers condoms broken bottles rags turds tissues cigarette butts filth grease scum and rot left as usual and always by the —

them! — the disrespectful California tourists. The sad untidy and depraved scum o' the earth.

But the sea is remarkably indifferent. Like the desert, indifferent, indifferent even to indifference.

help

Help

HELP

Fred and I, in a single night, consumed sixteen Roi-Tan cigars, a case of beer and a fifth of Old Echo Spring. Big Time stuff! And visions too, revelations, the discovery of brotherhood by dawn. Fantastic wit! Splendid song! Profound and magnificent discourse on the nature of the Eternal!

In factory work, from the worker's point of view, the important thing is not labor but time. We punch the clock, put in our time, punch the clock again and go home. Yes, we labor, but not hard; very little effort is required on most jobs, the work is easy and routine, and no sense of productivity — of making something — is felt. So it's all time, pure time — the minutes and hours on the big company clock. What we sell to the employer therefore (from our point of view) is not our labor, our help, our skill, but simply part of our time. Or, time being almost equivalent to life, what we sell to the employer is a big chunk of our lives. Sell — sold — no exchange, no refund. SOLD.

November 3, 1957 – Half Moon Bay

The stink of acres and acres of rotting artichokes. Groves of eucalyptus, Monterey pine, redwoods, oaks, gray lichen-splotched boulders, meadows of tough short tawny grass — the golden hills! sheet-metal lakes!

The child of divorce: "My father and his wife" ... or, "My mother and her husband."

Symbolism — used excessively in literature nowadays; weakens rather than strengthens prose and the idea.

Man is not an alien in this world, not at all. He is as much a child of it as the lion and the ant. Nevertheless, it is true that the natural world does *not* return our love, that it is indifferent to our ideas and that, after all, the heartbreaking beauty will remain when there are no hearts to break for it.

(Gulls on the shore, the sough of wind among mountain aspens, the red-tailed hawk soaring over the silence of the desert. . . .)

∞

[Wallace] Stegner: has most distinguished-looking bags under his eyes.

∞

We will now hear a few words from GAWD: "Friends. Are you tired, confused, uncertain about the meaning of life?"

∞

END OF JOURNAL IX

Road map: *Journal X — which opens in California and closes in New Mexico — is considerably enlivened by two reports of major adventures: the story of a float down the Colorado River through Glen Canyon in a rubber dinghy, prompting the first rumblings of what eventually would grow into Abbey's infamous "monkeywrenching" philosophy of environmental defense; and a detailed and spirited accounting of the author's first experience with hospitalization and surgery.*

JOURNAL X

January 1958 to November 1960

∞

January 29, 1958 – Half Moon Bay, California

Today I am thirty-one years old, which isn't nearly old enough. I still feel like a child. A gifted child, of course, but still a child.

The pot boils: *Brave Cowboy* appears in England, as a paperback reprint in the drugstores and finally is sold (for $7,500) to Kirk Douglas, movie actor. Unbelievable. Exasperating and unbelievable, yet there was the contract, there's the check, and did I make any attempt at any point to queer the deal? I did not.

Stanford and my writing fellowship: another fellowship like this and I'll claim bankruptcy. Rita is substitute-teaching, I'm swindling the state of Utah (unemployment compensation) in order to survive. Why? We *should* be able to live nine months on $2,500. It worries me that we cannot. Mostly carelessness, I believe: we could do it if we *had* to do it. Disaffiliation and the art of poverty, eh? That's right.

Night and the sea. The ocean rages at my nerves.

I shall soon write three Animal Stories:

(1) "A Dog's Life" — Chief the mongrel hound: his mysterious background, his troubles . . . gunshot, poisoned, strangled, kicked around and finally starved to death, etc.

(2) "The Lonely Horse" — A wild — well, half-wild — old bay gelding named Bill, who lives in a lonesome canyon in the most lonesome corner of Utah.

(3) "Hard to Kill" — An idle, distracted man, wandering the seashore, attempts and fails to kill a crippled sea gull.

∞

Comes Abbey again, still grinding his axiology.

Recently read: pommes — Eliot, Crane, Rexroth, Holderlin, Frost, Pound and Stevens. Novels and books — Kerouac, Traven, Miller, Freud (*Civilization and Its Discontents*), Austen (as much of *Mansfield Park* as I could endure), portions of *Middlemarch,* and maybe something else? All these books are worth reading if you have nothing better to do. For my part, I know I read too damned *many* books.

And also, Ginsberg's *Howl,* the best poem written in America by an American since — well, since Pearl Harbor. (So far as *I* know.) Yes, a beautifully shaggy little book. Wild and shaggy, and also highly accurate: "Moloch whose heart is a cannibal dynamo," etc. Very touching. My wife hates it, of course, just as everyone else I know does. They're all so *superior* to that kind of thing, you know. After all, they imply, Ginsberg is no poet — only a kid. (Like Chatterton? Rimbaud?) Only a crazy, hopped-up kid. About thirty-five, forty years old. But in America, that means nothing. We all mature slow and late, if at all, in this country.

Sycophancy seems to be a disease characteristic of the literary aesthete: Consider not only Lash, but such figures as Stendhal, James (H.), Proust, Scott Fitzgerald, Walter Scott, Rilke (that pathetic little lap-dog!), Yeats, and of course many others, most of them — *but not all* — second-raters.

∞

Confessions . . .

The American West: Robbed by the cattlemen, raped by the miners, insulted by the tourists.

Among metaphysicians I'm a G.P.

First day in the army: a Bible placed in one hand, a bayonet in the other.

Paradise: Any thunderstorms in Paradise? Any buzzards? cactus? flash floods? Any violence, mountains, sand dunes, scorpions?

No? Then keep it.

Essay: "Literary Crickets and the Herd Instinct."

Santa Fe: A dirty phony little town crawling with queers, promoters, creeps, thugs, vandals and parasites.

Los Alamos: An evil dirty little town.

Albuquerque: A large dirty sinister town, subsidized by war, dedicated to death and famed for its money, ugliness and vulgarity.

And Taos? Where the fairies and Buddhists live, and the rich ugly useless old women. Town of many hatreds.

April 22, 1959 – Albuquerque

Autobiography: The nadir. Yes, I've reached a low point. I'm bogged in the slough. Inert, frightened and angry. What a coward I am. No guts, that's my trouble. As simple as that — no guts. The chronic Abbey disability. The one thing we need most — courage — we haven't got. Black, bleak, barren. No job. No home. Another baby on the way. My little pile of movie money flowing away like sand down a wash. My latest and greatest book (*Black Sun*) rejected by one two three publishers. [Not the same novel later published under that title.] So far. And me quite unable to start a new one.

Losing my hair. Losing my old friends. Nasty grueling quarrels with Rita. Hidden hates and frustrations chewing up my bowels. Premonitions of the ultimate ulcer. Bloodshot eyes. Can't hold my liquor. A little beer-belly at my bow. Can't write. Can't love or live. "To kill love is to kill life."

The economic aspect of the situation is worst. Continual insecurity, frequent moving about with all the nagging chores and perplexities that entails. In the last three or four years, we've lived in — how many? — at least a dozen different places: Albuquerque, Moab, Hoboken, Moab, Half Moon Bay, Beavershead (Hoboken for Rita), Santa Fe, Casa Grande, now Albuquerq again. A maddening waste of time and money and effort and nerves. No wonder we're always snarling at each other, me and Reet.

And the near future looks just as bad. The same weary pursuit. Can't find the right job or the right place. Driving ourselves nuts in a half-ton Chevvy truck. (As I write this, I can hear, through the kitchen door, the tired barking of my wife, the sullen affected whining of my son Joshua, age three.) Somehow we've got to break out of this awful trap, this treadmill. Or else give up. Divorce. Maybe that's the one thing we need more than anything else, a divorce. (But Gawd, I dread another defeat, another failure.)

And stupid jobs with the Park Service. Wrangling dudes, picking up Kleenex, answering tiresome and childish questions five-thousand times a day. Desperately lonely among the genial mediocrities, the crew-cut bald-faced time-servers who operate the various Park Service outposts. The tourist nurseries and nursemaids.

What I want, should get and should keep is a fire-fighting job with the Forest [Service] — especially as a lookout. Instead, I allowed myself, through the usual cowardice, to be pushed into a Civil Service exam for a career job with the incredible U.S. Park Service. Shameful.

Do I still want to be a writer? Or am I ready to surrender that final illusion? Almost — but not quite. I still have a few cards left to play. I'm not whipped yet, though I sometimes act as if I were. Dedication, devotion, conviction, confidence, energy and courage. But the last above all — courage. Gawd, give me courage! Please, old man, a little courage!

(Yes? But where then, Abbey, is the center of your life? Where's *your* rock? Off in the canyon country, where junipers agonize and buzzards loftily meditate under a winedark sky? Forever and forever? Where nothing *ever* happens? Stasis, stillness, beauty and death. Ah shit, the olde death wish is upon me. I have nowhere to turn. I smell Him at my side, his filthy breath is on my neck.)

May 28, 1959 – Albuquerque

ATTENTION: Aaron Paul Abbey is born today. My second son. May he, like my first, be blessed by Heaven and Earth, grow straight and strong in the joyous sunlight.

∞

If the world of men is truly as ugly, cruel, trivial, unjust and stinking with fraud as it usually appears, and if it is really impossible to make it pleasant and decent, then there remains only one alternative for the honest man: stay home, cultivate your own garden, look to the mountains. (*Withdraw! Withdraw! Withdraw!*)

∞

Reverie and experience: *Solitude: Pages From a Desert Journal.*

June 25, 1959 – Glen Canyon, Colorado River, Utah

[This detailed chronicle of Abbey's float trip through a dam-doomed Glen Canyon consumes a full third of Journal X and has, of necessity, been abbreviated here. For more, see "Down the River" in *Desert Solitaire*.]

∞

We started [from Albuquerque] Tuesday morning, Ralph Newcomb and I, my pickup loaded with two rubber boats, paddles, spare tires, water and gasoline cans, lots of dried and canned grub, bedrolls and other equipment. By that afternoon we were lost in the maze of awful new truck roads in the Aneth oil field area [of southeast Utah]. Just before sundown, we met a carload of oil workers who guided us out of the maze to the newly paved road between Blanding and Bluff. We camped, first night, a dry camp, on a mesa overlooking the Four Corners country. Had chili beans, canned peaches, coffee and tobacco for supper.

Next morning, we drove on to Bluff, which looks pretty much as it did ten years ago, except for a new motel and a coupla new gas stations. (Saw Hovenweep National Monument that first day: no ranger in the ranger shack, trash in the spring, fine old ruins in the midst of all that desolation.)

Gassed up at Bluff, went on to Mexican Hat, saw the San Juan roaring fiercely down its narrow channel, bought more groceries (bacon, oranges, chocolate, etc.), drove up the new connecting road to Natural Bridges, where we lingered for a while. All as ever. No ranger in residence, tho; I should apply for a job there.

Onward thru the great red and white desert to White Canyon and Hite's Ferry. Here we had some beer and advice, and were a little alarmed to learn there *are* rapids in Glen Canyon and life jackets are *de rigeur* — we had none. Nevertheless, we went down to the river and made our preparations: inflated the boats, divided and packed our gear in canvas, paraffined a box of matches, experimented with the boats.

The river looked enormous, powerful, brown, the rubber boats so fragile. I was scared, to tell the truth, and half-hoped Ralph would suggest backing out. The boats seemed dangerously small and soft, their bottoms sinking like jelly under our weight. Still, we went ahead. I parked the truck in a lady's backyard, walked back to the launching site and got in my boat. All was ready. I paddled out into the river while Ralph took pictures. Finished, he put his camera away and we proceeded downriver, the roar of rapids around the first bend.

It occurred to me that the boats might be easier to handle if we tied them together, side by side. That way, we could each paddle on the outside, and together. As it turned out, this was the best idea we could have had for running the rapids. The two boats, lashed fast together, formed one large raft that flopped and folded over the large waves much better and easier than the boats could have done singly.

And so together we hit the first rough water, Trachyte Rapids, only half aware of what was going to happen . . . the growing roar of fast water, then our first glimpse of whitecaps, choppy seas and big waves — the shore glided swiftly by and we were in!

We settled deep into our boats, paddling only enough to keep our bows headed into the waves. Immediately we began to ship water and spray; I soon became wet as faster and faster the current pulled us into the heart of the rapids. The roar was overwhelming. A great boulder loomed up before us — Ralph's boat hit it, slid halfway up, clung there for a moment until my boat, twisting round in the flow, dragged his free; we could do very little with our paddles.

The water continued rough and choppy, but we were already thru the worst. Our first run through rapids was over in a moment; everything happened so quickly that we were on smooth water again while still poised with paddles ready for action. Both boats were half full of water, but they floated well enough; we had no bailing can then.

Relaxing, leaning back, laughing with delight and relief, I nearly fell out of my boat — more of the heavy brown silty water poured in; I sat in a pool of it in the stern while my bedroll, on which I was sitting, soaked up more. But we were happy. We lolled in our wet boats, lit our pipes and watched the towering canyon walls roll by.

Then we hit a second group of rapids, almost as rough as the first. Over-cautious, we went too far out of the main current and ended up aground in the shallows. We had to get out of the boats and drag them over the pebbly bar till we were back in knee-deep water. Hard work for one-legged Ralph, but he managed.

We drifted on for a few more miles, admiring the golden sunlight on the far walls and buttes, the elaborate strata of Moenkope mudstone beneath the naked masses and rounded humps of the Navajo formation resting upon it. The sun had gone out of sight and, seeing a beach far ahead, white sand with green young willows, we bore for it, paddling strenuously across the current. (We usually seemed to be on the wrong side of the river when we wanted to make a landing.)

Beached, we unloaded. I pulled the boats ashore and tethered them to the bole of a willow. My bedroll, when I opened it, turned out to be soaked thru and thru; I draped it over some young willows and built three small smoky fires beneath. (The bag still smells of willow wood smoke.) Ralph built a campfire and prepared supper. A lovely quiet evening with nothing human in sight, the great river murmuring a few feet away, frogs and cicadas chirping, a few nighthawks zooming thru the twilight gulping bugs.

After dinner and an hour or so of quiet pipe-smoking by the embers of the campfire, Ralph turned in. I stayed up for another two hours, firing my sleeping bag, trying to dry it. Little progress; I gave up at last, spread the wet thing on the sand and crawled inside. Oh wretched sensation! Cold and damp, I managed nevertheless to obtain at least a few hours of sleep.

Morning on the river. Up with the dawn, before the sun, Ralph still sleeping, strange birds calling and croaking, I washed the night's dishes and fixed a breakfast of bacon, beans and coffee. Unknown birds creaking and chirping on all sides — I could recognize only a few: canyon wren, pinon jays and a Mexican finch. Ralph awoke, washed in the silty water, pomaded his full beard and mustachios. We ate.

Thirsty already as the sun rose over the rimrock, we finished our canteens of spring water. And so, before noon, we were drinking from the great river itself. Not bad, the water laden with silt, brown as mud, but cool, clean-tasting. We'd dip tin cans into the river at our elbows, then set them on the gunwales of the boats to give the silt time to settle to the bottom. Good water, really, and plenty of it. Little chance of pollution, with Moab the nearest town [along the river] and it about 150 miles upstream. So much water — how could it be unclean? That was our belief. (Justified, apparently; no ill effects yet, three weeks after . . . radioactive?) [This is a reference to Abbey's concern over possible pollution from uranium mining along the Colorado and its feeder streams.]

The river, high with spring run-off, had water backed up, sometimes for a considerable distance, into the mouths of tributary canyons. High on the thousand-foot walls we saw occasional water seeps, sweetly green with ferns, watercress and sometimes willows, occasionally even with a small acid-green cottonwood or a group of dull-green scrub oak trees. Usually, these seeps or springs were set in the heart of deep recesses, alcoves, grottoes, shallow caves in the walls. We also saw, now and then, what might have been the ruins of old Moki [Anasazi] cliff houses.

Launch-off; we began our third day on the great river. The rapids turned out to be mostly nothing — we didn't even get wet. Then we resumed our leisurely gliding drift down the river (down the river! down the river!).

More great cliffs, sandbars, shores where jungles of willow, tamarisk, oak and cane sheltered mysterious and largely quiet birds. Solitary bird calls, little ripples and gurgles of water, the puffing of our pipes (*a la* Huck Finn!), occasional queer uproars in the water as the silty river bed altered its conformations.

Ah, so wild, lonely, sweet, primeval and remote — far far from anywhere: Blanding the nearest town at least a hundred miles away — nothing around us in any direction but miles and miles of naked wilderness; if not *pure* wilderness, certainly primitive. And original — bare rock, those hummocks of sandstone, pink as ham, buff as sand, extending ten twenty thirty forty miles away from the river. Now and then, as our twin boats turned in the current, we were offered a farewell glimpse of one of the Henry Mountains — rising above and beyond the canyon walls, far off, green and gray and blue and tan.

Every bend in the canyon promised new visionary delights, and seldom failed to deliver. It seemed to us that Glen Canyon became more beautiful and wonderful with every mile. We cursed the engineers and politicians who had condemned these marvels and the wildlife sheltered by them to death by drowning.

How much dynamite, we wondered aloud to each other, would be needed to destroy the dam? How delightful and just, we imagined, to have our dynamite so integrated into the dam's wiring system, that when the president or the secretary of the interior and the Four Corners' governors, together with their swarms of underlings, the press and hordes of tourists had all assembled for the Grand Opening, it would be the white pudgy finger of the biggest big-shot, pressing the little black button on the be-flagged switchboard, that would blow to hell and smithereens the official himself, his guests, the tourists, the bridge and Glen Canyon Dam. A sad and hopeless fantasy. . . .

Late that evening, well after sundown, we beached our boats and made camp on a sandy spit near the outlet of a deep, narrow, labyrinthine side canyon whose name, if it has a name, we did not know, and which I explored for part of its length before returning to the beach for supper. Within the depths of this unknown canyon I found a charming creek and water of remarkable beauty — crystal clear pools in bowls of rock and sand, perfect, free of weeds and litter, harboring schools of tiny fish.

Hungry as hell, we had corned beef and baked beans for supper, with fruit for dessert and tea and tobacco afterwards. A splendid night surrounded us — clouds like clipper ships, scattered stars, the fat white half-moon hanging over the edge of the crag that towered a thousand feet or more above our little camp. We searched out a couple of level places on our sloping sandbar and bedded down for the night, while the river murmured nearby and an unsteady wind hummed and whistled thru the willows.

Dawn and day again. We made a bacon and pancake breakfast, using the last of our bacon and the last of our pancake mix. I put too much water, then too much powdered milk into the mix, and the results, tho edible, fell far short of what might have been.

Afterwards, I went back into what I think of as "Labyrinth Canyon" to fill the canteens. I reached the farthest point of the previous exploration, a deep pool filling the canyon — which was no more than six or seven feet wide here — filled the canteens, undressed, swam the pool and continued farther into the heart of this strange and lovely glen, all bare rock, sand and running water, until I reached a place where giant boulders wedged into the canyon, forming a waterfall and checking my advance. Above, a narrow strip of blue; below, the smooth rock and clear water winding thru a luminous golden glow of refracted sunlight, and here and there, at certain bends in the grotto, patches of direct sunlight. After a pleasant swim, I sunned myself in one of these patches, then returned to camp where Ralph was waiting, sweating, beside the boats. I washed the dishes, we packed, loaded and shoved off.

This day we passed the entrance of the San Juan River, which looked quite small and trivial compared to the broad flow of the Colorado. I began looking for Music Temple [a huge alcove so-named for its acoustic qualities by explorer John Wesley Powell in 1869], but never found it. As I later learned, Music Temple is reached only thru a narrow entrance, hardly visible from the river. And we were probably on the wrong side when we passed it! One of the disadvantages of the self-guided tour.

I began thinking about Bridge Canyon, the path to Rainbow Bridge. We bore left and tried to keep close to the east, or south, shore. I had little clue as to how to recognize Bridge Canyon when we came to it — all I knew was that it was somewhere below Navajo Point, with rapids close by. We'd simply have to stop at each likely looking side canyon and hunt for evidence.

The first side canyon appeared (on the left). We paddled ashore. I climbed out and tied the boats to the willows. Ralph stayed in the boat, reloading his camera. I found a pathway leading thru the jungle of brush and apparently up into the canyon. I thought to follow it a piece, see what evidence I could find, but cut off my progress by accidentally starting a brush fire.

It happened this way: I saw scraps of tissue paper beside the trail, where some dirty swine of a tourist had stopped to crap. Conscientious as ever, I touched a match to the paper, the paper burned and was nearly consumed when a gust of wind blew the scraps into some dry grass hummocks close by. Instantly, the grass was afire, the flames multiplying rapidly. I tried to stamp them out; too much for me — smoke and fire flared in my face; I had to retreat.

The fire spread into the dried brush, the ivy, the willow thickets. Billows of gray-yellow smoke gushed up, nearly filling the mouth of the canyon; the flames glowered at me, red and furious, thru the leaves and stems of the little jungle. I retreated again, back to the boats, where I found some difficulty in explaining to Ralph what had happened.

The fire roared and crackled not very far away, cutting short my explorations. I untied the boats, got one leg into mine and pushed off into the current. We watched in amazement, as we floated past, the unbelievable clouds of smoke choking the deep side canyon. I felt pretty foolish, and mighty regretful too, at having possibly ruined my only opportunity to reach Rainbow Bridge.

Light in the east. Cloud banks on fire with the rising sun. I crawled out of the sack and bathed in the river. Even washed my shirt and underwear. Made breakfast — pea soup — with our last box of raisins set aside for lunch. Refilled the canteens in the boulder-strewn wash of the canyon. A great delta of boulders: good evidence that this particular canyon reached clear back to the slopes of Navajo Mountain.

We dressed (half the time, we moved around camp bare naked; felt good), reloaded the boats, pushed off. Into the rapids. Which sounded bad but failed to equal Trachyte.

Last day on the river coming up, though we didn't know it, thinking we were still a good two days' float away from the landing place. For breakfast we had catfish. Damn good. If only we'd known it, we could've lived on catfish the whole way down the river. Big, plentiful, delicious, easy to catch, easy to cook, easy to eat. I washed the dishes, we packed, loaded and paddled off.

Shot thru a rapids and glided down the broad bosom of the river. More magnificent scenery, including a colorful butte — a great monument of red and white sandstone perhaps two thousand feet high, perfectly banded in black and green around its middle, which we spent most of the day drifting below as the river meandered around it.

Then there was the terrifying side canyon we explored, deep and so narrow it was like a tunnel or cave, with the overhanging and interlocking walls completely shutting off the sky. Full of quicksand and pools of cold muddy water. And absolutely lifeless — not a blade of grass, not a bird, not a lizard, not even an insect did I see in that awful catacomb. I explored it as far as I could, to a point where the two walls of the canyon drew so close together that further progress would have been possible only by wedging myself thru sideways. And dark. And me half naked in cold water up to my knees.

Returning, I heard a holler from Ralph and found him back near the boats, stuck firm in quicksand. I pulled him out, we took a few photographs then paddled out of there. The hot sun on the wide river felt good.

And drifted on. And on and on. Mostly in silence, smoking our pipes. As noon approached and the heat became more intense (after the first day,

we kept ourselves well covered), we sought the shady side of the canyon —
when there was shade and when it was possible to reach it. We didn't talk
much on this voyage. Ralph seemed unusually quiet; maybe I seemed the
same to him. Most of the time there was no need for speech.
Wonder and contemplation were enough. And smoking. And munch-
ing raisins. And now and then dipping a canful of water from the river for
a drink. And sometimes paddling a little to avoid a rock, or to turn the
boats for a different view.

Late in the afternoon. Sun in our eyes. Drifting quietly along. Ralph is
asleep. I see an odd unnatural gleam on the right-hand shore, about a
mile-and-a-half ahead. A queer metallic glint. As we slowly near it, I
decide that it may be an automobile or house trailer and that we are
approaching *El Vado de los Padres,* for which we've been looking all day.

And then, on the left shore, not far ahead, I see a white rectangular
object. A sign! A billboard! Curious, I paddle closer and am able to read
it: "All boats must leave river at Kane Creek Landing one mile ahead on
right. Absolutely no boats allowed in construction zone." — U.S. Bureau
of Reclamation.

I woke up Ralph; astonished, he read the sign. We could barely believe
it, so certain were we that it'd take us at least another day to reach our
destination. We were half right. The answer to the puzzle lay in the fact
that Glen Canyon Dam was forcing us off the river [early], at the Crossing
of the Fathers.

So, paddling like mad again (for as usual we were way over on the
wrong side), we bore to the right, hoping nobody was watching our labor.
They weren't; when we landed, we found the place deserted of humans,
though a motorboat, outboard, car and house trailer (U.S. Park Service)
were on the place. We made ourselves at home, cooked supper, lay on the
warm rock and watched the moon rise over the river, wondering where the
hell we were — Kane Creek, yes, but where was Kane Creek? Not on my
map And finally went to bed. Our voyage was over.

August 13, 1959 – Albuquerque

The Wise Simpletons:

Tolstoy to Rilke, who was pestering him about techniques in writing: "If
you want to write, write!"

The dying Thoreau, asked by some damned cleric if he was ready for
the next world: "One world at a time, please."

William Morris on politics: "No man is wise enough to be another man's master."

∞

Appearance *and* reality? Appearance *is* reality — the only reality we know, will ever know, will ever need to know. (Keep it clean. Honesty is the best policy.)

Is it not possible to assemble a view of the world based only on what we know? Do we *need* the unknown, the private vision and fantasy, the speculative, the wishful or the possible?

August 15, 1959 - Albuquerque

Style:

Conrad. To write of — no, to do for the desert what he did for — of — the sea. But I must avoid his rich flowing organ-valved almost lush (tropical) style. Emulate his passion for the exact. My style: something almost harsh, bitter, ugly. The rough, compressed, asymmetrical, laconic, cryptic. Cactus. Old juniper. Rock, dry heat, the stark contour.

NO FOG. NO GODDAMNED FOG.

Mood, tone, feeling.

Combine intensity (not density) with clarity. *Clear* and *intense.* Like the desert landscape, the desert light, the desert atmosphere — clear, intense and infinitely suggestive. Hard distinctions, precise outlines — but each thing, suggesting, somehow, everything else. As in truth each thing does.

∞

San Francisco! Miller, Jeffers, Ferlinghetti, Rexroth, Leon Kirchner, Diebenkorn and Harris! And now Lash, too — and the great Al Sarvis — and many others. Damnit, maybe that's where we should be! I'm homesick for the sea, and the fog, and the sweet city in the hills! Sometimes I think . . . ah, but no, I am a desert rat! A desert rat!

September 16, 1959 - Albuquerque

JAZZ: Music for sophisticated patriots. Night music. Midnight music. Lonesome afternoon music. The blue sax. The squealing trumpet. The obedient drums. Amazing virtuosity exercised around a pill. Insipid. Tame. Deliberately dull. Ah, tedium! (Who wants to live forever?) An idiot's paradise. A tight narrow badly constricted kind of art. Can't break the limits without self-contradiction, without ceasing to be jazz. A long long way from Leadbelly and Big Bill Broonzy. A long way down.

Jazz: The destruction of melody. The rigid meter. The elaboration and direction of deliberately banal tunes.

Nightclub music. Cigarettes and boredom. The music of boredom, bored people. The urban ennui. Big-city music. American? The American Negro loose in the slums. Crafty, cunning, subtle, arid music. Cool and dry. No emotion, no passion, no blood and guts. The mechanical meter. (Shuffle-dance.) Industrial rhythm. Classicism, factory-style.

To hell with jazz!

So damned casual, urbane, smooth, sophisticated. Stylish. The casual, relaxed performance. ("Look at me, I'm not scared.") The casual applause. The jazz cult: professors, monographs, addicts, puritans. The terrible fear of emotion, significance, direct statement. Music for aesthetes, purists and cold-bellied geometers.

November 15, 1959 – Taos

What am I doing here? Why am I the editor of a weekly newspaper called *El Crepusculo de la Libertad* — meaning "The Dawn (or Twilight?) of Liberty." A fantastic situation, certainly.

It began without warning. One Saturday morning in Albuquerque I received a phone call from one Craig S. Vincent. He wanted to know what I was doing. I told him I was looking for a job. (True.) He wanted to know if I'd be interested in editing a weekly newspaper. I told him to come on over, we'd talk about it. He came, we talked. I was reluctant; I knew instinctively the job would be a big pain in the ass. I tried to talk him out of hiring me. But the next day I drove up to Taos, saw and talked with Phil Reno, acting editor, and decided (still reluctantly) that I ought to give the thing a try. Told Phil to tell Craig I was interested.

A week later Craig called again, asked me to come on up to Taos. I said I'd come on a two-week trial basis. He agreed. And we agreed on a salary — $100 per week.

So here we are, living in a big beautiful adobe house close to the office, in the heart of Taos, and me working my half-ass half off trying to put out a decent paper every week. It can't last long though — maybe a year. That's all I'll allow myself, a year. Unless the job shakes down into a smooth effortless part-time routine. Otherwise, I'll have to quit. I'm neglecting my vocation here, what with sixty to seventy hours a week of journalism. Which I've always despised. And do now more than ever, and with far better reason.

Rita likes it here and so does Joshua. Rita wants to buy a house, make a home here. My heart falters at the prospect — I don't like this arty hate-filled town, I don't like the bleak cold somber olive-drab landscape that surrounds us. I dream of and long for the desert. But we need a home. . . .

February 11, 1960 – Taos

What am I doing here? Nothing.

I quit my job two weeks ago. No more newspaper racket for me. Finished.

Couldn't get along with the boss. Vincent was too hard on my nerves, me on his. Thank Gawd it's over.

I have applied for sixteen different Park and Forest Service jobs. Also to a prep school in Colorado. (I feel discouraged. Terrible self-doubts. Can I do *anything*?)

Sent five pomes and four stories to Gilberto [Gilbert Neiman] for his "Between Worlds" review. Sonofabitch better print some of it, Gawddamn him.

(Good Christ, the amazing therapy of words: Even writing the above snatches has tugged my spirits up a few notches — I feel better already . . . somewhat better.)

April 17, 1960 – Veteran's Hospital, Albuquerque

"A HOSPITAL JOURNAL"

Sunday. In government pajamas and government robe I sit on a bunk in a two-man room in the veteran's hospital, waiting to have a torn cartilage scraped out of my knee bones. Hit a mogul at thirty-five mph. A moving mogul. Skis went two ways, I went four. Can't quite straighten the leg, can't bend it very far. Painless but stiff. Surgery called for, it seems.

So far, nothing much has happened. I checked in here last Friday afternoon, had my clothes and baggage taken away from me in exchange for a G.I. robe and pajamas. Escorted to Ward 15 by a nice old volunteer lady — a long walk over green lawns, birds twittering sweetly, jets roaring in the background, sunshine.

At the ward, a nurse did a routine check of my blood pressure, pulse, weight, height, temperature, then led me to room and bed — where, after an hour's wait, a young black intern named Brown came in, cocked the wounded leg around but rendered no opinion. The medical son of a bitch.

The officious head nurse seems a bit too eager to assert her authority over temporarily disabled men. What kind of women become nurses? Most are gentle, sweet, truly caring. But these others — is there really any tenderness in them? Or is it love of power? Women adore a sick man. But such generalities are useless; nurses no doubt are as varied as any other group.

I notice that the most menial and unpleasant tasks in this leech lyceum, this quackery factory, are performed by men. Busboys. Orderlies. Nurse's aides.

In the bathroom, a young Chicano aide is reaming out an old man's asshole with a tube. "Oh, easy!" groans the old wreck. "Easy, it hurts!" "I'm doing it as easy as I can," the boy says.

Me, I depart. Quick. Quickly. Too squeamish for such scenes. A serious defect in a writer, this squeamishness. The brute facticity of the world is sometimes too much for me. Like butchering a pig back home on the farm: I could do it, but never really *enjoyed* it.

Since I checked in on a medical holiday — Good Friday — they told me I'd have to wait until Monday to be inspected by the chief, a Dr. Bronitsky. So, no decisions yet and I can only wait and hope. But undoubtedly there's something wrong with my leg; five and a half weeks after the accident I still can't operate it normally. (Goddamnit anyway!)

Tonight will be my first night spent in the hospital. Friday I escaped, with a pass, after learning nothing would be done over the weekend. I spent Friday and Saturday nights with Bill Currie and Ralph Newcomb. Saturday night we went to a beat nightclub called *Le Grave*, where Ralph and I, with guitar and flute, performed for the mob. Seemed to me it went all right, though I was too drunk to really know, or care. The place was crowded and noisy. Ralph and I were nearly drowned out by an expert banjo player who appeared in about the middle of our concert.

Back at the hospital now, I go exploring.

On the first floor, south wing, I find barred windows. Barricaded wards. Dark and quiet. A sign: DO NOT ENTER. What manner of horror waits hidden down that way?

Lights out at 2100. Bedtime for the sick childer [sic].

I lie awake and think: Sitting in the Lobo Theater, Saturday afternoon, I was haunted by something like the conviction of sin. An original sin? The feeling of nothing, of nothingness. *Nihil ex nihilo.* A terrible dread. Why? The belief that I was, that I am, pissing my life away.

> *"Any way you turn*
> *Any way you look*
> *You have pissed away your life."*

I am now thirty-three, like Christ, and in the middle of the journey, like Dante. If there is any greatness in me, if I have a spirit and purpose here, then I must very soon drag it out of my guts. Tear truth from my entrails.

A pretty young blonde nurse just came and went, offering me a sleeping pill, which I disdained. (I hope I can sleep despite all the muted noise around here: radio earphones, a TV in a room down the way, interminable conversations up and down the corridor.)

Monday. The great hospital. These great slabs and blocks of steel and adobe overlooking the mountain, the plain, Sandia Base and atom bomb factory, the radiant city — radiant at night, dim vast and dusty by day. Albuquerque, New Mexico. The Geiger counters buzz like rattlesnakes. This huge murmuring dynamo of sickness and death, healing and hope, pain, boredom and hidden (DO NOT ENTER) despair: hospital. The smell of trauma.

I think of all the sad empty old men I've seen here already. Veterans of three wars. Veterans of pain. Those masks of defeat. God, I must not end up looking that way. Better to die young (too late!), or even middle-aged, I think, than age like a rat in a cage.

Never fear, Abbey, a higher destiny waits for you. You shall drop dead someday, sudden and violent, tumbling from a rotten-rock cliff. I hope. Or else age like a saint, become one of Whitman's splendid and savage old men, die raging against the horror and the cruelty of this world. (Listen to that!)

The VA apparatus is gigantic. Almost everything appears to be provided, to have been anticipated. Pool tables and TV, chaplains and libraries, TB wards and psycho wards, dentists and social workers. All the heart could desire.

I was admitted with little fuss. Half an hour of filling out forms and interviews, a one-week wait and I'm in — without even presenting military discharge papers. Of course, that would have been necessary if I hadn't attended the University of New Mexico: the hospital admitting officer verified my veteran's status simply by calling the downtown VA office, which still holds records of my G.I. Bill days.

Quite a number of pretty nurses in this factory. Surprising. Maybe the girls really *are* attracted by the glamour of medicine, the hope of marrying an M.D.

How many vets in America? About fifteen million, I believe. And each and every one entitled to the same care I'm getting, in case of need. Socialism has arrived, truly.

Good.

I'm going to hate to leave this place. Perhaps I should cultivate more delicately and lovingly that mysterious ache in my heart. (How about the pain in your groin, *gringo?* That sensation like a toothache where you know you have no teeth? Look at that sweetheart in tight white skirt retreating down the hall: look at it move; those brave vibrations — she could chew peanuts with that thing!)

So quiet now. Nothing seems to be happening. All I've done so far is drain piss into bottles. The sun booms in through an east window.

While down in the mess hall, I hear that the nurses have been looking for me. I'm supposed to stay in bed, supposed to stay off my feet. But first, a blood test. Syphilis. (Syphilization.) I watch my rich dark venous blood flowing into the lab tube. Back to the ward.

Waiting. Doctor due at 0930. First the two interns, Fish and Brown, come in. Punk kids full of gibberish, wearing white smocks. Trying to look technical. They make notes about me and depart.

Good.

Finally, the great Bronitsky arrives. The Chief. Osteologist supreme. A short stocky muscular man with a heavy shock of black hair, mustache, glasses, gold tooth. The interns return. Bronitsky with the two rookies. Interesting technical talk as they feel and paw my stiffened leg.

Bronitsky asks questions.

The interns try, usually fail, to answer them.

Putting my heels up on the foot of the bed, Bronitsky shows his students how the bad knee is locked. Incomplete extension. Minimal flexion. Torn and displaced cartilage. He asks me for the history of the case, especially the details of the accident.

I describe the accident as best I can.

Bronitsky says the knee is locked because of the presence of a foreign body, in this case the displaced cartilage. Recommends an operation.

No alternative?

All alternatives logically eliminated, he says, except a permanent gimp leg.

I agree to the operation.

He says I'll be scheduled for surgery. Stay off that leg, he orders in leaving. Use a wheelchair.

Lying here, I think bitterly of all that might have been, should have been: Those ski safety bindings that weren't quite safe enough; skiing the rest of the day after the accident; Doc's mis-diagnosis and all the unnecessary delay; my bad skiing.

Why didn't I stay home that day? Well, if I had, I might have been run over by a car, *quien sabe.*

This is the worst line of thought possible: There is nothing more futile, nothing more stupid and painful, than melancholy brooding over what might have been.

STOP AT ONCE!

Waiting, waiting.

A sky-pilot came in half an hour ago. The Rev. Anderson Hicks, South-ron Baptist, fat black Bible in hand. After polite preliminaries he began threatening me with eternal torture in Gawd's underworld. We argued, fairly politely; he seemed just *slightly* disturbed by my atheistical attitude. No doubt he's encountered us free-thinkers before.

I needn't recount the argument. It followed familiar lines, the preacher relying heavily on his Book, me responding with considerations of a more general nature. Think of Hell, he insisted, think of bacon frying on a greased skillet. Smells good, I said. He was not amused, left in a huff. I pursued in my wheelchair.

More damned X-rays; four views of my knee. That makes the fourth time I've been X-rayed in the last five months, the third time in a week. How many roentgens now? And the bloody VA dentist wants to X-ray my jawbones!

Ole Doc Brown just came in, telling me I'm scheduled for the slab Thursday. Or maybe Friday. Vague, as always. I tried to ask him questions about the affair, though I lack confidence in his answers. He said I'd be walking again two or three weeks after the operation.

What precisely does that mean? I didn't dare ask.

Blondie comes in to inform me I'm to have "bathroom privileges only" from now on. Pissing privileges, eh?

Thermometers, needles, X-rays, pills and a restricted diet. For supper I get a dish of jellied cartilage with raisins. I'm getting tired of this shit. I want out of here!

Christ! Jesus! Holy Mary!

I don't care for this premature second childhood.

Tuesday. Slept well last night, despite petty anxieties. Telephone call from Rita: she'll be down from Taos Friday to help me through the surgery.

Bad news from Grand Canyon: They're offering me a dream job (fire lookout), which I probably can't accept. I'll ask the doc's opinion this morning.

Rita sounded a trifle annoyed with me on the phone — perhaps be-cause I sounded so Goddamned disgusted, as I indeed am. This stupid and silly and frivolous accident — at such a time. But good Gawd, why fret over trifles? That's the spirit. A year from now this business will seem the merest incident. A nothing. However, I'm not living in the future, I'm living in the here and now. And here and now I'd like nothing better than to spend the summer in a tower above the yellow pines on the rim of the great canyon.

Which attitude is correct?

The philosophical.

Why?

Because it's more pleasant. Better to accept the unavoidable with cheer and good grace than to fret and moan over what cannot be helped. Obvious truth. And yet — how difficult. How difficult to ride over bad luck.

And how easy — how natural? — to relax into bitterness, disgust, anger, defeat. For it *is* defeat to surrender to the dark emotions. Bad for the nerves. Bad for the face. Consider the faces, the sad gaunt faces of the defeated old men in this place — a kind of disgrace lurks in those slack jaws, those trembling hands, those watery eyeballs, those querulous cranky voices. The disgrace of surrender. The surrender to bugs, bacteria, bad luck. To sweet wine.

Yet some of these poor old bastards may be the survivors of mustard gas attacks in the First World War. Deserted by friends and family, they hang onto the joyless rag of life, sunk in misery but unwilling or unable to die. Can one blame them for looking like specters?

Not the point.

The point is to triumph over my own misfortunes. There is no misfortune, I say, that I cannot surmount with scorn, with dirty jokes, with a light heart and a gay head. Yes, a gay head, like on a hog. Be proud and independent, like a hog on ice.

Outside, the turbojets howl, bellow, moan and scream — demons from Hell. Screaming at our necks.

Wednesday. D-day minus one. Am I scared? I think not. Most of the time I think of anything, everything, but the operation. If I think about it hard enough — the preparations, the anesthesia, the knife in the knee — I do get that old feeling: fear stirs in my belly and the bowels crawl.

(Right now!)

But mostly, I'm simply annoyed, exasperated at all this waste of time and effort, most of all in losing that job at Grand Canyon. (All but certain.) At such times I curse Hartwick, curse Doc — oh do I curse him — five weeks delay! The very difference between solitude above the pines and hay fever in Taos!

But why bother? What difference does it make, under the aspect of eternity? (The great Bronitsky says I'll be here until June, probably.)

"Aspect of eternity." What crap that is! We don't live in eternity.

Here I go again.

No, I won't go again. The mad merry-go-round in the head. Stay off it. Rather, get off it.

Don't fret, Abbey . . . we're coming.

My book stagnates. Stagnates.

Gerber [a pseudonym used in a typescript version of this story that Abbey prepared for unknown reasons, and which was inserted into Journal X at this point] came in yesterday — a friend of mine — with books and a story. The story is: He and his wife are getting what most married couples want more than anything else in the world — a divorce. Mostly her idea, it seems. She wants to get rid of him because, according to Gerber, he is not man enough for her. She wants to be manhandled and he just doesn't feel like it anymore.

Can't say I blame him.

And the children? Alas, the children. He spoke of them as one would speak of pet animals — he'll stay in Albuquerque, so as to see them occasionally. But much more interesting problems are involved.

Gerber seemed unnaturally cheerful when he came in. I asked him what he was so damned cheerful about. The divorce, of course. He seems to think of it as a great liberation. A big step forward. I was shocked but swiftly decided to be as encouraging as I could, rather than — sympathetic. Rather than consoling.

I don't really have much confidence in Gerber. I believe he is weak and will probably shoot himself before the year's up. I really felt sorry for him, but I tried to hide my pity under a veil of cynical approval. "Takes two to make a good divorce," we agreed. "A good clean divorce is the finest work of man." "Gotta consummate this divorce." Etc.

But I wanted to weep for him, feeling already the loneliness about to overwhelm the man.

Did I do right? That's what troubles me. Surely I should have been truly open and compassionate with him, perhaps wept for him. For how can a divorce, in his case, after thirteen years of marriage, with three children — how can it be anything less than tragedy? I was near overwhelmed with a sense of the terrible loneliness that must already be shrouding him.

The trouble is that Americans expect too much of marriage, as they expect too much of life. Americans: the only people in the world who *pursue* happiness. Tragic chase. Inevitably, disappointment and frustration appear on every hand. Alcoholism and suicide in every head. A gray overcast of despair overhanging the land. Man's fate is sorrow and sickness and death. Also joy and victory. (Sometimes.)

Wednesday afternoon. The tempo steps up as H-hour approaches. I sign a permit for surgery. (Resembles a death warrant.) I wheel down to the lab for more flocculation, get a pin stuck in a finger. Blood type A-1, 3.2. Bleeding speed, 0.32 cfs.

A meniscectomy, that's what they call it. Most routine of operations — many skiers and most football players know it. A trivial operation.

Cold terror grips my guts.

The assistant anesthesiologist comes in to tell me I'm to have a spinal block.

A *spinal!*

A needle in the spine!

(Gotta get outa here!)

Well, not precisely *in* the spine, he explains casually, leafing through the *Vesalius* Gerber brought me, but in that horsetail of nerves just beneath the spine. The spinal is customary, he says, for such operations as mine. Nothing to it. I'll be "dead from the chest down" he says cheerfully.

Why not a local?

Not done, he says. Too much pain, too big a job. A major operation. (Christ!) Nice guy. He goes on to describe the horrors of the alternative — the gas mask, the tube down the windpipe, etc.

Pre-operative instructions:

(1) Sign permit for surgery.
(2) Deposit money, other valuables, with finance department.
(3) Shower with special antiseptic soap.
(4) Remove mustache and beard, clean shave. (*What?*)
(5) Eat or drink nothing after midnight, and no breakfast.
(6) Return special soap container to nurses' station. (Fuck that. Let the indolent sluts come and get it; goddamn nurses don't do nothing around here, avoiding patients as if they were diseased!)

Well, what the hell. Who wants to live forever?

After supper, an orderly wheels me into the bathroom, jams a tube up my asshole and sluices out my entrails. My very first enema and the last loss of my cherry youth. Now I know that I shall never grow up to be a virgin.

(Friend or enema?)

Back in bed, a nurse brings me one tiny little yellow pill. The first nice thing a nurse has done for me in several days. Sedative, probably.

Thursday. Early morning. Awakened around 0530 by an orderly with a thermometer. He puts it in my mouth, leaves. A few minutes later he returns, removes the thermometer and checks my pulse and blood pressure. The rubber band around my skinny arm.

"Am I dead or alive?"

"Too much alive," says he.

Changed my mind. Don't think I'll let them do this to me.

Nerves. Butterflies. Stomach lively.

Antiseptic shower. Fresh pajamas.

Waiting, waiting.

What's next?

Shorn. Baldface as a bank clerk. God, I look strange without the beard; like a plucked bird. Hospital life consists chiefly of one humiliation after another. The excuse was some medical garbage about the beard interfering with possible oral anesthesia. They lie like statesmen around here.

I wish somebody would give me another pill. Or a pint of bourbon.

Another sedation pill arrives, about 0630, followed by a pregnant nurse who shoots me in the arm with a loaded needle. Demerol? Seconal? She won't say. Always keep the patient guessing.

A last trip to the toilet for a final piss.

Shot taking effect. An uncomfortable numbing sensation drifts through my nervous system. Procaine? Codeine? Morphine?

I still feel nervous. Worried more about the phucking spinal than the surgery. What's a kneecap? Am I writing gibberish? Not yet. Gawd bless literature. Art equals love equals God.

I *am* writing gibberish.

Perhaps, in writing, I'm resisting the sedative. But I'm so interested in my own reactions. Groping for the pen. Grog. I'm groggy as a spiked frog. My mind crawls with obscenities. Relax, man, and let the drug do its kindly work. (I have the conviction I could fight this off if I wanted to, just as I fought off the pill.)

Twenty minutes after the shot, and I'm still alive enough to write. A barber comes in to shave my leg. The attention is flattering, of course. But I wish it were one of the good-looking nurses handling my thigh, my balls. Needs a woman's touch.

Bare-legged as a girl I am now; my wife will hate me. Bare face, bare leg, bare ass. I feel heroic, and very witty, but mustn't make too many jokes. Everyone is so cheerful and friendly, grateful they don't have to endure what I — probably — shall endure.

Goddamn Newcomb never came to see me. Wife due tomorrow. Judy [Pepper, destined to become the third Mrs. Abbey] called yesterday, offered anything I wanted. What I want most is out of here.

Feeling mighty groggy, half pleasant, half unpleasant. A tightness in my chest.

Thousands, maybe millions of women have spinals for childbirth. Common enough. Nothing to fear — except fear.

Little danger now, I trust, of Bronitsky knifing up the wrong leg.

If I'm swooning it's mighty slow. Lethe-wards I sink? I forget nothing. And forgive everything. Run for the hills? Too late. *Too late.* . . .

∞

Monday. Four days post-op. Still prone in bed. The operation was a great success. Now I can't do *anything* with my leg.

Courage, courage.

I remember it all quite clearly: The dizzy ride through the corridors under the lights, flat on my back on the wheeled stretcher watching the ceiling whirl past. Through the swinging gates, into surgery. . . .

I'm pretty well doped-up but cheerful, inquisitive, asking questions of everybody. Off the cart onto the butcher's block. Waiting for anesthesia. An assistant holds me on my side, knees up, fetal position. I make the usual foolish remarks about a return to the womb, which everyone ignores. The anesthesiologist, a woman, winks at me. Everyone is wearing pale green — green gowns, green caps, green masks. Four or five people in the room, plus the victim, all of us waiting for Bronitsky. Now reported to be on the way.

The anesthesiologist goes to work — on my backbone. I can feel the fine needle probing, probing for a hole through the bone. Into my spine. *Oooooh.* . . .

"There'll be some pressure now," she says. I feel a charge of cold electricity surge through my pelvis.

What is it?

"Conocaine."

The numb sensation spreads.

Some time later . . . they're pricking my leg with a needle. A slight tickling effect, growing sharper as the needle approaches my belly. I tell them when to stop.

A glimpse of Bronitsky's smiling face.

"Good morning," I say.

Ole Doc Brown is here too, looking interested. And Fish, looking nervous. Somebody shoves a grounding plate under my back: execution about to begin.

I can see nothing. Drapes over my face. Anesthesiologist at my head, checking the blood pressure every few minutes. Ticklish and jarring sensations in the vicinity of my knee. I keep talking and turning my head. A quart of dextrose hangs above, attached by tube and needle to a vein in my forearm. "Don't talk so much, try to sleep," the woman at my head says, and gives me another shot in the arm. I'm in love with her.

Time lapses, elapses, relapses.

I get a glimpse of needle and thread: they're sewing my kneecap back in place. Bronitsky is talking, talking all the time, lecturing to the interns. I see Brown wrapping my wounded knee in an enormous bandage. A giant ball of gauze, big as a hornet's nest. Insulation? Then Bronitsky, as he had promised earlier, shows me something like a worn-out rubber gasket in a small jar of bloody water: my cartilage.

All done: they wheel me out to the recovery room.

How long did it take? An hour or so, I believe.

I spend three hours in the recovery room, soaking up dextrose and getting my blood pressure checked by a pretty nurse named Lucero. Around three o'clock they take me out; I'm the first to go.

Back to the cell. Feeling miserable but not too miserable to eat a liquid supper. Soon get pilled off to sleep.

The next day is bad. Two shots keep me going. Bronitsky comes in, hoists my leg up and down, says I'm doing all right but he won't let me out of bed until I can lift that leg myself. (He must be bluffing. Good Christ I hope it's a bluff! For I cannot budge the bloody bandaged leg. Can't do it. Can barely twitch the kneecap and it hurts like hell. Three days of semi-paralysis.)

Time collapses.

Friday evening Rita comes, a sweet lovely smiling angel. What a lucky man I am to have such a woman imagine that she loves me. I am overwhelmed with gratitude. And lacerated by regret: I think of the times *she* was in hospital and I neglected her. What a *shit* I have been! Still am?

Saturday she comes twice, bringing me a stack of goodies. Washes my legs and smelly feet. Saturday night and she's on the bed with me, in the darkened room, and we're kissing and I'm. . . .

So now it's four days later and the problem, precisely phrased, is how to get the phucking leg up off the phucking bed. Sweating and cursing, try as I will, I cannot lift that phucking limb.

So — what next?

Monday morning. Doc Brown comes in early, asks me to lift the leg. I can't. He looks worried. Despair in my heart. In a sweat of anguish I wait for Bronitsky and more bad news.

He comes, tells me to relax, lifts my leg in the air. "Hold it there," he *commands*, letting go. I hold it. "Raise it," he says. I raise it. "Lower it slowly," he says. I lower it slowly. "Raise it again," he says. I raise it again. Joy. I say . . .

Joy!

Tuesday. Newcomb, that dirty skunk, has not yet come to see me. I'll remember this. Betrayal. The fake friend. There never was any genuine communion there, or even true communication. Two introverts cannot share anything; two monologues cannot make a dialogue. Haven't I noticed often enough that he never really listens to anything I say? The truth about Newcomb is that he's badly self-obsessed, worse than I. Not much sympathy, imagination or charity there. I feel ashamed — for him. (I did a little for *him* during *his* time of trouble. Ingratitude.)

Wednesday morning. Almost a week since the operation. I can lift the leg at will now, but it still ain't easy. Painful as hell, in fact. And a strange persistent *ache* in my heel. As if someone had been hammering on the bone with an iron mallet.

Gerber appeared last night. Told me the divorce was *off.* I knew that would happen. But he's still keeping bachelor's quarters.

I should get to work on my little book, *Le Soleil Noir* [*Black Sun*].

Boredom, loneliness, melancholy. How long?

Newcomb, that dirty skunk.

Thursday morning. Waiting for the Doc, in *stitches* of anticipation. Perhaps I'll get promoted to crutches today.

Currie was here last night. But no Newcomb. Damn.

Rita's coming this weekend, I hope.

A sick mind in a sick body.

As useless as tits on a motor.

Remember how the old man taught us to play poker? Paid us off for a week's work in the fields, then won it all back Saturday night. Remember? Oh yes.

"What do we have in common?" she asked.

"It's not what we have in common that interests me," he answered, fingering her pudenda.

This bloody hospital: Thronged by hordes of sick old men, dead gaunt hopeless ugly faces, with their repulsive feeble coughing and phlegm-hawking and continual spitting. My room-mate now is a desperate case, one leg already chopped off and the other doomed — poor circulation, dead toes, gangrene. "I need medical attention," he complains. Poor bastard has spent half his life in VA hospitals. He'd be better off dead, I think. But he would not agree. Wants to live. Why?

Sunday evening, May 8, 1960 – Albuquerque

Sorrow and disorder. Rita and the kids launched into the air last night, arrived in New York this afternoon. Problems. Old Witch Berninglaus [their landlady in Taos] is trying to evict my family — by June 1st. Bitch. Of course Rita told *la bruja* to go to hell, in effect. But she agreed to leave by July 1st. The only alternative, apparently, is to pay double rent, $100 a month. Oh the foul old bitch. Greedy old sow. The damned unfairness of it.

Exasperating complications are now created, especially if I get that job at Grand Canyon after all. But what does it matter? These are trifles. Are they? They bring into prominence once more the painful insecurity, instability and difficulty of our nomadic life. We don't even have a hogan. Not even a tent. Impossible to cultivate the soul, the mind, the body, under these painful conditions. As usual, no home, no job, no income, no book. (McGraw-Hill rejects *Black Sun* [not the same novel later published under that title] without a word of explanation.)

September 10, 1960 – Taos

Here we go again. The happy family on the move again. Same tedious old story. Low on money, job-hunting. My book floating around New York collecting rejections (I presume; no word). I'm about to establish Rita and the kids in town (Taos), then go off to Albuquerque, El Paso, Phoenix, Salt Lake City, seeking work and income. Still no home. Still no security. A severe trial for love.

Discipline. Concentration. Patience.

I want to become a man. I want to be a human being. I want to be.

I want to learn to love again. Somewhere between here and childhood I've lost the faculty of free spontaneous passionate love for the world around me. I want to be able to give. I want to give of myself. But if I am nothing? Then I must become. Something.

I want to love. I'm too young to die. I want to know joy again. Not happiness, satisfaction, pleasure or contentment — I want joy. Beyond confusion and doubt and distrust and hate. To respond. To share. To be able to teach. *To be.* Nothingness will come later.

October 25, 1960 – Taos

Hard Times. Still haven't found a job. Down to our last $40. Living in a big house in town now. Will have to borrow money from wife and father in order to survive. Still dreaming of Utah but too cowardly to get up and go.

Half dead as usual, steeped in weariness and melancholy. Very sick. Inert. Unable to start work on anything literary. Unable even to hope anymore. Lonesome. Tired. Defeated. How pitiful I am! Waiting for a miracle. For the moon to rise on the dirty devil. [Apparently a double entendre, referring to Abbey himself as well as the Dirty Devil River in Utah's canyon country.]

November 30, 1960 - Taos

Working now, as a bartender at the Taos Inn. A wretched job, of course, but I endure.

Not writing. Still waiting.

Tired. Self-pity is becoming my major vice.

There hath passed away a glory from the world. You've pissed away your youth . . . all gone. Strangled by marriage and domesticity? Perhaps. Or the rot in the bowels? Perhaps.

My thoughts gather like a dark cloud — beware of lightning!

Art! Art! Art! Art must be my salvation, there is no other, for me there is no other! Art or madness. Art or defeat. Art or nothing.

The man. The artist. The failure.

And then there's alcohol. And marijuana. And peyote. And flight, violence, crime. And if all else fails, the disappearing act. Exit with a flourish, in drama and mystery. *Vanish.*

Suicide — the only sensible solution?

Not yet, pal.

Next time 'round, I'll be a big-assed bird, a buzzard with stinking breath, lazy wings and a heart of stone.

∞

END OF JOURNAL X

Obscurely-remembered sign at fork in roads somewhere in W. Texas:
"Harting's road. Take the other."

Road map: *Due to the author's lapse in journal-keeping, the details of how, and why, Abbey went from tending bar in Taos to park rangering in Arizona sometime between the November 30, 1960, final entry in Journal X and the February 21, 1961, opening entry in Journal XI are unknown. The passages below, however, tell us that he and Rita were once again on the outs, and that she had returned to Hoboken, where her father was dying of cancer. In June, Ed joined her there for yet another reconciliation and remained throughout the course of this journal — hating his office job, aching for the southwestern deserts, and generally feeling blue.*

JOURNAL XI

February 1961 to November 1962

∞

February 21, 1961 – Painted Desert [Petrified Forest National Park, Arizona]

I say, this is a detestable chickenshit sort of place. To work in, I mean. Have applied already to thirty-eight different places, including U.S. Senator Clinton P. Anderson, in hopes of escape.

No word from the wife for ten days. [Divorce] proceedings? Third thoughts? Give the old man another chance, Rita. I'm right for you, you know, though you don't know it yet. Our destiny — to suffer together for another forty or fifty years.

Lee's Ferry. Resident hydrographer. The ideal job? Perhaps. If I can get away for at least a month every summer. Father-as-substitute? Perhaps. Rita? would she live there? Probably not. Great for the kids among them canyons, by the river, except — how far to school? Horseback to the highway, walk home. Great. Page [Arizona] forty-five miles, Kanab [Utah] eighty, Flag[staff, Arizona] 130, Phoenix 250. Not bad. Feasible. Gawd knows *I'd* like it — if only a woman, any woman, almost any woman, was willing to share it with me. Red walls two-thousand-feet high. The sacred river; Colo-rado!

Ah desolation! Isolation! Bereavement! Now I know, now I know, the delicate agony of sorrow. Sorrow.

Now.

Here.

Carpe diem? The day has seized *me*. I am confiscated and heart-busted, alas. Yes.

March 2, 1961 - Painted Desert

The heavy heart. Christ, I can't fight it down. Can't fight it down. Her last letter, yesterday: [Here Abbey quotes Rita saying, in essence, that she feels more in control, more her own person without him.]

Of course she's "emotionally at ease." With me writing her mad, despairing love letters twice a week, working for her, while she has the kids, her studio and — possibly — that phucking eunuch boyfriend. (HATE).

∞

The screenplay for *The Brave Cowboy* — now *Lonely Are the Brave* — by Dalton Trumbo, arrived yesterday. It's very good — the dialog much livelier, heartier, wittier, than my own. More authenticity in the jail and truck scenes. Swift pace, no drag. Follows the original in all essentials. In short, I'm delighted with the play — except for the change of title. I must put up a fight on that.

Where to film? They want my advice. Why not Albuquerque and the Sandias? Yes, but they can't get a truck up in there for the chase scenes. Difficulties. . . .

My new book, *Vogelin's Ranch* [*Fire on the Mountain*], proceeds slowly. Slowly. In fact, it is still only seven pages long, as it was on the end of the day on which I began. Too hard to write, too cruel hard, with this cold heavy defeated heart weighing down my spirit.

I sit at a table in the Desert Inn, me and Scott and his wife and McLenore and his'n and we chat cheerfully; I chat cheerily, they chat cheerfully, about travel and music and cities and mountains and I — I sit there, smiling and talking with death, in, my, heart. Death.

Red eyeballs. Aching nuts.

Oh desolation. Some things, you said, some things would never fail you — like sun and wind and desert colors. Lie. False. That was an untruth.

Do not forsake me oh my darlin' — too late. I'm forsook. And high time too, what? I is had it.

∞

Rejection of *Black Sun* — the biggest publishing blunder since Simon & Schuster rejected the New Testament.

June 23, 1962 - Hoboken

Reconciled with Rita. Future a bright gray. So much for that. Love? We need each other. One more try.

I just quit a horrible job for NYC Welfare. Truly horrible — the paper nightmare.

Rita's father is slowly dying. Her mother is an irritable, guilty, irrational wreck. Our apartment is crawling with cockroaches, the windowsills are coated with black New York soot, everything is layered in grime. Rita herself is sunk in dread and emptiness.

A dream: Rita and I, driving a fat new car, come to a flooded stream crossing. I wade in to ascertain the depth of the water, find it over my head. I sink deeper and deeper, entangled in underwater vines, and know at once that all is lost. And do not care. Down, down, no bottom.

Saw the movie *Lonely Are the Brave* — my movie (*The Brave Cowboy*). Somehow an embarrassing experience, tho it's really an honest and lucid film that follows my book quite closely. Embarrassing for Rita and me, perhaps, because it seemed so personal, intimate, revealing, almost an invasion of privacy. And I was troubled as always by the anachronistic character of the story; a mythical figure — the Cowboy — portrayed in a realistic, contemporary setting. But most of the movie reviews have been very friendly, especially those in *Newsweek* and the *Herald Tribune*.

July 8, 1962 - Hoboken

What are they doing to Rita's father? They will not let him die in peace and dignity, but insist on keeping him hideously half-alive on drugs and mechanical organs. His head in an oxygen tent, a tube in his bowels, intravenous tubes in his feet and wrists (the *Stigmata*). He cannot eat, can barely swallow — but they've kept him suffering for close to six months while he slowly wastes and rots away. And all this in the name of mercy?

Medical science (no longer an art) at its most gruesome. Joe was right in not wanting to go back to the hospital — that hall of horrors. And the double-talking doctors — now promising one thing, now another, and always wrong. Now they've put a tube down his throat and propose to "operate" again, insert a tube direct thru his belly into his stomach, keep him artificially alive for a few more weeks or months.

It's all like some kind of nightmarish experiment: the mad scientist, once a creature of fiction, now lives everywhere, and dominates our lives.

Scapegoat: that's my job. Load your grief and your guilt on the scapegoat, send him out into the wilderness of loneliness.

The presence of death. The Presence — his odor pervades.

Annihilation. Nil. *Nihil.* Nothingization. But not really that; a transformation rather, following decomposition. A Re-Union with the elements of earth and sky. Certainly, the consciousness is lost — how could it be otherwise? The unique individual is gone forever. Only his works — if any — remain behind, and his memory — if any — in the minds of others.

Death shall have no dominion? False. Death is an essential part in the way it is — without death, there could be no new life. Death clears the way for new life, new works, new opportunities.

And yet — and yet — how can we accept this iron scheme when those we love are sacrificed to it? My own death I can acknowledge and accept — but I could never accept the death of my wife — or my sons — or my parents — or my brothers. No, no, the very thought fills me with anger and rebellion and a kind of blind hatred for the forces of nature. And anything less, any lesser emotion, would seem like treason to the human spirit.

The only way to overcome the fear of death is by accepting the necessity and inevitability of death. Those who cannot face and accept the eventual certainty of death are condemned to spend their lives in trembling dread, in spiritual hiding, in moral cowardice, or else to search for the comforting dream of life after death.

Who cannot accept death must fear death.

Out of nothing into nothing. Out of darkness, a day in the sun, into the darkness again. The endless procession of humanity across an endless plain, against the iron sky, the march, the long march. . . .

∞

In the Jungle: Not to break the heart striving to accept, comprehend or master the iron nightmare — the point is to turn your back on it, walk out on it, repudiate it, defy it, resist it, die fighting it.

∞

The New Yorker review of our movie calls it "a shoddy and simple-minded song of hatred for twentieth-century American society."

Exactly! Exactly what I meant the book to be. I am quite pleased by the reviewer's observation. He stated the issues clearly. The only review that did so, so far as I know.

∞

Revisions to *The Brave Cowboy*, or *Lonely Are the Brave* (?): drop the prologue, delete "passel of spicks," change files to hacksaw-blades, Whisky [horse's name] to Rosie, Virginia deer to mule deer, change ending — ambiguify "death" of the Cowboy, delete the word "dead" — etc. — change title? Use part of "Cowboy's Lament" ("Streets of Laredo") for epigraph.

July 16, 1962 - Hoboken

The nightmare here continues, day after day and night after night. Rita grows more frantic and desperate all the time, haggard and pale, and lashes out at me, in revenge — I suppose — for her own feelings of guilt and futility. Her father hangs on, somehow, unable to live and unable to die — the body fights for continued existence, although nothing lies ahead but more and more pain and certain death. Drugged and doped, half-conscious or unconscious — Demerol, Thorazine, morphine — he wanders through a dream-world of — what? — fragments, apparently, from the past, muttering unintelligible words, staring with dazed, half-closed, half-blind eyes at nothing.

Rita insists this shameful and disgusting torture has some Purpose — but what that Purpose is, she cannot say. Except, perhaps, in her eyes, to expose the indifference, or weariness, or cowardice, of all concerned. She cannot understand why I cannot *share* her feelings. It is not enough for her that I respect and admire and honor her devotion — she insists that I share it. I wish I could, if it would make this agony any easier for her — but it would not, and I cannot.

I cannot overcome the feeling of revulsion the spectacle of slow and ugly death inspires in me. To me it seems so wrong, wrong, wrong — something that should never have been allowed to happen in this way. I cannot imagine my own father submitting to such a gruesome end — I cannot imagine myself permitting such an end for him, anymore than I would wish it for myself. Better by far to blast out your brains with a shotgun, to dive off a cliff, to plunge into the river, than inflict upon yourself and upon those who care for you this piecemeal, inchworm, smelly, messy, rotten and horribly prolonged dying. It's unfair not only to the victim, but also to everyone who is forced to attend it. Worst of all, it is a sort of insult to human dignity, to the human spirit.

But who's to blame? At this stage, it makes no difference. The doctors have done their dirty work and washed their hands, left the scene.

September 16, 1962 - Hoboken

Nothing. *Nada. Nihil* & *nihilo.* One sinks. The weight of a nameless doom, something more immediate and strange than physical death, from which the only possible escape seems to be through insanity. Nothing is more real than nothing.

The sound of darkness rising from the heart of the self. Correspondent to the awful silence of the vastness surrounding our world. The inability to reach out and touch — another soul, a god, a spirit, a solid ground. A cavern of despair, where tormenting hope falls, drop by slow drop, out of blackness into blackness, the toneless flat amusical noise. . . .

Only the scientific madmen and the technological idiots are happy in this crowded Hell, busily constructing their complex machines of destruction and futility and meaningless abundance. An absurd redundancy of junk. While the self falls inward, stale and fatigued, emigrating deeper into that desert of the interior where lunatic wolves howl forlorn under the moon-mad eye of the blind horned owl. Dejection stains like an inky poison the white body of my hope, my lost youth, my forfeit honor.

THE TRAP. Can I be a part-time writer? Can I write novels in the evenings, weekends, two-week vacations? Glenway Wescott says *not*, and he's probably right. Especially novel-writing, which requires total daily uninterrupted absorption for at least four or five hours per day. And then after that, preferably some sort of simple physical outdoor activity. That's what I want, what I need, now as much as ever. And who prevents this?

October 5, 1962 – Hoboken

Reminiscence: Early morning snow falling in the desert — the bright vast land — coffee and hotcakes on the stove — all around, golden silence spangled with bird cries — the feeling of something splendid about to occur — a setting for visions, pageants, dreams, cavalry battles — Balanced Rock at Arches, snow-covered mountains beyond and me squatting on sandstone in the clean clear chill air, coffee cup in hand, sun blazing down on snow already beginning to melt from juniper, cliffrose, dead pine, pinnacle, ramada — brief bliss.

That must have been my last year of youth and confidence; ever since, nothing but struggle and terror, the horror in the heart.

And earlier yet: Beyond Cabeza [Prieta National Wildlife Refuge, Arizona] with Muller and Oden, eating tuna from a tin, lost in the badlands, brilliant appetite for life, for every moment, for every detail; the big house in Taos, full of music, fires in fireplaces, snow on the adobe wall; the shack at Malcolm's [the Brown house, Albuquerque]; the isolate lake below Truches Peak high above Santa Fe, the open meadow with the dark wall of fir and spruce on the far side and above a blue-black sky that somehow *vibrates*. . . .

178

∞

New York City is like the war. NYC is like the army. Darkness and tedium. Hurry-up and wait. Huddled masses of humiliated men rushing about in gloom and damp and discomfort, burdened with worries, briefcases in hand, the automatic newspaper to shut out the faces, the horrible suffering faces of their neighbors.

October 20, 1962 – Hoboken

Analysis: I guess, like she says, there's something seriously wrong with me. I'd rather be living in the bright open Southwest than the smoky iron swamps of New York. (You're sick, man.) And I'd rather be doing man's work, with my hands and body, out-of-doors, than sitting in an overheated office all day, necktie-strangulated, with a horde of middle-aged females, pushing papers and pressing dictaphone buttons. (Yes, man, you are in bad shape.)

And not only would I like to live in the Southwest, and work in the air and sunlight, but also I would like to have my wife and my children with me. (Wow! my Gawd, you'd better see a doctor quick!)

And this, none of it, as it might be for other men, is for me an empty fantasy, not at all. For me and my family, such a place, such a job, such a way of life were all within the realm of concrete actuality, all within easy reach. We could have done it. But we didn't — the boys and I had to give it all up. And why? Yes, why? (And she wonders at my bitterness.)

The subway passes with a *blast* of *iron!* Gawd, what could be more heart-crushing than those terrible New York subways . . . absolutely so dismal, bleak, gray, hopeless: Abandon all hope ye who enter here. Nothing so ugly could be in any way good, or even useful. The means have again destroyed the end desired. Nothing good can emerge from this iron wasteland.

There are some things a man must stand and face. And there are some he'd be a fool not to flee. Perhaps it requires more courage to do what you really want to do than what you believe you have to do. But what do you really want? Yes, you know, you're sure you know. But — when choices have to be made — what then? What then, brother?

∞

The necktie, sign of servitude. Tight white collar, symbol of slavery, badge of bondage. The uniform: tight sharp shoes, tight dark suit, tight-furled umbrella, strangling collar and narrow tie, tight little narrow-brimmed hat, black reticule (dispatch or briefcase), etc. The man in the gray flannel straitjacket.

October 30, 1962 – Hoboken

My love, my enemy. How can I love she who is my most immovable enemy? Yet how can I hate she who is (aside from the children) the only person on earth I love? Bittercruel insoluble heartcracking dilemma. No matter what I do — I lose. No way out. An absolutely impossible situation.

November 9, 1962 – Hoboken

The almost irresistible urge to violence which comes to me at times — the lust to break, smash and destroy things, to hurl chains through windows, fling a brick at the TV's eye, crumple automobiles into lamp-posts, rip doors off their hinges, push walls aside, overturn office desks and toss typewriters and dictaphones out fifth-story windows, to heap all papers, forms, letters, documents, photostats, manuals, booklets, phone books into a pile, drench with gasoline and ignite, to smash traffic lights, cut cables and wires (the nervous system of syphilization), uproot mailboxes and fireplugs and phone booths, bust through the glass barrier, level all billboards. . . .

Oh God, there is a fearful tornado of Nothingness spinning in my soul. Raging against my own inner deadness — I have cut myself off from so much, I can barely reach my own children, my own wife, I truly love no one. I live in a vast solitude. . . .

∞

Most of us have no more *awareness* of the grandeur, beauty, mystery, complexity, vitality, form and infinite possibilities of the world of earth and space, than the ant has of the landscape beyond the denuded perimeter of his anthill. Why? Because most of us are exclusively preoccupied with the human sphere only — or not even that much — obsessed with the interhuman, the personal, subjective, internal region. . . .

∞

All formal religion is based on fear: some on fear of death (Occidental), others on fear of life (Oriental) and all to a large degree on fear of both.

November 14, 1962 – Hoboken

Autobiography: Perhaps I, like Boswell, am neither neurotic nor psychotic but a type of psychopath: "intact intelligence, defective superego, self-destructive tendencies, social maladaptation, unpredictable behavior, intense narcissism, weak ego — this type often very gifted, even brilliant and creative" (From the book *Great Men*). Certainly the description suits, satisfies, even pleases me — I am particularly eager to accept the final terms of the diagnosis: like any other psychopath, I'm perfectly content to be sick if I can also be clever.

Self-portrait: Inescapable feelings of inferiority, incompetence, helplessness; terrifying lack of self-assurance; almost always stiff, awkward, constrained, ill-at-ease in the presence of others; slavishly lustful — all pretty women excite me; an inclination to silliness; spineless compliance with the desires of those around me; in most things a follower rather than a leader; no leadership ability at all — teaching, for example, wrecks frightful strain on my nerves; cowardly — inclined to avoid any antagonistic confrontation with others; dull, reserved, apathetic, slow-witted.

November 20, 1962 – Hoboken

Going under, Abbey, going under, down down, vicious spiraling downward circle, piling bitterness upon bitterness, hate upon hate, grudge upon grudge, losing your wife, losing your friends, may even lose your children. Better stop, Abbey, better stop. A change of heart, a change in outlook — relax a little, accept a little more, don't be so in deadly earnest. Don't become a monomaniac.

∽

END OF JOURNAL XI

I did not come to solve anything.
I came here to sing
and for you to sing with me.
— Neruda

Flute

Desert sunrise song

Road map: *"What a life. From Hoboken to Sunset Crater to Santa Fe to Death Valley to Santa Fe to Hoboken." This entry summarizes Abbey's frenetic peregrinations during the forty-four months documented by Journal XII. To complete the litany, add Las Vegas, Moab, and California.*

The most significant event of this period, a knee-jerk act for which Ed never forgave himself, was the desertion of his family in Las Vegas. Soon after, Rita filed for divorce, while Ed, now in his mid-thirties, flung himself headlong into the romance that would lead promptly to his third marriage.

JOURNAL XII

December 1962 to July 1966

∞

December 5, 1962 – Hoboken

"THIS IS WHAT YOU SHALL DO " [Walt Whitman]: Love the earth and sun and the animals. Stand up for the stupid and crazy. Take off your hat to no man.

On Literary Criticism:

So-called American literary criticism is a hoax and a fraud, because it makes a pretense of objective judgment in a field where only subjective preferences are valid. *It has no authority or validity whatsoever.* The only reason it appears to wear an air of authority is because it is inculcated through years of public schooling and because the opinion of any given critic is usually shared by all other professional critics. This near-unanimity does not give the critic's evaluation any weight: it merely demonstrates the strong herd-instinct of the literary professors, who tend to move in unison like a flock of starlings or a school of fish. Their erratic flights reflect merely the transience and mutability of literary fashions.

The men who make a good living writing about the work of their betters would actually be more appropriately occupied in the designing of women's apparel. Otherwise, failing this, they should stick to their classrooms and not presume to impose their private opinions upon the public under the pretense of established, authoritative judgment.

The professors tend to support one another not only out of "professional ethics," but because frank and open dispute among them would expose their game for what it really is, i.e., private preferences of taste and/or personal worldviews imposed upon the captive audiences of classrooms and a gullible public under the masquerade of a consensus of established evaluation.

This writer can testify from personal experience that to object to this dogma by questioning, for example, the greatness of Jane Austen or Henry James as a graduate student in a standard university English department, is to bring upon oneself not only the penalties of the grading system and the scorn of the professors, but also, and consequently, to jeopardize one's chances of an academic career.

In the field of literature, as in politics, we can only follow the democratic dictum of "one man, one vote." When the critic dislikes a certain author, let us say, because of personal animosity, or disputes the author's point of view, he is on legitimate ground. But when he pretends to pass judgment on the overall worth of an author's work on certain canons of literary aesthetics, he is perpetrating a fraud and a hoax.

If we allowed these people to meddle too much in literature, then all literature would soon consist of nothing but the careful, cautious, correct work of such as Austen and James.

January 19, 1963 - Hoboken

Another wet cold gray day in the Megalopolis — typical!

Gloom deep in my heart, deep, as I go once more through the dreary familiar routine of filing job applications with the Park Service, various county welfare departments, all that tedious crap all over again.

"The Writer"
On a cold sea, empty of life,
Appeared
A solitary craft.

The book *Fire on the Mountain* has been a complete flop, of course — so far not even a reprint sale has been made. Oh well, what's the use, what's the use? Almost thirty-six years old and still struggling, still unable to establish some sort of sane rational way of living.

The book racket wouldn't mean a damn, of course, if I were free to live the kind of life I enjoy: if I were doing what I like, living how and where I please, I would not give another thot for the rest of my life to the literary racket. I might not even ever write another line. There are, after all,

several things more important than art. Like a pine tree on a mountainside. Like a juniper in the red desert. Like air and sunlight.

> *A simile is like an understanding*
> *Smile of love—*
> *warm, deepening*
> *And full of grace.*

∞

Projected [books to write]:
*Don Coyote, The Hermit of Slumgullion Pass, The Tower and the Abyss, The Good
Life, The Mine on the Dirty Devil, Solitaire in the Desert* (a journal), *The Border
Town, The Wooden Shoe Gang* (or) *The Monkey Wrench Mob* (a novel about the
"Wilderness Avenger" and his desperate band; sabotage and laughter and
wild wild fun).

∞

The significance of the desert:
  In the desert, a man comes directly upon a world that is *not* a projection
of human consciousness, a world that has *not* been interpreted by art or
science or myth, that bears no trace of humanity on its surface, that has no
apparent connection to the indoor human world: In the desert one comes
in direct confrontation with the bones of existence, the bare imcompre-
hensible absolute *is-ness* of being. Like a temporary rebirth of childhood,
when all was new and wonderful.
  Indoors and Outdoors: The human and the non-human. Privacy and
space. The manmade and the natural. All that is the product and projection of man and his mind, vs. all that precedes, underlies and surrounds
man and his mind. To go truly Outdoors is to escape for a while the
narrow limits of previous human experience (the cultural apparatus) and
to enter a world that is new, different, much greater, and of course largely
incomprehensible. A church, e.g., is a place in which to *hide* from the real
world. That's why they're so comforting.

∞

Pommes de terre ("Earth Apples"):
  The plow, the raw September earth, the massive-haunched mighty-
hoofed bay clomping and farting down the furrow, Father holding the
plow, my brother the reins and me with a sack, following, gathering the
fruits of the overturned soil, the earth apples:
  Richly abundant, brown fat potatoes, thick as stars appearing like mir-
acles out of the barren, weedy, stony patch, thousands of big hefty solid

spuds, bushel after bushel, a hundred bushels per acre, a wealth of treasures from the earth.

How the hand and eye delighted in that harvest, how gladly and freely we dragged our bulging gunnysacks to the wagon . . . a wagonful of potatoes! Dark brown, crusted with dirt, soil, earth, cool to the touch, good to eat even raw; we plowed the shabby field and turned up nuggets, plenty, abundance, more than we needed, riches unimagined!

May 29, 1963 – Sunset Crater [National Monument, Arizona]

Back in the West again, rangering again, lost and bewildered again as always, a bit lonely, but the air and light are exhilarating, the desert landscape almost as marvelous as ever before.

The brave, sweet, heartbreaking beauty of all wild and lonely things.

Wife and kids should be here in a couple of weeks, if I can rely on Rita's latest letter. She put me through the wringer again, she did; kept me guessing for two months and ain't through yet, neither, I guess, since she plans to visit her eunuch-saint in Taos on the way. More anguish, heartache and uncertainty for all concerned. But that seems to be what she likes — drama.

I am bitter, even though I understand that this weary game is partly my own fault. Perhaps, if I had been a good husband when she needed me . . . perhaps. But I wasn't . . . and now she's getting her revenge, grinding it in, and there's nothing I can do but endure it and hope for eventual good luck.

September 17, 1963 – Sunset Crater

Comrade, regret no more, regret no more, leave off these vain and foolish and painful regrets based more on *machismo* ego than anything else. Your seeming failure that bright sweet morning (Bastille Day!) was a liberal, a generous, a considerate failure — you could not take what was not willingly given. And gratitude rewarded you, and the spoken word of love, remember? (What bullshit!)

Love = Evil. Four-letter words: love, hate, evil, life, fear, fire, Gawd.

Gawd only knows, nothing in my own life has created as much misery as love — or my sorry attempts at love. What a sweet relief it would be to acquire a heart of stone, carborundum, or cast-iron, and never again feel a twinge of emotion for another human face . . . or form. (Love first begins as a prickling sensation in the hair of the balls.)

Love is essential? Yes. But sufficient? No. On all sides we hear this hysterical demand for love — for love! — FOR LOVE! — cries of panic and desperation — *liebe! liebe! liebe!* — like a herd of bleating sheep. They cling together in couples, out of terror — and wonder why love turns to hate, why marriage is not enough and fails. Aye! It's community we need lads, society, and not merely love.

May 26, 1964 – Hoboken

Arrived here the first of January. Back at work with Welfare. Finished *Down the River* [not the essay collection later published under that title] on May 20, 1964. *The Wilderness* rejected by all concerned. Reconciled with Rita and the kids; the future looks hopeful. Planning to write a play next. But how? On what? Who? (*Love in Hoboken*)

June 18, 1964 – Hoboken

Brother Bill is here on a visit, after two years with the Peace Corps in the Philippines, bringing with him a little Philippina — a sweet cute charming child named Vicki.

∞

The buzzard: ugly, skinny, solitary, cruel, indolent, lazy, contemplative, remote and aloof, soaring, utterly selfish and totally irresponsible, hungry, cowardly, ragged in poverty, lousy, essentially stupid but with intellectual pretensions, ridiculous, absurd, peripheral, proud — and always alone! How well we know thee, brother!

September 3, 1964 – Hoboken

Bastards, they're still a tryin' to sink me. *Down the River* rejected by Dial ("diffuse and meaningless"), Grove (no comment), Scribners ("too simple, too easy, tedious, piled-up lists, Kovalchick's tedious fundamentalism, values at odds beneath all the raucousness and tired reductions, banal, etc."), and McGraw-Hill ("most disappointing, a good writer gone badly wrong, the less said the better").

The Wilderness also being kicked around. Even my agent, Don Congdon, doesn't like either book. I'll think about this next: *Confessions of a Literary Failure* — a frank and detailed account of my experiences as a writer. (*Vendetta.*) All the ups and downs, the cruel disappointments, the gyps, the rejections, the ravages wrought on family life, the writer's envy and jealousy, with reminiscences of other writers I have known (Stegner, Creeley, Mailer, Eastlake, Granat, Nieman, Woolf, etc.), agents, editors, fans, public, etc.

October 30, 1964 – Hoboken

Jesus! Midnight in Hoboken. What's a man to do? Girls. Places. Books I want to write. Old friends I may never see again. The confusion and regret and anger and bitterness and dull despair forever stirring inside my own head . . . little dust devils in an empty cavern. *Gotta get to work.* Rotting away in passive torpor, rotting away, the very veins and muscles of my limbs cracking, aching, through dis-use far too long continued. My god, I have too long been city-pent. My own life is slipping through my fingers like . . . water.

Rita, sweet and tender, trying so hard to love me yet doubtful, fearful, uncertain. And with good reason. Despite my earnest intentions I remain as restless, bored, discontented, irresponsible and unreliable as ever. The buzzard. Red dust of Utah.

My father. Those long vine-covered hills in my dreams, where smoky birds whistle tunes older than my father. My father, back from Idaho with a truck full of rocks, writing letters to the editor again, confirming enemies.

I don't know what the hell I'm doing here. Do you? (What *am* I doing here?) Bitterness and bitter frustration — not enough money, not enough sex, no real friends, no *work*. Out of work. I miss light on rock, the sun on my bones, the smell of a sweating horse, the bright thirsty air of the high plateaus.

My god I'm homesick. And lonesome. (So nothing has changed? Nothing ever changes.) Corruption and cynicism are boring into my soul. Lee's Ferry. Dandy Crossing. Sunset Crater. North Rim. Pariah. Ah, the places, the wonderful places I have known. And the girls, the sweet unbelievably lovely girls. . . . The universal discontent.

Thermite, dynamite, sugar in the gas tank. Falling billboards, falling in flames. D.A.C. — direct action committee. What else can we do? Oh God, what's the use? What's the use of complaining? Your self-piety and self-indulgence make me sick. More driveling *à la bouche*, comrade. Near the summit now. Looking back, the rearguard. Over the hump, soon, and down the far side. Into the darkness.

October 31, 1964 – Hoboken

Caseworker with the Hudson County Welfare Office. Relations with Rita are very good at the present. Plans call for a move to the San Diego area as soon as a job can be secured. San Diego — a compromise between Moab and Hoboken — almost the only place in the whole West where *both* Rita and I are willing to try to make a home. (Frankly, I'd sooner go to Australia.)

So be it. We'll do it. At least the great Al Sarvis is there [a college professor friend and model for the fictional characters Doc Sarvis in *The Monkey Wrench Gang* and Ballantine in *Black Sun*], and [San Diego is] adjacent the Baja wilderness, a thousand miles of primitive Mexico. Not to mention other obvious attractions. Into the hotbed of American Know-Nothingness. Oh well, what the hell.

What a life. From Hoboken to Sunset Crater to Santa Fe to Death Valley to Santa Fe to Hoboken. And the girls. And poor mad DePuy [John, a western landscape artist Ed met while living in Taos in the fifties; see "My Friend Debris" in *Down the River*], crafty Creeley, noble Malcolm Brown, remote Ralph Newcomb, wild and lost Hugh Hudson. The fabulous wonders of Grand Canyon and the Kofa Mountains and Pariah and Pipe Spring (oh loveliest of oases!) and Zion on a misty evening and the Nevada desert and North Wash and Furnace Creek and Telescope Peak and White Canyon, New Mexico, and White Canyon, Utah, etc. etc., and her white blonde naked moonlit body running embracing and seeing the blue!

L'homme sensuel. It seems to me I am more obsessed than ever by sex. Perhaps this is an illusion. But the desire, the need is there. Surely half my waking hours (and much of my dream time) are spent in meditation upon sex. Lust rides me like a monkey, panting in my ear continually; hardly ever a moment's rest.

Well . . . it's the fate of most men, I suppose. Aldous Huxley, quote: "I have never met a man who was *not* obsessed by sex." Wide-ranging lust, which craves every young pretty female within sight as object and prey. How boring is monogamy. How can any honest man deny it? Never get enough. More than anything else, one desires variety. Variety. Novelty. Fresh young stuff everywhere I look and none available. Maddening, maddening.

This cruel city, perhaps the only great city on earth where this male need is not recognized and accommodated. No wonder so many men are driven into camp — queer — homo. All these lovely girls with that valuable article between their legs; they won't share it easily, by god, and they mean — if not deliberately — to make men sweat for its possession.

November 4, 1964 – Hoboken

Johnson wins in a landslide.

My life is meaningless to me. How can I seize it, grasp it, view it clearly and as a whole? — before it's all gone? Oh Christ, we've been through this before. Coming fully alive? — Gawd, who knows. How hopeless it seems, after all. And me nearing forty years. Armageddon. Judgment Day. Dreams, idle foolish dreams, sick with longing and nostalgia. That's me.

Out the window and whaddya see? That awful gray sick dull Hoboken scene.

Still full of crap, comrade; you're leaking again.

Peace is hell, said Patton. Bloody peace, said Churchill. Good Christ, what's a man to do? Haven't got a can of beer. Or tobacco for my pipe. Lee's Ferry, the Navajos hangin' around the beer joint near the bridge. Vermilion Cliffs beyond loomin' two-thousand feet into the Utah blue. Looking up. Unscalable cliffs, cape after cape. The dark buzzard there, wings in scrawny dihedral, floating without effort on currents of hot silent air. Silence. The silence. The terrible silence. Nature, hostile or indifferent? Or neither — supportive and sustaining rather, bosom of our mother. Earth Mother — and Daddy a long-connected bolt of lightning, striking down from sky to tree to bosom soil.

It seems to me that yesterday I had an idea. Not today. Where oh where did it go?

∞

Visited the old folks at home last weekend, the long long drag through the raggedy woody hills of Pennsylvania and the rural Allegheny slums. Back to ye olde lonesome briar patch. My poor sad rejected mother and father, their sad and lonesome lives.

Mother so terribly thin, pale, tense, constricted, a soul in a straitjacket, worn-out by overwork and over-worry. Why the hell can't she unbend a little, relax, take it easy? (Why can't I?)

And the old man, moaning over his minor physical afflictions as if he were Job reincarnate — a bone or calcium spur in one heel, hemorrhoids, a bit of the grippe, boredom and fatigue. Says he can't work more than two hours a day, tho he's only sixty-four, for chrissake. Has nothing to do, don't know what to do. Complains about the neighbors cheating him. (Life has cheated him, and vice versa.) Yet he still retains much of the old charm and good humor, can still be gravely handsome in certain light, certain angles. So bitter and resentful, with much justice, of course. Yet he does nothing about it. The martyr complex. In this he is almost as bad as Mother — the worst type of martyr.

Gawd how I dislike these domestic martyrdoms! Why don't they *do something?* Sacrifice, sacrifice, but always in self-pity, resentment, bitterness. Ah, the decay and bitterness of old age. Old man Postlewaite, e.g., so senile now he couldn't even recognize me; ninety-two years old. Yeah, that's what we have to look forward to: decomposition and deepening bitterness and childish bad temper. Christ, the bore it is! Better to die in middle age, with a sudden sweet violence. A prophecy of my own death, *con brio:* it will be sudden, violent and sweet, under the sun, on rock, with cousin buzzard hangin' in the air nearby. Smell of broken flint. The ancient chaos and stone.

∞

French: Of all forms of sexual perverseness, the most obscene is chastity.

Don Juan: How can I be true to one without being false to all the others?

November 20, 1964 – Hoboken

Remember Jerome, Arizona? The big old pipe organ in the old church? You bet. And way out in the valley, the red ramparts of Sycamore Canyon? Oh God . . . and me sitting on the railing there, Jerome, above the abyss, pretending to fall backward, feet hooked snugly behind the lower rail — help me, Claire, I'm falling! Crossing the bridge on the Verde: I love you, she said. And the grim journey to Perkinsville and Perkinsville to Williams, gas gage signifying empty? But we made it. Anyhow. Is all the best now in the past?

The Grand Canyon hours: Those too were bitter ones. In June of '61, with a heart heavy as lead, Josh and I, struggling up the trail toward the North Rim, watch a lone man with a string of pack mules ambling down the trail, the man a-whistling some cheerful tune, all the way down — down, down, he goes, alone but quietly content, down into the great canyon, diminishing to a point along the meandering switch-backs and my gawd how I envied his peace of soul!

Two years later, I'm on a lookout on the South Rim with Rita and the kids, minutes after a fateful secret farewell, and again with heart black with despair, I'm almost ready to vault the rail and leap into the chasm, so bleak and empty seemed my life. Yet again, a few months later, I'd be wallowing in luxurious good fortune, followed again by loneliness, forsook and desperate — a mad thief barreling across the bulging continent to my hostile spouse — ice in my heart.

November 28, 1964 – Hoboken

I think of my friends: Ralph Newcomb at Coos Bay in his little shack in the woods, with his wife and kids and goat and chickens, his fishing boat and beat-up truck, and the book about the war he's been trying to write for some six or seven years. Poor Scotty [Mrs. Newcomb], teaching and hating it, and poor Ralph feeling guilty but not doing anything about it.

There on that rain-drenched coast, mostly alone except for the animals, how does he go on? What does he feel. Think about?

I think of DePuy at that fairy-tale villa in Ranchos de Taos, finally sundered from wife and kids after almost two years of struggle. Now living with his old man, his father, the two alone in that lovely place. Though apparently he now has a girlfriend. (The lucky fellow!) And he, John, still painting his romantic landscapes — I presume — and hiking over the hills of Taos. Last month to Navajo Mountain and Rainbow Bridge. What will become of him? Poor mad John — a good painter, a good friend, a wonderful hiking and drinking companion.

(What will become of me? Suffocating with boredom here on the bosom of my family, but scared to death to try to leave.)

And the Great Al Sarvis, most beautiful of friends but also, in his way, absurd and desperate. Now teaching art at San Diego, fighting and struggling with his wife no doubt, drawing, fucking, etc. One hopes.

HOW DO THEY BEAR IT? The tragic loneliness. This separation, over and over. HOW DO I BEAR IT? And why do I suffer so from this fatal envy that imagines their lot any better than mine? And why do I want so much to plunge again into that course which has brought me so much anguish, loneliness, guilt and grief before?

Friendship's a rare and elusive gift in this shattered, chaotic, frantically moving society of ours.

The Problem of Leisure: What would I do if I had more time?
— Write more books
— Build a house
— The outdoors: hiking, camping, exploration, nature study
— Read and study: literature, philosophy, science, history
— Music: flute, harmonica, piano, songs
— Travel
— Politics
— Contemplation, meditation and *prayer*
— And . . . *la chasse.*

March 14, 1965 – Hoboken

Events: Got fired from the welfare job after a nasty argument with Stapleton the witch. Got a job offer from Las Vegas but do not intend to accept. May go with the Park Service this summer. Received a contract from McGraw-Hill for two books: (1) *A Desert Journal*, and (2) *Lives*, or,

American Lives — a study of welfare clientele and their actual way of life; $2,500 advance now, another $2,500 on delivery of acceptable manuscripts — two-year deadline but hope to finish both within a year.

More terrible, bitter, lacerating quarrels with Rita because I wish to take a river trip in May. Naturally, spoils everything. But I am determined not to endure any more of her hysterical bullying; no more.

I have so much to do and I sit here doing nothing. Two books to write. Letters to write. Plans and decisions to make. A wife, a girlfriend, old friends to placate and touch. (Abbey, you treacherous bastard, always playing your old game of both ends against the middle!) No wonder I'm going stark naked insane.

Abbey on his serial polygamy: "I guess I'm not the domesticated type."

June 2, 1965 - Las Vegas, Nevada

"Song from the City"

There is a columbine that blooms
by a natural spring;
it has the brave, heartbreaking beauty
of any wild and lonely thing.
Under a desolate sky, far up
on the mountainside, the snow
is melting now and the cold torrents
rush downward, thru the alpenglow
where the rock wren sings
with the heartbreaking beauty
of all wild and lonely things.
Evening smoke rises, uninhibited,
from a campfire. A bird calls,
still, alone, in the clear dark.
My heart falls. My heart falls.

I finally saw the fabled Wolf Hole (nothing), and Toroweap (almost everything): What a refuge! What a place to hide: the rosy pink sandstone, the tall graceful agave stalks about to bloom (curved like shepherds' crooks), the flowers — purple four o'clock, prickly pear, cliffrose, yucca, paintbrush, penstemon, primrose, larkspur, mallow, asters, golden crown-beard, moonflowers (sacred datura) and others I could not identify; the clear cool rain-pools in the shallow basins on the plateau's edge; the cliffs and the rich clouds and the magic distances; and of course the great abyss itself, three-thousand feet down, down, down.

No word from my loves. They've abandoned me to my harsh and sterile fate . . . nobody's fault but my own, of course — my cowardice. One must at times have *the courage to be cruel.* I haven't — and thus have made the worst of the situation, causing confusion and heartbreak everywhere, including within myself, if I have a self.

I remain obsessed by sex. An overpowering lust is driving me mad — everywhere I look I see only ripe young female flesh — cunt, ass, thigh, knee, swelling breast and soft lips parted to receive my torpedo of love — ah! As the Scotch say, the standing cock hath no conscience.

July 14, 1965 – Moab, Utah

Bolted. Left wife and kids and job for exile in the desert. Am I mad? Literally, clinically insane? Must be — no other explanation is possible. Such incredible folly is otherwise impossible to explain. My only hope now is Judy [Pepper] — good sweet delightful Judy — only she can save me now from the solitude worse than death. (But perhaps suicide is the only sensible solution?)

Park rangering at Arches again — reliving the past — retracing my steps — I've traveled a complete circle — My God I really *am* lost! Rita is now at last divorcing me, of course — can't blame her one bit. Aye! My bitter fate!

∞

I must, simply must get to work on the book. No other possible cure for these terrible blues that oppress me — oh this awful burden of grief and regret and guilt and remorse! Canst thou not minister to a mind diseased, and with some sweet oblivious antidote pluck from the memory the roots of sorrow?

No. No sir.

Then throw physic to the dogs, I'll none of it!

The ultimate solution: down the river. Cataract Canyon. Into the Maze. No more Abbey — never seen again. Ah! what a romantic exit — and why not? After all, thirty-eight years . . . I've had enough, my share, outlived Keats Byron Shelley Crane Thomas Lawrence and a million others. Exit smiling. But — *one good book.*

Terrible but true: We live in the kind of world where courage is the most necessary of virtues — for without courage, all other virtues are useless.

July 24, 1965 - Arches

Camping out: My god I need a grill, a little grill for my fire. A pretty little doe-eyed dove-soft duck of a grill to take some of the heat out of my infernal internal fires. Plutonic love.

All the pretty girls — Abbey's downfall, his destruction. And his only regret — the ones he missed. (Judy, come! Quickly!)

I wish my arms were around you now and your legs around me and my tongue down your throat and your fingernails in my back and my hands on your bottom and your hair in my eyes and your nipples on my chest and my et cetera in yours, et cetera. And my feet against the wall. Day-dreams.

Judy: I've become a convert to Judyism.

September 8, 1965 - Arches

August flood: the [Colorado] river comes down today a rich dark orange-red, like the color of tomato soup.

Silver-blue sand sage streaming in the wind. Hosts of jocund sunflowers.

September 9, 1965 - Arches

At times I am caught in a terrible impatience: Why should I put up with the second-rate? Why tolerate bores? Why give even courteous attention to all these dull pigheaded swine who stifle me with their banalities, crush me under their heavy passive benevolence, smother me with courtesy and kindness and empty goodwill. Yeah! Good swill to all men! Piss on earth! *Why?*

As Celine said, "I piss on you all, from a considerable height."

∽

A woman said this to me, apropos of whoring: "No girl can be a swill-can to all the world and still retain her self-respect." Perhaps. No doubt. But how about the courtesan, the geisha, the call girl — all who are selective in their customers?

September 20, 1965 - Denver airport

Taking off for NYC and my sweetheart, my love, my one and only honey-pot, Judy Pepper. My God how I've missed her — it's been a long and lonesome five weeks. Wet snow and slush on the runway, the sky socked in — but we'll be climbing to 33,000 feet, *above it all.*

Here we go — the great surge of power — the rain on the windowpane streaks by in thinner and thinner, strained and tenuous lines. Up into the clouds — all is whiteness around us now, white on white, growing brighter, brighter, like the ascent to heaven. Absolutely nothing can be seen outside except this opaque WHITENESS — pure evil? pure good? Still brighter as we soar higher — distant rush of air, thin whine of the jet engines in our rear. Now I can see the sun, coming closer — Judy, my sweet, my darling, I'm coming, coming, coming, in a great crescendo of an orgasm, at six-hundred mph. Wow!

Frivolous question: Judy my sweet: Will you still love me when I am bald and fat and old and cold and impotent?

America's obsession with sex? Studies of monkeys reveal that their sexual activity is much greater in cages than in the jungle; in other words, captivity leads to sex as compensation for lack of liberty — no doubt the same principle applies to human beings. (cf. *African Genesis*)

Georgia, USA: Where they sell "white chocolate."

The Mormons of Utah:

— Joseph Smith and his two-ton gold tablets.

— Heroic Brigham Young with his seventeen wives.

— Their agrarian socialism, communal feeling, healthy and sane way of life. A good way of life.

— Beautiful sandstone-block homes, lovely farms.

The religion is ridiculous, but no more so than Christianity with its heavenly orders, fire and damnation. Buddhism with its life negation. The sick fecundity of Hinduism.

"The Mormon Constitution is divinely inspired." What about the amendment and its subsequent repeal — apparently God changed his mind.

Liberal friends look down their noses, but should they? There is much of value in the Mormon feeling for decentralization and home rule . . . 3.2 beer, however, is unforgivable.

Lord's Anointed: the flaw in the anointment.

Yes, I dislike Communists as much as everyone else. I mean, I dislike them as much as I dislike everyone else. As far as I can see, a Communist is no better than a Christian. ("Smug as a Christian holding three aces.")

Nor will you find deep thinkers on mountaintops.

Distant thunder heard on a hot still afternoon from the Needles [Can-

yonlands National Park]: Eliot's *Wasteland* always sounded good to me —
his dry silent desert is more appealing than any gilded Dantean heaven . . .
I mean, I liked the poem for the wrong reasons — and disliked it for the
right ones.

June 16, 1965–[?]

Art of the arty novel: The Problem —
To say as little as possible in the greatest possible number of words.
(I.e. — James, the cathedral built around a piece of string — and Son-
tag — and Updike.)

ORDEAL OF A WRITER —

In Professor Stegner's creative writing workshop, Stanford, 1958, someone from the Ford Foundation asked for suggestions on what to do with
their millions. Abbey said, "Why (the fuck) don't they give it all back to the
people they stole it from in the first place?"

September, 1965 – Boulevard East, New York City

Divorced August 25, 1965 — Married October 16, 1965. (Idiot!)

July 1, 1966 – Mt. Harkness, California

In a fire lookout tower 8,045 feet above sea level in Lassen Volcanic
National Park, all alone with my new and lovely and delightful wife Judy
P. Writing the book in the middle of the great mountains and magnificent
trees (incense cedar and sugar pine) of northern California. Page 191 of
Desert Solitaire — two-thirds completed thank Gawd.
After this, the Welfare Mess book (*Scum of the Earth?*), and then — yes,
then what? The Great Novel at last! But which one?

Ordeal of a Writer: Secrets of a Literary Bum:
— Always throw in a little or a lot of rubbish in your book, so the
publisher's editor will have something to cut out, something to
do — otherwise, he'll try to cut something important and give the
author a bad time.
— Editors and agents are usually wrong: axiomatic.
— Detail financial rewards, very interesting to neophytes. (I owe
McGraw-Hill $2,500. No wonder I can't write.)
— The book as a paper club to beat enemies over the head with.
— All art is didactic.

— The problem novel: What other kind is there?
— Only two kinds of novels: good ones and bad ones.
— The story of a movie: *Lonely Are the Brave* and how I got screwed
 . . . change of title, consultant, bit player, failure of Pocketbooks,
 Dodd-Mead to reprint.
— The ruination of marriage and family life by literary ambition; the
 torture of mothers and children and parents-in-law.
— Beginnings, correspondence, contact with other writers (Stegner
 and Stanford).
— Reflections on the star system: best-sellers — roulette-wheel deal;
 sour-grape juice.
— The endless search for the right job, for economic independence,
 for the time and freedom to write.
— Interviews with editors, publishers, agents; royalty reports; total
 sales of each book, advances, contracts.
— A writer's worst enemies are other writers.

Love: Is it this or that individual whom we love, or something larger, greater, more general? The *fact* that our love moves freely from person to person, sometimes including several at once, seems to suggest that love is an *internal* force demanding expression and not simply a response to an attractive object. The love of a man for a maid is really his love of beauty, of life, of the world. (E.g., one will do as well as another.)

I've had bad luck with natural disasters: Have never been in an earthquake, flood or legitimate forest fire; missed the last eruption of Vesuvius by one year; and the only time a tornado ever passed through my hometown, I wasn't there. Etc. Missed Hurricane Betsy in the Everglades by only two months. Born a few years too late for the Johnstown flood.

On taking sides: Why have I always, instinctively, immediately, in every sort of social conflict, sympathized with the underdogs, the working or peasant class, the lower, weaker or oppressed side? Why do I tend to identify with them and not with the others — the powerful and rich, the established, authoritative, dignified caste?

Why? Well, partly the Socialist heritage bequeathed me by my father — because I come from the peasant class myself, and am still a member of the outsiders. Partly a sense of natural justice: let each pig have its turn in the trough. But mostly, because I *hate* the rich and powerful, and those who support *them* while not *of* them — servile and sycophantic natures: the servants, lackeys, court jesters. They I despise more than any other.

OASIS — A home in the Desert:

Anywhere? Yes, most anywhere — Nevada, New Mexico, Utah, Arizona, eastern California or SW Colorado — just so it's *outback,* way out, beyond all pavements and power lines, out of sight, sound and smell of my fellowmen.

Half for Judy and me, half for Josh and Aaron. Let Josh help with the design — he's got his heart set on a *home* (poor kid) — with M. Brown as architectural consultant.

Design of the house will depend on location, lay of the land, climate, times of occupancy and the nature of native building materials — rock, adobe, wood, beer cans, etc. . . .

[A parenthetic note has been added here in feminine script: "Dear Ed: Indoor toilet very necessary. —J.P."]

July 23, 1966 – Mt. Harkness

Do I seem to write only of the surfaces of things? Yet, it seems to me that only surfaces are of ultimate importance — the touch of a child's hand in yours, the taste of an apple, the embrace of friend or lover, sunlight on rock and leaf, music, the feel of a girl's skin on the inside of her thigh, the bark of a tree, the plunge of clear water, the face of the wind.

END OF JOURNAL XII

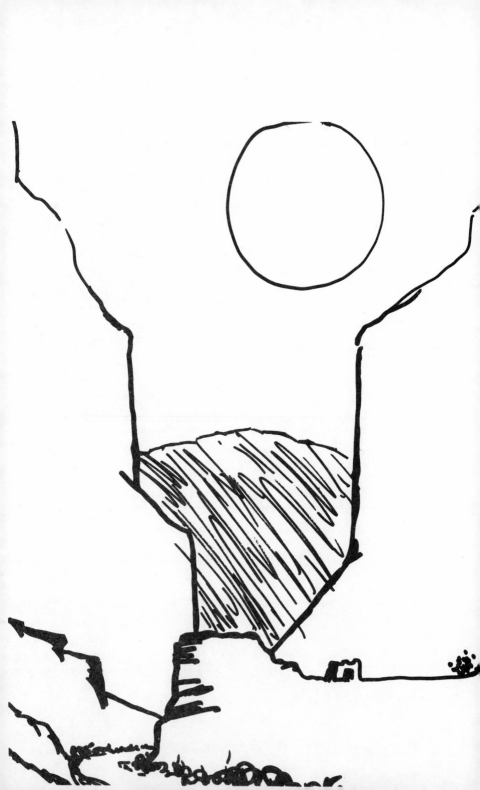

Road map: *Happily married to Judy Pepper, Abbey continued his dual identity as park ranger and "famous unknown author." From fire-watching in northern California, he moved down to Death Valley, where he drove a school bus while completing* Desert Solitaire . . . *then on to Lee's Ferry, Utah, for a stint at "motorboat rangering" on the Colorado River . . . followed by a pleasant interlude in San Francisco en route to Tucson, where Judy was completing her master's degree . . . another park ranger job, this time at Organ Pipe National Monument, Arizona . . . and finally, back to Judy and Tucson.*

JOURNAL XIII

September 1966 to April 1968

∞

September 5, 1966 – Mt. Harkness Fire Lookout, California

Home in a stone tower: fire lookout. All around me spread the drab-green coniferous forests of Northern California. West stands the plug-dome volcano of Lassen Peak, northwest the shining Fuji-like form of Shasta, fourteen-thousand feet high and eighty miles away.

Finished *Desert Solitaire* two weeks ago; shipped it off to Congdon. No reply yet. One chapter, "Water," to appear in *Harper's* this fall. A good book? Yes. My best so far. Everything about it pleases me, except the more egregious errors on technical details — it's a *solid* book. No waste, no excess, except certain obviously superfluous passages I inserted deliberately for the editors to remove. (They've got to earn their salaries, right?)

Bound for Death Valley in October. Will finally get started on *the* novel — but which one? Not sure yet.

The big issues in my life at present: An accommodation of some sort with Rita, so that I can visit my sons regularly and often; finding a Southwest homesite for Al Sarvis and (we hope) myself; writing a good solid novel; fulfilling my obligation to McGraw-Hill (still owe them a book on the welfare mess); making a living of sorts, so that I can make support payments and not be entirely dependent upon Judy (bless her sweet, generous heart!); helping Judy get her M.A. — since her heart is set on it;

and finally, ideally, reaching a clear understanding of and with myself. Ah! But that job seems too much! Too difficult! Impossible!

Resumed correspondence with that maundering moralist Bob Granat [a writer and philosopher friend from Taos]: trying to explain to him why I'm a great novelist and why he and Creeley are not.

(Say! Remember the afternoon on Malcolm's lawn, a boiling thunderstorm overhead, Debris [John DePuy] and Malcolm watching, when I teased, shocked and exasperated poor Judeo-Catholic Granat by pointing an iron crowbar at the sky and challenging God to strike me dead? A childish stunt, of course — and yet, how pleasing! Almost as good as that evening at Dead Horse Point when I hurled the flaming spear-and-flag off the brink, to the immense delight of John DePuy and the horror of my father — he thought I'd get killed.)

∞

Thots on Marriage:

Most men naturally crave and need variety in their sexual provender. Thoroughly domesticated types like, e.g., Bob Granat, who apparently are content to stick with one woman for a lifetime, are rare. Others, the majority, do so not out of love or contentment but out of caution, sloth, cowardice, the fear of risk, the dread of effort and search.

All over America we see them, couples clinging together out of fear of isolation and loneliness — and because of it, expecting and demanding too much of each other, making their lives a mutual hell. It is precisely because they hope for so much and need so much from marriage that most Americans make a mess of it, seeking in romantic love and marriage the kind of spiritual fulfillment which actually can be found only within oneself and in interaction with a larger world than marriage.

Why this insane demand upon marriage — which is really only a conventional institution set up in European cultures for the rearing of children — and the constant, hysterical, sheeplike bleating *for love?*

Because our industrial-military-commercial-urbanized culture has broken up society, destroyed community, scattered the family and atomized in fearful isolation the solitary man and woman. And nothing has yet appeared to take the place of what has been destroyed.

Thus, naturally, men and women when they join, attach themselves to one another with desperate fervor and like cannibal leeches attempt to suck from each other the blood of emotional life, which neither has to offer. The inevitable results: disappointment, frustration, bitterness, anger, hatred — and a break-up in one out of four marriages. And in the rest, resigned, quiet desperation.

Love and marriage not only do not go together like horse and carriage, they are usually — given our frantic and atomized way of life — antipathetic. Opposed. Love, romantic love, is usually found before, outside of or after marriage; when marriage begins, love begins to end. "Romantic love is an illness for which marriage is the perfect cure." Quite so.

This is not a case against marriage; I am in fact in favor of marriage. But we must not demand too much from it, or expect too much — on pain of wreckage.

September 13, 1966 – Mt. Harkness

The deer (blacktails) — bony scrawny starving things, like giant mice, stare at me in motionless fascination when I play my flute for them — not amused or amazed, or puzzled or frightened or pleased, but simply . . . fascinated: silent wonder. They gather around the lookout and in the crater below in herds, as many as fifteen or sixteen at a time, counting fawns.

Giant vermin, they'll nibble at anything for a taste of salt — they even lick up my urine from the cinders. There seems to be a pecking order among them: each doe has one other doe she can frighten or kick around, and one other she must stay away from. Few bucks appear, and these are small young ones — spikes and forkers. Nothing big or venerable; perhaps the ruling stags have no need to climb the mountain for feed.

There is also a pair of golden eagles nesting nearby. Every day I see them soaring and sailing around the mountain, hovering on the wind or plunging down like projectiles below the rim into the woods — I have not been able to observe them catching anything.

September 14, 1966 – Mt. Harkness

On the Biological Basis of Female Beauty:

That which men call beauty in woman, which lures them on in endless pursuit, mad and helpless as any other animal, is not something abstract or idiosyncratic or in the eye of the beholder only, but rather *her* apparent readiness for reproduction — in a word, woman's *nubility*. This quality, in optimum, is equivalent to what we call "beauty" and generates the compulsive attraction to which all healthy men are susceptible.

What, then, does feminine beauty consist of?

(1) *Youth:* between fifteen and thirty — ideal childbearing age, and most naturally found in conjunction with . . .

(2) *Good health:* bright eyes, glossy hair, clear skin, sweet breath, full and normal bodily development, strength, agility, sexual appetite, good disposition and attractive figure — meaning a normal and healthy body (neither too thin nor too fleshy); and . . .

(3) *Genetic fitness:* a corollary of the second, above, usually implying straight and regular facial features (at least in the European races), intelligence, good health, shapely (meaning healthy) limbs, absence of any physical or mental deformities.

Taken together, these three attributes make up the sexual attractiveness of the human female — and all are indicators of reproductive fitness. Men "fall in love," as we say, with this or that pretty girl, and pay great tribute to her appearance while laying siege to her chastity. But what draws men on and in (and for this purpose any good-looking female will do) is that hidden essence buried in her genetic make-up — her promise of bearing good children. That is what nature is concerned with, and that is the *only* thing nature is concerned with.

A "plain" or "ugly" woman, on the other hand, is one whose appearance reveals that she would probably not produce sound children — this based on man's instinctive and correct assumption that the offspring will tend to resemble the parent. For example, the woman is too thin, or fat, or bad-complexioned (indicative of poor health), etc.; or she is too old, past the ideal childbearing age, this revealed in those symptoms opposed to "beauty": wrinkled skin, lusterless hair, dull or watery eyes, a flabby or run-down body, sagging breasts, wide and sloppy buttocks, etc.

And thus we see the pathetic spectacle, in all cultures where aging is not accepted, of woman trying desperately to preserve her youth (for in that is her essence) — and failing — in an attempt to deceive by imitating with artificial aids the simulacre of the female young: she dyes her hair; she paints, treats, stretches her skin; she caps her teeth; she darkens her eyelids to make her eyes seem brighter; she exercises; she inflates or implants with foreign objects her old, worn-out and useless breasts — a tragic and futile contention with the relentless, irresistible, irreversible processes of biology, of aging . . . of that which we call, simply, time.

Most males are unaware of or indifferent to the tragedy of woman, and ignorant of the real nature of that blind but purposive lust which enslaves men, drives them on in the eternal pursuit and makes them therefore as pathetic — *subspecies eternitatis* — as the aging women whom they neglect or discard.

Furthermore, men too are subject to similar criteria of beauty, subject to the same process of flowering and decay, with however very important differences in degree: Since the germ plasma of the male is largely independent of his age and health, hermetically sealed, his reproductive value is therefore not so identical with youth and health and he enjoys a much longer sexual career than the woman, whose destiny is so wholly involved in her anatomy.

Man enjoys a second great advantage as well: Since he dominates the world, controls its power and wealth, he is also able to dominate, control and buy women; in fact, while men are attracted by youth and health and genetic fitness in women ("beauty"), women are chiefly attracted by wealth and power (in their numerous modes and variations) in men. That is, women are attracted not so much by male beauty as by the signs and symbols of status, achievement and the power to offer security.

It may seem crude, even cruel, to reduce all the delightful phenomena of romance, love, sex and marriage to these few hard brutal facts — and indeed it would be fallacious to assert that love consists of *nothing but* these biological compulsions — but it is nevertheless necessary if we wish to face the truth squarely.

And only if we face the truth can we surmount, transcend and escape the menial role nature has assigned us, men and women both. Only by seeing and accepting the biological basis and limit of human life can we free ourselves from its animal bondage, cease struggling against it or denying it or lying to ourselves and to each other — and then, on that accomplishment, perhaps begin to realize the potential of mind, personality and spirit; and through sympathy, mutual aid, justice, creative work (the true forms of love), establish at last on earth a community and society where every man, every woman, will be free to fulfill the highest desires of the human soul.

The ideal robot is simply a properly processed human being. The social machine sorts men out as a factory grader does different sizes and weights of eggs, potatoes, etc., dropping each grade into appropriate slots. Because of its special requirements, an administrative apparatus accepts and rejects according to formula, and a certain kind of well-rounded adaptable *mediocrity* is best fitted for the higher administrative positions; thus, our "leaders" are generally and chiefly distinguished by their appalling ordinariness, blandness and banality — i.e., Truman, Ike, Johnson. . . .

Romanticism was not merely an aberration. Not merely the negation of literary classicism. Rather, it was and is a great expansion of man's collective consciousness, potent as LSD, which opened up new modes of feeling and perception, and discovered for us a whole new (additional) world of truth — i.e., the past and the future, the lure of adventure and the unknown, non-European cultures, the primitive, the passionate, the personal, and nature — the natural.

My philosophy, I guess, insofar as I still have one, would fall under some such heading as Romantic Naturalism.

Fourteen days since I took my wife and sweetheart (yes, both!) to Reno and the bus depot. Today, this afternoon, this hour, I am in a blue funk of loneliness and boredom — a strange childish terror of being alone, with nothing to do. A kind of panic and horror grips me — I can easily understand why solitary confinement is the cruelest of all tortures, easily sufficient to drive a man mad.

At bad times like this, I realize all too painfully how vulnerable I am, how far, far from self-sufficient — the beauty and grandeur of mountain, sky, cloud, volcano, forest, hawk, wind, sunlight and silence are not enuf, not enough! Nor is my own companionship enough — my own head, heart, soul, hands, ideas, pen, notebook — no, alas! not enough. (*I need you.*)

"MORNINGS IN SANTA FE"

The tomatoes were still green
your coffee black and bitter
but the taste of your honest brown nipples
in my teeth reminded me
that I was home again.
Home at last, I thought, sliding in,

as if for once my weary drive
back and forth across this bloody continent
had come to a real garage.
Mirage. Within ten weeks
our idyll would be smashed
in the valley of rock and alkali
horse shit and movie actors
and all my pretty hopes
banged out of shape again.

September 1966 – Death Valley, California

A Modest Proposal: Sept 66, Mt. Harkness or DV

That honorific prostitution should be viewed as a plausible stepping-stone toward the ideal utopian society of free love, liberty, personal fulfillment and the most human, humane world now imaginable (*a la* H. G. Wells and his Eloi?). Who knows what energies such an erotic and free world might release in the human kind?

Ah, you say, but for good — or ill?

And I reply: How could human life become much worse than it is already? Free love would tend to reduce the perverse and sadistic, especially with the new generations.

Our present puritanical code is a gross violation of human nature: thus the widespread discomfort, discontent, disease and desperation. Hypocrisy makes matters still worse by poisoning the spiritual atmosphere with a smog of cynicism, pornography and commercialism.

Community whorehouses might even be sponsored by the churches (which are already involved in prostitution through their real-estate investments, particularly the rich Roman Catholic, Episcopalian and Presbyterian sects).

I envision:

• Apprenticeship for young girls — professional training in the finest arts of love; free-lance work to be permitted but not encouraged — competition from the House would be too stiff for most girls; the House to be open to all women — any age, shape or color — absolutely democratic.

• Each girl to be completely free in her choice of customers and in her style of service; residence in the House not compulsory; girls free to name their own fees (demand and supply, etc.) and to leave and return, or quit and return, or marry or not, or fall in love, each entirely at her own discretion.

• Each and every act to be completely voluntary — no compulsion, no degradation, no "perverseness" except as agreed between consenting adults; each girl to be protected in her person by powerful guards stationed in the corridors, on call by electric signals (free enterprise under social supervision).

• All fees to be paid directly to the girls — no profits for the manager or Madam, who will be paid salaries from the State — or perhaps a small admission might be charged to cover overhead costs (socialized free enterprise).

• Each House will emphasize the beauty, dignity, traditions and profound significance of sexual love; the interiors will include the finest works of art, past and contemporary, relevant to the place, in all media; various forms of entertainment will be offered in addition to the erotic.

• And this most important of all: that "whore" become a laudable, respectable, honorific term, equivalent to courtesan, geisha, mistress, artist. It will be understood that the whore sells not her *self*, not even her body, but only her professional services, and can no more be regarded as debasing herself than the M.D. who sells his special knowledge, the professor who sells his brain to the university, or any other artist, artisan or technician. The whores' high incomes will reinforce this elevated social status. (A whore even now is more honest than the model, pin-up, actress, etc., who offers nothing worth the price.)

As Shaw said, the only difference between a whore and a lady is the way she's treated.

Presumably, since their earnings will directly depend on it, the girls will do their best to attract and please; but no vulgarity — all in the highest mode, as will necessarily follow from the recovered dignity of their profession.

The American obsession with sex is based on frustration; insufficient sex. We have lots of talk, pictures, pornography, but not enough of the genuine article; provocation everywhere (current modes of dress, for example) but damned little outlet for the need.

Prostitution would provide that outlet.

And marriage? It would be stabilized, rationalized and based solidly on its only purpose, function and justification — the production and rearing of children — freeing it from the awful, insane demands of passion and romance . . . with the end result a vast improvement in morals and morale for all concerned. Moreover, prostitution would provide diversion, satisfaction, pride and extra income for the middle-aged house-wife whose husband seems to have lost his interest in her.

But would this destroy romantic love?

Possibly — but probably not. It would, however, reduce love to a wholesome proportion, strip it of the malignant and dishonest elements and require women to have something really valuable to offer their suitors — they could no longer depend solely upon his need for that furry jewel between the legs. Love would be restored to its traditional honor, as glorified in most pre-Christian and non-European civilizations.

Even at its worst, prostitution is never so evil as institutional war, prisons, poverty, hypocrisy, censorship, prudery and all the other social vices to which we have become accustomed.

The whorehouse could become the shrine, the temple, the cathedral of the future town: a holy place, the sanctum sanctorum of mystery, delight, joy — and beauty!

October 26, 1966 – Death Valley

Death of the spirit. A terrible lassitude has overwhelmed me now for a month. Unable to act or feel. Caused no doubt by various small disappointments (such as failure of the movie deal) taken together, and by my lack of creative work. Trapped in the swamp between books, I find it impossible to extricate myself. Blocked, Christ! Might as well have taken the job of garbage collector, which I could've had here if I'd really wanted it. At least then I'd be earning money.

December 13, 1966 – Death Valley

From a letter to Al Sarvis:

"Frittering my life away"? Perhaps. I don't know. What *should* a man do? I'm assailed at times by a sense of desperation — in seven weeks I'll be forty years old and still don't know with any precision who or what I am. Or why. Booze is but a palliative and my one experiment with LSD was an uncomfortable and inconclusive failure: the stars quivered in a cloudy cobweb but the big spider-God failed to appear....

I am resolved, therefore, to continue on my present course: to compose somehow the one good novel; to try to be good to my wife; to run Cataract Canyon in a kayak; to raze more billboards; to build that solid house of rock and wood far out somewhere, where my sons and grandsons can find at least a temporary refuge from the nightmare world of 2000 A.D.; and to be ready, with rifle or rood, for the apocalyptic showdown which yet may come — I hope — in our lifetimes. . . .

January 12, 1967 – Gravel Gulch, Dead Valley

Still moribund. Paralyzed. Why? Dribbling my days away in petty routines — now I'm a school-bus driver, just like the old man. Why? I don't know.

The clear cool sunlight of Death Valley, beautiful in its way — somber grandeur and incomprehensible vastness, the colors of the mountains and hills, the sunset clouds, the icy mount of Telescope Peak shining, glazed, dangerous (two men fell to their deaths there this winter). I have explored so far almost all the usual places plus Chloride Cliff, Surprise Canyon, Honapah Canyon, Echo Canyon, Sand Spring.

Compared, however, to regions in the Southwest, Death Valley is less interesting: almost barren of plant life and the rock formations (except perhaps to a geologist) less appealing to the eye, less colorful.

One obvious thing wrong with Death Valley is simply far too many roads — everything is too easily accessible — no mystery, therefore, no adventure. One does not feel here the sense of wilderness, of remoteness, still available in other parks. You cannot *see* wilderness from a road. What you see from a road is something different — a scene, a panorama, a picture; but you do not *feel* anything. [Death Valley is] a good example of a badly overdeveloped park. It is big, yes, relative to other parks, but so is Texas, and what could be more monotonous and dreary?

My writing program for this winter: another fifty pages for *Desert Solitaire*, plus a straight magazine-type article on "Industrial Tourism and the Parks."

January 25, 1967 – Death Valley

Death Valley is the true test of the desert rat. Here is the ultimate in North American deserts: a grim vast barren place, ugly, fiercely hot and dry — highest temperatures, lowest humidities of anyplace on the continent; the huge alluvial fans bare of all life except a few scattered crouching shrubs, and the IRON mountains, barren of almost everything except rock, jagged ugly rock, black, gray, brown, red, bitterly dry and hot.

Across the flat floor of this immense sink (for it is not a true valley), beyond the long shimmering planes of the salt flats, rise the Panamints like red hot iron in the morning sunlight, like cold blue steel in twilight; mountains rather conventional in general outline.

Psychedelic and all that.

February 28, 1967 – Death Valley

Literary disgrace. My *Harper's* article, "Water" (and *Harper's* is bad enough), is reprinted in (Gawd help me!) *Reader's Digest.* Aaah . . . the lures of mammon. And fan letters — about twenty so far — more than I ever received from my books. [I also received] an offer to speak at the University of Nevada — and a critical review in *Western Review.* Could the ice finally be breaking?

E. Abbey, the famous unknown author.

August 6, 1967 – Lee's Ferry, Utah

The motorboat ranger. I have twenty-three miles of river to patrol — fifteen upstream, eight down. Up to the dam [Glen Canyon on Lake Powell], down over the Pariah Rapids and on to Badger Rapids, a major obstacle. I have been here since June 10th or so, will probably stay until October. Then to Tucson to join Judy in her grad studies — the M.A. pursuit.

The madness of my life. "A chaotic improvisation from month to month." Somehow somewhere soon I've got to settle *down* for a few years, write a BOOK, raise some KIDS. (Josh! Aaron!) Seems I never know what I'm gonna do until I do it.

The Great Al Sarvis arrives, accompanied by his sweet and charming and ultra-sexy friend Annie Blaylock. After a day on the river, during which I mash a boat prop on a gravel bar — too much bourbon, too little bikini — he and Annie take off for northern New Mexico, land hunting, home hunting, for us all.

I must, simply must get to work on the book. Judy is two-thousand miles away [visiting family on the East Coast] and my heart is riddled with loneliness, anxiety, the ancient nameless dread: all the terrible things that could happen to her — a plane crash, a tumor, a love affair — what would I do then? A mad crazy dirty old man, masturbating his life away in these personal obsessions.

Ah, to be a buzzard now that spring is here!

The vanity of vultures. Abbey and his red bandanna 'round the neck.

Pre-incarnation impatience. An impertinent, presumptuous and perhaps dangerous impatience.

October 1967 – San Francisco!

Gawd what a sweet town. The first time I think I've ever really *loved* a city. A *city*. I, Edward Abbey, hater of cities, have fallen in love with a city. And with its people — but then, city and people, how to tell the one from the other? The wave from the water? The dancer from the dance? City of light, of pastel fogs, of silvery smog, city of hills — like the hanging gardens of Babylon! And city of love. Never in my life so many pretty girls in one place — and so many bold, brave, handsome boys. You look in vain for a sick, corrupted face. (Now comrade, you exaggerate. Aye! But not by much.)

Color everywhere. Defiance, sweetness, pity, anger. A breakout. Shattered prisms litter the streets. Bach and Beethoven soar above the power-line poles. And the girls. And the beautiful bearded young men. And the fine old ladies. And the gentlemen.

Saw my sister Nancy the other night. Sister Nancy, so bright and gay, and her three golden children — Bill, Abigail and Kelly. Abigail Abbey Hartsell. Very much the independent woman now, [Nancy] since her divorce. *Her* divorce. Says she's happy enough. Moderately happy, like any other Abbey. Still looks good — not pretty, no, but beautiful.

November 22, 1967 – Tucson

Literary Notes: *Desert Solitaire* is "almost" selected by Book-of-Fucking-Month-Club. *Almost.* Too bad about them. Well, what would I do with twenty or thirty thousand dollars anyway? Get fat and insolent, prob'ly.

The book, incidentally, looks OK. A solid, handsome little book — I'm pleased with it. It should last for many years. (For a century at least!)

With appreciative notes from Krutch, Lea, A. B. Guthrie, Clark, Eastlake — good generous men; I'd do the same for some other struggling young punk someday.

The book may do well. It should at any rate *sell* better than my poor misfit quixotic cowboy nuvvles. And will undoubtedly get better reviews — in the *East!*

Went down the Grand [Colorado River], all the way, with Ron Smith & Co. [river guides] in October — Lee's Ferry to Temple Bar. A great trip — a sweet adventure. Worked my way as "#2 flunky," and mighty hard work too. But well worth it. I am eager to do it again, with my own hand on the tiller. Much exploration to be done down in there. All them lateral canyons — all that marvelous uninhabited wilderness! I flew back, above it all, with Earl Leesburgh; dropped a beer can on Dick Cook's house in Lee's Ferry.

∞

What is Time?

Are there not several kinds of time? I.e. (1) clock time, (2) solar time — day and night, winter and summer, and (3) biological time — life-time, time as measured by the birth, growth, maturation, reproduction, decay and death of a living organism. And the time of poetry — and the time of music — and the time of love.

Past, present, future: mystery. To live fully in the present — yes — but could the present have any meaning, any value for us if we did not also believe in the ineluctable reality of the past? And therefore, also, inevitably, of the future.

Sidereal time — the life of the stars. Sidereal. . . .

Desert time. River time. I am haunted by the specter of river time.

And love — the birth and blossoming, the fading and dying of love. (Oh, but I can see through those weak-hearted ideas!)

January 11, 1968 - Tucson

Melancholia — I've got it and bad. A fear of death? Hardly — almost the opposite — a longing for death. Cowardly, shameful, sick despair. Why? What do I want? Need? I am still, so far as I can judge, in perfect physical health — though now well into middle age, with gray whiskers and a few gray strands above the ears. Despair — melancholy — and a sick, secret, furtive longing for — what? For that mystic landscape — that ultimate loneliness — that final peace. Is that what I want? Or is it simply the shame of idleness?

For two months now I have done nothing — almost absolutely *nothing*. My only salvation is work, work; I know this well. I've discovered it (have I not?) a thousand times before. (Yet, I take a perverse kind of joy from my sorrow — I *want* sorrow — as if I were addicted to this subtle form of self-destruction.)

Not suicide but — *to vanish.* Disappear. Fade off into the wilderness, never return — that decadent romanticism of nihilism haunts me still, apparently I'll never never never outlive it. Forty-one years of searching.

A sickness. A disease. Melancholia — dread — the sick sad heartsick yearning for something lost, remote, past, future, forever out of reach. An absolute love for something absolute. Infinitely good and sweet and pure and beautiful — immutable. Forest — mountain — desert — sea!

January 23, 1968 – Tucson

I interviewed Joseph Wood Crutch a week ago. Nice gray old genteel professional man, quite amiable and condescending (as Austen would have said), with an impressive facility for the pedagogical monologue — talk talk talk. Admirable in his conservative-liberal way.

Krutch has a nice sweet old short fat gray French wife named Marcelle. A calm, cool, clear-minded old man, but definitely old-fashioned, still living largely in the '20s. Good ole gray fuddy-duddy, J. W. Krutch. [Though] a bit of an equivocater on the Vietnam War issue — has he forgotten Thoreau?

January 31, 1968 – Tucson (Tet!)

Seventeen Vietcong commandos seize the U.S. Embassy in Saigon and hold it for *seven hours!* Never before in human history have men armed with little more than courage, boldness and conviction fought so splendidly against such terrible, incredible odds. Men against machines, just as in Budapest, Santo Domingo, etc. Fantastic!

Dave Rehfield, draft-resister: A real man on the campus of what seems to be a university of 22,000 sheep [University of Arizona]. In a land of sheep and wolves.

Secrets of a Literary Bum:
The story of America's most famous unknown author — the man, the artist, the failure — a young man who descended the ladder of success rung by rung from the time of his graduation from one of the nation's top cow colleges, with real Ph.D. potential, to his middle-aged collapse on the bedrock-bottom of honest poverty.

A complete and distinguished literary failure whose numerous books have gone unpublished or, if published, unsung unreviewed untranslated and unread in almost every nation on earth. This is the story of that deep, abiding, unshakable satisfaction in life that only complete failure can bring.

But at least he wasn't a professor. He fought off that fate for as long as he could. When a writer starts accepting pay for doing nothing but talking about words, we know what he is going to write: nothing but words.

His lecture tour: "Why Write Novels, for Chrissake?"

His brief teaching career: canceled the final and gave all his students Bs, regardless of race creed or coloration.

Abbey: He wanted the same things all writers want — fame, money, beautiful girls. An *audience!*

February 6, 1968 - Tucson

A sympathetic review of our *Desert* book in the *New York Times* by that old bird-watcher Edwin Way Teale — the best so far. Nothing else except scads of hick-town newspaper reviews (one nice one in *People's World*) and a brief notice by Clifton Fadiman (oh no!) in the *Book of the Month Club News*. But nothing else. Another book dropped down the bottomless well. Into oblivion. The silent treatment.

There is nothing more infuriating to a writer — need I confess it? — than to be totally ignored. Even ole buddy Creeley has apparently failed to come across with a good word — little enuf to ask. I'd certainly have done it for him. Ah, the bitterness of it, the bitterness. But oh well, what the hell. It's hard but it's fair. The old wheel keeps turning. Fortuna, goddess of misery. (Besides, there's always time for one more effort. The effort Supreme, addressed to emptiness.)

Time heals all wounds . . . but does it really? Some losses are inconsolable. Those painful, poignant memories of my Grand Canyon days. So much that I loved and will always remember is associated with that baffling abysm that divides the earth at Kaibab. Guilts, sweetnesses, transient triumphs . . . the charming banality of [Ferde] Grofe's music brings it all back. Or aerial music. Painted Desert overlook.

March 17, 1968 - Organ Pipe Cactus National Monument, Arizona

Had a fight with Judy over some discarded [love] letters. She left me here *sans* typewriter, *sans* clock, *sans* towel, *sans* stew pot and *sans* wife. Trying to finish *The Iron Gates* [to be published as *Black Sun*]; two-thirds through. An excellent little novel, in my opinion. Very romantic. In fact, I think I'll call it "a romantic novel," or maybe simply "a romance." Judy hates it, of course, thinking it the story of one of my old love affairs, which in a way it is, but only in a greatly altered and much exaggerated way. If only she understood that there's nothing deader than a dead romance.

Mad Debris is here. A good man, a good comrade, and an *artist*. Has only one vice: garlic.

∞

Reviews of our *Desert* book in the *Park Association* magazine (of all places), and *Natural History*.

"The author seems motivated by resentment." — One line from a jolly know-nothing review in the Flagstaff [Arizona] news-rag. "His credibility is rimless." — Like the reviewer's glasses? "His reservoir of misinformation . . . inexhaustible." I should write a letter to this jerk, Budge Ruffner, just for the laughs if nothing else.

∞

The Indiana County [Pennsylvania] Tourist Promotion Bureau writes, nominating me as "Ambassador of Indiana County, 1968" for Chrissake! They want me to come to a banquet at Rustic Lodge. (Class re-union!) Will I go? Maybe — if they pay all expenses.

Signed a contract for *The Good Life* a few days ago. Now I'm a slave to World Literature for the next three years!

Saturday afternoon, March 23, 1968 – Organ Pipe

Solitude. And loneliness. And a furious eroticism that is driving me mad . . . nothing but hard-ons all day long . . . satyrmania, Abbey's vice. The satyr-maniac. The more it gets. . . .

April 7, 1968 – Organfeeler National Orgasm

To my infinite chagrin, *The New Yorker* is the first national magazine to run a review of *Desert*. Brief but highly favorable. My favorite general-purpose magazine. Written expressly for little ole ladies from Dubuque.

April 21, 1968 – Tucson

Midnight on the desert. *La Bohème* on the radio. Love in my thoughts. Judy (bless her) is sleeping in the next room. Farewell to old Organ Grinder National Pipedream for a while . . . maybe I'll return next winter. Who knows? Who cares.

Will I live that long? Sometimes I think I'll live to be a wild old shaggy man of ninety-odd — a witch doctor. And then I think I'll die tomorrow, in some way utterly absurd: motorcycle knotted 'round a telephone pole, heart stopping, fall from a rock. On my head. Mysterious disease. Or simply disappear. Disappear, even from myself. Does it matter? But I must live a little longer . . . sense of haste, urgency, panic: so *much* remaining to be done. Books. Places. Persons. Events. "Inner" achievements and all that rubbish. Ah well. On and on. On and on and on.

∞

END OF JOURNAL XIII

Road map: *And the stew boils. In Journal XIV, which glances across more than five years, Abbey experienced dark times following the death of Judy in 1970. But by journal's end, he had climbed to new heights of joy, aided considerably by the birth of his first daughter, Susannah, and by the company of young Renee, soon to become his fourth wife.*

JOURNAL XIV

May 1968 to November 1973

∞

May 22, 1968 – Atascosa Lookout, Coronado National Forest, Arizona

A golden eagle floated by under the kitchen window this morning as I poured myself a cup of coffee. Hot, dry, windy weather.

This lookout is merely a flimsy old frame shack perched like an eagle's nest on a pinnacle of rock 6,235 feet high. Built in the 1930s by the CCC, of course. Held together by paint and wire and nuts and bolts. Shudders in the wind.

I'm sitting here idle as an abbot, wearing my *huaraches.* My Jesus shoes. Doing nothing much positive except letting my whiskers grow and brooding, of course, as always, over the anguish and delight of my tormented heart. (The frivolous forties.)

Well then. I left Organic Pop Caucus National Monument on [April] the 21st, went soon after to Denver where I whored it for a week, trying to peddle my book. TV, radio, a public speech that was at least provocative enough to rouse the hackles of some and cause others to walk out (tax motherhood; get out of Vietnam; resist the draft, etc.). Ravished by Denver, my heart cracked like a nut.

Anyway, the high life. Too much booze, too little sleep, but I succeeded anyhow in writing a review for the [?] *Times*, as well as the last five pages of *Black Sun* — a sweet lyrico-erotico "romance," which I sent off posthaste, special delivery, to [Walter] Clemons at McGraw-Hill — 202 pages — and now three weeks later, am still awaiting his/their/its decision.

(A jet rumbles by overhead. Like the Devil on roller-skates, tearing a rent in the sky.)

Father was here for a week. He spent several days in the lookout tower with me and I must confess, he got on my nerves a bit. Why? Well, the old boy is half deaf — making conversation difficult. And worse yet, though I hope he never learns this, he is now also tone deaf: couldn't carry a tune in a bushel basket. Nevertheless, he insists on singing or whistling almost all the time. (Mother's joke: "Maybe there's a little electricity left in the wires.")

When I was a windy little boy, how I adored, cherished, thrilled to the sound of the old man's cheery whistling — *"Father's home again!"* I loved him then, between bouts of hatred, and I love him now, though he is not — anymore than I — entirely a lovable man.

Life, said the Viking chieftain, is a bird that flies out of the night, into the lighted hall, circles once and flies out again, back into the night. . . .

The Negroes: America's only true aristocracy.

June 5, 1968 – Atascosa

Robert Kennedy was shot last night, as I toiled up the obscure mountain by moonlight.

Alone on my mountain, feeling oh so lonely and desolate. I wish Judy would come. I wish Al [Sarvis] would come, or Gus, or *somebody* for Godsake. Even God.

Good old Bartòk on the radio — insufficient consolation. Howling winds outside, the sky full of dust and smoke — condemned Arizona, lonesome Abbey. And this is what I think I love? Solitude? Well . . . sometimes. (Terrible dreams lately . . . those wails of anguish.) Gotta get to work on my masterpiece.

A great grimy sunset glowers on the west. Plains of gold, veils of dust, wind-whipped clouds. The big aching tooth of Baboquivari far and high on the skyline.

Oh Lord have mercy. Mercy. Not justice. Mercy. Forgive me if you can my meanness and selfishness, my cruelty and stupidity. For I cannot. Darkening now. The light is going out. I cannot.

June 8, 1968 – Atascosa

He loved them all, that was the trouble. Could never willingly give up any of them, could never forget. He wanted them all around him, all his life. Never did he *want* to lose one for another. But they, of course . . . they never understood. And so, one goddamned tragedy after another.

The anguish of longing. This filthy disease, romance. This yearning for something afar . . . forty years of torment . . . forty years in the wilderness. Forty years of searching. How to stop this madness?

July 5, 1968 – Atascosa

Woke up this morning on an island in the sky, surrounded by clouds. Wild swirling banks of vapor, flowing and passing to reveal brief glimpses of rocky crags, dripping trees, the golden grassy hillsides far below.

August 28, 1968 – [?]

Susannah Mildred Abbey born today; 7-1/2 pounds, blonde. And beautiful.

October 8, 1968 – Cullowhee, North Carolina

Like a bloody idiot, I accepted a teaching job here at Redneck U. All for monetary greed (and of course for other somewhat less-mentionable considerations — what Al, that sonofabitch, calls the fringe benefits — though I have yet to see any fringes); $7,800, or almost $1,000 per working month, good wages for me.

But oh! The horror the tedium the *drudgery* of academic life. How I despise it. How I loathe it. All those pink faces in the classroom three fucking hours, five fucking days per week. All them unspeakable truly hideous little bluebook themes ("How Reading Historical Novels Helped My Weak Eyes").

All them fellow-faculty. (Except Al himself, the bastard, who dragged me here, of whom I never tire.) And the hours and hours of preparation, reading filthy garbage like Homer and Shithead Plato and Dante and that ancient archaic bore Wm. Shakespeare. The ceaseless pressure of the fucking job — no time to relax — always there's tomorrow's shit to prepare, to read, to grade, etc.

October 20, 1968 – Cullowhee

Haven't made up the feeble mind yet if I'll stick it here through the winter, or quit at the end of this quarter. Judy is on my side, bless her sweet soul; it's only us two (and Susannah) against all of them.

Of course, I could always shoot myself. But I haven't even got a gun.

November 22, 1968 – Cullowhee

Done it. Gave "Model T." Crum my resignation letter. Leaving here 12-10-68, back to Organ Pipe National Orgasm. What a rogue and peasant slave. Clown. Self-disgust and self-hatred cloud my mind. (AH, SHIT!)

January 17, 1969 – Organfeeler National Monument

Ah well, what the fuck, as old Jerusalem Slim would say.

The magic has flown, for the time being. Ah well — Wordsworth had this trouble too, though only a poet. That's the problem with being a middle-aged romantic. Romantics are supposed to die young goddamnit, and here I am, stiff and wrinkled and forty-two in a week, still fucking around *alive!*

April 12, 1969 – Organic Pipette

Men love ideas more than their lives. A man holds to his ideas regardless of their truth or falsity — perhaps all the more strongly the weaker they are. His ideas cannot be separated from his self. They become his self. They are his self. Thus, a man can no more give up his ideas than he can give up his soul — they are one and the same.

∞

Tolstoy's publisher to Tolstoy: "For Godsake, Leo, stop scribbling!"

April 25, 1969 – Organ Pipe

Off to North Rim [Grand Canyon] for the summer. Fire lookout. Vindication?

June 6, 1969 – North Rim Lookout, Grand Canyon, Arizona

Back at the old stand again. The cabin in the woods. The steel tower. The sea of treetops, spruce and fir and aspen. The violet-green swallows and the hermit thrush. The crooked forest. Lightning, red flash, smell of ozone in the air. The wind. The quietness between. . . .

June 20, 1969 – North Rim

Whose hand will part her lovely thighs?
Whose touch will close her eyes?
Whose mouth will fill her ears with tender lies?
Whose love — her heart?

June 26, 1969 – North Rim

The sweet clear silver song of the hermit thrush, morning and evening, every day. A flute music from the dark woods. (From the heart?) A bittersweet, faintly melancholy tune — so perfectly in key with my own feelings. The bird is common here, I hear them singing all around . . . and yet I very seldom see one.

June 27, 1969 – North Rim

I believe in marriage. I love my wife. I love family life. And yet, I can't bear monogamy; there's the rub. For me it's unnatural. Cruel. Painful. Unbearable. I like girls: can't seem to get over it, or outgrow it, or sublimate it — in fact, the more active and creative I am, and the happier I am, the *more* I crave sexual excitement. Which means, for me, a new girl now and then in bed.

Is there something wrong with me? Am I sick? Am I truly a satyrmaniac, as Judy thinks? Do I really need a shrink? Or just a good deep fuck now and then with some fresh young thing out of the blue? Sex is one of the few outlets we have these days for a man's inherent lust for adventure. The only remaining frontier — besides science, and maybe revolution, and maybe (doubtful) art.

June 30, 1969 – North Rim

A summer with a girl ranger. Big sweet friendly good-lookin' blonde Californian. Screwing in the sunshine, on the pine needles. In the cabin while it rains. Up in the lookout tower, on the floor. In my VW here and there and everywhere. In her hot and musical Springdale apartment (Near Zion). In the Towne House, seventeenth floor, Phoenix. In Taos. Many sweet and delightful weekends. Oh yes, and at Point Sublime! An absolutely splendid girl — I should never have let her get away. Climbing the tower behind her, looking up. (Those delicious rosy cheeks!) So good-natured, even-tempered and — compliant. A real woman. Will make some kid a wonderful mother. I loved her, in my way.

September 30, 1969 – North Rim

Abbey vs. Abbey: Case #4373, Superior Court, Tucson, AZ.

Good ole Rita, she's even got around to having a couple of attorneys named Frost and Pleasant (!), NYC, attach my royalty payments from McGraw-Hill. Not that they amount to much. I'll bet a dollar to a doughnut that was ole Buddy Sarvis's idea: according to Clyde, he's been scheming with Rita for some time to put the blocks to Abbey. Tighten the screws.

October 7, 1969 – Indiana, Pennsylvania

Back home, where you can't go, said Wolfe. Why not? says Wendell Berry. I'm with Wolfe. To me, this town, this place, this area is nothing. I feel nothing, no emotion whatever. Might as well be visiting Fargo ND for all it means to me.

Everything has changed. No, not everything — but much. The town is now three times bigger. Pittsburgh is much closer; only an hour's drive away, with Indiana now practically a suburb. New houses all over the hills outside town — devastated farmland — hills disemboweled to make room for highway interchanges — new factories and coal-burning power plants — the old teachers' college is now ten times grown and called a "university" — schools and children everywhere.

The post-war baby boom has exploded on us now. All the old-style general farms are gone; the only serious farmers now are specialists: dairy, beef, pigs, truck, Christmas trees, cabbages. Most work their farms only on weekends; work in stores or factories the rest of the time. A dismal scene, man.

Female rumps: I know why I like them, but I don't know why I like them so much. (The ass-man cometh.)

Kathy, on her middle-aged lover: "He was a slow comer."

Ah, it's a poor barbarous Christian superstition as says a man can love only one woman. Or only one woman at a time. Why, I say (and *I know*), a man can love two three four or more women all at once. Love is indivisible. Not a quantity but a quality. I am full of love (for beautiful things), and the more I love, the more I am capable of loving. (And the more I, the more I.) This is written most soberly, comrades. Can not a man love more than one friend? One brother? Then why in Christ's name not more than one woman?

October 10, 1969 – Indiana, Pennsylvania

Alone again. Judy has left, swears she'll never come back, that I'll never see her again.

So be it. I'll survive. (Somehow.)

October 16, 1969 – Indiana, Pennsylvania

Still not a word on my book. I'm sex-starved, can't seem to think of anything but thighs, belly, breasts, lips, eyes, small of back, buttocks and — ah! — cunt. It's like an obsession. What's wrong with me?

October 24, 1969 – Indiana, Pennsylvania

Last night I made love to a bonnie bonnie lass. Ah! The sweetness and the beauty and the madness of that hour. And her name: Bonnie! An unusual, almost Asiatic beauty. A Hollywood Indian princess. "I want to be dominated," she said. How true!

June 15, 1970 – North Rim Lookout

Judy is back east in Mt. Sinai Hospital, slowly dying of acute leukemia. Her chances are forty/sixty of "making it," according to her doctor. She will not live a year, according to two other doctors. "Critical list."

How could something like this happen to someone so young (twenty-seven), sweet, innocent and good as Judy? Who can answer me that? "What fucking rotten luck," she writes.

I'm hoping to get her transferred out here to Kanab Hospital in two or three weeks, if "remission" takes hold. If not, I'll have to fly east again. She's already planned her own funeral: cremation, ashes scattered on the Colorado River, music: a flute and a drum. Some poems (Dylan, Donne, Shakespeare).

July 11, 1970 – North Rim

Judy died on July 4th, early in the morning at Mt. Sinai Hospital in NYC, while rockets and firecrackers rattled in Harlem. There was nothing anyone could do. Acute leukemia, in the most virulent form; poor kid, she never had a chance.

I spent the last two weeks with her, slept in the same room with her during the last few nights — except the very last two, when I could no longer bear to watch and listen to her suffering. On morphine every four hours, she nevertheless still had half-hours of agitation, pain, anxiety, fear, confusion. ("Oh Ed, there's something terribly wrong with me. . . .")

I wish I could forget. Oh, more than anything, I wish I could forget Judy's pain and fear, and all the hurt I gave her during our 4-1/2 years of marriage. Perhaps writing it all down will help. Or will writing only make it worse?

Should I record what that evil disease did to my sweet wife? The weakness, the gradual loss of strength, the swelling of the gums, the multiple infections of throat, stomach, bowels, the wracking gas pains, the perpetual discomfort that no position on the bed could relieve, the yellowish cast to her skin, the gauntness of her face, the purplish welts (from needle punctures) that would not heal, her nausea (from the cortisone and other drugs?), her loss of appetite. All the physical torments, in short, of a Hiroshima victim.

And the repulsive degradations of the hospital routine: the I.V., the transfusions of blood and platelets, the rectal tube, the Cantor tube (down her nose and throat, with the slippery little bag of mercury on the end), the continual blood-letting and pricking and pressuring as the medical engineers measured her decline; and the catheter, and the bedpan of course — the whole hideous chamber of horrors! And the Demerol and morphine. The X-rays and fluoroscopes.

Yet, none of this monstrous procedure seemed really to degrade my Judy in any essential way. During the last few terrible days, she seemed to me somehow more beautiful than ever — more sweet and good and brave. She wanted so much to live! She tried so hard to do everything the doctors asked her to do — she knew more about the pills than the nurses did. She became, near the end, under the influence of merciful morphine, like a sweet, docile child. Except when coming out of the drug, she felt no physical pain. She was so easy to please. Sweet words made her smile. I assured her of my love. She replied that she loved me.

Delirium and disorientation: she wanted to go to a movie; she thought she was in Salt Lake City; on the last afternoon I was with her, she wanted me to bring Suzie so she could hug her. "I want to hug Suzie!" (Sitting up and staring out the window. The bleeding nose, her panic. The trips down to X-ray. The cup of ice.)

Oh God, I should not recall these things!

I wanted so much for her to win, to survive, to live, if only for the three- or six-month remission the doctors promised. And then, about Wednesday, when it became obvious that her condition was utterly hopeless, I wanted so much for her to die — quickly, easily, painlessly — and I began to hate the doctors and the nurses and the hospital and the whole gruesome medical apparatus because, it seemed to me, they were too much bent on keeping her alive as long as possible, prolonging her suffering — hers and mine. No doubt those last three days I suffered more, her brother Henry and her parents suffered more, than Judy did herself.

I was lying awake, in bed, in Henry's apartment on 36th St., when the phone rang and some intern at the hospital gave me the news. Poor Judy, poor Judy, poor Judy!

The family gave her a nice quick Jewish funeral the next day, with a little old white-bearded rabbi presiding who didn't even know how to pronounce her name. Buried at Mt. Moriah, near Fairview, in the family plot, on a hillside, with a nice view of the Jersey meadows, the Newark smogs, the turnpike, the sky and the clouds.

The intern assured me she died peacefully, under the morphine, no struggle, no last-minute attempt at a temporary resuscitation. (I hadn't even anticipated any such monstrosity as that!)

And Suzie is with me (to her grandparents' sorrow). And Judy is gone forever.

The thought that tortures me more than anything else, sometimes outweighing the pity and absurdity and total unacceptability of her death, is that I betrayed Judy at the end by not telling her the truth. I allowed the doctors to persuade me that it would be better to encourage her with lies, to seek a "remission" on the thin rationale that during the next few months some combination of drugs might yet be discovered that could save her life.

Oh the falsity of it! I should have told Judy the truth, while she was still whole and rational, and given her the *choice* of the hideous hospital ordeal or of taking her own life, dying quickly and with dignity and with a minimum of pain. She had a right to an honorable death — and we denied it to her!

She and I had often agreed, long ago, that we would do as much for each other, if it ever came to a terminal illness. And yet, I did not do it. It never even seriously occurred to me to do it. I was so certain that medicine would achieve a reprieve for her.

When should I have told her? On the night we went to Manhattan together to see a movie? Or else on the day she called me in Tucson to tell me she was going to Mt. Sinai the next day? Or maybe even two weeks later, in the hospital, when she was still well enough to beat me at chess?

But I did not. On none of those occasions did I even seriously consider the idea. All I could think of was giving her mental aid, comfort and encouragement. As the doctors advised. Were we all wrong?

Yes? (But she did not *insist* on the truth — perhaps she did not really want to know.) [The preceding parenthetic sentence appears to have been inserted at some later date.]

How do I know? Because I know without any doubt what I would prefer for myself. And Judy was certainly as strong and brave as I — maybe stronger, braver. I cannot escape the conviction that we betrayed her: the doctors, because they knew best what was in store for Judy if the drug treatment failed, as it did; and I, because I knew best what a brave girl Judy really was.

What now is the aim of my life?

To sit on a rock in the desert and stare at the sun until the sun goes black.

July 11, 1970 – North Rim

Suzie is with me, being looked after by Ingrid, whom I have yet to mention in this journal. Why do I have this fatal attraction for sweet good innocent Jewish girls? (Rita, Judy, Inger?)

Anyway, Inger's a fine girl: wise and compassionate, tender and understanding, cool and clear and clever, and very pretty, sexy and young — only twenty-two. Much too good a girl for a dirty, treacherous, hairy old man like me. But she seems to love me anyway, God knows why, and I love her too, God knows, and need her very much, especially now. Without Ingrid, how could I ever have brought little Suzie (twenty-three months) out to this man-forsaken wilderness? Or bear my guilt and loneliness?

I first met Ingrid at Organ Pipe, under Earth Day auspices. We have been together almost all the time since — at Logan [Utah], in Cataract [Canyon, on the Colorado River] with Ken [Sleight, a river and back-country guide and close friend of Ed's] and now at North Rim.

What does she hope or expect from me? I don't know — but I'd like her to be my mistress and buddy for about twenty-five years, then I'll drop dead. Off a cliff, I hope.

July 22, 1970 – North Rim

Judy — her death. Just too goddamned cruel and unjust and absurd and unnecessary to be borne. As Bobby Kennedy used to say (and how sweet *his* memory now seems), this is "unacceptable." (Oblivion. Annihilation. Nothingness.)

Two-and-a-half weeks now. Every now and then, it hits me like a blow in the soul, and all I can do is weep. Oh poor sweet good doomed Judy, wherever you are now, forgive me for all the wrong I did you, and remember the good and happy times we had together. Think of Lassen and Moab. Think of *Le Rendezvous*. Think of Organ Pipe and Everglades. Think of Suzie. Think of me.

August 18, 1970 – North Rim

Grandmaw's gone, Inger's back, thank Gawd. [Sister] Nancy's here on a brief visit. John Debris and his Judy are here for the rest of the season: good. All my reservations about John I now abjure: he's a good man. A fine man and a great artist and the best friend, maybe the only man-friend, I've got anymore. I am grateful. My comrade — we'll die together.

September 16, 1970 - Logan, Utah

Sent little Suzi back to Grandmaw and New Jersey today by air with Ingrid. [Abbey's spellings of his daughter's name vary from entry to entry, even within individual entries, in the journals — Suzi, Suzie, Suzy, Susie, etc.] Desolation in my heart. Sweet utterly lovable little Suzi — I feel I've betrayed her, forsaken her. But there was nothing else I could do. Nobody would help me. It's so difficult even to find a decent place to live in Salt Lake City.

I am teaching "creative writing" at the University of Utah this fall.

November 18, 1970 - Salt Lake City

Snowstorm outside.

"Just remember how she was — and write her off. You have to do it sooner or later. Do it now."

If only I could be sure I'd never see roses in a glass in a quiet room again. Never again hear Bach in the background — the suites for solo cello. Some things are too much. Most of the time, I do not think of her — but when I do, the sorrow is still there, still here, as bitter and baffling as ever.

The novel *Black Sun*, which I never clearly understood (although I wrote it), now has meaning for me: it is a novel about death — which, in the case of one you love and need, is an inexplicable *vanishing* — an unaccountable *deprivation* — an *opaque void* — a hopeless *disappearance* . . . a meditation upon death.

February 28, 1971 - Kanab, Utah

Inconsolable memories. Inassuagable grief. Her hands groping in the air. The torment of her pain. The moments of panic and despair. Her brave valiant efforts to do what they asked her to do. That courage of hers, which was more heartbreaking than her pain and fear. (Oh, there are times when I think I shall rise up at night screaming with the agony, the unendurable torture of these memories. . . .)

Time to be thinkin' of work, man. Time for the wild bunch to ride again, the wooden shoe mob, THE MONKEY WRENCH GANG! Strikes! Again!

March 9, 1971 - Kanab

The Program: What must I do? Meet my obligations: write a book or books, make money for Suzi and Josh and Aaron. Make them a home somewhere, somehow. Pay off my debts. Some way.

Be good to my good Ingrid.

Keep my body alive, even if the soul is dead. Get out in the wind and sun every day. Do not abuse the poor, faithful beast that has served you so well for over four decades. Getting close to half a century!

Try to go beyond your morass of personal affairs. Think of others more. Be cheerful and sympathetic, or at least try to be, or at least feign it and maybe the honest emotions will follow. Transcend thyself, man.

Write your three pages each day before you allow yourself any indulgences. Daily labor is good for the spirits.

Chop wood. Make things. Play with your child. Share with your friends. Grow something. Moderate your wrath, moderate your anger, pacify your hatred. Build a cabin in the woods or a hut in the desert. Avoid the cities.

(ACEDIA. . . .)

May 18, 1971 - North Rim

Sweet Ingrid is chopping out my heart for supper.

May 19, 1971 - North Rim

Suzi is with me: a sheer delight. Such a gay, bright, clever, joyous child — a joy to have and hold. I can lose all else, but not Suzi.

Sad and bitter quarrels with Ingrid. She's been brooding over all the wrongs I've done her over the past year. But — she hasn't left me (completely) yet. Which means, I suppose, there is still hope. ALL MAY YET BE WELL. And Suzi seems to like her.

Of course I have a couple of other lady-friends waiting in the wings (Boston, Berkeley). But none so beautiful and young and wise and witty as my Ingrid. The best by far.

Ah yes, what to do? The old dilemma.

∞

Black Sun — a thundering lead balloon so far. Brief notices in the papers, but not a decent review yet. Maybe it really is a lousy book. But *I* like it.

May 26, 1971 - North Rim

Me father was here a week ago. The old man. He spent a week with me and we hiked the Canyon together, rim to rim. He looks awful in the face, ravaged and gaunt, sunken eyes, yellowish complexion. Nevertheless, he seems to be still in good shape; he walked the old trail happy and whistling and never faltered, in fact walked almost as fast as I would have walked, though he stopped much more often.

I fear I was unkind to him, much of the time, unable to conceal my irritation. I love him, I love him — but I can't bear to live with him day by day. Petty tragedy.

Sunday morning, his last day here, he walked up the trail-road to say good-by: "I don't approve of everything you say and do, Ned," he said (he did not approve of *Black Sun*, naturally), "but I love you anyway." We embraced. "I love you too, Dad." And he walked away, looking quite handsome then, in his big coat and silver-gray Stetson and his white hair. My poor old Paw.

June 10, 1971 – North Rim

Where was my Ingrid last night? Sick with longing and anxiety, I searched for her for an hour. Oh where? "I loved you so much . . . I will miss you for a long time." Oh yes!

∞

Gave a speech at Aspen [Colorado] High graduation ceremonies last Friday eve, June 4th.

Aspen: lovely girls in minimal skirts. Maddening lust! "I was insatiable," said Tolstoy. Alas, yes. "Will I never be rid of this demon that rides me night and day?" (Sophocles?) Apparently not. Do I want to be? Hell, no. "Oh Lord, make me chaste . . . but not yet." (Augustine? Auden? Me?) No wonder dear sweet Ingrid has given up on me.

June 10, 1972 – Aravaipa Canyon, Arizona

[During the "year of silence" referred to here, Abbey made no journal entries.]

A year of silence. That golden stuff.

Exactly one year. Odd, what.

So what the fuck am I doing here? (My language has degenerated; I've become very crude and foul-mouthed lately; symptoms of sloth and acedia, no doubt.)

Well, it's just another fucking cocksucking goddamned stupid fucking job that's all: so I'm manager, or "coordinating custodian," of a wildlife refuge: forty-thousand acres of rugged canyon and mountain country. I should be happy as a pig in shit. And I am.

October 9, 1972 – Tucson

No getting around it, some men are queer for women.

A lovely rainy day here in the arboreal desert, sweet sweet lovely melancholy rain . . . fucking Mozart on the stereo. . . .

Am I really so simple and crude and ugly as I sometimes seem in these vulgar pages? No, I am not. I am a sensitive young punk, poetical, melancholical, romantic, fastidious, fond of Mozart and marigolds and cats and cunt and delicate varieties of fruit such as watermelon and buckbrush nuts.

October 31, 1972 – Tucson

Writer's block. I got it. For a year and a half now, I have not writ a word on *MWG*. For a full month, I have been lounging about the house trying to write and getting nowhere. Fuck!

Two more masterpieces — *MWG* and *The Good Life*. Then the desert, and music, and mysticism until the circle closes. An eternity in each silver moment.

Christmas Day 1972 – Tucson

I've been living with Janet for about six months now. A crazy and neurotic but also very pretty, sexy, funny, clever, delightful, kind, sweet and generous girl — in most ways, the best girlfriend I've ever had.

There is nothing so obscene as an American Christmas, about which I wrote the following note to my parents, out of bitterness, to wit, viz:

"Merry Christmas and all that, but I must say that never has Christmas in America seemed to me so obscene as now — this national orgy of gluttony, fake religiosity, nauseating and hypocrite music, the cobweb of official lies and deception while the B-52s are doing their shameful and cowardly work in Vietnam. 'Peace is at hand,' said Kissinger, our Machiavellian Metternich. I am utterly disgusted with this country, with this smug fat brutal people. I hope and pray that the wrath of God, if there is a God, will destroy this nation soon. We deserve it, just as the Germans did. . . ."

∞

The Canyonlands. What's the use: no matter where I go, what I do, I can't get the canyon country out of my heart. A love affair with a pile of rock. Will I never be content until I make my home on the rim of Utah, at World's End, under juniper, lightning and cloud, Temple Mountain, Labyrinth and Desolation canyons, Mollie's Nipple and the Bishop's Prick? Guess not. The current scheme involves a homemade sixty-five-foot adobe houseboat — a hide-out afloat on "Lake" Powell — death sudden and violent, plenty of blood and ecstasy. What the fuck.

I do not fear death. I fear loneliness. And torture. Prison. And power. If only I could be as strong and brave as others say I look!

June 10, 1973 - Aravaipa (one year later)

Still here! Longest I've held a steady job since . . . since when? Since I was drummed out of the army in '47.

Despite the lugubrious tone prevailing through most of these erratic journals, I am, most of the time, a rather happy man. The air of self-pity comes from the fact that I generally write in this book *only* when down, dejected or in trouble. And this book [Journal XIV], please note, is now more than five years old.

I am in good health, "just fine as a frog's hair," as old Cliff Wood says. Walked forty miles around Navajo Mountain [just north of the Arizona-Utah border and east of Lake Powell] a couple of weeks ago. I can still fuck three or four times a day, if decently stimulated (though not *every* day). I can ride, swim, dive, play tennis, climb rocks — in short, the old (forty-six years) body will do nigh anything I ask of it. More than I ask.

And I look good, better than I ever have before. My weight is up to 190 pounds — I *look* big, solid, muscular. Well, shit, I am. Sounds as if I'm falling in love with myself. Quite true; I'm as vain as Narcissus; I love mirrors and running around stark-raving naked. And I enjoy amazing success with girls; I could pick up a new one every week if I wished. But I don't; too much bother. And besides — after a whole year! — I'm still largely pleased with my darling Janet. And Renee — my "Natasha," my "Sandy," my forbidden delight.

The world is full of good things. An abundance of sweet things — fruit, ideas, women . . . rocks, trees, snakes. . . .

But I must stop this adolescent gloating, this inventory garbage. I am not writing enough; *MWG* proceeds, limps along, much too slowly. And I'm not even sure it can be published. A difficult book.

But I really am a fairly happy man. I enjoy being alone, as I am today, and I enjoy the company of friends, as I did yesterday and the night before. My mind is clear, my head on straight, my body functioning properly, my heart alive and throbbing — and them blues, they don't come knockin' on my door no more. (Knock on wood!) As for women, with a daughter like Suzi, I think I could survive quite well without any more heavy romances cluttering up my golden years. If necessary.

July 3, 1973 – Aravaipa

Susan G. — the violence of her passion! She came so hard and so fast and so often, I could hardly come myself. A wonderful girl, the sweetest cleverest prettiest — ah, but you say that about them all. True. And it's always true. I love them all. The lists, the stockpile, mean nothing: I love the girl I'm *with*, here and now. Whoever she may be.

Women *are* better than men. I ought to know. Not only different — but better!

July 5, 1973 – Aravaipa

I'm tired of "hippies," "freaks," that whole sick crew. I find, more than ever, that I respect only *men* — and *women* — who can *act*, who can do good things well, who are responsible to others, who are honest in all ways, who *really care* about this earth we live on. Letting your hair grow is not good enough; nor does a headband make an Indian. I'm tired of soft weak passive people who can't *make anything* — except babies. (You sound tired, Doc.)

∞

Javalina: a wild, piglike animal. (Sounds like *Peacock* [Douglas, a close friend and model for Hayduke in *The Monkey Wrench Gang* and *Hayduke Lives!*].)

August 12, 1973 – near Redstone, Colorado

Stranded. Goldang ole truck give out on me last night with fouled plugs, burnt-out points and now today the battery is dead as a doornail. I paid two-hundred hard-earned dollars for this here truck, and I wuz robbed. Ole '62 Dodge V-8 carryall with tall tires, an altimeter on the dashboard, four-speed stick-shift. Was doing fine until a few days ago, when the fucker began to miss and I noticed she was a-burnin' oil too. And I was getting fond of this hyar beast. Still am. Gotta get a mechanic up here from Redstone or Carbondale, I reckon.

I was on my way to Aspen ("that grim and squalid playground") to hear Ben Lipman play Elliott Carter's piano concerto. No soap. Never made it. So here I sit, full of spite. Couldn't hardly ask for a prettier place for the old truck to croak, I guess, with the Crystal River down below, spruce and fir and aspens all around and me — *à solitaire* — in the middle!

September 20, 1973 – Aravaipa

From a memo to the *Tucson Daily Citizen*, re a recent interview:

"I did *not* say 'We are heading for catastrophe.' I said, 'We are heading for Fredonia.' "

November 17, 1973 - Aravaipa

A nasty scene with Janet. I'm afraid it's all over with us.

Renee — a splendid girl. The best ever — lovely and warm, humorous and bright and witty, gracious and sophisticated. She's the first girl I've known, since Virginia L-D, who has that rare, fine, excellent quality the vulgar call *class*. My teen-age sweetheart. (Grown up at last — eighteen a week ago!)

November 20, 1973 - Aravaipa

A cold sunny day at Aravaipa. The heartcracking loveliness of this bloody, incomprehensible world. Cardinals and thrashers, woodpeckers and wrens and gilded flickers, cowbirds and doves in the air. And I, lord of it all, custodian and janitor of a seventy-thousand-acre wildlife preserve. With a fine novel to finish and a sweet young absolutely delightful girl to love and a bright jewel of a daughter and the body in firm fettle and what is there to despair about, anymore? Except despair. I have been and am a very lucky man. And I have earned and I deserve every fucking bit of it.

And I rejoice.

And I *am exceedingly* glad.

And I shall piss and whine no more, nay, nor moan and bitch, nor take the name of My Lord in vain, for he has been *exceedingly* good to me and lo! his servant Abbey waxeth *fat,* and *prospers,* and curseth not so much as formerly, nor shaketh fist at that old, ancient, heartbreaking, wild and iron sky that seals and shelters us from (peace!) that (whatever) which lies beyond. *I am blest.* Amen.

∞

END OF JOURNAL XIV

MOONRISE AT
BALANCED ROCK

Road map: *During the almost three years recorded in Journal XV, Abbey continued his gadfly existence, living serially in Arizona; Moab; Glacier National Park, Montana; Moab; Arizona; and Moab. Throughout all these moves, he remained relatively happy, his marriage to Renee more or less sound. Ed also won a Guggenheim grant and published two more books: the novel* The Monkey Wrench Gang *and the essay collection* Journey Home. *Feeling shunned and misunderstood, Abbey's contempt for the eastern literary establishment grew ever more bilious.*

JOURNAL XV

February 1974 to October 1977

∞

February 10, 1974 – Aravaipa Canyon, Arizona

Married once again and — I swear — for the final time. If this one fails, for any reason, I shall resign myself forever to the call of solitude, wander the world with my Suzi and maybe a small friendly homely dog.

But it won't. Renee is the right one, at last, after twenty-seven years (!) of searching. Very young — eighteen now, sixteen when I met and fell in love with her — she is not only beautiful and sweet and gentle and full of love for me, but also — so to speak — unspoiled, free of all those neurotic tics and nervous fears that older women invariably reveal after the honeymoon begins to fade. Spoiled, mostly, by men of course, by mistreatment or what they imagine is mistreatment. Anyway, I've found the one *I* want. And by Gawd, I'm going to keep her!

6:14:02 p.m., May 4, 1974 – Aravaipa

Currently on page 647 of *Monkey Wrench.* A splendid hilarious tragic book. Four little humans against the Glittering Tower of the Power Complex, Mega-Machine. Should dedicate it to Lewis Mumford. He'd disown it. Not his type. One-and-a-half chapters and an epilogue to go. Then FINIS.

May 30, 1974 – Aravaipa

Fired from my job with Defenders of Fur-Bearers [Defenders of Wildlife]. Why? Fell out of favor with [Ted] Steele. Why, how? Don't know. Now what? On to Utah! Build the boat. Bitterness. A shabby, sneaky, cowardly thing to do, what *they* did. Not quite honorable. Not quite *gentlemanly*. "My Dear Edward," he would say. Ted Steele — that semi-senile capricious tyrannous old man. Fuck the DOW! That old woman's organization, of all ages, all sexes, fuckers. I'll probably spend a couple more months here anyway.

∞

Transcendence. It is this which haunts me night and day. The desire to transcend my own limits, to exceed myself, to become more than I am. How? I don't know. To transcend this job, this work, this place, this kind of life — for the sake of something superlative, supreme, exalting. But where? Again, how? Don't know. It will come of itself . . . like lightning, like rain, like God's gift of grace, in its own good time. (If it comes at all.)

∞

Mexico. The Revenge. Population rising from fifteen million in 1900 to somewhere close to sixty million in 1975 — a five-fold increase in three generations — with *half* the present population *under* the age of seventeen! Dare one mention — or is it impolite and impolitic? — their real and pressing problem? And the only solution? Which no amount of *turismo* or *industrialismo* is going to solve? May one? *No, gringo, mind your own fucking beez-ness and geeve me peso!*

∞

Tom Wolfe (*Pump House Gang*, etc.) — a pretentious fad-chaser and apologist for the techno-tyrants. That faggoty fascist little fop: the pom-pom girl of American letters.

September 15, 1974 – Moab, Utah

Moved up here in July. Bought a crumbly old house a month ago for $26,000. Regrets, vain useless regrets about selling that beautiful old stone house at Sabino — the only real-value property I ever owned. We also bought twenty acres up along Green River. For $3,000. Good deal, there, for once. Abbey as businessman: sell cheap, buy dear. . . . Christ, I shouldn't have to waste valuable minutes fretting about such trifles. Should give all my money to the Sierra Club and be done with it. Ah! the bliss of poverty!

MWG turned down by Knopf (Gottlieb) and Random House; Simon & Schuster is interested but wanted one-third cut; McGraw-Hill and Dutton [made offers].

October 5, 1974 - Moab

MWG contract signed. A movie option "probable." No paperback deal arranged yet.

I'm embarrassed by this sudden wealth. Except, of course, it's all really fantasy. A bunch of paper. One-third to the IRS, one-third to Rita — leaves me what? Practically *nada*. Enough to buy pinto beans, maybe, for a year or two.

Drinking too much again: insulting cell tissues, all them brain cells rotting away, cirrhosis of the liver, kidney stones, the shakes — Jesus Christ! Gimme a drink!

Rabbit Redux: these third-rate novels by fourth-rate novelists published by Knopf.

Fear of Flying, Erica Jong: banal and boring; typical psycho-hang-up New York Jewish fem-lib bullshit.

Castaneda: a teenybopper intellectual's writer.

Desert Solipsism by E. Abbett, LDS, famous unknown arther.

Bill Eastlake: a master storyteller from whom we learned much and borrowed more.

Rock: imitation Afro industrial music; music to assemble Mack trucks by. Slave-labor music. Music to hammer out fenders by.

Billboard for new housing development near Phoenix: "Five Different Lifestyles to choose From."

We've got no life, only lifestyles.

November 30, 1974 - Moab

Nearing the final end of agony in revising *MWG*. I am tired of obscurity! I want to be famous! Like everybody else! At least for fifteen minutes. (Like Andy Warhol promised.)

February 6, 1975 - Moab

I'm feeling depressed. Why? *Can't say.* Sibelius chanting in the background (the Fifth) helps some, but not enough. I want to weep. Why? *Can't say.*

Renee is also depressed, and not well, and has to call her doctor today, and is bored with me and [this place] and wants to go back to school.

DePuy [replying] to a young mocker: "I'll live to piss on your grave!"
American Indians: imitation rednecks.

Unrequited lust: that feeling like a toothache where you know you got
no teeth.

Mexican women don't shave their legs; *porque*? Because [body] hair
shows Spanish rather than Indian ancestry; caste before beauty — they're
proud of their hairy legs.

Mexico — the India a'burning on our southern border; the cactus Cal-
cuttas of Juarez and Nogales.

March 21, 1975 - Moab

Guggenheim finally came through with an award, beginning this July.
Shall we head out for Vienna my dear? Thanks to Larry [Lawrence Clark]
Powell.

I'm planning a little walk along the White Rim [Canyonlands National
Park], sixty miles, but mostly on the level. The only problem is water; I'm
waiting for a good rain or snow in the area (potholes).

The Guggenheim grant, by the way, is [to allow me to work on] *The
Good Life* [an autobiographical novel, never finished, about growing up on
a farm]. I must start thinking about that work — the farm, the old man,
the glory and tragedy of hard work, etc.

I have little to say in my journal these days. Why? Because I am so
contented, busy, happy, et cetera? Probably. Or because I have little to
say? Not so much introspection anymore? Haven't heard from myself for
a long time.

Still no settlement with Rita. She's got a judgment against me now in
Arizona for $13,000. Have paid $4,500 on it, but received absolutely no
concessions in return. Hiding. Secret addresses. Oh, the humiliation and
indignity of it all. The unforgiving woman. Vengeance. The fury of the
discarded wife. And alimony is not even tax deductible.

∞

Had a nice walk along the White Rim, from Murphy Hogback to Little
Bridge Canyon, with a twenty-mile side-trip down through White Crack to
Green River. Splendid, lonely, fantastic country. All delightful — except
the last ten miles on a slushy road in the dark through a phukking bitter
blizzard. Full moon over slickrock, potholes full of water shining under
stars, blackbrush and junipers *gleaming* with snow.

These are the happiest days of my life and I hate it! Where's the misery
to which I'd grown so comfortably accustomed?

∞

DePuy: "Seen my latest masterpiece?"
Abbey: "Haven't seen your first one yet."
(The *retort discourteous.*)

∞

Those pitiful weak egos of those who rejoice in our government's little triumphs, sink with each well-earned defeat; that is, all their pride is invested in the nation-state: they have, it seems, no pride in themselves apart from "America."

May 17, 1975 – /Moab

Turned down a fire-lookout job at Jacob Lake [North Rim, Grand Canyon] because the Forest Service had no accommodations for my wife. Now that was a dumb thing to do! We could have camped out in the truck in the woods.

June 7, 1975 – /Moab

The tragic fallacy of *Joy of Sex* and all other such training manuals is that what a man really desires is not 144 different positions, but 144 different women.

"Beauty, charm and novelty — and the greatest of these is novelty."

June 20, 1975 – /Moab

Just back from NYC. Interview with John Baker of *Publishers Weekly*. Hit on the head with two deadly double-dry martinis, I babbled like an idiot — can hardly remember what he asked or what I said. Never again. I hate that sort of thing.

July 10, 1975 – Numa Ridge Lookout, Glacier National Park, /Montana

So here we are, me and Renny, seven-thousand feet above sea level, in a square wooden shack on a rocky peak looking down down down on a million acres of piney woods and the peculiar, milky-green lakes of Bowman, Akokala, and the North Fork of the Flathead River. What gives the water here its strange color? "Glacial milk," they call it, the powdered rubble ground from the rocks by the ponderous movement of the glaciers.

Above us loom a number of bare, grim, craggy, snow-dappled peaks: Reuter, Kintla, Numa, Chapman, Carter, Rainbow, Square, Vulture, Great Northern and Logging. The highest in sight is Kintla, over ten-thousand feet. The roughest-looking is Rainbow, which has been climbed by only thirty-five people in all of human history. So far as known. I shall be the thirty-sixth.

Wildlife: We've seen a few black bears, one cow moose, deer, a golden eagle. Mountain goat tracks on the trail, also elk droppings and bear shit. There is indeed, as Doug [Peacock] says, something "titivating" about a woods wherein Grizz, *Ursus arctos horribilus,* is known to prowl. One stays alert. One pays attention to strange noises back in the brush. One looks about for climbable trees.

Renee is a delightful companion in this situation. Cheerful, clever, sharp and unafraid, and growing prettier every hour — I have never loved her so much as I do now. How fortunate I am, ugly hairy smelly morose old man, to have so good and strong and beautiful a wife.

Bears, beans, bores and bugs: Numa Ridge Lookout.

July 21, 1975 – Glacier National Park

Shakespeare: Certainly, he was a master poet — but his plays are archaic bores: the childish humor of his comedies; the farcical nonsense of his tragedies; the tedious sychophancy of his histories. One of the many things I dislike is the total absence of any real, free, independent men in his world — all we have are masters and slaves, bosses and the bossed, and the prevailing slime of servility by which the hierarchical machinery is lubricated; in short, no MEN. Therefore — no heroes, no tragedy.

Shakespeare, the immortal bard — vastly overrated. Really belongs in the company of other distinguished hacks, such as S. N. Behrman, J. T. Racine, Ben Jonson, J. M. Barrie, Gilbert & Sullivan, etc. etc. . . . characters I admire most in Shakespeare are his villains: Jack Cade, Caliban, Edmund the Bastard, Macbeth, that chap who married Hamlet's mother, what's his name, etc. In all of Shakespeare, there is no Spartacus — not a single one.

Ah, you say, but such a figure could not have been regarded as heroic in Shakespeare's time, and Shakespeare was very much a product of his time. To which I reply — Precisely. I think it unbecoming of a writer to submit, supinely, to evil institutions merely because they constitute the prevailing order of things. Raleigh serves as an example of a man who was able, unlike Shakespeare, to rise above and see beyond the narrow limitations of his own time. Marlowe was another.

I'm a narrow-minded sonofabitch. I lack that generosity of spirit and easy tolerance of others I so much admire in a man like, well — who? Henry Miller? I suppose so. Yet he too is impatient with fools. He says.

∞

Mon ami DeBris: fancies that he looks like Zapata, whereas in reality he resembles much more an organ-grinder from the Lower East Side without his monkey; tall skinny gray-haired, wild-eyed furtive nervous and shifty-eyed. *Mon ami* . . . and yet I love him. Despite his defects, which are, after all, of no more serious consequence than my own. How must *I* sometimes appear to *him*? If he really sees me at all? (Which I doubt.) Or to others (most of the human race) more perceptive? One prefers not to think about that.

DeBris: his tendency always to . . . *over-exaggerate*. The melo-romantic.

August 10, 1975 – Numa Ridge Lookout

Most writers write the same book over and over again. Certainly I do. Trying to get it *right*. Just as Bruckner wrote one symphony nine times, striving for the perfect Brucknerian symphony. *And almost made it.*

Goddamn cocksucking motherfucking reviewers and critics and fellow writers refuse to take my books seriously, even when they're not serious. Bastards! And of course they [Abbey's books] don't sell either. Shit. Piss. Cuckoo-eruptions!

August 25, 1975 – Numa Ridge

MWG appears a flop so far. Turned down by book clubs, no progress on movie screenplay, no big advance sales and no raves yet from reviewers or other writers. Nice mentions in *Audubon*, *Playboy*, a few newspapers, but that's all. Oh well, so it don't sell. That — as Gaddis says — is the publisher's problem. Of course, the official publication date is still seventeen days away. One more book down the well of oblivion.

Doubtless I'll be accused of a rash of crimes now. Every time some Boy Scout sugars a bulldozer, or shellacs an earth-mover, they'll come looking for me. The men in blue, with their tiresome questions. Ah well, martyrdom, I'll try it on for size. Though the cut of the garment doth not appeal.

∞

This wet dark clammy-cold Northwest. A somber landscape of pine and peaks, in a minor key. [I hear the] thrilling cry of a loon from Long Bow [Bowman] Lake, three-thousand feet below. Hungry eagles cruising by, checking out our chipmunks. The nervous, paranoid deer. The sullen, red-eyed, irritable grizzly bear, crashing through the dark forest, muttering to himself. (That dance they do, when bluffing, or threatening, or pondering a charge: stamping with the forefeet, first one then the other, growling.) *Les Grizz.*

Staggering up the trail to the lookout, through the dark and dank and heavy woods, I just *assume* any Grizz I meet will be understanding, accommodating, forbearing, if not outright friendly. You know me, Pooh.

The dark cold wet Northwest. I dream of Vermilion Cliffs, of White Rim, of Grand and Slickhorn gulches, of Waterpocket Fold and San Rafaeal Reef and Book Cliffs and my little hay farm and gopher ranch on the banks of the golden Green.

Southern Utah — a "depressed area," meaning really, merely, non-industrialized.

What's wrong with northwest Montana? Not enuf aspens. Too much fire suppression. All them smoke-jumpers waiting in Missoula.

September 20, 1975 - Moab

A day so heart-rendingly beautiful (clear, bright, sunny, breezy; cumuli floating above the mountains) that it breaks your heart to think that someday this will all go on without you — or what is worse, that you (as the mystics say) might have to go on without this sweet desert earth.

November 6, 1975 - Moab

Dejection. Loss of nerve. Awake at four in the morning, full of fear. A manic-depressive, I am now in the depressed phase. The apparent failure of *MWG* doesn't help; still no reviews in the goddamn NYC media. (Has sold only about ten-thousand copies to date. Bad. No foreign sale. No paperback sale — waiting for the movie. *I* think it's a jolly, jocund, joyful, jubilant book! Not angry, not porno-violent, but good-humored, happy, ending on a note of reconciliation as all good comedies should. Rollicking! Exuberant! Joyous! Goddamnit!) Loss of the house in Tucson. Swindled on Green River farm. Renee losing interest in me. Economic insecurity (no job anymore, of any kind). But worst of all, facing that blank page: *Another book to write.* Ahhhhh! (Shee-it!)

One-hundred years from now we'll all be dead. Good.

Always, anytime, he'd sacrifice the finest nuance for a laugh . . . anything for a cheap gag — like the trapeze artist who dropped his partner.

Hayduke, of course, is a *hajduk, heiduk:* a Magyar, Serbian, Turkish word meaning "brigand" or "robber" or Balkan bandit-resister (*Oxford English Dictionary*); or (thanks to Katie Lee), in Hungarian, "foot soldier."

The one-eyed stranger in *MWG* is really the reincarnation of Jack Burns, the "Brave Cowboy" — some fan pointed this out to me; I'd never thought of it; incarnated a third time as The Old Man in *Sundown Legend.* [*Sundown Legend* was Abbey's working title for the novel eventually published as *Good News.* Incidentally, Jack Burns eventually was incarnated yet a fourth time as the patch-eyed "Lone Ranger" in Abbey's final novel, *Hayduke Lives!*]

December 8, 1975 – On the train to Chicago

Recently visited my sons in L.A. and Vegas. Josh and Aaron. Fine tall handsome talented and intelligent young men. I am so terribly proud of both of them. Josh the actor — I've written to Kirk Douglas, David Miller [and others] trying to get him a bit part in some film. Joshua, so impressive in his good looks, self-confidence, ease and grace. Already, at nineteen, he is more grown-up than I ever was. Best of all — despite all — he likes me. Loves? Maybe.

April 19, 1976 – Moab

The mountains stand like great vanilla ice cream cones above the watermelon mesas; trees and fields in spring green; flowers alight and bees alive! Glory glory *GLORY!*

∞

My favorite animal is the crocodile, my favorite bird the fly, my favorite bush the cactus.

∞

Alaskan bumper sticker: "'Happiness is a Texan headed south with an Okie under each arm."

October 29, 1976 – Moab

MWG finally reviewed in *New York Times!* — one year late — by Jim Harrison. Favorable notice; but misrepresents the book as a "revolutionary" tract for the old "New Left." Jeez! No mention of the comedy, the wordplay, the wit, humor and *brilliance!*

I'm reading *MWG* for the seventh time — not bad, but too many words. Too fucking goddamned many fucking words. Urgently needs a ruthless blue pencil. Alas, too late. "Arch, uneven, verbose verbiage." (*Publishers Weekly*)

The Avon paperback edition contains about a hundred typographical errors.

November 20, 1976 – Moab

Rage rage fury and outrage: They move in on us uninvited, they camp in our kitchen, they seem indifferent to the crudest hints ("Are you trying to get rid of us?" he said, laughing) — good fucking Christ! What does one have to do?

Like Cavangero or whatever his fucking name was: asks if he can stay overnight, then shows up with wife and babe-in-arms, stays a week. Besieged in my own house by strangers, *I* have to leave. . . . Zounds and gadzooks. Effrontery and insolence and insensitivity.

How to speed the departing guest? Good god! Suppose they won't even depart but just lounge around in your house day after day, eating your food, drinking your Michelob, wiping their asses on your toilet paper, doing nothing but knitting and eating, for holy sweet motherfucking Christ's sake!

I don't know.

One should be brutal and direct, courageous. Say, "Look here, mate; nice to have a beer with you, even a meal, but for godsake you've made your visit, you've seen me; now, for the love of God, go!"

November 29, 1976 – Moab

Mailed the first ninety-eight pages of *Sundown Legend* to [Frederick] Hills at McGraw-Hill, via [Don] Congdon, today. Is it any fucking good? How the fuck should I know? Not my problem.

∞

One definite advantage of being a conservative is that you never have to trouble your conscience about selling out; a conservative is a sell-out from the beginning, an ass-kisser and power-sycophant by definition.

∞

Sent two chapters of *Sundown Legend* to *Mother Jones*, 1-10-77 (first and third). Rejected! 1-20-77. So, well, fuck 'em.

∞

T-shirts, posters, postcards, arm patches: on becoming a "cult hero" — "I don't write for hippies or college sophomores; I write for literate, educated people like yourself, who enjoy a good story told with style, passion and wit." (As told to Grace Liechtenstein, *New York Times*.)

∞

"You corrupt honkey." — [Thomas] McGuane

Re: my letter to *Harper's*, published in November (?) '76 issue, attacking "Tom Wolfe" as a sycophant to the rich and powerful, and suggesting that his so-called "Happiness Explosion" is fueled largely by booze, dope and Valium. In reply, he accused me of faulty logic and hiding in my den. *Touché!* (That faggoty little fascist fop.)

The Edward Abbey of my books is largely a fictional creation: the true adventures of an imaginary person. The *real* Edward Abbey? I think I hardly know him. A shy, retiring, very timid fellow, obviously. Somewhat of a recluse, emerging rarely from his fictional den only when lured by money, vice, the prospect of applause.

January 27, 1977 – Moab

Fifty years of old. Been stumbling around, sweating and whining, on this dirty old planet for nigh half a century. Fifty years. Had a great party anyhow: Renee made a cake with fifty burning candles on it — the booze flowed freely — Father Sandy was there, and Quist, and T.K. Arnold and many others. But I lost $12 in a poker game afterwards. (Detrimental to faith in my fellow man.)

February 23, 1977 – Moab

Fifty years old! Haven't I done most everything I ever wanted to do? I've enjoyed the friendship of a few good men, the love of several fine women. Fathered three sound, healthy and superior children (superior to their father). Wrote a couple of novels I'm not ashamed of, and some other books. Enjoyed a modicum of fame and glory, sudden money and easy living. Been fairly good to my parents, fairly generous to my friends and lovers and wives. Seen a bit of history in action. Seen some of the world's most beautiful places. Camped in solitude on the rim of a high plateau, overlooking eternity. And so on.

And yet — and yet — of course, I am not satisfied. There must be something more. Something more I wanted to do . . . or be.

VALUES:
— Courage ("without courage, all other virtues are useless")
— generosity: kindness, gentleness, sharing
— wisdom: knowledge and understanding; search for truth
— health
— good useful work to do
— love and friendship
— sanctity of all life, of all forms of being (including rocks, hills etc.)
— intelligence and humor
—music, poetry, drama, fiction, ideas
— Nature
— fruit, nuts and beautiful women
— easy money and fat girls.

Just returned from a week on a fantastic, lovely desert island: *Isla de la Sombra*. A hauntingly beautiful, desolate place — the desert and the sea, side by side — ah! too much. I was sea-sick with beauty! *Encantada.* . . .

My readings in Tucson, at U of A, were apparently a great success. The auditorium was packed *two nights running*, aisles jammed, people in doorways — biggest audience since Neruda, said one lady. And yet, I feel I did not do my best for such an eager, appreciative crowd. Too much playing to the gallery, going for the cheap gag and the easy laugh. I read them my "Profane Love Poems" — much laughter. And "Revelation" — and dumb fan letters — and "The BLOB comes to Arizona." Not good enough. I feel I let them down a bit, those nine-hundred or so enthusiastic young people.

I played the clown instead of the sage. Was that wise? They came, presumably, for wisdom and beauty; I gave them jokes. The Entertainer. Not enough. Not good enough.

— REMORSE. . . .

∞

All these letters, speaking invitations, etc. But never have I received any letters from old friends at UNM, or any kind of invitation from that school. Letters from strangers every day, but never a word from those I'd most like to hear from.

March 5, 1977 - Moab

My father was seventy-six last month (born 1901). My mother is now seventy-two. My grandfather John lived eighty-one years, my grandmother Eleanor seventy, my grandfather C.C. ninety-two years, and Mother's mother? I don't know. Anyway, it looks like it's going to be a long haul. (Is that why I awake so often, in the gray dawn, with a heart full of dread? fear? panic? What am I afraid of? I don't know. The unknown?)

∞

Jack Burns: *one* eye!

How to write the difficult novel: Get on a slow boat to Fiji, with nothing but a typewriter, two reams of paper and a dictionary.

Hey! Remember — hurling the flaming spear off Deadhorse Point, while my father and DeBris watched?

March 22, 1977 - Moab

Gotta be good to my wife. I mean, better. For I'll never find another woman better than Renee. Or even half as good. And I know it. And yet I keep making these careless, thoughtless, mindless gestures toward break-up and disaster. Out of sheer sloth! stupidity! Some atavistic blind urge to self-destruction. As if I *wanted* to be lonely and miserable again. As if my present contentment and happiness were not tolerable. As if dejection were my natural norm. As if I hated my good fortune in marrying a girl as pretty, sweet, clever, intelligent and loving as Renee. As if I wanted, once again, to sink into despair, touch rock bottom of the soul one more time. Why?

Is happiness a bore?

God, the absurd pain we inflict not only on one another, but also on ourselves!

April 28, 1977 – Moab

Visited Josh and Aaron in Lost Wages [Las Vegas] last weekend. With Suzy. We four had dinner on Top O' the Mint. Played tennis.

I'm going up on Aztec Peak in the Tonto [National Forest, Arizona] next week. Fire lookout again. I hope finally to finish the fucking novel once ensconced up there. *The Sundown Legend.*

Should go to Australia, become a sheepherder.

Gave a reading at Utah State, Logan, on April 19th. Big hit, I guess. The hall was packed and they laughed at every line. Read them "Notes Found in a Beer Can: A River Journal." Answered a lot of questions, both pertinent and impertinent. Then a drunken party at Le Bistro. Dim memories of crawling over and under the table. (Legs and tits. All over the place.)

Agreed to write "Smoky the Cop" bit for *Outside.* They finally paid for "Desert Island."

May 7, 1977 – Aztec Peak Fire Lookout, Arizona

Lookout job. A beautiful place: yellow pine and aspen and spruce, eight-thousand feet elevation. Spectacular view: Roosevelt [Reservoir], Superstition Mountains, Four Peaks, Mogollon Rim, Salt River Canyon, Sierra Ancha Wilderness, buttes and mesas of the Fort Apache Reservation.

Winds have been howling for three days now. Nobody here but me and Ellie, our black Labrador mutt.

The lookout is a live-in, new (built in 1960), on a fifty-foot tower. No woodstove, unfortunately — only stinking propane. Cistern with rainwater and one decomposing rat, which I removed.

The old man was here, briefly, about twenty-four hours. Absolutely absorbed in his fears — heart trouble. Stroke. He wouldn't stay longer because he imagined he was having difficulty breathing at this altitude. He wants sympathy, but if you give him sympathy, he sinks into self-pity. And if you don't, he does anyway. No solution. What an abject, miserable way to end your life — in fear. I want to be proud of my father, but he's making it difficult. Or am I being too callous, indifferent, unfeeling? How would *I* feel and behave if I were in his situation? More bravely, I *hope*. But who knows for certain?

July 7, 1977 – Aztec Peak

Many newspaper reviews of *Journey Home* all over the country, but once again the goddamned NYC press seems united in giving my book the silent treatment. Suppression by silence. Same goddamn shit as buried *MWG*. Lousy cocksucking motherfucking tri-sexual sonsabitches. Only exception — a fairly good (but condescending) review in *New Times*, by one G. Wolff. Bastards! It ain't fair.

Should I complain? But to whom?

What the fuck. The press attempts to suppress my books. Old friends never write. The critics ignore my work. But what the fuck. I shall continue despite this shit, this ignorance and harassment. I still have a few books in my soul that must take form and body, must be born. If not for the good of the world, then at least for my own fucking sense of honor.

The reviewers consistently *misrepresented* the character of *MWG*.

∞

Letters I Wrote That Never got Answered:
"Dear Judy Collins . . . bring sleeping bag. . . ."
"Dear Gary [Snyder], I like your stuff too, except for all that Zen and Hindu bullshit. . . ."
To the Editors, *Ms.* Magazine, NY: "Dear Sirs. . . ."
"Dear Jean Sibelius: Happy Birthday."
To bill collectors and lawyers: "Edward Abbey regrets. . . ."
"Dear Ambassador Dobrynin. . . ."

— and Letters To Me That Never Got Answered:
"Dear Edward Albee. . . ."
"Dear *Senor* Abbey, please send two (2) pr cowboy pants. . . ." — Mario Roderigo Rodriguez-Silva ("call me Rod")
"Dear Mr. Abbey, Do you have any idea how funny you are? In a sick way, I mean. . . ."

August 11, 1977 – Aztec Peak

I'm sitting here at 1400 hours waiting for the lightning strike. A constant fizzing or buzzing noise (like frying eggs) emanates, apparently, from all metallic objects here as the charge builds up. That vast transfer of surplus electrons about to take place . . . the singing of excited electrons . . . the light crack of the whip, the flash, the awful crash! I can feel my tower shake beneath me — the smell of ozone — pink lightning strikes through the mist, followed by that rumpling, rolling, crashing reverberation of thunder — like toppling towers of masonry — echoing from mountain to mountain.

[Now comes] a dainty stroke with something like a fireball flung at the tip of it — great balls of fire!

The high thin cruel excruciating scream of the charge begins to fade somewhat now, as the heart of the storm moves beyond me into the west.

∞

B. Traven, Dreiser, James Jones et al — their prose is so bad, so crude, so stupid, that it's painful to read. And yet these lads often wrote better books than such master stylists as Henry James, Nabokov, Proust. Why? Perhaps there's something in great verbal felicity that misleads the writer, that betrays him into technique for the sake of technique; while the simple-minded prose writers, free of such allurements, are able to keep their attention fixed on the subject of their interest — the real life of actual human beings. Thus, their work, while repellent in style and detail, achieves great cumulative power through its steadfast devotion to fact, which equals and in the long run is equivalent to, the supreme poetry of truth.

The greatest writers were those, are those, capable of both powers: i.e., Tolstoy, Conrad, Chekov, Hemingway, Cervantes, Steinbeck and so on.

October 12, 1977 - /Moab

Oh Jesus Christ — my life is sinking into a bog of details, little ego trips, petty gratifications — this was not what I wanted. Not what I wanted. What I really want to do, to be, is something different. More difficult. My father is now seventy-seven; I am fifty; and love seems so fleeting, my "minor classics" and "regional notoriety" so vain and trivial, and the world — the bloody beautiful heart-breaking world! — so much more painful to understand than I had expected.

∞

END OF JOURNAL XV

Road map: *Finally, Abbey seemed to be narrowing the scope of his world — Moab, Tucson, Aztec Peak fire lookout, a brief vacation with daughter Suzi to the California desert — Journal XVI reflects a remarkably sedentary two years relative to his traditionally mobile lifestyle. This was also an introspective time for Ed, as suggested by journal entries that are by turns self-critical, angry and defensive. But also creative and productive; during his long tenure on Aztec Peak, especially, Ed enjoyed the experiences that would stimulate him to write several of the essays later collected in* Abbey's Road *and elsewhere. He was also hard at work on the novel* Good News. *His relationship with Renee appeared to be winding down.*

JOURNAL XVI

October 1977 to September 1979

∞

October 24, 1977 - Moab

Onward.

I saw Aaron and Joshua this weekend. My tall, handsome and talented sons.

∞

"This decaying, demented slaughterhouse of a planet." Where did I write that? Quoted in a review of *The Journey Home*.

Two books of mine, so far, give me that sensation Nabokov called "esthetic bliss": *Black Sun* and *The Monkey Wrench Gang*. All the rest is juvenalia or journalism.

All of my books have been hastily and carelessly written, in violent desperate spasms of last-minute effort to meet some publisher's mad, invented deadline. The only book I ever took pains with, actually labored over, was *Black Sun*. And all the reviewers hated it. (I think it's my best, most deeply felt.)

November 26, 1977 – Moab

Making a fresh new enemy: [Edward] Hoagland is very angry with me now because I called his friend [John] McPhee a temporizer and fence-straddler — no balls. [Hoagland] accuses me of envy and jealousy because McPhee's books get better reviews than mine do. But how can that be? My books don't get reviewed at all.

[Hoagland] even accuses me of envying Annie Dillard because her book [*Pilgrim at Tinker Creek*] was selected by Book of the Month Club. Is that true? That's awful! I made that cheap wisecrack about Dillard and Thoreau because Dillard is, I believe, the only contemporary "nature writer" who deliberately attempts to imitate him: the transcendentalist style, the high-flown (fly-blown) rhetoric, the raving about God. People who rave about God make me nervous.

January 23, 1978 – Moab

"God" — a word for not thinking. "Mystery" is better because it suggests questions, not answers. "'Why" is always a good question, the one question that distinguishes us from the other brutes.

Outdoors! Outdoors! Outlive the bastards! Joy, shipmates, joy! Piss on their graves! Keep their ulcers bleeding! Us nature mystics (and satyrmaniacs) got to stick together.

Marilyn's mother in Green Witch Village: "I've never seen so many young men out walking their toy poodles."

Grace L., girl reporter for the *New York Times*, once accused me of being thirty years behind the times. "*Thirty* years?" I said, insulted. "I'm a *hundred* years behind the times!"

Lord Chesterfield on sex: "The pleasure is momentary, the expense exorbitant, the position ridiculous."

May 17, 1978 – Aztec Peak fire lookout, Arizona

Alone on my mountaintop again. Rejoice. Me and my dog, my pipe, my bourbon, my pen.

Josh is coming for a visit soon — I hope.

The wind has stopped for a moment. Quietude surrounds me.

Bought a cute little desert house on 4-1/2 acres near Tucson. Lovely spot. A financial bind is possible.

Scribbling trivia here, busywork, waiting for profound thoughts to come. They do not come. No matter.

June 23, 1978 - Aztec Peak

The longest day. Yesterday evening, about 7 p.m., while walking down the lookout trail, I came almost face-to-face with a bear. I knew he was there, in the brush — I'd heard him. Standing still, waiting, this big golden-brown black bear appears, quite suddenly and silently, from behind a flowering locust. Head weaving a little, sniffing the air. Cousin Weak-Eyes.

I don't think he saw me, though he was less than fifty feet away. Fleas and midges hovered 'round his furry head, his black muzzle. He looked like a big dog. I waited; another moment and he caught my scent, snorted in alarm and rushed off, crashing through the woods.

Anyone who'd destroy that rare, beautiful, delightful beast for the sake of a rug on the floor should be — tacked to a barn wall for a dart board.

July 5, 1978 - Aztec Peak

Some goddamn cocksucking motherfucker tore the nylon flower off the hood of my motherfucking car yesterday, down in Globe [Arizona]. Glob. The Globules.

July 22, 1978 - Aztec Peak

The Hack's Progress: They keep demanding interviews — Miller for *Voice*. *Pipple* magazine, *Mudduh Jones, New Times, US'n, Mariah*, etc. What to do? My instinct is to crawl into my cave, refuse to see any of 'em. On the other hand, who's going to buy my books if nobody's ever heard of me? Edward Albee — who? I owe it, you might say, to my books. God knows I never get any help from the reviewers, or the critics, or my fellow scribes. (Thanks, fellas.)

The Windhover: Watching a redtail hawk poised on the wind; wind at twenty-five to thirty-five mph; the magnificent bird balanced in space, head twitching back and forth, watching below; the bird suddenly veers down, stooping (?), not in a dive, but feet-first, legs dangling — disappears into pines — reappears with a small brown thing wriggling in one talon — the hawk drops or loses the mouse for a moment, which falls diagonally, blown by the wind, back toward earth — hawk plunges after, re-snatches it, swoops to the top of a pine tree — pecks at mouse — glimpse of blood, red flesh — then gulps mouse whole, swallows, takes off again high into space, hovering about, indifferent to my movements and glasses.

In its swift sudden descent, the bird resembles a lady in skirts jumping off a bridge.

Saw my first authentic peregrine falcon yesterday. Exciting and beautiful, a true prince among birds, harassing the vultures — once I saw feathers fly. The falcon swoops, veers, hovers, planing and skating on the air; the vultures soar and sail, wings waggling in a shallow dihedral vee.

[I also saw the peregrine] eating a mouse in mid-air. Hovering and stooping, at terrific speed, head-first (unlike the redtail) into the forest. It perched for a while on a nearby pine, where I was able to make positive identification: the black mustache, the gray back, the narrow tail (fanned out in flight), the pinkish, speckled breast.

Dark clouds, a lightning storm beyond.

Do I want to be a hawk or falcon? No; I've had enough of extreme passion, anger, horror, pride and victory in *this* life; I'll settle for the contemplative insouciance of the turkey buzzard. Neither a Stoic nor an Epicure, but a Cynic. A Zen cynic.

Einstein was no doubt a great mathematician. All the mathematicians tell us so. But his true greatness lay not in his specialized talent, but in his humanity — in the fact that he cared about what is happening to our world. His greatest practical gift to humanity — the nuclear bomb — does not impel much sense of gratitude.

Nothing could be more foolish than to base one's moral philosophy on the vagaries of science. Whether the world began with a Big Bang, an act of special creation or always existed, has nothing of importance to do with the way we treat one another, our fellow creatures and this sweet planet earth.

The most common fallacy of contemporary scientism is the attempt to apply far-out, exotic scientific theory (relativity, e.g.) to ordinary, everyday, inductively empirical reality. Most scientific doctrines are based on, and require, extremely elaborate and long strung-out chains of inferences. They are seldom or never based on direct sensory experience. Therefore, they do not constitute knowledge. Information, yes; science gives us information. But not knowledge — *knowing* — and far less, wisdom, understanding, sympathy, love — each implying and entailing the others.

August 5, 1978 - Aztec Peak

Renee has been gone for eighteen days, off on her third dory trip down the Grand, and me feeling very lonesome, much forsaken, deeply unnecessary. I miss her!

Saw Suzi last Monday and that was good. My sweet, bright, clever, cute, loving and lovable daughter. She's almost ten years old now — the big One-O. I love her so much — and see her so little since we left Moab. Consigning her to Grandmaw once again, so that I'll be free to play, travel, waste a term at Idaho. Absurd. Absurd guilts. Self-torture. Remorse, etc. Shit and double-shit. Why do I wallow in this pit? Get to work! Get out of this! Of course.

Where's Josh? He was supposed to come this week. And Aaron — what ever happened to him?

Jack and Kathy [Loeffler; Jack is a musician, ethnomusicologist, and fellow anarchist; Kathy is a bookbinder and artist; both were among Ed's oldest and closest friends.] were here Tuesday, bringing gifts: steak, wine, apples, plums, a kaleidoscope, a book on flute playing by Johann Joachim Qusntz (1697–1773).

Aztec — evening and alone: My wind chimes tinkle gently. Storm cells growl and flicker in the north — thunder, lightning, curtains of rain. The sun going down in a solemn radiance of purple clouds, rimmed in scarlet.

Quietude. The distant cries of a hermit thrush — that flutelike song, deep in the dark and piney woods.

Why, in all this peace and beauty, should I trouble my soul with thoughts of war, politics, the endless battle to save a little of free, wild, agrarian America?

Why?

I don't know. Some vestigial sense of honor, I suppose. The less honor we have left — after all these decades of compromise, trade-offs, cowardice, evasion, temporizing, equivocating, fence-straddling — the more urgently we cling to what sense of honor still remains. I love the hills and the fresh wind, the desert and the sea, the forest, the swamps, the rural towns of America. I am obliged, therefore, morally obliged, to defend these things against the Enemy. Honor requires it.

The Enemy? We all know who the Enemy is. The Enemy speaks to us all the time — from the radio, on the television, on billboards, in the newspapers and slick magazines, in the halls of Congress, at the state capitol, in city hall.

And the Enemy says, "Behold, how sleek and fat I have become. Am I not the wonder of the world? Am I not the richest and most powerful beast on earth? Would you turn against the thing which has enriched you, which has given you safety and security and comfort, which promises you still more wonders in the future — electronic toys, computerized thinking, a life air-conditioned from womb to grave, an existence of endless novelty, luxury, diversion, things and more things, a universe of sport and adventure and romance and travel in the softness of your armchair, the ease of your V-8 four-wheel-drive wheelchair tourism, the sedation of your living room? A painless, discreet, sedated death? And all this for so little, so very little — merely for the price of some of your independence, a bit of your freedom, a little part of your manhood or womanhood, for only a little sacrifice of your humanity and honor. . . ."

Law and Order are not enough. Law and *Justice* is what I want. To hell with order! To hell with the law! I'll settle for justice, though the heavens fall.

(I realize this attitude is not merely a nuisance, but a great bore to almost everybody. I wish I could change; I wish I could adapt; I wish I could accept, with peace of mind, the standardized, institutional view of things. But I can't. There's something wrong with me. I'm a sick man, no doubt about it.)

September 7, 1978 – Aztec Peak

It occurs to me, now and then, that my solitary life here on the lookout much resembles my old fantasy of living alone in a stone hut deep in the desert — carrying water, wandering about naked, reading, writing, thinking, playing flute, dreaming, doing nothing at all; simply being.

But one does not really do much *thinking* alone. Not much. Most thought, I suspect, is generated in the company of others — by problems, conflict, disorder. Of course, in a way, reading and writing (if published) serve as a fairly adequate substitute for face-to-face contact. In some ways it's better, especially for slow-witted types like me who do not function well in extemporaneous debate.

Heidegger in his alpine cabin. Zarathushtra in his cave. Jesus alone in the wilderness. Nietzsche alone in his madness. The silent monks of the Crystal Mountain. . . . What do they know that we don't? They may be simply hiding from their creditors — or from their wives. *My* wife has long suspicioned that the holy beggardom of Hindu mystics, adopted in mid-life traditionally, was mainly an excuse to desert the care, trouble and aggravation of wife and family.

All solitude, too long endured, becomes madness.

September 8, 1978 – Aztec Peak

I have a good sweet loving wife, to whom, like a fool, I'm always exposing the worst aspects of my character: my melancholia, my volatile irritability, my jealousy and suspicion, the most narrow of my prejudices. Better be careful, try a little harder, or I'll lose this one too. And I don't, I really don't, I really *must not* lose again.

Yes, Virginia, there really is a Heaven. There is an ideal world. And we find that world in the realm of music. (I mean real music, of course, not our commercial "sounds.") In Bach, Mozart, Beethoven, Bruckner, a hundred others, we find that perfect world delineated, expressed, made real.

Proust was aware of this fact but, in his usual confused and fumbling way, went too far beyond the truth, into fantasy, by suggesting that the ideal world of music *proves* the existence of the traditional Christian notion — an actual 3-D Heaven *up there*, beyond time and space, where we can all disport ourselves after death. ("Mind is everything.")

Waking in the morning near the head of Cherry Creek Canyon. Salmon-colored clouds, surreally streamlined by the wind, sail slowly across the green and silver sky of the east. This is the world, *muchachos*. This is *our* world, mate, comrade, friend, lover. I want to share it with you. (Through my words, mainly.)

Susannah was born the night of the police riot at the Democratic convention in Chicago. August 28, 1969. And me going back and forth from Judy in the labor room to the TV in the waiting room. Two desperate struggles competing for my attention. I wanted to take a full part in each.

And oh God, how the beasts who run this country, and the sluggish swine who submit to their rule, how urgently both want to forget the whole thing: Chicago. Bobby Kennedy. People's Park. The draft-card burnings. The beatings, jailings, exiles, ridicule, hate, fear, murder. Kent State. The candlelight marches. Vietnam. . . .

(Clubbed down, we will rise again.)

My "friend" Hoagland says, in his *NY Times* review of *The Snow Leopard* [by Peter Matthiessen], that I am some kind of mystic, and guilty of "cranky quasi-political pronouncements" . . . *Cranky!* I say, that's not nice. And what the phuck does he mean, anyhow? I've always ridiculed mysticism — which is why my books sell even worse in California than in New York.

"Cranky"! What does he mean, "cranky"? (The wound begins to fester.)

October 19, 1978 - near Bodie, California

Suzi and I, camped out above Owens Valley: I wake early in the morning, Suzy still fast asleep. I go for a walk — too far and too long, as usual. I hear a thin high desperate cry, far away. Suzi? Returning hurriedly to camp, I see a small dark figure scurrying down the road toward the highway — Suzi, of course. I call and call; she finally hears me, stops, returns, crying with relief.

Poor little kid. She said she thought I'd gotten lost or killed — was dead. (Waking there alone.) Terrified, she'd dressed, then started down the road lugging my heavy briefcase. Too heavy, she removed from it my sheath knife, this journal, my address book and an envelope containing some checks — our money. The knife was "for snakes." The journal for . . . she "thought she'd want to read it sometime." Poor melodramatic Suzy!

The cardinal values: To love and be loved — a good wife, family, friends; good health; good work to do; intelligence, humor, sympathy, gentleness, strength, generosity; courage — without which all other virtues are useless; obvious necessities like sufficient food and shelter obtained without servitude; a beautiful home in a good place; or a humble home, any old shack, cabin, but in a free, wild, beautiful place; music, whiskey, art, poetry, sex, nature. . . .

Inbreeding. My Gawd, even the country-western singers are singing songs about country-western songs. Just like the highbrow literati, writing their novels about writing novels. (E.g., *Garp*, etc.)

And me, I'm doing too much of the same. Writing about myself. Writing about writing. The pathetic, pitiful, almost shameful longing for fame, money, money, fame . . . even mere shithead *publicity*. I too have been infected by the malaise. Reading magazine stories about myself. Admiring photographs of my simple semi-handsome hairy face. Compromise, compromise. The sell-out syndrome. I must be *very careful* from here on out. Hide. Work. Work. Hide.

November 7, 1978 - Tucson

I have enough money in the bank now to buy enough beans and rice for twenty-five years. To the end (sometimes longed for). Why not kidnap Suzy and sneak off to the life of a semi-hermit? A tempting, constantly tempting idea. Hide out up in Red Canyon, or Dirty Devil, or Trachyte Canyon under the Little Rockies?

Peace. Simplicity. Order, ceremony and ritual. Voluntary poverty. An end to clutter and this vulgar, stifling, crushing burden of things — junk — trash — *things!* — that weigh so upon our lives. I need some love in my daily life. Some loyalty. Some beauty. 'Tis a gift to be simple. 'Tis a gift to be free. . . .

December 9, 1978 - Tucson

The Hack's Progress:

Sent my Bodie "Ghost Town" bit to *GEO*. A dull, tedious, uninspired piece of prose. Much to my astonishment, they accepted it.

A lady editor at *Quest* calls me a "pisser" and a "blowhard" (in rejecting "Confessions of a Literary Bum").

Sent the final, copy-edited manuscript of *Abbey's Road* back to Dutton a week ago. Not a bad book, perhaps, but there is a lot of foolishness and a lot of plain bullshit in it.

Silence. Genius asleep. Quiet. Sleeping. Henry sleeping here. Zzzzzzzzz.

January 30, 1979 – Tucson

Fifty-two years olde [on the twenty-ninth]!
Confessions of a Barbarian — a comic hero.

February 27, 1979 – Tucson

Back from Salt Lake with the flu. But I had a lively two days with my river-rat friends. In bleak, cold, dismal, smog-veiled SLC.
Met Clarke Cartwright — a darling!

∞

Must set myself a daily regimen and stick to it:
— 8 a.m. — walk — run like hell if necessary
— 9 a.m. — to work (no respite until a minimum of five pages have been written)
— 5 p.m. — walk
— 8 p.m. — to work (three more pages).

March 10, 1979 – Tucson

"In Defense of the Redneck" was published in *Penthouse* a week ago. (Yes, *Penthouse* and *Playboy* are sexist magazines. They exploit men.) Nothing to do now but sit back and wait for the libel suits from the Ruins Bar, Antonio, Glob Chamber of Commerce — and goons layin' for me up on Aztec.
(Someone does put a bullet through the driver's door of my VW fastback — parked in a Glob alleyway — when I'm absent. Why?)

April 1979 – Tucson

"For the rest of my life. If I live that long." (Where'd I use this old gag?)
I am plagiarizing myself quite a bit these days. In my decline. Failing powers, fading vision, diminishing energy. Only my self-pity seems as powerful as ever. Fortunately.

May 7, 1979 - Aztec Peak

Up on the mountain again. Cold, windy (forty to forty-five mph), hazy. Several desert fires already. The lookout cab is full of millers, which I find intolerable; I smoke them out with a cigar. The windows are broken again, as usual; the trap-door chain in the catwalk was cut through — somebody lived up here for a few days. No ladybugs yet. The aspens are greening-out down below. The road is in horrible shape. Good.

May 10, 1979 - Aztec Peak

I'm $52^1/_2$ years old and I still suffer from lust for women. Everywhere I go, I can't stop looking and longing. Such a wearisome burden — and yet to yield to the drive would be even more trying for a happily married man like me. All the necessary lying and sneaking around. Not worth it.

What is the solution?

Obvious: the traditional; some form of legal, sanitized prostitution, by which a man could satisfy his need for sexual novelty without risking his health or his marriage or his sanity. But this, so much needed, our society does not provide.

War of the Sexes — Foreplay, penetration, ejaculation, sleep — the feminists say that old time-worn format has got to be changed (*The Hite Report*). Well . . . okay . . . we could drop the foreplay. Or sleep longer. Save the foreplay for later.

I still can't overcome my bitterness at the condescension or total indifference with which my books (especially *MWG*) are treated by the NYC Literary Establishment. But why should I be surprised by it? I've always been a loner, an outsider, a misfit in all respects; why should I not also be the same in the literary world? Why expect those institutions that you condemn to respond with praise, money, prizes? You're only getting what you asked for.

Besides, to tell the whole truth, for twenty-five years in the literary business, you've written very little. And of that little, to complete the truth, none is really first-rate or of much importance. Your real work still lies ahead. Then or never! *Now* . . . or never!

Perhaps we should restore dueling; it might improve manners. Next time some literary asshole insults me, I shall send him my challenge.

(Abbey, you're becoming a dyspeptic crank. Like Edmund Wilson. A professional curmudgeon. Well, what the hell, why the hell not. Somebody has to do it.)

May 29, 1979 - Aztec Peak

Visitors come and visitors go. Some sonofabitch shit on the *floor* of our old shithouse. Swine. So I'll have to lock that one up too.

Renee was here for a couple of days. Tells me we're through; she's bored with our marriage ("lacks intensity") and fed up with me — says I'm away too much, that I don't talk to her when I *am* with her, that I'm indifferent, that I don't love her, etc. She suspects me of fooling around with other women; doesn't trust me. Says she wants *out*. Wants a divorce.

I told her she was wrong, mistaken, crazy, etc., to little effect. I said I would not give her a divorce. More weeping. A day later she left, went away without saying what she was going to do. Ah Christ! More pathos, more pain, more sorrows, more disorder — will nothing in my life ever come out right?

Josh is coming for a visit in a couple of days. He says. I hope he does.

Another embittered letter from Rita demanding money. (Rita goes to France *via Concorde* for the summer, Josh tells me.)

Suzi will spend one week with me here, then off to summer camp at Prescott [Arizona] for eight weeks. Poor Suzi — no mother and not much of a father. Renee is torturing herself with guilt over Suzi; I tried but failed to console her.

May 30, 1979 - Aztec Peak

So. Again. Divorce and loneliness loom ahead. Can I endure it all again? If I must, I will. One thing for sure: no more hasty or impulsive marriages for me. Me and Suzi will go it on our own for a while.

Me, a "conservation writer"? Read my books and you'll discover that only about ten percent of my words are concerned with conservation issues. The rest is play. Entertainment.

Or, as I said to Hoagland: "It is no longer sufficient to *describe* the world of nature. The point is to *defend* it." He writes back accusing me of trying to "bully" him into writing in my manner. Which is true, I was. He should.

∞

Rednecks: A local rancher, whose over-grazing permits had been cut back a bit by the Tonto National Forest rangers, retaliated by capturing a coyote alive, tying a diesel-soaked rag on its tail, igniting, and turning it loose in the forest. Not all ranchers are like this — but too many are.

Another local rancher voluntarily reduced his herds in accordance with professional range guidelines; his allotted range then improved so much, in a few years, that he was able to increase his herds. As a result, some of his neighboring ranchers suspect and accuse him of receiving special favors from the Forest Service.

September 12, 1979 – Aztec Peak

Abbey's Road runs into feminist buzz-saws in the Sunday *NY Times* and *New Republic*. Who says vaginas can't have teeth? Some do. Dentate vaginas . . . *vaginae dentata* . . . All those literary ladies from the rubyfruit jungle. . . .

September 16, 1979 – Aztec Peak

Got a nasty letter from some *femme* in Tucson accusing me of being "tired of women." Eh, what? Me? I wrote back that everything I write is in praise of women, that "for love, sex, companionship, I find women infinitely preferable to men." I could not, actually, figure out what she's getting at.

Now on page 152, final revised version of *Good News*. Halfway! Author's Note: "Grateful acknowledgment is hereby made to Mr. Marcel Proust, of Paris, France, and to Mr. Zane Grey, of Steubenville, Ohio (two of my favorite modern novelists), for a couple of ideas borrowed from their work. Alert readers will discover . . ."

∞

The function of football, soccer, basketball and other passion-sports in modern industrial society is the transference of boredom, frustration, anger and rage into socially acceptable forms of combat. A temporary substitute for *WAR;* for nationalism; identification with something bigger than the self.

∞

265

I'll never make Renee happy. I still love her, I'm very fond of her, but I'll never be able to make her happy. Why not? Well, because I'm a restless, roaming, discontented sort of man. I still feel that something important is missing from my life. She calls me "joyless" and "distant." Quite so. She would think so.

There is nothing worse than cruelty. And yet, I have been cruel. Many times. Mental cruelty to others. Especially to my wives. And no form of suffering is any more real than the anguish caused by doubt, uncertainty, the loss of love, the fear of loss.

No wonder I can't sleep some nights. I suffer too — from guilt. And regret. And bitterness. And petty resentments. And anger. And all the other miserable little sins that flesh and mind are heir to. I envy the Catholics with their confessionals, though they show no sign of being happier, or less evil, than any others. How can I free myself from the bondage of these passions?

So wallow in your sense of guilt, shithead. And do nothing about it, as usual.

September 26, 1979 - Aztec Peak

My next-to-last day here. Probably my last season also. Not that it seems less beautiful than before — it has never been more beautiful! — but I have become bored, restless, anxious for new adventures. This job is too confining. I must explore the remainder of our glorious Southwest before it's all overrun and destroyed.

Oh Gawd, there's so many of them, these lovely and lonesome, wild and way-off places. And all, apparently, under the sign of DOOM. The Doomsday book.

September 27, 1979 - Aztec Peak

Owls and bats swoop around this tower at twilight. And the giant Luna moth, big as a hummingbird, with its red eyes shining in my light.

Night. The west wind moans and mumbles outside the windows of my tower, feels and gropes and fumbles at the door. The unrelenting, unceasing, eternal wind.

The eternal is now. The present moment, fully lived, is the eternal; the only eternity we can know. The purpose of art is to *fix* those moments for all eternity. Or for as long as eternity endures. Eternity is but a moment.

Mysticism is a relaxation of the mind. "God" is a substitute for thought. The supernatural is a failure of the human imagination and an insult to the majesty of the real. Imagination may be only a substitute for understanding.

Death: I fear dying, pain, suffering, but I do not fear death. The earth has fed me for half a century; I owe the earth a meal — that is, my body.

"He sleeps with that old whore Death." — Ernie

∞

END OF JOURNAL XVI

Road map: *During the three-and-a-half-year course of Journal XVII, Abbey lost Renee and gained his fifth and final wife ("the woman I've searched all my life for," he once told me), Clarke Cartwright. By this time, Ed's celebrity had grown to the point where it intruded upon his life in ways alternately troubling (openly antagonistic or merely ignorant literary criticism) and gratifying (spirited book sales and legions of fans). But overshadowing all else in the following pages are Abbey's reactions to being informed — at age fifty-five — that he had terminal cancer and only six months left to live.*

JOURNAL XVII

November 1979 to May 1983

∞

November 19, 1979 – Tucson

Back in syphilization. Very good. Just returned from a hectic three-week lecture and reading tour: Phoenix (a thousand or so at the Heard Museum), Salt Lake (about 2,500 at the U. of U.!), Tempe [Arizona] (five hundred), Boulder (1,500!), New Hampshire (five hundred). I was even invited to Brown [University] but turned it down, on account mainly of sloth.

Six days in clamorous Manhattan, where I listened, all night, in my hotel room (the "Executive") to the roaring whine of garbage trucks processing garbage, and the noise — it seemed — of bombs going off, and screams and shouts and laughter, all night long. And then two days and nights in cold brown drizzly Home, Pennsylvania. And then — the long flight home.

My last day in New York, Hoagland showed up for a Chinese lunch. A nice fellow — small, grinning, half-bald, professional-looking in his thick glasses, tweed jacket, necktie and dungarees. A nice grin, but his stammer, or stutter, is painful to witness. So much so that I pressed his hand in sympathy, and he smiled at me. One simply waits patiently as, twisting and ducking, jerking his head, he tries to get started into normal speech. Once he gets started, and does not stop, he does okay.

The awful clanging clamor of New York. The cold drizzle. The endless, harried, hurried, jostling crowds.

The *Penthouse* office full of secretary-models: terrifying sensuality. What else?

Oh God, my brief visit Home. A walk in the woods with the old man. He's feeling better these days. Helped him split some locust logs into rails — uses two wedges and a sledge, that's all.

Silent embraces with my mother, who says she thinks she's going to die in a year or so. Nonsense. I urged her to spend the winter with us in Arizona. She refused: "My roots are here."

Saw Aunt Ida, still bright and vigorous at eighty-three. (Oh, but it's a long haul for us Abbeys.) "Yes, I'll be dead pretty soon," she said, "and frankly I don't give a damn."

And a few short hours with brother Hoots [Howard], a real horny-handed workingman. He dyes his beard dark brown, he confessed, but has less hair on his head than I do. Cheerful and taciturn, as always. No news of [brothers] Johnny or Bill. "Johnny hates us all," Hoots said. ("The Abbeys are a strange people," I told Hoagland; "I'm the only normal one in the bunch.")

How good to alight in the small-town atmosphere of the Tucson airport, to walk in the dry air and bright sunlight again, with the view of purple craggy mountains all around. Yes, the Southwest is indeed my home. My dear, sweet, beloved and only home. The place where I belong, where I shall live and die.

∞

The Hack's Progress:

Desert Images is now in the stores. $100 per copy! I'm embarrassed. Oh well, next year, as I tell my friends, there'll be a cheap paperback edition — only $49.95. Not a coffee-table book, but a dinner-table book. I've autographed dozens of them here in Tucson.

Promised "Poison Ivy and Sex" to Ingrid for her *Garden* magazine.

The novel [*Good News*] is now on page 242; I promised the whole thing to Jack Macrae by the end of November. Tomorrow — we get to work!

Dutton says [sales of] *Journey Home* now at 32,000 copies, *Abbey's Road* 24,000 (in print). And *MWG* 270,000. Don't know about *Desert Solitaire* or the others.

∞

Memories — I have enough for a thousand years of sober reflection. And I have a poor memory. Memories of the women I've known. The places I've been. The books I've read. The troubles I've seen. The times I've had

... I could retire right now, if I wanted to, and like Proust live on my memories for the rest of my life. If I live that long.

Die now and avoid the rush later.

November 1979 – Tucson

It's his *work* that makes the artist interesting to us. But then why, after a while, do we begin to find the artist more interesting than his work?

∞

The more immoral, or unjust, or ignoble an activity or belief, the more ferociously do its adherents feel obliged to defend it, and the less tolerant they become of any whisper of dissent.

In myself, I find a tendency to hate or oppose or despise anything I cannot do or cannot understand: e.g., mathematics, physics, ballroom dancing, gourmet cooking, Henry James, Jane Austen, etc. And in fact I'm beginning to feel a deep revulsion against the whole goddamn human race, excepting a few friends and loved ones. Only Nature engages my full sympathy anymore. And art.

The war of mankind against other living things: Man has multiplied to the swarming stage, become a scourge and a pestilence upon the Earth, a threat to all life, including his own. *Man the Pest.*

December 21, 1979 – Tucson

Sent the last of my *Good Noose* to Congdon ten days ago. I hope the damn book is finally finished.

No word from those swine at *Oregon Rainbow,* who've been sitting on my "Sonora" essay, unpaid for, for at least a year. And I don't even have the fuckers' phone number or address.

To Nepal with Bob Godfrey in April? Who knows? I don't really want to go. My real life is right here, at home, with my good sweet lovely Renee, my Susie, my work.

January 1, 1980 – Tucson

Renee walks out. *Disaster. Catastrophe.* (Etc.)

"I'll miss you," she said. A straw for a drowning man.

"Come visit me," she (L.) says.

January 16, 1980 – Tucson

Guerrilla war in Afghanistan: Let's go! I wrote a letter to *GEO* requesting an assignment there. The way I've been feeling lately, the more dangerous, the better. Maybe I'll spend the next six months running rapids in a

Sportyak, *solo*. Or why not smuggle guns into Mexico? Dope into Tucson? White slaves into Libya? (*Desperation*. . . .)

January 30, 1980 – Jackson Hole, Wyoming

Just spent a week here with L., a beautiful, generous, brave, talented and clever woman. I first met her in Moab nearly three years ago, at an after-concert party for the Utah Symphony.

Icicles three feet long hang from the eaves of L.'s cabin. Snow on the roof two feet deep. At night we can hear trees cracking and groaning in the woods: sixteen below zero. Coyotes howling out under the moon. Elk tracks on the road. Birds in the afternoon that seem to be trying to sing the opening motif of Beethoven's Fifth. Trees fat and heavy with snow: spruce, fir, aspen, lodgepole pine. The snow is squeaky-cold underfoot. The stars blaze like candles. There is a frozen crust on the deep snow, not quite hard or thick enough to support my weight; I sink in to my knees.

Splitting wood: the chunks part with a single blow of the axe; with a sound like that of stone hitting stone. My vaporized breath floats before me. I split kindling: nice neat thin splints of aspen, fir — clean, sweet-smelling wood — my axe cleaves each chunk with ease. I carry an armful into the cabin, stash it under the stairway.

We carry in snow to melt on the stove. Or stoves — L. has two — a woodburning heating stove and a woodburning cookstove. We grind buckwheat in her hand-powered grist mill. She bakes several loaves of sweet, delicious sourdough bread. We sit by the stove, feet on the fender, snowflakes falling beyond the (Thermopane) windows, and we talk, and we read. L. is an omnivorous reader: everything from Abbey and Agatha Christie to Nabokov and Wilson. A very well-educated woman: Stanford and the University of Southern California.

Ski touring. On the skinny skis. No heel bindings, just the three-pin toe clamps. Led by L.'s friends Rob and Shelley, we go high on the ridges in Teton Pass. Way up near timberline. Deep, soft snow. Trees shagged with snow, golden in the afternoon sun. We practice *telemark* turns — too difficult — I give up easily and contemplate the scenery. [We make] suicidal plunges into the forest below. As always, I am consoled and comforted by the ready availability of death. An end to it all. Out of it. ("He's out of it.")

Two days later, we venture into Yellowstone Park on skis, following a stream that leads, after a mostly level three-mile trek, to a cluster of hot springs. We strip to the skin (four women, three men) and lie in these hot, steaming pools, and talk, and drink wine. A flock of Canada geese flies over us. Later, a lone bald eagle. A light scrim of snow falls around us, but in the hot pool we are perfectly comfortable. Sitting on a gravel bottom, we are presented with a panorama of red, pocked butts when all finally arise. I feel too drunk and enervated to make it home, but I do, we do, in easy bliss — the hot soak keeps us warm all the way. Striding along on my skinny skis.

Survival thoughts: Lost in a blizzard, no axe, no matches, a man could probably survive the subzero night here by staying in the hot pools.

At the highway, we watch a procession of snowmobilers pass by. Lights on, motors whining, faces masked and goggled, the men-machines roar past us with only a hand lifted in greeting. The Great Division apparent once again.

And what about Renee? The last words I heard directly from Renee were: "Stop loving me." I suppose I shall never — never! — fully recover from the pain of that separation. (Took about six months.) [This parenthetical phrase obviously was appended at a later date.]

Sent a twelve-page piece called "Getting Out, Getting On, Getting Off: A Free Speech" to *Rocky Mountain* about ten days ago. Writ in a deep alcoholic stupor, through a fog of pain and despair.

August 1980 – [Glacier National Park]

My fingers, as I write this, are purple from huckleberry juice. I'm just down from Doug [Peacock] and Lisa's Huckleberry Mountain fire lookout at Glacier NP. We saw one beautiful marsh hawk, one ptarmigan and absolutely no phucking bears at all.

Damn. Is the whole GRIZZ epic a hoax?

August 15, 1980 – in the air from Glacier to Denver

En route to Denver via Billings, Montana — next morning (after the party).

"I will drink no more forever," says young Dan'l O'Sullivan, horse logger. Dan's a disciple of Doug Arapaho Peacock, also known, to some of his friends, as Igor.

"Is Igor out of the woods yet?"

Fat Igor: "I will eat no more forever."

Doug inspecting the horizon from Huckleberry lookout: "Ain't that Mt. Motherfuck over there? And Cocksucker Peak down that way?"

I'm drunk as a skunk myself. Two free vodkas, compliments of Frontier Airlines.

Only six dollars in my pocket. How am I going to get home, when I finally arrive at the small, friendly, homey airport of good ole' Tucson, AZ, USA?

I could always walk.

Front Range. We descend upon Denver. Home to [many old girlfriends and temptations]. What's the use? My life is a hopeless miasma of confusion, heartache, guilt, remorse, regret, wild longing and vain aspiration.

Every moment is precious. But not precarious. Thank God I have children, three fine beautiful wise children, who connect my wretched existence with the infinite future. My link to the life to come.

Joshua. Aaron. Susannah. I love all three.

Sitting around, two hours, three, in this wretched clamorous rotten and crowded fucking Denver airport. Christ, you have to wait in line for *every* damn thing here.

Time to move to Australia.

To Australia. Where else is there for a man like me, who *requires* some elbow room, to fucking go? Maybe Clarke would go with me — sweet bright lovely Clarke. (Oh, she's a fine woman! I'm in love!)

October 16, 1980 – Tucson

Clarke is here, living with me now. I do love her, very much, but she remains a bit cautious. I fear that she's a little bored. An active, intelligent, competent woman, she needs something challenging to do. I hope she stays. We've been together since July 20th — almost three months — and all the time I like and appreciate her more. She is sweet, pretty, bright, delightful in every way; a splendid woman. With her in Montana, Utah and here, I've recovered from the malaise of loneliness and rejection. A fine woman; I want and plan and hope to marry her, even make a child with her. With the blessings, I hope, of her parents.

Henry Miller is dead [Miller died June 7]. Wherever there is joy, wherever there is laughter, wherever there is love, he will find a home.

January 11, 1981 – Tucson

Good News is another bomb, down the well; the usual mediocre reviews in NYC, Washington, Chicago, L.A. ("Doomsday Book of the 1980s"); no movie option, no paperback sale; reviews vary from bad to very bad — but I'm accustomed to that.

But *Good News* really is an *optimistic* book, in that it forecasts the imminent collapse of the military-industrial State. The title is not ironical, but the plain truth, which of course makes it incomprehensible to simple-minded reviewers who look for irony where none is intended; the collapse, followed by the triumph of love, life and rebellion. Reviewers are self-deceived, or baffled, by my title.

Traded my .22 for a .357; ready for the wars.

∞

Macho: hunters trappers rangers cowboys soldiers surveyors and such, men who spend their working lives out-of-doors, always seem to possess interesting personalities and basic knowledge and good stories to tell. Alas! It is too late for me, now, to become a real man; I have condemned myself to the menial role of — entertainer!

Good News: The highest form of literary subtlety, in a corrupt social order, is to tell the plain truth. They'll think you're kidding. Reviewers can't understand that I mean what I say, and say what I mean. E.g., *The Brave Cowboy* is about a brave cowboy. *GN* is about ... the villain is the quixotic one here, embarked on his venture to "rebuild America." A lot of people seem to have disappeared, that's true; but we're all going to die anyhow. Each of us owes the Earth a life, a body.

Every little bit helps.

∞

Warning to writers: Beware of granting interviews to ambitious journalists, especially those who come into your home in the guise of old friends.

∞

El Salvador (courtesy the U.S. government) — the clinging fire of napalm, acid spray, rubber hoods. . . .

Freedom begins between the ears.

∞

"Utah, where men are men and the sheep are nervous." — Utah Phillips. A great performer, a commanding voice, a wit, a musician, an anarchist, lover and hobo — a beautiful man.

April 21, 1981 – Tucson

Trudging up the Bright Angel Trail [Grand Canyon], my refrain was: "I ... pass ... everybody. . . . Nobody ... passes ... me. . . ."

Evening News:
"Right-to-lifers demand mandatory death penalty."
"Ayatollah Falwell and his Immoral Minority."
TV football: one team wins, the other loses. So?

August 16, 1981 – Tucson

I am in a home-building home-making mood these days. I can even accept the prospect of another baby without panic or terror. Hell, Clarke really is a good woman. The best I've ever known and loved.

John Irving on the cover of *Time* (September '81). That magazine never fails to bestow its blessings on the mediocre. (Salinger, Wouk, Updike, Sloan, Wilson, J. C. Oates, Toni Morrison, *et alia.*) The enriching but fatal kiss.

Some Essayists: Wendell Berry is solid and good. Guy Davenport is brilliant. Hoagland is buoyant and tough-minded. Abbey is "quirky." Didion is cool, nihilistic, another crypto-fascist like so many these days.

Royalty check from Viking: $29.50!

Discipline, that is the secret. Self-discipline. It's a secret all right — been a secret from me all my life.

I'm 54½ years old. Not a hell of a long time left.

Henry R. Lightcap, where are you? George Heiduk? Jack Burns? Bonnie Abbzug? Come rescue me. [Characters from various of Abbey's novels.]

October 1981 – Tucson

CLARKE — *Funeral instructions:*

My body to be transported in the bed of a pickup truck and buried as soon as possible after death, in a hole dug on our private property somewhere (along Green River, up in the LaSals, or at Cliff Dwellers). No undertakers wanted; no embalming (for godsake!); no coffin. Just a plain pine box hammered together by a friend; or an old sleeping bag or tarp will do. If the site selected is too rocky for burial, then pile on sand and a pile of stones sufficient to keep coyotes from dismembering and scattering my bones. Wrap my body in my anarch's flag. But bury me if possible; I want my body to help fertilize the growth of a cactus, or cliffrose, or sagebrush, or tree, etc. Disregard all state laws regarding burials. Hang a windbell nearby.

Ceremony? GUNFIRE! And — a little music, please: Jack Loeffler and his trumpet. Maybe a few readings from Thoreau, Whitman, Twain (something funny), Jeffers and/or Abbey, etc. That should be sufficient. No speeches desired, though the deceased will not interfere if someone feels the urge. But keep it all simple and brief.

Then — *a Wake!* More music, lots of gay and lively music — bagpipes! Drums and flutes! The Riverine String Band playing jigs, reels, country swing and polkas; I want dancing! And a flood of beer and booze! A bonfire! And lots of food — meat! Corn on the cob! Beans and chilies! Cake and pie and ice cream and soda pop for the kids! Gifts for all my friends and all who come — books, record albums, curios and keepsakes. Invite everybody (we like)! No formal mourning, please — lots of singing, dancing, talking, hollering, laughing and love-making instead. And I want my widow to take a new man as soon as she can find one good enough — for her.

It is not death or dying that is tragic, but rather to have existed without fully participating in life — that is the deepest personal tragedy.

∞

This above all: Give me truth, wherever it may lead.

Kidney-stone fever: Am I gonna have to give up beer?

All havens astern.

In medias res, God fucking damnit, *in medias res!*

"What demon possessed me that I behaved so well?"

"He done his best." (I done *me* best.)

And on the gravestone, inscribe these words: NO COMMENT

November 28, 1981 – Tucson

So here I sit in me lovely little writing cabin by the wash, watching one more desert sunset over yonder western hills. . . .

Those submarginal hominoids with a penis problem — driving their tractorlike 4×4s up and down the squalid streets of Tucson. (Big truck = little penis; big nose = big penis.) [Abbey had a big nose.]

December 11, 1981 – Tucson

Just returned from a six-day, 110-mile walk across Cabeza Prieta Wildlife Refuge/USAF Bombing and Gunnery Range. A beautiful, golden, glowing ordeal, which I shall treasure for the rest of my funny life. Read all about it in my forthcoming essay, "A Walk In the Desert Hills." [Following the lead set by Abbey himself with the Spanish Journal (V), the extensive notes from this long walk have been printed to follow, rather than interrupt, this journal.]

[After the walk] Clarke meets me in Ajo [Arizona]. We have a sweet, sexy, passionate reunion. Then all is clouded next day because she goes prying into my notebooks of the walk, finds something silly I'd written about what a great lover of "many women" I have been. Oh dear, what a dreary business. I must learn to control my pen. That habitual rhetoric with a will (hardly a mind) of its own.

Wrote a nasty letter to [*Rolling Stone*], complaining about what [they] did to my "1981 symposium" essay. The bastards. Didn't even warn me. Now people whom I admire will read that mutilated fragment and think I'm an idiot. Oh well. What the fuck. My fury will fade. Like Clarke's, I hope.

January 28, 1982 – Tucson

Tomorrow I become fifty-fucking-five years old. So?

Curious: my personal life seems to get better and better, year by year, while this country and world I live in seem to become worse and worse, year by year. A curious correlation. Or is it some warping in my vision of things? There's always room for self-doubt, however self-confident I generally feel.

Joshua is living in NYC, apparently loving it. Aaron is at U.S.C., too busy to write. Susie is growing tall, slim, very beautiful, a heartbreaker, happy at the prospect of going to Verde Valley School this September.

I'm back at "work" at my university job. The scam. I feel slightly dishonored by it; it's somehow wrong to be encouraging all those young people to become writers when they should be learning how to hunt, fish, carpenter, weld, lay bricks — survive the coming breakdown. But vanity and greed keep me at it. And my own economic fears: I am very sorry I gave up my fire lookout job. An honest job. But with the funding cutbacks, I probably would have lost it anyhow.

Looking forward to June, river trips, building something at Cliff Dwellers, getting out of filthy Tucson, touring Australia again, maybe Africa, maybe Europe — one last time.

January 1982 – Tucson

My asshole schmuckhead neighbor, who works for the copper companies, is now hard at work scraping his property with a front-end loader. I've finally figured out what he's doing: trying to make his home look like an open-pit copper mine. And of course he also feels comforted by the constant whine, roar and jangle of heavy equipment in operation.

∽

Most people should not be allowed to have children. Look around you. Look at them.

May 5, 1982 – Tucson

My Susie: she is growing up so beautiful, so clever, so talented, so sweet and loving and lively — my Gawd but I love this kid of mine. She's the joy and delight of me decrepit middle-age. A wonderful girl. If she only knew how much I love her — more than anything in the world — she'd never have doubts about me again. Bless her.

Friday morning, May 21, 1982 – Tucson

Clarke and I are married! Yay! Hooray!

May 25, 1982 – Tucson

Received my dossier from the FBI; disappointing — 130 pages of tedious dithering over that anti-draft letter at Indiana [Pennsylvania] State Teacher's College, and my alleged (false) presence at something called the "International Conference in Defense of Children" at Vienna in 1952; some humorous interviews with unidentified informants, in which I am described variously as "polite," "quiet," "well-liked," "argumentative," "quarrelsome," etc. Very disappointing.

∽

My own favorite books so far? (They always ask me this.) Well, probably *Down the River* and *Good News* — those two are the most carefully crafted, richly ambiguous and deeply felt books I've been able to build (so far).

July 12, 1982 – Dead Cow Ranch, Alamosa, Colorado

A lovely place. Belongs to Jim Carrico, ranger and gentleman. Old log cabin, restored and semi-winterized. No electricity, no plumbing. Lotsa firewood, wood cookstove, fireplace. Sign above mantel: "This is a high-class place. Act respectable."

Down the River was officially published two months ago in a first printing of twenty thousand. A damn good book, my *best* nonfiction so far. Apparently it's selling well, at least in western towns. (I'm always on the best-seller lists in Glob, Tuba City, Moab, etc.) About a dozen awkward misprints. Good cover design (mine), nice illustrations (mine). The usual dumb reviews in the eastern press, except for a fairly good one in the *Washington Post.* No magazine reviews at all, as customary. My books never get reviewed in *Time, Newsweek, New Yorker, Harper's, Atlantic, Village Voice,* etc. Hardly ever.

Stacks of fan mail already, which I solicited this time. Book-signings in Denver, Boulder — good crowds. Lined up for hours. Hard to explain. They love me out there, some of them. Gawd knows why. Rejoice, Abbey, Gawd fucking dammit, you really are an author. And a good one.

The *MWG* movie option expires at the end of this month. Then what? Gary Snyder, in a letter to Dave Foreman (Earth First!), says they'll never make a movie of *MWG.* And why not? Because *MWG* attacks not human lives — cheap — but property. And in our culture, property is sacred, valued far above human life. (The neutron bomb, e.g.)

∞

Why would it not be possible to create a sane, healthy, happy human society based on principles of common sense? On what we actually *know,* the simple truths of living experience, rather than on abstract doctrines of a life hereafter, or a life before, or on techno-utopia or the worship of power and domination? Eh? Why not? Stranger things have taken place.

August 12, 1982 - Santa Fe, New Mexico

LAST RITES — Some final chores:
— Sperm bank deposit for Clarke
— Make Clarke executor of will
— Review will
— Inform Congdon, have royalties paid to Clarke
— Recover Mauser
— Copies of medical records
— Write letters to Clarke, Susie, parents, Josh, Aaron
— A public letter to my friends and fans
— End with a bang, not a phucking whimper
— Write Jack, Wally, Debris, Ken, to join me on final outing (?)
  [This entry was lined out.]
— Why not a raid on the new uranium operations up Kanab Creek?
— Answer fan mail
— Change dedication of *Down the River* (to "for Clarke")

— Ask Congdon to arrange publication of two more books: (1) a selection of essays from the picture books — *Nature Lover;* and (2) an *Abbey Reader*, edited by Wendell Berry, or Hoagland, or Donn Rawlings perhaps, if I don't have time to do it myself

— Say good-bye and go for a walk "in the spirit of adventure, never to return."

September 23, 1982 – Tucson

For about two weeks, I looked death in the face (no eyes) — given six months to live — and was not frightened. I felt a great sadness, yes, at being forced so suddenly, abruptly, prematurely, to leave my beloved Clarke and Susie, and the desert hills and sunsets, and music and books and my friends and my work, but — strangely — I felt no fear. Nor panic, anger, despair. Only a great sadness and a calm acceptance of what I've always known to be inevitable. *Continuity!*

Infantile paralysis again. For two months now I've written scarcely a word (except letters), either on the novel or in this here humble journal. Of course, I thought I had a good excuse; I thought I was dying. The doctors pronounced me dead, of pancreatic cancer. The "good-bye kiss," as Greg Gorman, Santa Fe M.D., put it. Six months to live, probably. But the cancer was not in me; it was in their X-rays, CT-scans, sonic probes, ERCPs, arteriograms (catheter up the groin), liver biopsy, etc., etc. In the eyes of the beholder. Not in me.

Six doctors, three hospitals, sixteen machines, and a $23,000 bill (for Blue Cross) — and they could not kill me.

Gallstones, an "angry pancreas." Nothing more, apparently.

"The full rigors of Western medicine." Yes, I've had it: a fourteen-inch stitch, like a centipede, across my abdomen. Gall bladder removed, appendix removed, nothing else to do. My obstructed portal vein had been bypassed by a network of new veins. Six weeks on the medical RACK.

But I'm still sick, and weak, and down to 175 pounds, five weeks after surgery and eight weeks (or so) since the onset of this wretched, nauseating, miserable illness. (Coke and toast.)

I think of malpractice. Was the operation necessary? Or even justified? Brendan Phibbs [a doctor and long-time friend] says it was. But I keep wondering.

September 1982 – Tucson

The Hack's Progress:

"A Walk in the Desert Hills" rejected so far by *New Yorker, Atlantic, Smithsonian, Audubon,* who else?

My op-ed piece on illegal immigration rejected by *NY Times* on grounds of "no room." Swine. The lying, cowardly swine.

The movie option on *MWG* is renewed for six more months.

Down the River gets rotten little reviews in *Nation* and *Progressive;* good reviews in *NY Times, Washington Post, Chicago Sun-Times, Playboy, Denver Post, SLC Tribune.* . . . Of others, I know not.

∾

Joshua has been here for several days. A big strong handsome serious intelligent wonderful young man.

Susie is not happy at Verde Valley School. Homesick, lonely. I should never have sent her to that detention camp for unwanted teen-agers of wealthy families. How could I have been so dumb as not to realize what a prep school really is. A lesson for me. The rich, really, are *not* good people. They are selfish, spoiled, greedy, cliquish, clannish, mean-spirited. That's why they're rich. That's how they came to *be* rich.

I'll bring Susie home this weekend. Hell, I miss her as much as she misses me.

∾

According to Rita's doc, Robert Beliveux, I have both acute and chronic pancreatitis, requiring a strict dietary regimen for the rest of my life (if any). I.e., no more alcohol in any form. No more caffeine. A severe reduction of animal fats, dairy products, pork, beef. "Permanent damage" to pancreas, he says. Shit.

Jesus Christ! A spartan life, an ascetic's diet.

Poor Debris has amebic dysentery. And maybe gallstones as well. But he's better off than I.

∾

Just read Matthiessen's *Snow Leopard.* Good writing, but — there's something ludicrous and pathetic in the spectacle of these rich Americans going all the way to Nepal, trekking through the Himalaya, followed by a string of porters bearing the white man's burden, spending thousands of dollars, in order to — "find themselves"! Good Christ! Why didn't he just stay home and hike the Catskills? Traverse Long Island on a skateboard? The colossal egoism of these soul-searchers. What makes them think their useless pitiful souls are so godawful important?

October 4, 1982 – Tucson

Re Dennis DeConcini, Mo Udall, Barry Goldwater, et al: "We have the best politicians money can buy," as Will Rogers once said.

Quislings all, ready to sell their mothers' graves if the price is right.

∞

Is it true the word "paradise" is derived from an old Persian word meaning "wilderness"? The Garden of Eden = pre-agricultural life.

∞

Looking Death in the Face:

At Santa Fe last August, Doctors Gorman and Pinkerton agreed I had "less than a year" to live. . . .

My first reaction was, Well, at least I won't have to floss my teeth anymore.

I did not panic. Nor even feel despair. I felt instead a calm resolve to do what would be necessary. I was *not* going to die in a hospital, or by slow ugly humiliating degrees, in bed, under sedation, at home either, by Gawd. I made my plans, aided and abetted by Clarke, Jack Loeffler, and even Richard Hughes [an attorney friend], who looked into certain legal matters for me.

I felt no anger, fear or dismay or any of the alleged five stages of the terminal patient (fuck Kubler-Ross). I would hold out as long as possible, settle my affairs, do what literary work I could, and then, as the pain and debilitation became too much, I would take a walk. . . .

Susie, who knew all, was so wonderfully brave. And so was Clarke. We wept only once, Clarke and I, when we lay on the Santa Fe hospital bed, in each other's arms, listening to Bach on the tape player. To be forced to leave all that beauty — of music, of nature, of human love — so soon! So prematurely! Yes, that hurt.

But I felt I could bear it all. I'd been preparing for this very hour for the last thirty-five or forty years of my life. I felt calm — sad, full of sorrow, but calm.

But a funny thing happened on my way to the grave. . . .

Now what?

Gawd but I'm a wreck. Guts, gums, big toenails, ears, hay fever, arthritis, everything is falling apart. Prostate.

So, what now?

After age fifty (as Don Spaulding says), it's nothing but patch patch patch.

ego

Hoagland nominates me for the National Institute of Arts and Letters (he says). Why? The name Edward Abbey needs no adornment. (To paraphrase B. Shaw.)

ego

Why I Write:

Not so much to please, soothe or console, as to challenge, provoke, stimulate, even to anger if necessary — whatever's required to force the reader to think, feel, react, make choices. Such is my aim. (What's yours?) And, of course, to entertain. To generate tears and laughter.

Or, I write to amuse my friends, and to aggravate — exasperate — ulcerate — our enemies.

The fine art of making enemies: I've become remarkably good at it. Which is probably why reviewers give me such a hard time.

October 25, 1982 – Muley Point, Utah

It's as marvelous as ever up here. The tremendous stillness. The tremendous infinity of sky. One raven croaking. The inevitable raven, guardian spirit of this place. Sunlight on the beaches down in the Goosenecks of the San Juan River.

"A Poem for Clarke"

High in the redrock canyon land
We come for our honeymoon;
Married in bliss near the end of May
Would it last till the end of June?
You're selfish, she says, and mean and crass,
And dirty and ugly and old.
Quite true, I admit, but you have a sweet . . . !
If I may be so bold.
So we love one day and we battle the next,

And the music goes round and round;
We're on top of the mountain on Thursday eve
And by Friday underground.
Rising on wings of delight to fly
Just as high as lovebirds can sail;
Then sinking, barge-like, to the floor of the sea,
Low down as the shit of a whale.
But we'll struggle on through and outlive our tears,
Whether marriage be joy or a joke;
I don't give a damn if it takes forty years,
I'm cleaving to Clarke till I croak.

November 10, 1982 - Tucson

Wrote a letter to John Nichols in praise of his *Nirvana Blues,* especially his "gift for satire," but advised him to "avoid ideology." I also said that he "sentimentalized" (or "romanticized"?) the Meskins of New Mexico, whom I described as a people now devoted mainly to drugs, crime, spray paint, ward-heeling politics, cars and the monthly welfare check. That was over a month ago — I thought he'd be pleased — but no reply. Have I made *another* enemy? Not unlikely.

November 27, 1982 - Tucson

Money means power, not merely wealth. Money gives us power over others — to command their labor, their minds, even their souls. Even their behavior, conduct, attitudes. No wonder money possesses such glittering attraction for those who crave power. If all people were self-reliant — a nation of artisans, craftsmen, hunters, trappers, farmers, ranchers — the rich would have no means to dominate us. Their wealth would be useless.

Cities: The realm of masters and slaves.

Our dream is to escape the hierarchical order: neither to serve nor to rule. The classic American dream. A society of equals.

December 1, 1982 - Tucson

Got a nice contentious letter from Nichols, with two of his books, signed; guess we're not enemies — yet.

MWG is now in its ninth printing . . . the FBI is probably tapping my phone now, right now.

December 20, 1982 – Tucson

The New West of Edward Abbey, by Ann Ronald, a professor at the University of Nevada — a good sympathetic scrutiny of my books, though she takes 'em all much too seriously.

Clarke is pregnant!

February 2, 1983 – Tucson

At Notre Dame last week, I met Susan "Creamcheese" Sontag, a tall slim dark handsome woman about fifty years old, very cool and gracious and dignified, who answered each question from students with an immediate oral essay. Her reading — of a story called "Baby" — attracted a standing-room-only crowd. Much bigger than my audience, which bugged me, of course, a bit, until I got the check in hand. Barry Lopez was there; I like him. And [Richard] Brautigan.

Our enemies, Reagan and Co., et al — they really *do* want a simple society of masters and slaves, in the good old-fashioned historic tradition.

April 1983 – Tucson

Russel Martin, lit cricket, called me "petty and self-obsessed." Could be true. Must watch it. Clarke calls me "inhuman." Could be. David Roberts, in the *Boston Globe,* calls my fiction "sappy" and "cartoonish." Swine! "S.C." in *National Review* called *Abbey's Road* "smug and graceless." Denise Drabelle in *Nation* called me "puerile, arrogant, xenophobic, dopey" and — I forget what else. Not everybody loves me. Frank Waters thinks I'm a racist.

My self-graded report card, à la Vonnegut:

       Jonathan Troy: D–
       Brave Cowboy: B
       Fire on the Mountain: C
       Black Sun: A
       Monkey Wrench Gang: B
       Good News: B
       Desert Solitaire: B

Abbey's Road: A
Journey Home: C
Down the River: A

∞

Just read William Least Heat Moon's *Blue Highways*, a damn good book.

May 12, 1983 - Tucson

I do not want to become a grouchy, growling, grumpy old man. Do not want to become cranky and quarrelsome. Would rather be like some Zen saint, cheerful and careless and reckless and foolish and generous and patient and somewhat detached and comical and ironical and imical (not inimical) and spry and relaxed and lucky and happy (life is too short for grief, even good grief) and healthy and nimble and active and sexy and zany and hexy and gamy . . . and what the hell!

He done his best.

∞

END OF JOURNAL XVII

Road map: *Abbey recorded two long solo walks in Cabeza Prieta, a Sonoran Desert wildlife preserve and military bombing range west of Organ Pipe National Monument in extreme southern Arizona. The first walk took place in December of 1981 and covered 110 miles in seven days. The second was in March of 1984 and had to be aborted, due to medical problems, after four days.*

Ed subsequently organized his notes from the '81 walk for a reading at the fourth annual Belkin Lecture at the University of California, San Diego, in April of 1982. An abridged version of the "long walk" first found print in a 1983 issue of GEO (R.I.P.), while a fuller account is the lead essay in the collection Beyond the Wall, *under the title "A Walk in the Desert Hills."*

Because Abbey recorded his walk notes in pocket-sized spiral notebooks under difficult conditions — scribbling by moonlight or during brief rest stops in the scanty shade of an anonymous saguaro — they are choppier than his chronological journals. Reading this rough notebook version against the polished and published "Walk," at least for those of us interested in the mechanics of literature, is an informative and entertaining lesson in Abbey's note-to-essay method.

A Walk in the Desert Hills

∞

December 1981 – Cabeza Prieta National Wildlife Refuge, Arizona

First day (Friday). Hiking in the moonlight, granite hills: ironwood, creosote, cholla, saguaro, ocotillo, white sand of the old Tule Well Road, down along the west side of Cabeza Prieta beneath the Copper Mountains. Half moon. Fantastic beauty. No sounds whatsoever except the passage, once, of an Air Force helicopter.

Second day (Saturday). Morning: red skies, the plaintive bleat of one phainopepla off in the bush, great craggy granite hills, the distant mountains of Mexico, blue mists hanging in the valley floor, the next range ten to twenty miles away across the flats. Brittlebush, flies, beetles, lizards, elephant trees, no sign of other life.

Buck Tank nearby — then Cabeza Tank, then Tule Tank, then Buckhorn Tank. Recent rains; water should be no problem. And I have a full gallon on my back, a quart in hand, two fat cold oranges aching in my belly.

289

Overcast sky, cool, pallid sun, looks like rain. I jump a giant jackrabbit, come to boundary of "Game Range," am now between Copper Mountains and Cabeza Prieta Mountains. Distances begin to seem rather awesome, what? And I've walked only fifteen miles last night and this morning; about twenty from here to Tule Well; twenty-five back to Wellton (my joints hurt — fear).

I recall Mt. Sinai Hospital: walking from the nineties to Thirty Fifth St. every night, trying to find sleep through exhaustion, hoping some mugger would appear so I could kill him; but the muggers are never around when you need them.

Almost two years since Renee walked out! Two years!

And a few miles ago, thinking I was already in Cabeza, I thought it was all too easy, was even disappointed.

The west side of Copper Mountains is beautiful — all that desert flora and rotten granite.

No jets today, so far. Profound stillness out here; I hear only the blood singing through my head — let's get moving.

Cool, overcast, silent; one lone phainopepla off in the distance, bleating; that bird flies in what seems to be difficulty, as if just learning, wings beating hard but making slow progress.

This fifty-pound pack on the back is a pain in the neck; about 125 miles to go; maybe I'm not strong enough for this; haven't done this long a hike for years. Maybe I won't make it, have to wait by Tule Well for Clarke and Doug [Peacock] to come rescue me. (Damn, forgot to phone Clarke from Wellton! Last chance; I feel bad about it.)

Heavy somnolent silence. Coyote scat on the road.

I come to a sign:

ENTERING WILDLIFE REFUGE	
Permitted	*Prohibited*
Wildlife observation	Firearms
Hiking	Collecting
Riding	
NO VEHICLES	

About eighteen miles to Tule; got to get at least that far. Oh the tediousness of marching with pack on back. Count the steps, 5,280 feet per mile, so about seventeen to eighteen hundred paces. A self-imposed ordeal. Why? The need, I guess, for authentic experience, as opposed to the synthetic (books, movies, TV). Why should I carry all this water all these miles? Should have a good drink, pour out the rest — but I can't make myself do it — can't throw away water while in the desert.

Out on the flat: "Coyote Water" according to the map. The distant sound of jets, trucks — "that busy monster mankind." My head sweats, sweaty brain, secreting thoughts as the liver secretes bile.

This is going to be a long fukking march, and I could enjoy it too, were it not for this pain in hip, this pain on back.

One flogs oneself into movement again, getting under and into the pack, groaning and grumbling, like a camel into its load. Tired and sleepy. Big fat black ants sluggish in the chill. Am I gonna rain?

Is it gonna die?

Obsessive repetition — my besetting vice; like Mozart, writing the same symphony forty times.

At Tule — spoze the windmill ain't workin'?

Walking in moonlight, hear hoot owl. Arrive at Cabeza Tank intersection, check with map. OK; camp here for the night, water only three miles away. Clear, cold, glittering Orion. Dreams of lost love: "I don't love you anymore," Clarke says, evading my embrace; her new boyfriend appears in the bedroom doorway, an ugly, pale, redheaded fella.

Rodent digging in sand nearby, I spot him with my light: kangaroo rat. Big Dipper on its tail. Silence. Sleep.

Third day (Sunday). Awake in chill dawn, cloudless sky, pretty, cold, my knees are cold inside [the sleeping] bag.

Arise, build a fire of paloverde twigs, saltbush twigs for tinder, heat water for tea. First glints of sunlight on mountain peaks — those bare jagged steep little Alps half-buried in their own debris, rising at forty-five degrees from the flat desert floor.

Hear phainopepla, cactus wren, thrasher; saw *big* gray owl flop out of a tree at dawn, flap down the wash to another tree; the sharp black-crested silhouette of a 'pepla perched on topmost point of a creosote — of whatever else it perches on.

Third and last cup of tea, time to move — but which way? Three miles to Cabeza Tank, eight or ten miles to Tule Tank? With or without pack?

I nudge a [.50-caliber military] shell casing with my toe, a little gray lizard scampers out, scuttles away — he was living in there. Bits and pieces of mangled metal here and there: target fragments, shells, rocket assemblies with tangles of wiring like spaghetti (but spaghetti you can eat).

Jet jockeys all in church this morning, praying for peace, no doubt, while hoping for war, combat, promotion, medals — I know the type — they make good soldiers but terrible rulers. But all rulers are terrible. Deep ecology; the egalitarian outlook.

Uh-oh, sun on my back; time to move. Little gray titmice in bush; flit about with a sound like a cat purring. Fuzzy teddy-bear cholla glowing in light. Last night, my sentinel saguaro pointing straight up at Rigel on Orion's belt; constellations: the invention of bored sheep-herders waiting out the night. Dark bunches of mistletoe on trees.

Water: survival. Third day and I haven't even got to Tule Well, have yet to see any water in any tank (that small tingle of fear in the heart). Food is no problem: I can live off body fat for thirty days.

Nothing like the deep satisfaction of a good defecation in the morning; why carry two or three pounds of shit around all day?

Jet jocks rushing overhead with their hideous howls — devils on roller skates. Gawd, I hate them — theirs, ours, *all of them!*

Walking to Cabeza Tank. Lovely country. Agave (*lecheguilla*) interspersed with saguaro (thus the name, Lecheguilla Desert).

I pass a sheep hunter's camp. Huge $15,000 4X4 [truck], beer cans, egg shells. On the truck are stickers for the National Rifle Association and something called the Bighorn Sheep Society of Arizona. Nobody home. A five-gallon water jug on ground. I'm tempted to steal water but don't. Wanta see Cabeza Tank anyhow.

Absolute silence for a while — one fly buzzing. I leave the road to follow an old dim game path. Risky — but should be a shortcut. Down a cool dank ragweed gulch. Sand is damp an inch under the surface.

Desert Fantasies: *Treasure of the Sierra Madre.*

So quiet out here I hardly dare make a sound; delicately I turn the pages of this notebook.

"Abbey's Last Walk"

or

"A Little Walk in the Hills"

Nice title. (Once a scribbler, always a scribbler.)

Mixture of granite and dark old basalt in here, thus the peak's name, *Cabeza Prieta:* Dark (or Dirty) Stone Head.

Cabeza Obscura?

Little pointy hoof marks in the sand — deer? Sheep?

A brittlebush in bright yellow bloom — alone. A handful of water in a basin on top of a boulder. (Christ! I see more things out here in this "lifeless wasteland" than I can possibly record.)

Dead saguaros like scarecrows.

Hummingbird bush in red bloom.

Must approach the tank with care; hunters may have it staked out.

Lava fields, basalt-colored lizards, foot paths, remains of an ancient Indian sleeping circle (windbreak), lots of cactus out here in the dark country.

Sweat drips from my eyebrows onto this notebook as I write (like tear stains).

Up the faint worn trail (definitely manmade). Petroglyphs: A cross or X in a circle, and another I can't make sense of.

The tank is full of sweet clean cold amber-colored water (tastes good). It's true, Nature really does know best (and bats last), her pools properly designed, like scoops, allowing sand to wash out as well as in, leaving water behind — while an Anglo dam serves as a sand trap, probably filled with sand at the very first flood. Deep ecology, man!

Above pools, a stone cave full of sheep shit; a resting place with good views in most all directions.

Much water in mountains now; sheep will be hard for hunters to locate (I hope).

No sound here but the humming of bees. Dam built 3/17/48; probably thot they were improving on nature.

Cannot see the great dark Cabezon from down here in the gulch; means we're close.

Sweating: in December! I *must* find water.

I see the tank ahead, a gray cement dam built by [U.S. Fish and] Wildlife Service (for benefit of bighorns and bighorn hunters). Preliminary basins are damp but empty; even from here I can see that the dam is full of sand and greasewood — and saltbush?

SILENCE.

Limberbush and brittlebush growing side by side.

Spider balloons high in the air, drifting, shine in the sun.

Trickle of water in gulch.

Lots of H_2O, as I knew there would be.

Swarms of honeybees; I rescue one from the water.

Water in lower pools a dark green; slight seepage around sides and base of dam (eight feet high, twenty-five feet wide, one foot thick at top).

Despite dam, this is a beautiful holy place, an ancient primordial water hole.

The Old Ones: *metates* (grinding holes) in boulders nearby; more petroglyphs I can't make sense of.

A cave *tinaja* [natural stone water catchment, or pothole] nearby, also dammed up ("3-26-63, U.S. F&W Service, Bill Pirr, Roy Beals, Al Mounts, Sam Miller"). Almost eighteen years ago; a different age! (A retaining wall to keep out sand?)

Saguaros and their nurse trees; Gila woodpeckers yammering in yonder dead paloverde; streams of white granitic sand flowing between dark somber hills of broken basalt.

Mesquite along wash.

Pack rat's nest — furry with cholla balls.

I stand in the cool lean shade of a saguaro.

Dead cholla: death warmed over.

I leave camp at Cabeza Pass intersection: Onward!

Ten miles to Tule Well — make it tonight or bust.

Eight miles!

It's 3 p.m., December 6, and I'm dripping with sweat — goddamn desert!

Six miles to Tule Tank!

El Cabezon, dark brown like cocoa, looms now to my northeast; good.

Four miles.

Going south, sun to the southeast, keeps glaring in my right eye, tho my shadow now is seventy-five feet long; will that bloody nagging winter sun never set? The moon like a silver egg high on my left in the clear southeast; not a trace of cloud all day (so much for "red skies at morning").

Jumpin' a blacktailed mule-eared lagomorph every quarter mile; they bound away on rubber legs.

Twilight at last: I pass the gap to Buckhorn Tank — water only half a mile away; but I don't need it.

Rest stop at Camino del Diablo [Devil's Road]; sublime spectacle here, looking south toward the jagged Tule Mountains along Mexican border.

Twilight, silence, moon and evening star.

I recall the old black geezer on the bus who thot there was "nothing out there."

Coyote sign *hic et ubique* [it's everywhere].

Arrive at Tule Well by moonlight: *no water!* Windmill has a broken pump shaft. Something to think about as, too tired to sleep easily, I go to bed. Cold night.

Fourth day (Monday). Up with the red dawn. Cold, dewy. Breakfast of tea and Fig Newtons. Now I go to check the water situation.

One mockingbird in the mesquite tree above my bed this morning.

Morning wind turns the windmill, upper part of shaft goes up and down, connects to nothing. Small tank with tap is dry; but big tank set on ground sounds half full when I thump its side. Outlet valve is padlocked. Hatch on roof is also padlocked. Thanks a lot, men. (Lack of funds, no doubt, is what they'll say; too much paperwork — and they're right.) Anyhow.

Hedgehog [or] barrel cactus? Fat trunk; clustered, long pink thorns slightly curved.

Rocky Himalayas in all directions; they look so immense, tho rising only fifteen-hundred to two-thousand feet above desert floor; bare rock peaks.

About the water: half-ladder on tank, propped with board and pipe, reached ladder, climbed to roof, managed to wrench open hatch by its rusted hinge end. Tank two-thirds full, water about six feet down. Returned to ground, got my jugs, baling wire, two stove lids for sinkers (out of an old tin shanty near well); lowered jug, it sank, when bubbles stopped I pulled it up. Full. Water!

This Tule Well water very hard, alkaline, but potable. Drinkable. Barely. It'll do, altho tank water (rain-filled) is much better.

I declare a day of rest: brush and floss my teeth, air out underwear, socks and sleeping bag. Will resume anabasis late this afternoon, near sundown, walk all night till moon-set. Aye, but which way? Southeast to Papago Well, northeast to Heart Tank and Sunday Pass, west to Altas Tanks or north back along the Cabezas past Buckhorn, Cabeza, Buck tanks? A long long walk whichever way. Neck is sore; hip aches; hot spot on ball of left foot. I'll take it easy today, tho I feel the urge to get moving.

Steady wind from northwest. The old windmill creaks and clanks, like a dyin' machine. Alkali on surface of ground; soda in water; "the water makes men sick."

Fallen saguaro, still green, starting to decompose, looks like a dying octopus: soft, puce-green limbs draped on one another.

I climb a hillock near Tule, look around — nothing but stony hills, rocky peaks, creosote flats, winding dry washes lined with trees, a few dim jeep trails and a vast brown arid desolation for fifty miles in every direction — wonderful!

Lecheguilla Desert on the west, Sierra Pinto east and northeast, Camino Diablo going southeast past Tule Mountains across Tule Desert, over Pinto Sands, Malpais Lava Field to O'Brian Hills and Papago Well and safety (I hope). No water by this route except Tuseral Tank, four miles out of the way (two each way). What to do?

All that trouble at the water tank was unnecessary; [I found] an open trough nearby with float valve in working order; water. Tamarisk near the tank; I should have seen it; good water sign. I wash my face with soap, rinse out my two bandannas.

Grave at Tule: "G.D. Slob, died 1976, Caught Littering," two rusty cans embedded in slab of cement, which some other slob has wrecked.

Which way? Tule to Papago via Diablo Camino? Or via Senita, Heart, and southeast down west side of Sierra Pinto to O'Brian Pass? And on to Papago?

On impulse, I take the safer way, stick to the road, the known route. Thirty miles to go, two gallons of water on my back — sixteen fucking pounds I probably won't even need, shit.

About 3½ miles past the turnoff to Tuseral Tank, I come upon a grave site; ancient stones arranged to form a hollow cross. Flat grave. Nice view of Sierra Pintos beyond grave. A good resting place for me as well as the resident; I halt for a few minutes. This is gonna be a long night march past the lava flow to Pinto Sands if possible — twenty miles. (If I didn't have all this pig-iron on me back, I could do it easy.)

A half-mile farther, another grave, another mound of stones in the form of a cross — nameless, like the other.

Dry desolate volcanic hills, stones and rubble. [I'm] writing by moonlight.

Out into the creosote flats, the flat desert valley.

Grave in lava field:

1871
NAMEER

Fifth day (Tuesday). Radiant rosy dawn wisps of salmon clouds — soft lambent light on the dunes around me, the Schotts' (?) cholla, the withered creosote (even they can't take it here).

Jettisoned a half-gallon of water last night, [another] half-pound this morning; just sick of carrying all that weight (may regret it later).

Leisurely preparations; banana chips, walnuts, cheese and water for breakfast. Then attend to feet; blood blister on right. I incise, drain, bandage, change socks. Dry out baggage in the sun (lots of dew in the desert now).

Hoot owls last night. A great chorus of coyotes at dawn. Cactus wrens too. But now, after sun-up, all is silent again.

O'Brian Hills awaiting about ten fucking miles away; must have walked nineteen or twenty miles yesterday afternoon and last night; what a trudge, especially those rocky five or six miles through the lava field — strange, eerie country by day, even weirder by moonlight. Gave up waiting for the moon to set and sacked out when I came to Pinto Sands beyond the lava. Saw some lovely dunes last night by lunar light.

Cold pale sand with a few saguaros and mesquites, but mostly paloverde, creosote, the low nasty ugly Schotts' cholla and other vegetables even more obscure and lower class.

[I can] see Agua Dulce Mountains beyond the O'Brians, and farthest off, the rugged outline of Kino Peak, forty to fifty miles to the east — and the Growler Range (odd name).

Now the moment I dread! Hoisting fucking pack to back, marching off on sore feet and aching fucking back!

Pass a jeep trail ("No Vehicles") heading north to Pintos; so, I'm nine miles from Papago Well.

Down in playa: mud, damp, scrubby mesquite, dead creosote. Playa is to the desert as Arkansas is to the West.

Center of playa, puddles of water in road ruts, creosote in bloom, flocks of sparrows darting about, towhees in underbrush.

Afar: wild yapping of coyotes on the hunt. I love that sound and know they hunt out of need, not for "sport."

Saguaros ahead: higher ground.

Bursage and creosote, bright green with happiness.

O'Brian's grave: a stony mound with cast-iron cross for headpiece (miner, prospector, died — ?).

Clouding up again; I've still got forty-seven miles to [the town of] Ajo — Christ! Ain't thirsty but I'm nearly out of water; there had better be water at Papago or I'm in trouble.

Hoofprints on road. Deer? Antelope?

Jets again; the pigs!

Nice to just sprawl in the sun and rest. Forty million people in the U.S. and only one in Cabeza — me! And the black raven circling over, curious: *Awk! awk! awk! tok, tok.*

I have now walked seventy-five miles since Wellton. But still have seen *nada* of Pinto Mountains (must get to Heart Tank someday).

Five days now I've been living in the open — no roof, no walls. God but I'm stiff and sore, and me poor dogs hurt. How long will it take to get lean and hard and fast again? Too old? What's the difference? That which we are, we are, and if we now are less than once we were, still even so we are what few men ever dream or hope to be.

On to Papago Well. And what if there really is no water there? Don't give it a thought. Until necessary.

His aching stiffening crusty limbs; arise? Can these bones live? Ravens object to my lounging on old man O'Brian's grave anyhow.

Not much tread left on me poor old jungle boots; worn down to the threads.

Tok tok.

Lollipop saguaros.

Old ironwoods, sick from mistletoe (rusty brown clumps).

Mexico: Their contempt for democracy. Their contempt for the *Indios*. For the environment, the arts, science. Their filth, squalor, oppression, poverty, superstition, irresponsible breeding rates (too many of them). The story of God and Mexico — the catch. The *patron* system.

Papago Well!

A quiet afternoon at Papago; I have declared this a day of rest and meditation, lie naked on the sand in the sun and think of my sweetheart; only five days but I miss her so much. She should be here; she'd love it as much as I do. Well, I'll see her Friday, make up for a lost week.

Flies buzz around my bod, unwashed and sweaty; erotic fantasies! Clarke's my darling!

Late afternoon; sun about to sink behind the O'Brian Hills; Growlers show dim thru Ajo smog. To Bates Well tomorrow. Yes? No? Maybe? So lovely here, plenty good water, lots of food remaining in pack. I'm tempted to lie around another day, let my sore feet heal. Could still make Ajo by Friday, probably. Too tired to write. . . .

Mountains, mountains, in every direction mountains. The rocky jagged craggy spired and pointed peaks of the Arizona desert. You may not think of the desert as mountainous but ours, at least, certainly is. Rising sharply from the desert floor, half buried in their own erosional debris.

A hawk swoops by toward the open water tank. Various birds twittering all around. In the brush. In the bush. A flock of doves by the tank, gray feathers in the water.

One nice thing about this place: no goddamn fucking domestic cattle infesting every nook and cranny like in national forests and national parks. A blessing — no flies, no dung, no polluted water holes, no dusty trampled eaten-out ground everywhere you go — cattlemen have been having a free ride on the public lands for a century: EAT LESS BEEF.

But they gotta make a living. Yeah, I know. Like the Hindu farmer in his beard, turban and diaper, got no fertilizer cause he's got to use cattle dung for fuel, got no wood cause he cut down the last living tree ten years ago. Like this naked dude says, "Hey man, like I got to make a living, man, you know? Don't bug me."

The cholla.

Evolution: has the ring of plausibility. Creationism: has the ring of tribal myth.

This cholla!

Dawn, no wind, the windmill (tho it's not a mill but a pump) absolutely still; more coyotes yapping last night. The cholla, the old mine in the moonlight — !

EAT LESS BEEF!

Should declare the beef cow a game animal when found on public lands, open season on KOWS. Sakred Kows: the Hindus and other Orientals believe quite passionately in the right of their people to go on reproducing, multiplying forever, and the obligation of us Amerikans to keep them fed while they do it.

My concern for wilderness is not aesthetic but physical, sensual, empathic, spiritual, political, but above all *moral:* all beings are created equal, all are endowed by their Creator (whatever — God or Evolution or Nature) with certain inalienable rights. Among those rights are the right to life, liberty and the pursuit of happiness, each man in his own way.

I say these things because few others will; it is the writer's duty to speak for the voiceless, especially the defenseless. Humanity has four billion desperate advocates, but how many has the mountain lion, the snail darter, the eagle, the bighorn, the ibex, the Siberian tiger, the eland and the elephant? Human needs do *not* take precedence over all others. We must share this planet with all — "For I say unto you, as you do to the least of these, so you do unto me." The willful destruction of a single creature, as of the extermination of a species, is a crime against God, a mortal sin against Nature.

Have pity for our human children, yes, for they are not yet guilty of the collective crime. But have pity also for the children of the falcon, the whale, the pupfish, the leopard, the rhino, etc. Yes, you say, but what about human needs? In service of human need — this is the argument relied on finally by those who destroy wilderness and exploit men for the sake of profit. We must deny them, learn to moderate our needs, conserve our resources and, above all, control and begin to gradually reduce our human numbers. We were given this planet as a garden to enjoy; thru brainless fecundity we are transforming it into a slum, a workhouse, a prison, a techno-military police-industrial Hell.

But about the cholla: exploring old Papago Mine by moonlight (an evil and sinister place), I step into a tiny six-inch baby teddy bear cholla. One thorn needle pierces the leather toe of my boot and sinks into my big toe; feels like a rattlesnake bite, the sharp instant pain, the furry ball of spines cling to toe of boot. I need two stones to disengage it (you can't touch the thing with fingers), then remove boot and sock and pull out the needle. An aching pain remains, like an injection of poison. No fate more unpleasant than to fall bodily into a nest of cholla, as did the villain of a recent novel (*Good News*), thus reaping a satisfactory punishment for his tortures and murders.

The mine: deep dark grottoes in the rotten rock, the smell of something stale and sick. I drop big rocks into pits, they crash down, clattering; bats fly up, gibbering at me. An old mine, a century old. Hand-built road along the hillside, each rock of retaining wall obviously placed by hand. Pick and shovel engineering, burro and mule and man power. But gaping wounds in mountainside: these miners were not like the old men in Traven's wonderful novel, *Treasure [of the Sierra Madre]*, who restored. No.

But even so, I admire those old-time hard-rock miners. No bulldozers for them. No pickup trucks to whisk them each night back to trailer house and TV and beer joint; just lonesomeness and incredibly hard work. Where did the pit props come from? Where the boards for the frame houses below, now in ruins? A long haul. Those old photos: lean fierce mean-looking men. Did they enjoy this life? Don't look it. But they were posing formally, trying to look serious and stern. No Disney smiles for them — did Jesse James ever say "Have a nice day" to his clientele, as he was leaving? Doubt it. Even the water had to be hauled from three miles away, assuming Papago Well even existed then. Probably did, if it's a hand-dug well like Tule.

Time's a'wastin'.

Sixth day (Wednesday). Sweet little red clouds in a green east dawn. Plenty coyotes nearby last night, sniffing out my cheese and salami, probably. Thudding of hooves near water tank but too far, behind brush, can't see — deer? Pronghorn? Horseshit, very old, near camp.

Today I march on to Bates Well, more or less right on schedule. Thinking of cutting my load down to essentials, caching the remainder here. Will carry only one quart water — there's *got* to be water at Bates; old Henry Gray lived there, and the National Park Service maintains it with retired caretakers. I would like that job myself. Or better yet, to be a patrol ranger for entire Cabeza Prieta (by truck and horse).

Agua Dulces across the south, Antelope Hills to the north, Mohawk Valley northwest, Growler Valley northeast, Sierra Pintos northwest.

Saguaro with their drooping nurse trees; maybe young can get a decent start here, if [James] Watt don't bring back the fucking Kows.

Eating: mustn't leave crumbs about for ants; spoil the little critters. Let them find their own food like I did. The little fuckers.

Separating baggage; will go for the minimum load. All these many items, each so light, but packed together they make forty pounds. So, lots of water for brunch, lots of cheese and salami (heavy stuff) to build up me strength for the day ahead, duties ahead. Do solar laundry. Baby me dogs today: put on cashmere socks. Soak my shirt, wash face, hair and the old pits (sans soap, of course). Pack stripped down to grim essentials, wet headband on, hat on top. . . .

Ready to march!

All is silent here as I prepare to leave; nobody says good-bye, which is exactly the fuck as it should be.

I leave Papago Well circa noon Wednesday.

One mile gone.

Standing in the slim shade of a saguaro, I play with its rigid spines while pissing. They have a pizzicato tone, different notes dull and flat but potentially musical.

If I don't stop too often to write drivel, I might make it to Bates Well before dying of thirst.

More hazy vistas ahead, mountains and [valley] floors.

Have now walked around three ranges and across two basins (basin and range).

Walkin' along with my prick hangin' out, givin' baby some air. ("It looked so nice out this morn.") Delirium? It's all the same, yet it's all different (put your emphasis wherever).

Stately fluted saguaros like Greek columns; unfinished ruins.

A honeybee hangin' around; better put my cock in. Damn thing interferes with my walkin' anyhow, knockin' agin' my knees.

Saguaros look as if sunburnt on south sides (bronze color), some of them. One with an arm dangling to the ground like an elephant's trunk. Aluminum [Air Force gunnery] targets glitter on hillsides; dud shells, rockets, frags of metal.

Clusters of small anthills in road, each like little cinder cone. Sandy road, no clouds, shit.

Off with my earth-devouring stride.

Cholla concealed in bursage. Gambel's quail in wash. Sonic boom: *Wham-BAM!* Suppose some poor animal was copulatin' or giving birth now?

South of Sheep Mountains into Deer Hollow. South of Antelope Hills. Now I can see Kino Peak far away across the desert valley — my objective for tonight.

I pass a dry well, drop a stone down the twelve-inch bore, it falls a hundred feet; no splash.

Pass a tinfoil tow target [like a] twelve-foot arrow point, slashed with large-caliber bullet holes; red tape over some holes; this one must have been recovered once: wood, cardboard, aluminum, "1174."

I lie in the shade of a friendly paloverde, on cool damp mud. One forty-foot saguaro rises above me, gold-green in the late sun, a breeze whispering thru its whiskers; sky dark blue. No clouds. Here [I am], by the side of this dim winding primitive old road. Elves and gnomes and wizards might live in the dark, rough, nearby unknown hills. What was that warm buzzing friendly dream I had yesterday? The faint sadness in my heart today?

Seven miles to the Cabeza boundary — then seven to ten more to Bates Well? Better be water there or I'm in trouble. Feel fine now, but I've only one quart with me.

Clarke! Susie! Mother! Father! All my friends and all I love — there is no land more kind than home! Where you have found your happiness!

This road winds on thru the landscape of some medieval fairy tale.

Refreshed, I carry on. Steps. Step after step. Left right left. Walking: the only mode of travel *not* done in a sitting position. Sun at my back, fifteen-foot shadow before me and Kino Peak calling, only twenty miles away. Between us, Growler Valley, a flat wasteland of sand, gravel, creosote and cactus.

God what a difference this lighter pack makes! Walking becomes a pleasure again.

Black beetle ambling along, tail up head down as if following something. (Very interesting; touch it with a stick and it rolls on its back, legs splayed, playing dead.)

Mohawk Mountain [lies to the] north, a tall pointy butte north-northeast.

I have now walked about ninety miles; feet hurt but *I* feel fine.

Overlapping ant hills on road; ants hard at work in each, dumping sand into others' cones.

Kino Peak — like a rusty axe blade, my hope. Little toes pinched, boots too narrow.

From forty miles away, you can see the smelter smog of Ajo; that's the kind of world we live in.

Discarded quartzite rocks and rusty sardine cans, signs of the miner (old time).

March ... march ... into shade of mesquite — a moment of coolness — then into heat again, trudge trudge trudge.

Fat pale moon rising thru haze over Kino, near full.

Road junction: Papago Well nine miles, Tule Well forty miles, Tinajas Altas fifty-nine miles.

Debris and I once camped near here, years ago. Twinge of loneliness.

Nine miles from Ft. Papago, means about eleven or twelve to go, right? Right, man, right on. Across the flats, into the land of sere withered creosote again.

Aha! Approximate center of playa, road becomes muddy; jungle of mesquite and creosote ten feet on either side; puddles of water. Good. I drink what's left in my canteen and refill with puddle water; who knows, may need it yet; was gettin' a mite thirsty, to tell the truth.

Nada. There's plenty of that out here. But it's a positive nothingness. Tramp. Tramp. Tramp tramp tramp. Moonlight. Silence. The creosote horizon, flat as a board.

Sun rises, Earth turns.

Boundary fence.

Cabeza Prieta entry sign:

AVISO
WARNING
U.S. Air Force Installation. Unlawful to enter without permit of the installation commander (Sec 21, Internal Security Act 1950 USC 797). Personnel found in this area are subject to search.

Thursday, 3 p.m. In Ajo. Cheated a bit; accepted a ride for last fifteen miles. So, walked only 110 miles, plus side-trips.

Feel weary, dog-thirsty, sort of depressed. My great solo walk is done. Looking back, it now seems too easy, despite my sore feet, the kink in my neck from the goddamn pack. But I'm excited about seeing my darling again.

∞

END OF CABEZA WALK

Road map: *Journal XVIII is an eclectic record of random thoughts and activities and, therefore, a tough one to summarize. A couple of significant events do, however, stand out during the two-plus years covered here. First, in October of 1983, baby Rebecca was born to Ed and Clarke; in Ed's words: "I finally did something right." Second, Ed became painfully aware of the disease that was slowly killing him. His reaction was philosophic, stoic, and calm.*

JOURNAL XVIII

June 1983 to August 1985

∞

June 14, 1983 – Tucson

"Immigration and Liberal Taboos" is rejected by *NY Times* (op-ed), *Atlantic, Mother Jones, Harper's, Rolling Stone, Newsweek* ("My Turn"); sent to *Playboy*.

My letters on the subject [of illegal immigration] are printed in *Mother Jones*, the *Tucson Star* (third time), the *NY Review of Books*; [I am] interviewed on the subject by a reporter from the *Arizona Republic* (a hatchet job).

Stalking the Wild Taboo. I think I might like Garrett Hardin. He offers an excellent argument against immigration; against [Julian] Simon's cornucopia economics.

Racial, sexual, cultural differences: forbidden ideas; we're not supposed to think such things, much less say them out loud; yet it is fun to bring them up.

Taboos. Liberal taboos.

TABOO: the stir and rattle of old tired liberal hackles rising all around me.

∞

Ten more days and I'm off to Alaska for a float trip down the Kongakut River in the Brooks Range, with *Outside* magazine paying all expenses. How come I feel no pleasure, no excitement?

July 21, 1983 – Tucson

Back from Alaska; one month's interruption of work-in-progress.

Alaska's chief attraction is its very small, insignificant human population

305

and its very large wildlife population. Both attractions are now being rapidly diminished. The issue is not people or wildlife, but people *and* wildlife — or people and *no* wildlife; the only requirement is that we limit human population and greed.

July 31, 1983 – Tucson

Finished my Alaska story yesterday. Fifty-three pages long and a bit on the prickly side — they won't like it. Like Joe McGinnis, I report exactly what I see — and truth is never popular.

∞

These hysterical liberals who keep telling me they love Mexican culture so much. Then why are they living in the U.S.? And what *is* this much-loved "Mexican culture" anyhow? Tacos, tequila and ranchero music, sure — but what else? Culture means a way of life, the way people do things. Mexican culture includes not only the hot food and the pretty flag, but overpopulation, poverty and misery, filth and squalor, injustice and oppression, class and caste, corruption and cruelty, brutal police, a Nazi-like military, a fear and hatred of the natural world . . . one could go on and on.

August 11, 1983 – Tucson

Playboy rejects my "Immigration and Liberal Taboos" essay, the wimps. It was published, though, a month ago, in the Phoenix *New Times*, provoking the usual storm of abuse ("racism" etc.) from local Hispanic politicos, chickenshit liberals, knee-pad Tories.

∞

Dillard, Muir, Burroughs and other nature writers: I dislike poetical prose.

Most of my novels are simple in theme, style and construction. Voluntary simplicity is part of my creed. Of all modern writers, my favorite is Anton Chekhov, who says somewhere, maybe in one of his letters, that he decided early to say what he wanted to say in the clearest, simplest manner possible. And he succeeds.

The opposite school, e.g., Borges, Nabokov, Joyce, Proust, Kafka, James et al, gave us elaborate wind-up whirligigs that went straight from the authors' laboratories to the professors' studies. I greatly admire their fantastic inventions, but could not possibly emulate them, and do not think they serve the high moral purpose of our greatest literature. As Faulkner said, "They write good, but they don't seem to have nothing to say."

Music endures and ages far better than literature. Because lit is tied to words, ideas, social systems and history. Music is the only art that transcends time.

August 30, 1983 – Tucson

A plague of flies here at *chez* Abbey, thanks to our neolithic neighbor and his goddamn herds of sheep, his poultry, cow, jackass. Fly vomit. The fly rancher.

The Tucson-Sonoran monsoon goes on and on: cloudy afternoons, high temps, high humidity, occasional cloudbursts, two flash floods down our back-acre wash. It's becoming tiresome — beautiful but tiresome.

September 9, 1983 – Tucson

I indulged in a frenzy of irascible letter-writing this summer. Letters against illegal immigration, against Tucson's growth, against androgyny, against . . . ? Most of them were published — in *New Times, Mother Jones,* etc. — also in the local papers.

RACE: In conditions of conflict, when more and more people struggle for survival in a world of dwindling space and resources, it is natural and inevitable that racial strife should become more intense. Tribalism is basic. Each group looks to its own for protection. Biology. In a crowded chickenyard, the white leghorns and the Rhode Island reds become bitter enemies. The melting pot becomes a boiling pot. But the doctrinaire liberals, in alliance with the growing "minorities," are reluctant, are unwilling, are fearful of even beginning to rethink this situation.

Only the rich and powerful benefit from race conflict. They encourage it. They set the poor against one another, the lower class against the middle class, whites against blacks against browns against reds. (Affirmative action, etc.)

According to the morning newspaper, the population of America will reach 267 million by 2000 A.D. An increase of forty million, or about one-sixth, in only seventeen years! And the racial composition of the population will also change considerably: the white birth rate is about sixty per thousand females, the Negro rate eighty-three per thousand, the Hispanic rate ninety-six per thousand.

Am I a racist? I guess I am. I certainly do not wish to live in a society dominated by blacks, or Mexicans, or Orientals. Look at Africa, at Mexico, at Asia.

Garrett Hardin compares our situation to an overcrowded lifeboat in a sea of drowning bodies. If we take more aboard, the boat will be swamped and we'll *all* go under. [We must] militarize our borders [against illegal immigration]. The lifeboat is listing.

[America's] welfare system is a failure. A subsidy for baby production. [We need] some severe economic and political means for [promoting] birth control, population stabilization, population reduction. ZPG [Zero Population Growth] and then — NPG!

Abbey the crank. I'm becoming just one more cranky, cantankerous, dyspeptic, choleric, poker-playing, whiskey-drinking, cigar-smoking evil old man. The curmudgeon.

Good.

I'm getting — not old — but older. I feel it. And I'm only 56½. According to the doctors and their electronic scanners, I should have been dead six months ago. Maybe I am. Who can tell?

I have seen the world — and I am not impressed.

Why am I writing these semi-truths, these half-lies?

Dejection.

Joy . . . where are you? Where were you on the night of January 29th, 1927, in that lamp-lit room in the old farmhouse near Home, Pennsylvania, when I was born?

I may never live to see sixty. And what of it? That near brush with death a year ago did something to me. It cast a shadow over my soul from which I have not escaped. Melancholy most profound. It's as if I sometimes regret that I did *not* die then, when God wanted me to.

Had to kill a rattlesnake this morning. The poor damn thing got caught in the chicken-wire surrounding our patio. I approached with a spade; defiant and fearless, the rattler struck, leaving stains of venom on the steel. I severed its head with one blow; the head continued to bite, the body continued to writhe, both unwilling to die. Those fierce eyes. Throwing the remains into the ravine, I felt rotten — sad, guilty, failed. Should have found some way to save the poor beast.

September 1983 – Tucson

Just returned from nine days in New Mexico and Colorado. Splendid days in the crisp frosty aspen-gold San Juan Mountains near Creede, investigating the headwaters of *El Rio Bravo del Norte* [the Rio Grande] for *National Geographic*. We camped for two days and nights near Stoney Pass, walked twenty miles, to the twelve-thousand-foot level. Saw deer and elk and bowhunters and too many cows (the whole area is infested and stinking with domestic cattle) and rugged peaks glazed with new snow; babbling brooks, ponds and lakes, etc. Very nice — sure hated to return to hot steamy Tucson.

October 14, 1983 – Tucson

Rebecca Claire Abbey was born at 11:20 p.m., Monday, October 10th. Eight pounds, one ounce. Looks human. (Beautiful!)

It was a long ordeal for Clarke — almost twenty-three hours. The water sac broke at 12:30 a.m. Monday, and her long day's night began. She tried for a natural birthing, but the baby's head was too big for Clarke's small pelvis. The pain was great. Around noon, she gave up and asked for Demerol. And later, a shot. Still no progress. At 10 o'clock, we all agreed on a cesarean section. Prepped, then to the operating room. A whole team of doctors and nurses participated. I was there of course, at Clarke's head, holding her hand. I saw the baby drawn out, a strange fantastic space creature covered with silvery slime — the caul. A metaphysical experience. Baby is structurally perfect. Mother is recovering normally. All is well. We are both delighted by our Becky.

October 27, 1983 – Tucson

I do nothing. Nothing. But the money continues to flow in. Royalty checks from Dutton, Holt, McGraw-Hill, Avon, Harper. The movie option (*MWG*) is renewed again. Checks from *Outside*, U.N.M. Press, *National Geographic*, *NY Times*. Embarrassing. And so much of it will go on to the U.S. government for its Cruise missiles, H-bombs, foreign meddling, nuclear subsidies, the welfare-warfare State.

In January, it's back to the University of Arizona to preside over a couple of graduate courses — more easy, unearned increment. Shame, shame.

I live falsely. I do not practice what I preach. I wanted a life of freedom, passion, simplicity; I lead instead a life of complicated deals, petty routines, rancorous internal grievances, moral compromise, sloth, acedia and vanity. The only generous thing I ever do is write checks.

YOU MUST CHANGE YOUR LIFE!

Naw — you're too hard on yourself. Oh? Or not hard enough, not nearly hard enough? Always question authority.

November 15, 1983 – Tucson

Poem: "My Daughter Sleeping" (for Rebecca, age six weeks):

> *She lies upon her belly,*
> *Head aside,*

Eyes relaxed but shut,
A dimpled smile.
Whole nations, entire races
May crash in ruin
Before I'd sacrifice your smallest finger
To save them.
(The fanatic love of the parent
for the child. . . .)

∞

I am accused of being a hater. What those two-bit book reviewers cannot see is that every hate implies a corresponding love. I.e., I hate asphalt because I love grass. I hate militarism because I love liberty and dignity. I hate the ever-expanding industrial megamachine because I love agrarianism, wilderness and wildlife, human freedom, etc. Etc!

∞

In the desert, I caress an agitated rattler's throat with my walking stick. He likes it and quiets down.

One of my favorite sights: a lone windmill against a western sunrise. *Vox clamantis in deserto,* that's me.

Annie Dillard and the Great Christian Hangover.

I should stop being so mean to so many other writers. It will do me no good in either the long or short run. But damn, I do like to say what I think. Nobody else does.

In a nation of sheep, one brave man is a majority.

∞

Peacock has a good nose for wine — sticking his hairy nostrils into the neck of the bottle.

December 31, 1983 – Tucson

Brother Johnny has lost his wife, Dolores. After a year of fear and suffering, she's dead of cancer. The evil black plague of our time. Johnny is terribly depressed, plagued by loneliness and guilt — like all or most survivors, he feels he did not do enough to try to save her. It's useless to try and tell him there is nothing he could've done. I invited him to come visit during the Xmas holidays; he said he would, but failed to show.

No word from Aaron. A card from Josh. A call from Hoots. The family dis-in-tegrates.

∞

There's a sentimental notion abroad that the only way to improve the world is by changing human nature — the Christian notion, two-thousand years old. This implies, first, a contempt for man as he is, and second, a passive acquiescence to things as they are, because, as we really know, you can *not* change human nature without mutilating human beings.

The world is really nothing but an idea in the mind of God, say the physicist-orientalist-mystics. To which my response is: So what? Who cares? What difference does that make? We still have to live in the world of actual daily experience, of all those hard objects and firm living bodies that certainly *appear* to share the world with us. We are not alone.

∞

Good writing consists of having something interesting to say and saying it well. Message and technique, content and form — neither alone is sufficient; both are essential.

∞

[Premise for novel *The Fool's Progress*]:

Henry Lightcap [semi-autobiographical protagonist] as Job? Stricken with afflictions — his wife leaves him, his boss fires him, his doctors put him under sentence of imminent death (biliary tumor?) — he flees home to visit three comforters in New Mexico: Bildads [Ernie] Bulow [a New Mexico book dealer and longtime friend], Debris and [Malcolm] Brown. They cannot comfort him. He challenges the *Vox clamantis in deserto*, the whirlwind, the storm in the New Mexico desert, then crawls on homeward through varied vicissitudes to temporary shelter with brother Will Lightcap back in Stump Creek Hollow, Shawnee County, West Virginia. "Oh *Mort* . . . thou comest when I had thee least in mind."

As Henry advances toward Shawnee County, his language regresses into hillbilly idiom.

1927–1977. Fifty years is enuf for our hero, so book time is 1977 . . . the Carter interregnum.

January 4, 1984 – Tucson

A local paper will publish my diatribe against Growth: "How Big Is Big Enough?" More hate letters.

A long interview with *MEN: Muddah Eart' Noose.*

Wrote a long letter to A. Dillard, five pages of single-spaced sulfurous fulminations: should be sufficient to stifle *that* correspondence in its cradle.

"Monkeywrenching Abbey" in the December *High Country News;* delightful!

Oh Mort! We have nothing to fear but fear itself, so to speak. Or, to be or not to be, as it were, or, you might say.

I must write out a new will for Clarke; holograph it this time.

Most men fear death, and resist it, and invent pathetic, vain consolations to outwit death. But it is possible to accept the idea of one's own death, without embracing it, by seeing the death of the individual as an intrinsic, essential, natural part of the great life process.

For a Damoclean sword, Brendan Phibbs [a doctor friend] recommends aneurysm: sudden death. But is the terminus predictable? How about — varices? [This is the first mention in the journals that Ed is aware of the name of his own Damoclean sword, and may well have been added at a later date.]

∞

If Reagan did not exist, it would *not* be necessary to invent him.

∞

Why the critics always behave like a school of fish: Their authority with a gullible public requires unanimity. Like sectarian theologians. Otherwise, if disunity appeared, people might realize that the "experts" don't really know what they're talking about — i.e., like everyone else, they're merely dealing in opinions. And then — questions. For a defense of literary authority, see Edmund Wilson.

The only final test of literary worth is long-run popularity. The democracy of time.

April 15, 1984 – Tucson

Gave a reading at the University of North Carolina (Chapel Hill) on April 4. Was damn near rained out by a storm, but still 150 or so appeared. Turned down invitations from Harvard, Idaho, Yale, Sun Valley, Port Townsend, Wisconsin, and I forget what other places. This job of being America's most famous unknown arthur is getting to be a squalid nuisance.

Spring 1984 – Tucson

Letter from Ken Lash! The first and only letter I've ever received from any of the many people I knew at UNM, only thirty or thirty-five years ago. Whatever became of...? I have been in touch with Ralph Newcomb, Malcolm Brown, A. T. Sarvis, Rita ... somewhat ... but what about all the others?

What others? I can't remember many others, nor even the names of the many girls I thought I was in love with.

∞

A constant ringing in my ears. Fungus under my toenails. An ache in my belly. I must see an ear doctor, a toe doctor, a belly doctor. And a witch doctor for me disabled soul.

"I wish I was out of the whole mess," said [a friend] to me the other night. I understand the feeling.

May Day 1984 – Tucson

Whom do I envy? This man's gift, that man's blessings? Among those I know, none. I certainly would not exchange my lot for Hoagland's or Berry's or Lopez's or Peacock's or Eastlake's or [Alan] Harrington's or anyone else I can think of. Not that I am the luckiest of men — not at all — but my fate is *my* fate, my character mine, and I embrace it, for better or for worse.

May 3, 1984 – Tucson

On equality of the sexes:

In each social class (if not quite equally), the sexes share in the attendant power and privileges — or miseries and poverty. In general, it is much better to be a female member of higher class than a male member of a lower class — so far as wealth, amenities, comforts and graces of life are concerned. There has never been a modern, urbanized, civilized society in which the entire ruling class is comprised only of men and the entire working class comprised only of women. A fantasy!

Men and women share the same fate.

We need each other.

Men are bigger, stronger, more aggressive and generally dominant within each family and class, but this dominance has a biologically deter-mined function. Bio-sociology: we cannot repeal ten million years of pri-mate biology. The sexual act itself involves a necessary, unavoidable, mutually agreed-upon thrust of *violation* at the essence of love, the *penetration.*

We men are rangy animals, *driven* creatures who naturally and helplessly lust after *every* attractive female we see — that urge to sow our seed and spread our genes far and wide. Wild oats! If women felt like men, we'd all spend most of our time in nothing but fucking. But a woman, a girl, obeying the bio-imperative, requires more from a man than the transient enjoyment of sex: she requires protection, provision, the security of a lifetime relationship. Thus family, marriage, the human community.

Faggotry may be a flight from the difficulty and responsibility of normal sex.

May 27, 1984 – Tucson

Just back from seven days on the San Jew-ann [San Juan] River [Utah]. High, fast, muddy waters with some sand waves. The overgrazed dust-bowls of Navajo country. A tolerable trip, but I'd have enjoyed it much more if Clarke (and only Clarke) had been with me. Maybe this fall, the two of us. . . .

∞

A dumb review of *Beyond the Wall* in the Arizona *Sun*. Appears to have been written by some freshman composition student. No skill or understanding whatsoever of humor, irony, paradox, subtlety or the other literary arts. How to convince that gutless editor Auslander that book reviewing, like film or music or art reviewing, requires a minimum amount of skill, training, wit, competence?

The *Washington Post* and *NY Times Book Review* didn't do much better. For some reason, my books are always given for review to nature writers, naturalists, etc., who have only a dim comprehension of what I'm about. Just *once* I'd like to see a book of mine reviewed — favorably or unfavorably — by one of my *peers!*

But then, Robert Houston did write a truly good essay about *Down the River* for the [James] Hepworth [and Gregory McNamee, eds.] anthology [*Resist Much, Obey Little: Some Notes on Edward Abbey*].

∞

A big, noisy babbling party here last night. About twenty-two people plus dogs and babies. Ostensibly a going-away party for Peacock. Baby 'Becca fell off the bed onto her head on the concrete floor while in my charge; I felt guilty and miserable all evening after that.

I've come to dislike parties. Even those consisting mostly of my friends. They make me nervous and irritable; poor Clarke — me getting old, cranky, choleric before her eyes, as she enters her early thirties. She'll probably leave me someday — can't blame her — and I'll just lay down and curl up and die.

Trying to enjoy *our own* party, I drank too much bourbon. Now I've got a hangover, a sick stomach and the Blue Funk. Can't win for losing.

∞

I'm getting much too obsessed with this literary career biz. I should write my good nuvvle, then quit, take up shoe repair, horses, masonry, something useful, honest and sensible *while time remains.*

> *"But at my back I seem to [sic] hear*
> *Time's winged chariot hovering [sic] near."*

I should read — and write — more poetry.

June 6, 1984 – Tucson

Letters to *NY Times Magazine* and *New Age* re Bellow, urging him to move to the Ayatollah's Iran . . . "his kind of country."

A canker of bitterness is gnawing at my soul. Fungus under my big toenails. (The agenbite of inwit.) Stomach muscles still are not recovered from that ill-advised surgery near nigh two years ago. Dizzy spells — I'll never make it to sixty!

Joshua makes the movies! Saw a flash of his face in Redford's *The Natural*, his name among the cast. Hooray. At least he's now a member of SAG [Screen Actors' Guild], like me.

Daughter Rebecca, age eight months, grows more lovable, adorable, beautiful every day! What an angel, what an imp, what a marvel and wonder and spicy bundle of vitality and joy!

I finally did something right.

I want to be a good husband, a good father, a good *man*, more than anything else that life makes possible. Fame and money seem trivial now.

Sorrow, bitterness, melancholy, sloth — WASTE. I must overcome my tendency to too much morbid introspection. Pull down vanity. Become open to all, generous, loving, living. . . .

So easy to write these words. So difficult to live them.

Sister Nancy was here for two days. She is a sweet, wise, delightful woman — hardly recognizable as one of the twisted, warped, knotty, malformed Abbeys. Both Clarke and Susie loved her.

How tragic that we are all so scattered about. For Clarke and me both, those we like and love most live so far away, we seldom see them.

Then, fool, make true friends where you are. And clasp them to you with hoops of steel.

Clarke and Becky fly off to Salt Lake City [to visit Clarke's parents] for a month and I am one lonesome hounddog. Susie is still here, and she is good sweet company, but she too will be gone in a week (to Prescott). Lethargy. Sadness. I think I'm dying.

July 7, 1984 – Tucson

Longing, longing, longing — for what? Death. I wish I were dead. There, I said it, and it's false. I cannot go now. I have two sweet daughters, a young wife.

∞

Censorship and pornography: The cure is worse than the disease. Why is porn so popular? Why this immense sex frustration among men? The *boredom* of life in an industrial society.

August 15, 1984 – Tucson

Watching the twenty-third Olympics on the Tee Vee: the athletes were beautiful, most of them, but the slimy insistent advertising and the flag-waving cretins were sickening — an infantile combo of commercialism and nationalistic chauvinism, erroneously called "patriotism."

∞

We're now dabbling with the idea of moving back to the Land of Moab. 'Round and round and round again, my life revolves in overlapping spirals — to what end? God grant me a revelation!

September 23, 1984 – Tucson

Returned from Big Bend [National Park, Texas] exactly one week ago. Now I must write my travel piece. Boredom! Writing for *National Geographic* is like trying to jerk off while wearing ski mitts.

∞

Should have Terry [Moore, a friend and professional photographer] photograph me posing with a rifle beside my slain TV set; the hunter and his trophy.

∞

It's not enough to halt immigration. We will also have to find ways to reduce the birthrate among Negroes, Mexicans, Indians and — Mormons! Now *there's* a popular program.

∞

Arizona aristocracy: car dealers, land speculators, tract-slum builders, former dope peddlers, mafia gangsters, land and cattle thieves and their host of flunky, quisling politicos. . . .

The '80s are shaping up as another smug, complacent slum of a decade like the '50s. Hope is deferred to the '90s.

September 24, 1984 - Tucson

One punk slob on a dirt bike makes more noise takes up more space inflicts more damage than a hundred horsemen or a thousand walkers.

∽

Rebecca is walking!

R. Crumb [cartoonist] is doing drawings for the tenth anniversary edition of *MWG*. Good!

November 15, 1984 - Tucson

Just back from two weeks on the Rio Colorado in Utah. Seven days alone on the river, four at Spanish Bottom. Bliss. Lonely? No — too busy hunting for campsites and firewood, cooking meals, pitching tent — though I did think continually of Clarke, wishing she were with me, thinking how much she'd enjoy it.

Threatening weather, cold nights, but no trouble. "Discovered" (maybe) an elegant arch near the Doll's House. Confluence Trail. Hiked part of the Fins, found an exit near Lizard Rock. Was joined by the jolly Ken Sanders on the eighth day, at Spanish Bottom. Snow on mountains, golden cottonwoods, deer — splendor!

Trip to Baja soon? Then what? Then back to goddamn U of A on January 15. Ugh!

Been down with a lousy flu for two weeks.

Three.

Four!

January 2, 1985 - Tucson

That "lousy flu" turned out to be something called bleeding "esophageal varices" — in other words, a couple of weeks ago, feeling sick as a dawg, I fell down in a faint, had to go to the hospital, get eight units of AB+ blood (now — AIDS?) to bring me back to life. Damn near blew the whole ball game. Lost three-fourths of my red blood cells. Another twenty-four hours and I'd have been dead as Duke Leopold.

∽

Dillard will be a good environmental writer, once she outgrows her adolescent mysticism.

Sundog — [Jim] Harrison: Why write a novel glorifying some asshole engineer who roams the world building dams?

Truth: If the writer doesn't do it, who will? The Politician? The businessman?

January 15, 1985 – Tucson

My reply to Professor Link, I.S.U., after receiving his "you will" do this, "you will" do that letter:

"Dear Professor Link:

"I don't like the tone of your letter. I don't take orders from anybody, not for a measly $2,000 or for any imaginable sum. I 'will' do only what I first agreed to do ... etc., etc. ...."

Let's see what he makes of that.

Why do the truly clever and intelligent and educated often succumb to superstition — i.e. Yeats, Eliot, Proust, Auden, Bellow, Dillard, e.g. among moderns? Perhaps it's due to some fundamental brooding dissatisfaction with life as it is; a hatred of Nature and our basic primate nature, or fear of death, disappointment, a longing to get close to authority and power?

The real political issues: concentration of wealth, power, land ownership; immigration and differential birth rates; the nuclear arms race; destruction of human habitat. ...

February 8, 1985 – Tucson

Adios muchachos. ...

LAST WISHES:

Dear Clarke, my good beloved wife —

Intimations of mortality. If anything fatal should happen to me, whether by accident or illness, please dispose of my remains as follows:

(1) If needed, and I spoze it is, obtain an MD's certification of death. (Simply to avoid legal problems.) If my death is by accident, be sure to get verification by an MD and witnesses, if possible (for sake of mortgage insurance on your house).

(2) Then, as quickly as convenient, place my body, dressed as-is, inside an old sleeping bag and load me into the back of a pickup. (If hot weather, hire a pilot and airplane.) Take me either to our property at Cliff Dwellers or Green River (either would be fine) and bury me at once. Cover me with plenty of rocks so old Cousin Coyote cannot dig up my body. (Ask Ken Sleight or Sanders or Quist to help.)

If possible, or later when convenient, plant a shrub or a small tree (juniper, cottonwood, pine or such) in my grave, so that the decomposing body will nourish the plant's growth. That is the only monument I want.

A wooden marker with name and dates, nothing else, may be set on the grave if you wish.

(3) Then, hold a wake, as described elsewhere in these journals. A big party: friends, beer, bourbon, music, gunfire, poetry, loving. Jack [Loeffler] and his trumpet, Debris and his sketchbook, Doug and his guns, Sanders and his EF!ers, etc. Invite all our old friends.

(4) Give away those of my books, records, firearms, etc. (that you don't wish to keep) to my old friends.

FINALE: *Adios, muchachos, companeros de ma vida.*

February 27, 1985 - Tucson

The old bod is breaking down, falling apart, like an old car: one part goes, something else begins to malfunction — gallstones, portal vein obstruction, pancreatitis, burned-out stomach, esophageal varices, high blood pressure, abdominal fluid, anemia, enlarged spleen — and now another kidney stone. Thromboses. . . .

Hubris. My debauchery and arrogance have finally overtaken me. Thought I had the world by the balls; now Fate has a hard grasp on *my* balls.

Character and fate: A man's fate *is* his character (Heraclitus). By the age of forty, a man is responsible for his face (Abbey), *and* his fate.

I think.

March 7, 1985 - Tucson

Inflammatory letters published in the *NY Times Book Review* (re "Taboos" and covert censorship), *Arizona Star* (re C.A.P.) [Central Arizona Project; an elaborate scheme to bring Colorado River water to Tucson, thus allowing further development], *Bloomsbury* (re science). Nothing but trouble.

Gregory McNamee's essay in the *Tucson Weekly* places too much stress on my politics, no mention of the love and humor in my books. He makes them seem grim, which they are not; *au contraire,* [they are] too carefree and careless, hastily written.

April 25, 1985 - Tucson

The Tenth Anniversary Edition of *MWG* debuts this month! Maybe this time it'll get the reviews it should have gotten ten years ago. Maybe. Not bloody likely.

I feel no fear of death. (Perhaps because I do not fully believe in death.) But I do feel a great sadness, an irremediable sorrow, at the possibility that I may not live long enough to help our Rebecca become a girl, a teen-ager

(another insolent teen-ager!), a woman. That thought hurts. Otherwise . . .
I might say — enough. Enough. Enough!

∞

Missoula [University of Montana] — waving a huge (unloaded) .44 hogleg
about. The audience — standing room only — seemed to love my jokes.
Eating from the palm of my hand. I felt very tart and sassy in Missoula,
flaying the Kowboys and Sakred Kows. Shocked and outraged the local
journalists. Was insulted myself by some law students, but I gave 'em tit for
tat. Had fun at the lectern. Had dinner with Bill Kittredge, that jolly fellow
who writes those somber stories.

June 4, 1985 - Tucson

Off to the hills with wife and kid Thursday: Santa Fe, Taos, Telluride,
Durango, Salt Creek Mesa, Moab, SLC, Idaho . . . a summer of camping.
Things are looking up again. (Though the sword of Death hangs over-
head.)

June 20, 1985 - Salt Lake City, Utah

Done the camping bit. Drove my truck into a steel post set in concrete in
Santa Fe and wrecked the bumper, grill and radiator. $550. Helped Jack
[Loeffler] with his famous *cabrito* [goat] roast.

Spent a glorious week in the mountains near Telluride.

∞

I've unpacked the XVIII volumes of my journals in preparation for actually assembling this semi-book (*Pages*, or *Notes* . . .).

I've been off my cough syrup (codeine) habit for a week now, but it still
hurts. Withdrawal symptoms every evening when I get that run-down
miserable flulike ache-all-over feeling. Beer does not help. Nor coffee nor
ice cream. What to do? Heave to and ride her out. Tough it out, like a
cowboy or sailor *should*.

∞

State of the Bod:

Still suffering from general debility, although I can ride a bicycle around
town. Tried iron pills, as recommended by Doc Bauer here in SLC, but
they gave me a critical bellyache.

I broke, bent or sprained my little toe, falling on a slippery rock in South
Cottonwood Crick west of Blanding [Utah]. (How the pale gray cow-flies
did swoon and swarm around my shanks!)

August 3, 1985 – Durango, Colorado

After a tedious month of house-camping in SLC, we finally left. Then down here to Durango for two weeks (?) maybe a month (I hope) in the beautiful mountain cabin of Dusty Duck [Dusty Teal, an old river-ratting friend]. A great place. All is well — or should be. But I brood and brood, weighed down by futile melancholy, and this in turn angers and depresses Clarke, which makes me feel even more out-of-sorts.

Out of sorts. How do I get back into sorts? By the only psycho-therapy I've ever needed: scribbling my miseries in this wearisome journal.

Must assemble my notes.

Must somehow mollify my wife: she is so vulnerable to my passing moods.

Promised a reading from novel-in-progress [*Fool's Progress*] to a bookstore in Telluride, also for Dusty's bookstore [Maria's] here in Durango.

Trouble, trouble trouble. Except for sweet things like Clarke and Rebecca, my life seems to me a dismal failure. Good Christ! Fifty-eight years old and I've never learned to do *anything* practical, useful, sociable. I am becoming a cranky, bitter, embittered, dyspeptic old fart. I look about me at Dusty's workshop, his marvelous [self-built] cabin, and I feel so goddamn inadequate, weak, helpless, inept, slobbish.

Stop this sniveling! You have work to do, a good wife to support, a beautiful child to help raise! For the love of life, man, drag yourself up out of this slough of despondency!

OK.

∞

END OF JOURNAL XVIII

Road map: *Much of Journal XIX is flavored with Abbey's knowledge of his impending death. But he still had plenty of spunk left in him — sufficient to take long hikes and swim a major rapid in the Colorado River and write and speak and more. This stoic determination to live and enjoy life for as long as possible was redoubled with the birth, in March of 1987, of his third son, Benjamin Cartwright Abbey.*

JOURNAL XIX

September 1985 to January 1988

∞

September 4, 1985 – Tucson

Got home about two weeks ago — 106 degrees in the shade. Very dry. All the broomplant dead. Dog OK, house OK. Garden a desiccated ruin. My [writing] cabin full of cobwebs and the husks of flies, gracehopers, bees, etc. (Love that "etc."!)

September 12, 1985 – Tucson

To Moab and Arches in late October [to do a documentary film] for NBC's "Almanac." Must write a short script.

Summer's over here! Hooray! A delightful tingle of autumn in the air. One's thoughts stray to another walk across Cabeza, a float trip down the Green, a stroll along the White Rim.

But what about my great book? Fuck it.

What of love, life, death and immortality?

September 25, 1985 – Tucson

According to [Doctor] Ian MacGregor, me blood count is back within normal range. All the same, I feel kinda weak and puny most of the time. My guts are a mess. Tired every evening. *Un*-sociable: conversation is a wearisome chore. I'm not sure I'll live to see sixty. So?

Got the world by the tail — with a downhill pull.

Regret. A genuine regret: Reading *Naples '94* by Norman Lewis, I am reminded once again that I *should* have re-enlisted for at least one more year when I was [stationed with the army] in Italy, got a job as a motor-cycle courier maybe, studied Italian or German, really learned another language and another way of life. What's Napoli like now, I wonder? And Sorrento? And Capri? And all that wonderful, haunting coast south of Naples? (Overrun now, perhaps, with motors [automobiles]; shrouded in smog; the coastline crowded with villas and hotels. . . .)

October 11, 1985 – Tucson

Going to Utah about October 20th: hike with Debris, meet with the NBC crew at Arches, maybe hunt for a new home.

Mostly I feel simply overwhelmed with all these goddamn literary projects: novel, screenplay, TV skit — it's too much. Sometimes I feel so *sick* of writing. Can't cope with it all. Would much rather retire, build my cabin, spend the rest of my life contemplating rocks, buzzards, distant sunsets, remote mountains, and gradually gently by imperceptible degrees *fade away* into the desert . . . into the sunset. . . .

November 5, 1985 – Tucson

Returned from Utah. Did the TV skit ["Out There in the Rocks"] for NBC's "Almanac." Mostly fun, me and a red convertible. Saw [Ken] Sleight and [Jim] Stiles. Hiked from John's Canyon to Slickrock Gulch and up Comb Ridge with Debris: glowing sunlight, silver moon, golden cottonwoods, running streams in every gulch . . . Debris showed me some magnificent [Anasazi] glyphs near the ancient "Wolf Man" (circa 2,000 BC?) and a lofty cliff dwelling he calls "Eagle's Nest." In fact, a golden eagle circled above us when we went to see the ruin.

Gone for ten days; returned just in time for Rebecca's first real Hal-loween. Dressed as a black kitty-cat, she went trick-or-treating (with us) to the Peacocks', etc.

Typed up "River Solitaire" for Dave Petersen's new magazine.

∞

After five years, Clarke is showing signs of strain. She's not entirely pleased with me. Thinks I don't like people; thinks I'm unfriendly and unsociable; thinks I'm a lousy host and thus scare away potential visitors. Here we go again.

But I could not survive another marital break-up. I'd surely die. With-out my Rebecca, how could I live? For what? Nothing imaginable could possibly console me for the loss of my angel-child Becky. Or for Clarke either.

Josh is getting married to his Swiss girl Yve in Las Vegas this week. I am not invited. Rita specifically invited me not to come.

Life is a bitch. And then you die?

No: Life is a joyous adventure. And *then* you die.

November 11, 1985 - Tucson

Wind howling outside my cabin, moaning and rustling and fidgeting. Good. I like this beleaguered sensation. White woolies drifting across a blue sky. Big purple shadows on the mountains. Trees and shrubbery weaving in the foreground. Excellent.

Sent "River Solitaire" to Dave Petersen. Accepted.

January 1, 1986 - Tucson

Despondency. Had a quarrel with my dear Susie last night, a quarrel over nothing, really, and today I feel lower than whale shit.

(*Will I never know joy again?*)

The dogs bark, the caravan moves on.

Some days it seems like everything goes wrong. I awake with my heart gripped by dread — fear — terror. Of what? I don't know. That's the dreadful fearful terrifying thing about it.

Suicide is an always-viable option. The sensible solution. A rational alternative. A workable compromise.

January 22, 1986 - Tucson

Every time I hear Beethoven's *Ode to Joy*, I weep. Surely it is the most tragic piece of music ever written.

∽

ON THE EDGE . . .

Just back from a week in Mexico. Camped on the beach at Tepoca Bay, north of Kino, on the Sea of Cortez. Splendid desert, beautiful sea, miles and miles of lonely sands — perfect. Just us and the Loefflers.

On the return trip, near the town of Saric, thirty miles south of Sasabe, we were accosted by three men waving guns, signaling us to halt. No uniforms. We waved, grinned . . . and drove on by. They did not shoot — that time. Later, we learned the three were members of the local police force. Then, five miles south of Sasabe, we were stopped by Mexican soldiers in uniform, carrying automatic rifles — M-16s. We stopped that time, but they were fairly polite, nothing happened.

Will I ever return to Mexico? Not with wife and child, I don't think. Filthy stinking evil little country. Clarke caught the dysentery from a chunk of ice in her drink.

March 12, 1986 – Tucson

In our time, in our Amerika, too many of our poets novelists essayists seem to be taking the side of the State in that ancient and inevitable conflict between the State and the independent individual. This is wrong; that is not the natural place for a writer.

If it weren't for all these fools and fanatics running around trying to make things better, then most certainly things would get worse. We need this constant pressure against the barriers to change in order simply to prevent a collapse into total evil. The tension against wrong. To keep things from getting worse.

∞

We don't go into the wilderness to exhibit our skills at gourmet cooking. We go into the wilderness to get away from the kind of people who think gourmet cooking is important.

March 31, 1986 – Tucson

Into the hospital Tuesday (tomorrow?!) for removal of a kidney stone. Which has apparently set up residence in my bladder.

∞

A letter from Mother: The frogs are staging their annual Appalachian resurrection. And the old man's back in the woods, after a winter of doing jigsaw puzzles and reading — what? *Soviet Life?*

May 15, 1986 – Tucson

So? So — what?

It's true: In old age, like Byron, my thoughts turn more and more to avarice, less and less to sex, art, adventure and new ideas.

Ol' rockin' chair's done got me.

Shocking.

Dis-ease. Thank Gawd for cough syrup. Codeine.

∞

WHITE NOISE:

Religion, self-deception — the compulsion to believe in some form of life after death, without examining what such a disembodied existence

326

could consist of or amount to. Suppose there really is an intelligent Being "out there" — a transcendent God. So what? What good does that do us? Such an answer answers nothing. We are still confronted, God or no God, by the riddle of the universe, the mystery of existence.

Or — a technological effort to prolong life indefinitely? That makes some sense to me. On the whole, I enjoy this earthly career — so much to do, to learn, to enjoy. If it were offered to me, would I refuse an immortality serum? I would not.

However, in the meantime, we are left with the choice between accepting death with some pride and dignity, or groveling in fear and clinging with terror to a medicated survival for as long as possible.

Furthermore, without death, life would lose half its drama. Joy would seem pallid, beauty pale, danger insipid, adventure empty.

Our existence would become merely spiritual — off-white and ghostly. Sort of — idyllic but boring.

All the old rituals of death and birth would become meaningless.

Boredom, in fact, would become the *terror*. I can imagine the most cruel and terrible gladiatorial contests taking place, as a populace sick with *ennui* seeks to recover the thrill of death, the joy of victory.

Madre, madre . . . socorro [succor]. Faced with death, the body recoils in fear, in horror, in terror. The body *knows*. The pious pray, but the body *knows*.

Face to face with death. To look death in the face — see it, know it — and then . . . to go on. The heroic stoic.

Your turn. . . .

June 17, 1986 – Moab

Living in a cabin at Sleight's Pack Creek Ranch. Beautiful mountain country, sagebrush and cottonwoods, horses, horseshit and horseflies, at six-thousand feet above sea level. (Gnats, blackflies, mosquitoes also.)

∞

Cowboys, yahoos and rednecks: the bigger the belt buckle, the smaller the cock, say the girls.

∞

Immigration: The conservatives want their cheap labor and the liberals their cheap cause.

Individual humans here and there may be admirable — wise, beautiful, even heroic — and the common run are decent enough. But who can think of any group, class, nation or race (as such) that is unworthy of the vilest insult?

June 29, 1986 – Moab

The sky seems hazy all the time; I can hardly make out the Henrys, the Swell, the Books anymore from my high mountain meadow on Tukuhnikivats. Why? Because of that dismal evaporation tank called Lake Foul? Or the new power plants at Page, Castledale, Warner Creek, etc.? Most likely. No doubt.

The swine the scum oh God when will your vengeance descend upon these mean ugly greedy people? *I long* for the day of the coming Collapse.

Exasperation will take ten years off me life.

∞

The Fool's Progress: How to kill off me heroine? My hero is threatened with happiness!

July 17, 1986 – Pack Creek Ranch, Moab

Fine grand summer storms. Flickers of lightning across sunsets like grand finales to this foolish world. Patches of snow dwindling fast on the mountainsides. Pack Creek roaring in its channel. Wind rushing down at night from Mount Tukuhnikivats. Bluebirds, kestrels, robins, ravens, golden eagles. Hummingbirds. Pink morning-glories blooming on the asphalt berm of road. Minarets of the Moab Wall silhouetted against the sunset. Immaculate white marshmallow clouds rising above the mountains.

July 25, 1986 – Moab

Clarke announces she's preggers again. Oh my Gawd!

Say a man normally lives seventy years — three score and ten. Say each decade represents a day of the week — then I'm now in the Saturday evening of my life. One more night and one more day — Sunday! — remaining. Happy thoughts.

So what?

Out with the old, in with the new.

August 2, 1986 – Moab

Susie calls, says she's feeling "depressed." Why? She doesn't know.

I'm feeling depressed too. Growing older by the hour and nowhere nearer to living a clean simple ascetic life now than I was ten years ago. Bogged down, as always, in the endless complications of supporting a family.

But do I envy the single man, e.g. Malcolm Brown? No. Or even a childless fart like Debris? Well, yes, to some extent, until I look upon my

Becky sleeping and feel such a *rush* of unlimited love, boundless tenderness and desire to protect and nurture and cherish . . . that it nigh transfigures me. We are at our best when we live for others. No doubt about it. It's that quality of caring so much for others, always for others, that makes my Clarke such a fine distinguished woman. Like my mother. Like her [Clarke's] mother [Carolyn Cartwright]. Most women really are better than most men. No doubt about that, either.

September 9, 1986 – Moab

Autumnal winds off the mountains; patches of golden aspen appearing; new moon on the evening sky; almost time to finish the novel, head for the canyons!

Clarke and Becky return [from a week in Texas]: O joy!

September 12, 1986 – Moab

Hooray! Sent off 901 pages (+ XIV in the "Preface") of *Fool's Progress* to Jack Macrae, by express mail, today!

Never again to type another page: that is my dream at present.

∞

Hollywood's to make a move in Moab soon. Called "Hot." In choosing Moab for a movie about brain-damaged mutants, they sure chose the right place.

Moab, Utah: a mean ugly little town run by little ugly mean people.

October 24, 1986 – Tucson

Home again, after ten days of solitary wandering in the canyon country of Utah and Arizona. Haunting days of splendor, fear, beauty and loneliness. "A golden glowing on the mind. . . ."

My heart is heavy. Very heavy. Opus 132 by L.v.B. [Beethoven] suits my mood exactly. Music — my rampart. Good ol' Ludwig, old courage-giver, hero of Western man.

November 19, 1986 – Tucson

What kind of book is *The Fool's Progress?* Well . . . *it's an Edward Abbey kind of book.* (Goddamn it.) It's about a fool. It's funny, harsh, sardonic, sentimental. It's *picaro* [roguish]. It's a semi-autobiography. It's — a six-hundred-page shaggy dog story. It's a farce with funeral. It's the story of a man's life from boyhood into middle-age — fifty years. It's . . . a work with greatness in it, the best thing I've written yet, and I'm proud of it. Yes. Lightcap is an arrogant, swaggering, macho, obnoxious and eccentric character — but he learns some humility in the end. Good for him.

January 7, 1987 - Tucson

Kathy, Jack, Celeste [the Loefflers], Clarke, Becky and I spend a week traversing La Cabeza Prieta desert and visiting a small portion of the Mojave. Very interesting country around Picacho Peak along the Colorado River, classic barren desert northwest of Yuma.

Poor Jack, in a manic frantic harassed state. Overworked, he strikes me as a severely troubled man, driven and torn (like me) by inchoate yearnings for simplicity and a more physical, outdoors existence. (Before it's forever too late!) Yet also loyal to his wife and child. He paces back and forth, constantly, like a wolf in a cage. His jolly good nature makes him lovable always. But it seems to me there's a touch of desperation in his constant joking and laughter.

January 23, 1987 - Tucson

In one week I'll be sixty (60!) years old. Time to retire from this literary drudgery, this typewriter rat-race. Two more years and I start collecting social security — good!

∞

WEALTH AND HOW TO ACHIEVE IT:

Let us define the wealthy man as he who has everything he desires. How to reach that happy condition? Two ways . . .

(1) Through money: Work, sweat, scheme, grovel, cheat, lie, betray to acquire it. But there's no guarantee you'll succeed. Ninety-nine chances out of a hundred, you'll fail. Or . . .

(2) Do without: Reduce your needs to the minimum required for a healthy life. Get by on part-time work. Enjoy the leisure of the leisure class. That's the easy way to become rich, and anyone can do it; the success rate is one-hundred percent.

February 28, 1987 - Tucson

I am invited to contribute [an essay] to the *Antaeus* nature issue, but the editor said it must be "non-controversial." How can anything of any genuine intellectual interest to grown-ups be "non-controversial"? He didn't explain. [And Abbey didn't contribute.]

March 10, 1987 – Tucson

A letter from Irving Howe at the American Institute of Arts and Letters, etc., whatever they call it. He's pleased to inform me that I've been awarded $5,000 for "achievement in creative writing." But I have to go to NYC in May to pick up the check. Guess I won't. Too little, too late.

March 17, 1987 – Tucson

An absolutely splendid day out there. Fat clouds and radiant light over the mountains, over the range. For spacious skies, purple mountains. Wild-flowers beginning to bloom. Hawks on the wing. Great-horned owls hooting at night. A lonesome phainopepla bleating in the bush.

The grandeur and the splendor — of Nature. Of Beethoven's music. Of Tolstoy's heart. Of Bertrand Russell's mind.

The Wild Nineties are coming!

March 19, 1987 – Tucson

Benjamin Cartwright Abbey is born today, at 5:00 a.m., by cesarean section, at the Tucson Medical Center. Seven pounds, twelve ounces. Mother and child both are doing well. Hallelujah!

March 26, 1987 – Tucson

Springtime at *chez* Abbey. The little cottonwoods and the old elm are leafing out. Globemallow and desert marigold in bloom. Clarke's flower garden is a riot, as it were, of color, so to speak. Thrashers and wrens hurling up nests. Quail calling to one another in the creosote parks. Another baby is born, Baby Ben, pink as a boiled prawn, noisy as a fire-truck siren, sweet as a clove in an apple, cute as a button, fresh as a flower. *Ours!*

April 18, 1987 – Tucson

Just returned from two days up in the hills with Becky. We camped the first night in Molino Basin beside a trickling stream. Becky caught a frog and floated it on a pond in a tiny plastic boat. Later, we rode the chair lift to the top of the mountain, played and picnicked in the snow. Camped the second night at 5,500 feet on a mesquite and scrub-oak ridge down the back side of the mountain along the old dirt road to Oracle.

God I love that kid. She is so beautiful and can be so sweet and loving. Every night she cuddled in my arms as I told her stories of Bill the Bug, Kokomo Joe the Giant Lizard, Joe the Jackrabbit, Felix the Kat and a dozen others improvised and invented. She does love stories: no matter how dumb or dull my made-up tale, she seems to find it fascinating and always pleads for more. Rebecca my sweetheart my darling my treasure I love you I love you — "right up to the sky!"

Sunday, April 19, 1987 - Tucson

I am becoming a cranky old man. Quite. Extremely contentious. True. Quarrelsome, petulant and exceedingly irritable. Right. I have less and less patience with fools, bores, pedants and crooks. I do not love, respect or admire the human race. I think modern history is a horror story. I fear for the lives of my children. I regret and am outraged by the systematic destruction of the natural world for the sake of human greed. Exactly.

May 18, 1987 - Tucson

Backpacking in the Catalinas, I slept under a rock overhang during an all-night rainstorm. A great lightning show. A rattlesnake on the trail, I lift it gently out of my path with my walking stick. (The snake stares down at the tip of the stick, does not strike.) Waterfalls and lovely pools. What a place to bring a girl — a girl with the face of an angel, the morals of a slut.

Talked with ranger Zeke Smith in the Catalina Park parking lot. I'm his "hero," he sez. Well, he'll grow up. I walked sixteen miles, all down-hill, and got dog-tired and footsore anyhow. Limped home on a bruised heel.

Tried to hike up to a pass south of Table Mountain. No trail. Too hot, rough, rocky, thornbrushy — after an hour or two I gave up, limped back to my battered truck, crept down the hill, took a nude dip in an emerald pool, came home to Tucson.

May 29, 1987 - Tucson

"People are no damn good." — Martin Litton, canyoneer.

BUT — there are certain honorable exceptions to the above rule: Martin Litton himself, e.g., the Cartwright family, Dave Foreman, Chuck Bowden, Jack Loeffler, Barry Lopez, Mike Roselle, Don Spaulding, Dan O'Sullivan, Susie F. and Rebecca C. Abbey, Mildred Abbey, Paul Abbey, Marian Gierlach, Terry Moore, Bill Waller, Brendan Phibbs, Ken Sleight, Dave Petersen, Jim Ferrigan, the Quist brothers, Wendell Berry, Doug Peacock, John DePuy, Ian MacGregor . . . many more. (People I've actually met whom I like, love, respect and/or admire.)

∞

A. B. Guthrie, Jr. [in *Big Sky, Fair Land*] on "realists": "It was the realists, so-called, who gave us toxic wastes, poisoned our air, denuded our country. All in the name of good private enterprise. That's realism at work. That's the pioneer ethic."

Good man. By God, there is at least one genuine writer living in Montana. (You'll note he doesn't hang out with those movie actors, coke sniffers, horse lovers and literary *exquisites* of Livingston.)

∞

RANDOM NOTES:

Fool's Progress: An Honest Novel. Honest? Well, that's a teaser, a come-on, a secret between me and the reader.

∞

The so-called "minorities" in the U.S.A. are really advance men for the planetary majorities.

∞

A query for Alan Savory, Savior of the Beef Rancher: If our public lands could support vast herds of cattle, why not vast herds of buffalo, antelope and elk instead? Better public animals than private animals on our public lands — we could all then hunt the wild game, the sacred game, us tender carnivores — *or else decree range cattle as game animals.*

∞

Motherhood is a difficult, essential and *full-time* job: women who don't want to do a mother's work — who don't want to be mothers — should not have babies.

∞

There *must* be a Gawd; the world could not have gotten so fucked-up by chance alone.

Better a cruel truth than a comforting delusion.

∞

[I've been] reading Wilson's *Journal* of the 1950s: Fine, precise writing, rich with exact observations, sweet reason, bold iconoclasm. I love Edmund and wish he were still alive. No one like him around these days — both learned and radical, literary and political, sensitive and capable of moral anger.

June 1, 1987 – Tucson

June the first in Tucson Arizona and the withering desert heat of summer comes clamping down. All things dance and shimmer and shrivel and dry in the aching glare, the stunning heat. I like it. I love it.

June 11, 1987 – Tucson

Off for Moab in a week or two. Good. To find a real home at last, I hope. Maybe. Good.

Spent a day with Aaron at Petrified Forest. He's on a paleontological dig. A big flappy affable charming young man, 190 pounds, 6'3", big feet big hands big wide engaging grin. We took a hike in the Painted Desert but failed to find Onyx Bridge. Cooked our supper at Chinde Point and talked of many things. (But not of ancient painful wrongs.) Aaron sold his first short story to *Playboy* and is now hooked of course on becoming a writer, poor devil. Embracing at departure, he promised to write more often, to come visit sometime soon. I love him.

June 12, 1987 – Tucson

Jack Loeffler was here for a couple of days. I do love that man. How I wish he lived nearby.

Benjamin is becoming quite a sweet, delightful baby, slowly gradually overcoming the colic, jiggling and wriggling his fat little arms and legs in the liveliest way, and greeting me from time to time with a wide little toothless smile so charming, so lovely, so sincere and ingenuous, so absolutely heartwarming, it melts me cold Calvinist heart to even write these words.

Clarke and I, somehow, by some genetic miracle, have produced two of the sweetest handsomest brightest pinkest goldenest kids I ever imagined. I wish I could write that poem I have in mind, that rhapsody of absolute fierce violent savage *overwhelming* love I feel for both of them — and Clarke too. Aye, I'd leap into fire for them without a moment's hesitation!

June 18, 1987 – Tucson

Black ragged clots of shit in the cathole. Black as sin, black as the Congo, black as the heart of darkness. (This began Monday morning, June 15, after three days of bellyache.)

Fucking varices. I'm dying again. And I still haven't quite finished my novel [*Fool's Progress*]. Or helped Clarke raise our two sweet and wonderful children. Dang!

I feel weak, tired, trembly. The heart is beating rapidly. No doubt about it, [it's] the same damn thing I got slugged by two? three? years ago.

I'm so tired and *sick* of stinking hospitals.

Sick and tired o' dyin' . . . but feared o' livin'.

Dat ol' man ribbah, he jes keep rollin' along!

July 2, 1987 – Moab

Survived. Still alive. Back in the redrock country, among the gnats, black-flies, cowflies and rednecks, in Gawd's own country. Good.

Moab: Nowhere such an ugly town in such a beautiful place. But I like this town and many of the people in it. Despite the greedheads who run it.

July 17, 1987 – Moab

Peacock is mad at me because Dave Petersen and I went up into the mountains without him. After we'd waited two hours for Doug to make up his mind.

∞

Weariness and disgust threaten to overwhelm my soul. What do I really want to do? Same as always: complete one good novel. Help Clarke raise Becky and Ben. Make a good home, with trees and garden and water and animals, for my little family. Climb Mt. Wilson. Do another solo boat trip down the Green River. Die alone on a rock, at sunset or sunrise, in the fartherest innermost recesses of Eden.

July 26, 1987 – Moab

Swam through the Black Hole of White Canyon [Colorado River] with Glen Lathrop yesterday; a thousand feet and about an hour of fear (cloudy sky) and bone-chilling chatters; sure indeed knocked half the energy out of me. But awesome in its miserable way; like Dungeon Canyon but wetter; like Buckskin Gulch but darker.

Next time, I wear a wet suit.

Found a beautiful petroglyph of an owl near the mouth of Kane Creek Canyon. Must show it to Rebecca.

Hematocrit is up from twenty-eight to thirty-seven, but still below norms for a big fella (180 pounds) like me. A trace of blood in my stool. Iron deficient. Will I live another year? Who knows. Who cares.

September 14, 1987 – Moab

Fresh snow on the La Sal peaks — lovely! Stormy skies over the red cliffs — splendid!

September 16, 1987 – Moab

That sloppyminded asshole Alston Chase, in *Outside* (October '87) calls EF! and Sea Shepherd and animal rights groups "eco-terrorists." The scum. Must send a nasty letter to *Outside.*

October 12, 1987 – Moab

Going down the river (Green) this week by yak [inflatable kayak]!

Agreed to write a two-thousand-word essay for Dave Petersen's new magazine. Deadline, Thanksgiving.

Spent several days last week with DePuy and Loeffler on Muley Point. Found some petroglyphs. Too many tourists in the backcountry now.

Read the entire book of Genesis (King James) at Herdina Park. A delightful book, but followed immediately by the tedious horrors of Exodus.

November 7, 1987 – Tucson

A professional correspondent asks me to define the meaning of life. The flip truth comes out: "Existence has no given significance. This precisely is what makes our situation so interesting."

Thanksgiving trip: Down the Old Salt Trail to the Little Colorado; down the river and up Tanner Trail to Desert View. (A story for Dave Petersen?)

November 19, 1987 – Los Angeles

Brother Johnny died two days ago, age fifty-eight. Cancer, the doctors say. What do they know? Damn little. He'd been on heavy chemo-"therapy" for two months. Cured the cancer but killed the patient.

What do I feel? A dull sorrow, a poignant regret that I never knew him. Most of his life he considered me some kind of enemy, "just another bleeding-heart liberal." He quarreled with all of us, sooner or later, but forgave all in his holographic will.

Mother says, defiantly: "His life was not wasted. He made some people very happy."

January 3, 1988 – Cabeza Prieta

Am I a racist?

I cannot imagine any standard (intelligence, military power, morality, cultural achievement, athletic ability, musical ability, appearance) by which all members of any particular race can be adjudged innately inherently intrinsically *superior* to all members of some other particular race.

My notion of a superior race, if such a thing were plausible, would be harmlessness: which group has done the least harm to the earth, to other forms of life, to other humans, to each other? By that standard, the only superior races would be the Aborigines of Australia, the Bushmen of Africa, maybe the Hopis of Arizona. (But even there, the reason may lie simply in their lack of power and technology.)

Nor do I think it ever fair to evaluate the quality of any individual by reason of race. You cannot judge the worth of a man by his skin color, bone structure, I.Q., body chemistry or genetic inheritance. Japanese and Jews seem to be smarter, on the average — but that does not make them *superior* beings.

However, there are significant differences among the various races, both in character and in achievement. It is intellectually dishonest and socially condescending to pretend otherwise. If recognizing and stating certain facts about Africans *vis a vis* Europeans, e.g., constitutes racism, then I am to that extent a racialist, acknowledge it and stand by it.

In our weird taboo-ridden cult-obsessed hypersensitive creed-crazed culture, anyone who attempts to examine tough social questions in a logical, analytic, empiric manner, must learn to expect a blizzard of rhetorical abuse from all sides.

Anyone with any experience of the other animals takes for granted the hereditary nature of basic attributes. Only we humans like to pretend that we are superior to the laws of biology and evolution. Vanity, vanity, thy name is humanism — whether Christian, Marxist or "secular." (You too, Wendell Berry!)

The one thing both conservatives and liberals, Left and Right wingers, *hate*, is a free-thinker, a nonconformist. From either side. Unless you subscribe *in every detail* to one doctrine or the other, you will be denounced. Look at me.

I am out of it, I know. I despise *rock* — that slaves' music. I really do think women are different from men — and I love that difference. I really do think that European-American civilization, rotten though it be, is far better than anything available in the cruel, squalid, corrupt, overcrowded and miserable nations of Asia, Africa, Latin America. I really do think that if human life is sacred, then all life is sacred — or none. Even on a pragmatic basis: the function of the Anopheles mosquito, like the smallpox virus or the Ethiopian crocodile, is to help control and stabilize the growth of human populations. I really do think that the function of infant mortality, disease, venomous reptiles, is *quality control*. I really do believe that a wild free-flowing river is of more value, to itself and to us, than the lives of any number of fucking dam-building civil engineers. *Etc!*

January 4, 1988 – Cabeza Prieta

I will soon, in twenty-five days, be sixty-one years old. Coasting down the downhill side of life. Good. I done me bit. I done me best.

∞

In writing, I speak only for myself. But in speaking only for myself, I have discovered, through the years and to my delight, that I speak also for hundreds of thousands of *others*. Every one of my books since *Brave Cowboy* has stayed in print, and every single one has sold by now at least fifty-thousand copies. Not bad for the most hated, reviled and ignored of modern American writers.

∞

Joshua! He owes me a letter. Why doesn't he write? What's he afraid of?

And the Peacock Problem: Doug is like a brother to me. And maybe that's why, most of the time, I can't stand him. He's too much like me to love. And yet, on the other hand, there's a great zest for life about him, a gusto in living that I lack and bitterly envy. Many love him. He attracts people with magnetic charm.

And what do others think of *me?* I suspect that although I may be somewhat admired, possibly even respected, very few people actually *like* me. Understood. I am not a likable man. Understood and accepted — for what is even more alarming, I discover that I don't much care whether others like me or not. I would not want to be totally alone, but as long as I have a good woman in my arms and a couple of real friends, I am content. The best of companions are your own mind and soul. I do not lack for stimulating society, even in solitude.

And what's more, there's something about being alone out here in the wild that tickles my brain into jolly action — my pen cannot keep pace with my racing thoughts. Images, ideas, words and phrases come whirling at me out of the blue, a snowstorm of glittering — aperçus? (A detestable word.)

Morning, January 4, 1988 – Granite Mountains, Cabeza Prieta

Cold water and fresh fruit for breakfast. What a horrible way to begin the day. What I crave is sugar, grease and caffeine. The rotten habits of a soft lazy corrupt life — but mine!

So it's fucking Monday morning again. So what? I think I'll stay out here all fucking winter, slay a few deer, a few sheep, cook their brains and eat their guts. Be happy, healthy and hermit. The wilderness is our only true and native home.

Smog in the valley between here and the Growler Range. Fucking Phoenix. Fucking L.A. Fucking techno-industrial culture.

You know what? I wish Doug Peacock would suddenly appear, looking for me.

∞

END OF JOURNAL XIX

Road map: *By this time, illness and responsibility had reduced Abbey's focus to family, a few close friends, and work . . . most notably, completing his final novel,* Hayduke Lives!, *and suffering through a coast-to-coast promotional tour for* Fool's Progress. *Ed's one big outdoor adventure of this period, a solo camping trip into the wild heart of the Cabeza Prieta bighorn sheep preserve/gunnery range, became a painful survival ordeal.*

The last entries in Journal XX were recorded under March 2, 1989 — just twelve days before Ed's death.

JOURNAL XX

January 1988 to March 1989

∞

January 22, 1988 – Tucson

Yuppie Liberalism:

They hate segregation in South Africa (apartheid) but have nothing to say about the one-party dictatorships north of there.

They demand a Martin Luther King holiday while lumping Lincoln and Washington together in a single "President's Day."

They love Negroes, Mexicans and Indians (our official minorities), but prefer not to live near them or send their children to their schools.

They support Feminist fantasies but ignore discrimination against young white working-class males (affirmative action).

They support civil rights but seem unaware of or indifferent to the concentration of wealth and power in America (i.e., one percent of the population controls thirty-four percent of the country's wealth, while ten percent controls sixty-eight percent) as a threat to democracy.

They promote economic Growth while ignoring the effects of Growth upon our air, water, soil, wildlife, open space, wilderness, etc.

Neo-racism, yupster liberalism, New Age liberalism.

January 29, 1988 – campsite, Galiuro Mountains, Arizona

I am now sixty-one years old. So?

A great waxing new moon over orange cliffs of volcanic tuff. A lovely stream and pools in a side canyon of Canyon Creek or whatever this place is called. A quaint old stone house built into the base of an overhanging cliff. A permanent stream rushing by below, with sycamores and willows on the banks. Sun setting over the south shoulder of Catalina Mountains.

Did not sleep well last night. Bad dreams of death and transfiguration. The fatal shore of mortality. Getting older, I appreciate more poignantly the precious brevity of every moment.

Vanity Fair with Ralph "Laurens" on its cover, wearing his fake cowboy outfit on his Colorado "ranch." The androids are coming: Tommy McGuane and Gretel Ehrlich, now this clothing designer. Next, I spoze, will be Rex Reed and Andy Warhol. The West is truly going to hell. Write another phukkin letter! Sleek *litterateurs* are moving into my West — Abbey's West. Time to light out for the last good country: Dinkum Aussieland.

February 19, 1988 – Tucson

The *splendid* wrath of James, Chapter five, verses one through six:
"Go to now, ye rich men, weep and howl for your miseries. . . ."
Greed, the profit motive, is the ugliest thing in America, the closest we've got to pure evil; even the nuke bomb, SDI, the arms race, are based essentially on greed — greed for money, greed for power.

March 22, 1988 – Tucson

To Denver next week for a public reading, talk show, interviews, receptions etc. — all the horrible tedious farce of the Publick Author. Why do I do this nonsense? Vanity. Money. But is it worth it? No. I swear, this is my last time.

Weariness. Fatigue. I'm heartily sick of writing, typing, editing, reviewing — the whole corrupt and rotten literary world.

Or is it the splinter in my left thumb? The ache in me bowels? The constant worry over Susie and Becky, and poor little Benno sick again and our doctor as usual not available.

Finally bought my Pimpmobile, a '75 Caddie convertible. A maroon beauty, vulgar and gorgeous, with an eighteen-inch front overhang and white sidewalls and push-button gadgets, half of which don't work.

April 24, 1988 – Tucson

Just back from two days and nights at Cabeza Prieta. Peace, beauty, well-being — and then, the day I get back, come all the usual headaches, bellyaches, bad sleep, worries, that feeling of dread and despair in the heart, the heavy melancholia. Why?

May 28, 1988 – rim of Dark Canyon, Utah

Went on horseback down Grand Gulch with Ken Sleight and Grant Johnson. Later, into the Maze with John Debris. A highly satisfactory two weeks in the boondocks. But — who was that foxy blonde in the purple skirt, scratching the gnat bite high on her thigh, who I saw at Bluff Trading Post?

∞

Note to my fellow American writers:

What a gutless pack of invertebrates you mostly are. What a fawning groveling writhing genteel array of courtiers (male courtesans) — gutless temporizing trimming poetical-rhapsodical fence-straddling castrated gelded neutered craven equivocating tepid vapid insipid timorous timid high-minded low-bellied spineless cool hip crafty cowardly moral jellyfish you are! Banana slugs of literature! A living slime-mold on our intellectual life!

June 12, 1988 – Tucson

Call from Jim Fergus, *Outside* magazine. Wants to do a "profile." Reluctantly, I agreed to an interview on neutral ground, but declined to submit to a personal visit at home with my family.

The best thing I've done all week: spade Clarke's garden. Now there's true satisfaction.

∞

Going to Eagle Tank, Cabeza Prieta, for a bighorn sheep count on June 20th. Five days at 110 in the shade — if we get there before the monsoon.

∞

The swine are running amuck around Tucson. Degraded degenerates, cretinous high-school dropouts, shave-headed government gangsters ... devastating Sweetwater and Moraga, Tanque Verde Canyon, Catalina Highway, the Oracle area ... aye! And murdering two baby mountain

lions. Destroying southern Arizona while our corrupt congressional dele-
gation (without exception) are hard at work making sure the C.A.P.
reaches Tucson, thus guaranteeing further "growth" and giving the Drad-
mamanite land speculators, Hummelite real estate developers and Mur-
phyite tract-slum builders exactly what they want in order to complete and
cap the destruction of Tucson.

All this in the face of majority opposition. So much for democracy.

No wonder most of the adult public has given up on the political
process. Our courts are the flunkies of politicians, officials and bureau-
crats — who in turn have all sold out to the crude commercial avarice of
the Greed and Growth Machine. (Would it do any good to write one final
begging letter to that phony liberal and fake conservationist Moe "the
Schmoe" Udall, imploring him to defend Tucson against further
"growth"? No. It would not. Of course not.)

What we need now is confrontation. Direct resistance. Plain talk and
bold action. Otherwise, Tucson is clearly doomed to become no more than
another Phoenix.

Thursday, June 23, 1988 – Eagle Tank, Cabeza Prieta

Camped out near Ajo Sunday night; all seemed well.

Attended an orientation meeting Monday morning, after having breakfast with Bill Broyles and Byrd Baylor. Met them later on the road to
Papago Well: Byrd bound for Basiric Tank, Bill for Las Tinajas Altos —
the high tanks. Me, I took off north up Mohawk Valley and by 1600 hours
was stuck deep in the sand of a roadside wash about sixteen miles north of
Papago Well, ten miles short of Eagle Tank.

And there, for the next three nights and days, I struggled with the
horror and despair of trying to jack, crank, wedge my goldamn exasperating two-wheel-drive, free-wheel (no posi-traction) truck out of the sand
and dust. The horror of it. The hopelessness. I even called for help on the
CB radio the second night — Tuesday. Nobody heard me. Or nobody
responded.

I tried brush under the tires. Tried the bench covers, plywood and
dacron plush, from the camper shell in the bed of the truck. (Ruined them.
Should have deflated the tires to five p.s.i., driven out, re-inflated with the
hand pump.) I tried fins from [military] tow-targets. I jacked and shoveled,
jacked and shoveled, gunned the motor. Dug in again. Brief flurries of
progress followed by static spells of failure.

And all of this in the godawful heat — 110 in the shade of a tree, up to
116 in the cab of my truck.

I finally gave up and decided to walk the sixteen miles to Papago Well, at night, in hopes of catching Bill Broyles there on his return to Ajo. The walk itself was an appalling prospect, with the temperatures at 2200 hours still up around ninety. And me exhausted. No sleep in three nights. All my ice and cold drinks gone the first day.

Nightmare!

How I was beginning to *hate* the sight of that Hi-Lift jack, those rear wheels sunk to the hubs in sand, the shovel, the ragged bench covers, the tattered and scattered and half-buried fragments of target fins, the piles of hand-chopped mesquite brush. Hate. Despair. *Fear.*

How long would my water last in this horrible inferno? (I had about eighteen gallons with me, actually, and some ten gallons of it still untouched.) Always thirsty. I reached for my faithful Desert (brand) water bag last night, in the dark, where I'd hung it on a scrawny mesquite — no decent trees anywhere around, no real shade either — and found the bag alive with tiny ants as I raised it to my lips. Instantly, hundreds of them were swarming over my hand, arm, face, whiskers.

Well, OK, about 2230 I went to bed with my shoes on. Slept badly. Awoke about 0130 — after the moon was down — and went for a little walk to see if I could follow the dirt road in the dark.

Maybe. But suppose I broke an ankle, got snake-bit, and the rising sun found me still miles from Papago? I'd be a goner for sure; a horrible death in the heat. Thoughts of easing the process: I'd carry a knife, of course. And a flashlight. And two gallons of water, at least. Some food.

I returned to bed about two in the morning, slept fitfully if at all, and rose at 0400 with the first glimmer of dawn.

So? Resolve! Desperation!

In one final spasm of effort, I took my leather gloves and my little hatchet and walked off into the pre-dawn twilight to find another aluminum and fiber target. Found one a mile from camp, still standing, nose buried in the ground. I chopped off two big bright fins and dragged them back through the wash to my truck.

Came then that awful moment when the red desert sun appears, over the Mohawk Mountains, around 0530 fucking hours. The instant heat.

With more jack-work, more shoveling, I finally got the truck almost in line with the road and on the bank, set the fins under the rear wheels, started the motor, popped the clutch and . . . ?

Hooray! Progress: got halfway across the wash before bogging down again.

Well then, let's repeat the whole process: try again. And this time I *succeed*, reaching hard ground at 0700.

And thus I escaped — deeper into Hell, where I am now, sitting in this saguaro-rib [wildlife] observation blind before Eagle Tank. I'm now twenty-six sandy miles from Papago Well, fifty or sixty from Ajo. But at least there's water here. I'll live — if I stay.

I've seen no live sheep yet. Nothing but doves, Gambel's quail, a few other birds, and lots of wild honeybees.

The "tank" is actually a cave blasted into granite, about ten feet deep and six feet high, with maybe two or three feet of green warm water in the basin. Cleverly shielded from the sun to retard evaporation.

The tank is *roaring* with bees. Masses of drowned bees float on the water, others creep upon its edge, and swarms swirl and buzz in the cool shade of the cave. They seem not at all disturbed by my presence.

Still no sheep, but much fresh sheep dung in the area, as well as coyote scat, and maybe others — bobcat? Raccoon? Lion! (One hopes.)

On the job — three days late. A disaster. I only hope nobody heard my radio plea for help.

Jet-jockeys sceaming overhead all day. Several sonic booms. What does a sonic boom do to a bighorn sheep? They could never *get used* to it — nobody could.

So here I sit all broken-hearted.

Nineteen-hundred hours: Twilight creeping in, into Eagle Canyon, and not a single fucking sheep in sight yet. Why not?

In four days in this awful heat I've eaten almost nothing. Why? Ain't hungry. Too busy drinking water. *Survival*, that's the thing.

Boring here. No action: no bighorns, no lions, not even an eagle or rattlesnake.

Maybe I'll go home tomorrow. This expedition is a failure. Next time I'll bring three or four iceboxes packed with ice and at least one gallon of juice per day — I dream of cold cider, icy orange juice, chilled milk, cold cranberry juice, all of it mixed with club soda, garnished with lemon or lime — and, of course, a fucking four-wheel-drive fucking truck!

0600, *Friday, June 24, 1988 - Eagle Tank, Cabeza Prieta*

Overslept, enjoying strange happy rollicking dreams. Arose at sunup, thick and groggy, and padded quietly up here to my sheep-count blind: sat, ate an orange and read the conclusion to Santayana's *Three Philosopher Poets* [Lucretius, Dante, Goethe]. Such sweet fine precious writing! So finicky and fastidious a fellow! But all right . . . I liked his remarks on Homer — the sycophant — in the essay on Dante.

Passed a coyote on my way up to the blind, [he was] headed down-canyon on the other side — where bound? [I continue] into the morning sun, into the grisly heat, the sweet stink of *bursera* [elephant tree] and the arid waterless waste of rocks.

Half an hour in the blind, and I've seen nothing but the usual doves and bees — then suddenly, a quick gray fox appears at the lip of the cave. Nervous, restless, annoyed by the bees, it dashes to and fro — pointy nose, pointy ears, long bushy tail — dropping down, now and then, into the cave for a quick drink. Anxious, agitated, constantly checking for danger, the fox seems quite different from the relatively calm, self-assured and at times even brassy and insolent coyote.

But where be da phukkin ships?

The fox is gone. A second coyote has come and gone. No action at the tank now [except for] the usual flocks of white-wing doves ("Who cooks for you? Who cooks for you?") coming and going. They descend, enter the cave, come hurtling out excited and crying, then race down-canyon past me in my saguaro-rib blind like fat, gray-feathered bullets.

I am homesick, sick for home.

∝∞

The female ass and the whiskey glass
Made a loser out of you

∝∞

Proposed—A letter to Jim Cohee, SC [Sierra Club] Books:

How 'bout a companion volume to *The Best of Abbey (a reader)?* Say, *The Worst of Abbey: A Steaming Stew of His Meanest, Nastiest, Funniest Essays?*

July 7, 1988 – Tucson

Sent cards to Godfrey Reggio and David Quammen, praising their latest work. And to Barry Lopez. And to A. B. Guthrie, Jr. (*Big Sky, Fair Land* — essays). I'm such a nice guy. The only writer I know who does such a thing.

Did a two-hour interview with Jim Fergus for *Outside.*

July 9, 1988 – Amerind Foundation, Benson, Arizona

Rented a room here a week ago. Finally got started on *Hayduke Lives!* Begin at page forty-four today. I hope. This is a beautiful place, a lovely fifty-year-old house with thick adobe walls, a twenty-foot ceiling in the main room, twelve feet in my bedroom. Ten degrees cooler here than the summer inferno of Tucson. A very quiet, orderly, peaceful place. Except for the scorpions and kissing bugs.

(Writing gets harder, more painful, all the time. Why?)

So, by this drastic means, I've managed to get finally started on this bloody final fucking novel. This is the one good decent thing I can do for wife and kinder, leave them some money. (Assuming I may not live much longer.)

The rule is, self-imposed, I can't go home until I do forty pages. So, I'm away for four or five days at a time. If I can keep up the pace, then I should complete a first draft and fulfill my contract within ten weeks. I hope.

But oh me, I miss my sweet little Becky and Benno so much, so very much! And my sweet lovely sexy young wife also. I'm sixty miles, or about ninety minutes from home. A breeze, but far enough away to insure isolation, which is what I seem to need.

July 14, 1988 - Amerind Foundation

On page ninety! Going well. Very funny. I think. All the cheap gags I never used before, and some I have, I'm dumping into this stew. But is it any good? Is it a good book? How the hell should I know — that ain't my problem. I just aim to tell me little four-hundred-page story in the most entertaining way I know how.

But the richness, the complexity, of our noble English, our Anglo-American language: every paragraph, every sentence, every phrase a puzzle and a problem, because almost any idea, every idea, can be expressed in an apparent infinity of different modes, ways, details.

July 20, 1988 - Amerind House, Dragoon, Arizona

Diddle dawdle. About to start on page 101, chapter eleven, of *HL!* But it's already 1450 hours, 2:50 p.m., and I ain't done a word. Sick last night and this morning. Will I live another year? Who know, who cares? Don't babble like a fool. Anyhow, you've got to do it. Promises to keep.

A lovely thunderstorm rages outside. The light that never was on land or sea shines on the Dragoon Hills, the granite boulders of Texas Canyon, the oak and mesquite and yucca and golden glowing bunchgrass. The whine of wind, the pompous bombinade of thunder, the blue-white jag of lightning. . . .

July 25, 1988 – Amerind Foundation

Cadillacs: Until you've acquired one, you cannot believe how badly de-signed and shoddily manufactured they are. Ask the man who owns one. The American standard of motoring excellence? Maybe the older ones were better than my '75 Eldorado rag-top, but I doubt it.

July 26, 1988 – Amerind House

Sheet! Drove me Caddie all the way from Benson to here in fuckin' low gear. Didn't notice until the red idiot lights went on. Damn near burned up the engine. She's sittin' out there in the hot sun a-smokin' and a-sizzlin' right now. Ruint? Maybe. . . .

Giant beetles zooming like bullets through the twilight, crashing into walls and lamp posts and cars and human heads. Tarantulas, centipedes, solpugids [arachnids of the order Solpugida, also called windscorpions], rattlesnakes, kissing bugs and scorpions. Ah! The delights of the summer-time desert. Ants everywhere. Nighthawks soaring, bats flitting about, fat Junebugs dying on the window-screens. Fat dead solpugids on the floor.

Stepped (with sandals) on a big scorpion in the dark. That horrible crackling noise. The slimy smear. What hideous creatures these arachnids be; just can't quite learn to wholly love them.

Friday, August 5, 1988 – Tucson

Alone! (Since Tuesday noon.)

Ah, the luxury the bliss the absolute delight of solitude! The freedom and beauty and dignity of coming and going as I please, of playing *real music* loud enough to wake the dead, of doing what I want when I want, beholden to no one!

Been here alone for four days, though, and have written only two pages on *HL!* so far. Wasting too much time answering letters, gadding about (watched the lunch-time "fashion show" at Gus and Andy's with friend [Charles] Bowden. Sort of embarrassing, all that bare ass passing by my beef stroganoff).

August 18, 1988 – Tucson

One Life at a Time, Please and *Best of Abbey* reviewed, sort of, in the *NY Review of Books*. That nice young man Bill McKibben done it. Not bad, really, except, like most other book reviewers I've had to endure now for the past twenty years, he seizes on one narrow aspect of my writing (the desert-loving, deep-ecology bit), and ignores the other ninety percent, thus misrepresenting my books and falsifying my life. Should I protest? What's the use? I haven't seen a review of any of my books anywhere yet that I couldn't have written much better myself.

September 24, 1988 – Tucson

I'm living within a blizzard of [media] abuse — my customary medium. But it's better to write the truth for a small audience than tell lies for a big one.

October 2, 1988 – Tucson

Love love love. I must give more love to Clarke, much more. The only thing that really counts, finally, is the love we share with one another. It's so easy to love my darlings Becky and Ben, impossible not to, but I must also give, share, show, prove my love for Clarke. Make this marriage something better than merely another routine domestic *arrangement:* she needs my love, I need hers and we both have much much more to give each other. She is a permanent wellspring of love, which I, through indifference, cynicism, weariness, conflict, longing for the paradoxical impossible, have done too little to encourage, too much to suppress.

November 18, 1988 – Home, Pennsylvania

My mother was killed in a car wreck. She was eighty-three. Died instantly, thank God. Murdered by some careless idiot driving a truck.

We buried her, a week before Thanksgiving, in the family plot at Washington Church. A simple ceremony. The preacher read from Isaiah and Ecclesiastes and the 23rd Psalm — exactly my own preferences. About a hundred people standing about. A chill and windy day, scattered clouds, cold sunshine. We cried.

December 12, 1988 – Tucson

Just returned from a tiresome, tedious four-week book tour. Never again. *Never!* Sold a lot of books, I guess, but so far as I can tell, accomplished nothing else.

The *L.A. Times* gives *Fool's Progress* to some Chicano *psychologist* in Texas to review! The *Washington Post* assigns it to Denise Drabelle! A *lawyer!* What does she know or care about fiction? And she hates my guts too. The Tucson rags ignore the book.

My wife hates the first chapter.

Nevertheless, *FP* is a good novel. Perhaps a great novel. My best by far. *My time will come.* Now I must resume work on *Hayduke Lives!* and forget those excrement.

December 15, 1988 – Tucson

My final condemnation of existentialism: obsessive self-obsession. A completely homocentric egocentric anthropocentric view of life and the world ... unacceptable to me now. I think I sensed something of this way back in 1951, at UNM, when I objected, in a course on existentialism, that it was an "indoor philosophy," as jazz is an indoor musick and Christianity an indoor or man-centered religion. An infantile vanity lies at the heart of all these enterprises.

Humanity's view of the world as *our* property, *our* dominion, our stewardship, is like that of a child who imagines himself as the center of existence, with all other beings having no purpose but to serve him.

New Year's Day 1989 – Tucson

Fool's Progress is finally reviewed by *NY Times Book Review* (December 18), about two months late. A slight silly superficial review (buried on page twenty-two) by some "free-lance writer" I never heard of. As usual, the reviewer devotes so much space to attacking the author that he barely gets around to mentioning the book.

January 13, 1989 – Tucson

Fool's Progress is reviewed in *National Review* by Ed Marston, publisher of *High Country News*. He devotes ninety percent of his review to attacking the author's "racism," "sexism," etc., says nothing about the actual content of the book until the final brief paragraph. Never thought I'd be attacked in the *National Review* from the point of view of the most standard, doctrinaire, conventional *chickenshit* liberalism — but this is it. Exactly the kind of cant and sham and hypocrisy, intellectual dishonesty and moral cowardice, that has turned me finally against "liberalism" in general.

∽

Ives [Charles, American composer] to copyist: "Do not correct my wrong notes. The wrong notes are right."

Ives to critics: "Don't worry too much about the wrong notes. You'll miss the music."

∽

I felt pretty good at first.
But then the good feeling went away.
Now I don't feel so good.

February 2, 1989 – Tucson

On page 423 of *HL!* today. I've failed the contract deadline of February first. No matter. Two more weeks will finish the job. I may skip the courtroom trial [scene], however, just in case my guts don't hold out much longer. Let Doc, Bonnie and Seldom escape free and clear from the hijacking of the GEM, get off undetected, unidentified, and therefore never arrested or indicted. This way, we'd still have a complete novel, satisfy the contract, and I can croak, if necessary, in peace. (Doc Mac-Gregor sez I lost at least half my blood that awful Friday and Saturday, only ten or eleven days ago. It seems and feels to me that I may not really recover this time.)

"I've gone for a little walk. Into the West. I'll be home by sunset." — Thoreau? Ruess? Who?

Jim Fergus [in his *Outside* interview] — the sly backstab artist: "poison pen letters"; long quotes from enemies without giving me the elementary courtesy of a chance to reply. And his own sneak attack: the "horsewhip" business.

March 2, 1989 – Tucson

THE HACK'S PROGRESS:

Money money money. Here I sit, bleeding to death (look, Maw!) and the fukkin greasy money keeps pouring in as me tired old blood pours out.

Why book reviewers hate my books:

Because the books are really no good? Perhaps. But I think I've got a better explanation. Almost all reviewers, these days, are members of and adherents to some anxious particular sect or faction. I.e., they are lesbians or New Agers or fem-libbers or (even worse) male fem-libbers or techno-philes or self-hating white liberals or right-wing conservatives or Growth maniacs or Negroes or female Negroes or Third-World lesbian militant Negro poetesses or closet Marxists (Marxoids) or futurologists or academ-ical specialists or Chicano idealogues or ballerinas or Kowboy Kultists or Kerouac Kultists or Henry James Minimalist Perfectionists or one-tenth

Chippewa "Native American" Indians or at very least and all-inclusive Official Chickenshit Correct-Thinking Liberals etc. etc.

As such, any member of any one of those majority minorities is going to find *for certain* a few remarks in any of *my* books that will offend/enrage "s/he" to the marrow, leading inevitably in turn, on the part of such sectarian book reviewers, to a denunciation not merely of the offending passage, but of the *entire book*, and not merely of the book, but of the author too.

∞

Upon my arrival at NYC's LaGuardia Airport:
"Where to?" sez the cab driver.
"It doesn't matter," sez I; "I'm in demand everywhere."

∞

END OF JOURNAL XX

$\mathcal{P}$ostscript

∽

$\mathcal{J}$N THE SECOND WEEK of March 1989 — the selfsame week Ed, Jack Loeffler, and I were to have gone desert camping together — Ed began bleeding and fainted at home. Clarke, with the help of Tucson friends Dave and Nancy Foreman and Doug and Lisa Peacock, rushed Ed to the hospital emergency room. There he was revived with transfusions and — at the behest of doctors, family, and friends — submitted to a portal shunt, deemed the last best hope.

When it became apparent the surgical procedure hadn't worked, Ed had himself kidnapped from the hated institutional environment and carried out into the warm springtime desert to die in peaceful dignity.

Ironically, out there among the familiar saguaros, surrounded by friends and with Clarke lying by his side, Ed did not die but actually improved somewhat. At this unexpected turn, he asked to be taken back to his little writing cabin in the backyard of the Abbey home on the western outskirts of Tucson. There, he toughed it out a couple more days, falling in and out of consciousness.

About sunrise on the morning of March 14, with loved ones at his side, Cactus Ed moved on.

Former Vietnam combat medic Doug Peacock sat with Ed through that long last night and said that his old friend's passing was the bravest dying he'd ever witnessed.

In accordance with his instructions, Ed's body was placed in

355

his favorite sleeping bag and transported in the back of Jack Loeffler's pickup into the burning heart of a distant and remote desert wilderness. At road's end, Ed was carried — by the hands and hearts of Loeffler, Peacock, Clarke's father, Tom Cartwright, and her brother-in-law Stephen Prescott — an exhausting distance to a final campsite offering "an Abbey kind of view." There, among the rocks, sand, and cactus of "the only Heaven we'll ever know or ever need to know," with eagles and vultures soaring overhead and coyotes crying in each new day, Edward Paul Abbey now enjoys the ultimate desert solitaire.

A huge, boisterous wake was held a few days later at Tucson's Saguaro National Monument West — with food and booze and bagpipes and taps trumpeted by jazzman Jack Loeffler — exactly as Ed had wanted.

In May, a more formal and subdued memorial service was held along the old dirt entrance road to Arches National Park. The event was organized by Ed's good friend Ken "Seldom Seen" Sleight of Pack Creek Ranch. Guest speakers included Wendell Berry, Ann Zwinger, Barry Lopez, Terry Tempest Williams, Doug Peacock, Sleight, John "Debris" DePuy, C. L. Rawlins, and others.

Both the wake and the memorial were beautiful events and great comforts to the multitudes of mourners — but neither was quite able to raise the dead.

Edward Abbey was my friend and my hero. He gave me hope for a better world, and still does. I miss him. I miss his big wolfish grin and his lusty love of life, his joyful laughter, his unassuming wisdom, his impassioned polemics, his towering physical, intellectual, and spiritual presence, his ability to paint the West to vibrant life with an effortless brush of words. And most of all, I miss the moral courage and conviction Edward Abbey embodied. . . .

THIS IS WHAT YOU SHALL DO: Be loyal to what you love, be true to the earth, fight your enemies with passion and laughter.

Ed's sudden and premature passing blew a hole in my world as big as a big man's grave . . . a hole these *Confessions* help some to fill.

— D.P.